Research in Criminology

Series Editors
Alfred Blumstein
David P. Farrington

Research in Criminology

Understanding and Controlling Crime: Toward A New Research Strategy
D.P. Farrington, L.E. Ohlin and J.Q. Wilson

The Social Ecology of Crime
J.M. Byrne and R.J. Sampson (Eds.)

The Reasoning Criminal: Rational Choice Perspectives on Offending
D.B. Cornish and R.V. Clarke (Eds.)

The Social Contexts of Criminal Sentencing
Martha A. Myers and Susette M. Talarico

Predicting Recidivism Using Survival Models
Peter Schmidt and Ann Dryden Witte

Coping, Behavior, and Adaptation in Prison Inmates
Edward Zamble and Frank Porporino

Prison Crowding: A Psychological Perspective
Paul B. Paulus

Off School, In Court: An Experimental and Psychiatric Investigation of Severe School Attendance Problems
I. Berg, I. Brown and R. Hullin

Policing and Punishing the Drinking Driver: A Study of General and Specific Deterrence
Ross Homel

Judicial Decision Making, Sentencing Policy, and Numerical Guidance
Austin Lovegrove

Austin Lovegrove

Judicial Decision Making, Sentencing Policy, and Numerical Guidance

Springer-Verlag
New York Berlin Heidelberg
London Paris Tokyo

Austin Lovegrove
Criminology Department, University of Melbourne, Parkville, Victoria 3052, Australia.

Series Editors
Alfred Blumstein
School of Urban and Public Affairs, Carnegie-Mellon University, Pittsburgh, Pennsylvania 15213, USA.

David P. Farrington
Institute of Criminology, University of Cambridge, Cambridge, CB3 9DT, England.

With 9 Illustrations

Library of Congress Cataloging-in-Publication Data
Lovegrove, Austin.
Judicial decision making, sentencing policy, and numerical guidance / Austin Lovegrove.
p. cm. — (Research in Criminology)
Bibliography: p.
Includes indexes.
1. Sentences (Criminal procedure) 2. Judicial process.
I. Title. II. Series.
K5121.L68 1988
345'.0772—dc19
[342.5772] 88-17664

Printed on acid-free paper.

Typeset by Publishers Service, Bozeman, Montana.
Printed and bound by R.R. Donnelley & Sons, Harrisonburg, Virginia.
Printed in the United States of America.

9 8 7 6 5 4 3 2 1

ISBN 0-387-96764-8 Springer-Verlag New York Berlin Heidelberg
ISBN 3-540-96764-8 Springer-Verlag Berlin Heidelberg New York

To
my Mother
and
late Father

I often say that when you can measure what you are speaking about, and express it in numbers, you know something about it; but when you cannot measure it, when you cannot express it in numbers, your knowledge is of a meagre and unsatisfactory kind. (Mackay, 1977:148)

—William Thomson (Lord Kelvin), 1883

Acknowledgments

There are a number of people and organizations to whom I would like to express my appreciation for the part they have played in the research reported in this book. Dr. R. Sharwood of the Law School, University of Melbourne, was a source of encouragement and wise counsel when I first thought about studying sentencing; it was he who prepared the way for the submission of my initial research proposal to the Victoria Law Foundation.

I would also like to thank Dr. P. Pattison of the Department of Psychology, University of Melbourne, for the several profitable conversations I had with her about methodological issues.

It would have been impossible to undertake research of this nature without assistance. The Victoria Law Foundation recognized this and made a generous grant of over $55,000. The Faculty of Arts and the Criminology Department also provided supplementary financial assistance in order to facilitate the completion of this project.

One is conscious that the quality of a research project is to a large extent dependent upon the caliber of the research assistance. Helen Harbison collected data for the archival study and coded it intelligently, provided advice on the weighting of the material offender characteristics for the archival study, and drafted the fictitious cases for the sentencing exercises. Belinda Fehlberg assisted Helen in collecting the data for the archival study and carried out this task conscientiously and with enthusiasm. Moreover, the support of Mr. J. Buckley, Mr. S. Kelly, and Mr. A. Owen of the Attorney-General's Department (formerly the Law Department) ought to be recognized; they gave me access to the data upon which the archival study is founded. At this point one would be remiss not to acknowledge the cooperation of several members of the Attorney-General's Department who made the research assistants welcome and helped them find files, tapes, and other records.

One cannot overemphasize the generous spirit of the nine County Court judges who agreed to undertake the sentencing exercises. And I am most grateful to His Honour Judge Shillito for making the necessary arrangements with the judges.

Finally, I would like to record my appreciation to Helene Richards for typing the manuscript so diligently, to Christine McIntyre for supervising the word processing, and to the editorial staff at Springer-Verlag for their assistance in the publication process.

Victoria, Australia Austin Lovegrove

Contents

Part One A Perspective for a Quantitative Approach to Sentencing Policy and Guidance

1
The Task of Describing Sentencing Policy Quantitatively

Sentencing is about the imposition of punishment on individuals who have been found guilty of criminal behavior. The judiciary, in administering justice through the courts, exercise a discretion. Traditionally, in common law countries this discretion has been largely unfettered, in most instances confined only by broad statutory provisions, the most significant of which cover maximum penalties and available dispositions. Within these wide boundaries the judiciary have enjoyed the freedom of formulating and administering sentencing policy. In determining an appropriate sentence in a particular case, judges have traditionally regarded the harm caused by the offense, the offender's culpability and rehabilitation prospects, and whether justice required the exercise of mercy. This is individualized justice.

In the past two decades, particularly in the United States, there has been a flurry of academic, legislative, and community discussion and writing on the judiciary's use of its discretionary powers in the sentencing process. Of particular concern have been the courts' powers to determine whether a particular offender should be imprisoned and the length of the term of imprisonment. In relation to these powers, two perceived problems have dominated the debates. First, there is a widely and firmly held belief that the courts' fixing of penalties is characterized by inconsistency—like cases are not treated alike. Where these inconsistencies in sentencing occur within particular jurisdictions, and it is alleged that such disparities do occur, the administration of justice is seen as unfair, and in turn this elicits feelings ranging from disquiet to outrage and engenders within the community a lack of confidence in the courts. (For a succinct account capturing the mood and temper of the pioneering contributions in this tide of criticism in the United States, see Radzinowicz & Hood, 1981. Bottoms & Preston, 1980; Law Reform Commission—Australia, 1980, offer an introduction to the problem of disparity in the British and Australian contexts, respectively.) There is, of course, some empirical support for the existence of disparity, although this evidence is limited to relatively few courts and jurisdictions and is further weakened by the methodological problems necessarily besetting such analyses (Forst, 1982; Kapardis, 1985; Lovegrove, 1984a). Typically, the criticisms raised against these studies (e.g., lack of adequate controls) lead to doubts about the existence of disparity as little more than an artifact of the method. These studies, however, have other (rarely mentioned) features, such as the inadequate coverage of interactions involving the factor of judge, as well as the problem of the contribution of intrajudge variation to disparity, the effect of which would be to underestimate disparity. Nevertheless, the case for or against doing something about sentencing does not stand or fall on the strength of the evidence for disparity, because disparity is an inevitable consequence associated with the (second) problem to which this introduction now turns. This second concern centers around sentencing policy—the principles governing the exercise of the sentencing discretion. These principles cover the purposes of punishment, the case factors relevant to the determination of sentence, and the rules prescribing the way in which this information should be selected, classified, and aggregated to determine the appropriate goals of sentence and to give effect to these goals. In a system conferring wide discretionary powers on the judiciary, the judges are responsible for the development and enunciation of sentencing policy. The rising tide of intellectual concern has been directed toward the three previously mentioned aspects of policy: the validity of some of the possible aims of punishment, especially rehabilitation; the fairness of certain types of case factors sometimes considered relevant to sentence, for example, unemployment; and the high degree of imprecision associated with the specification and application of sentencing policy, captured succinctly by the notorious judicial aphorism, "each case turns on its own facts." Clearly, if this last criticism is valid, then it would inevitably follow that an unacceptable level of inconsistency would characterize the courts' administration of justice. Of course, a rigorous investigation of inconsistency can be made only in relation to a particular sentencing policy, since the notions *like* and *unlike* depend on policy for meaning. In the absence of a stable, comprehensive, and clearly articulated policy, the validity of disparity studies is seriously undermined and somewhat problematic. It is not surprising, then, that the previously mentioned intellectual forays against the judiciary and sentencing strike at not only inconsistency but also policy. Two of the academic leaders in the area of reform and sentencing policy are Ashworth (1983b, 1987) and von Hirsch (1976, 1985). Both call for changes to penal policy; both see the need for a more detailed statement of the principles governing the determination of sentence. Not that these commentators speak with one voice; but they are united in their distaste for the judiciary's traditional approach to sentencing. Indeed, Ashworth (1983b) has concluded, as if in disgust, ". . . the sentencing process is a disgrace to the common law tradition" (p. 450).

The present research arose from my unease over the current state of the art of sentencing and, in particular, the looseness characterizing statements of current sentencing policy and the rules governing the application of this policy. Indeed, the description of this aspect of the problems of sentencing as subjective, qualitative, and intuitive is both reasonable and diagnostic. Two undesirable consequences follow from this state of affairs. First, it is often difficult to ascertain whether particular case factors should be taken into account, the way in which material factors should be taken into account, and the importance to be attached to them in the determination of sentence. Accordingly, debates about the proper content of sentencing policy are restricted, with a consequent stunting of the development of sentencing policy. Second, a vague statement of sentencing policy must result in the inconsistent application of that policy. On matters on which there is no guidance or imprecise guidance, it falls to the individual judge to formulate policy and the rules for applying policy, and to the extent that sentencing lies with the individual judge, it will be idiosyncratic. Where this situation prevails, the discretionary powers are regarded as unstructured (or not sufficiently structured) (see Davis, 1969). The responsibility for this parlous state of affairs does not lie solely with the judiciary. Rather, the contention here is that the necessary conceptual framework and appropriate empirical techniques have not been developed and applied to the problem of adequately describing sentencing policy. The purpose of the present project is to develop and apply relevant concepts and methods so that the determination of sentence might be seen as more objective, quantitative, and deliberative. Specifically, it examines the potential of a numerical solution to the problem of imprecision as it afflicts sentencing policy. This goal would be achieved when a relationship had been established between various combinations of objectively defined offense and offender characteristics of cases and the appropriate quanta of sentence and then presented in a form that would provide guidance to the sentencing judge. Such a statement of sentencing policy is referred to as *detailed sentencing statistics* where it is applied as a description of current sentencing policy and, where associated with a deliberate attempt to develop (specify) sentencing policy, with guidance in mind, as *numerical guidelines*. This represents one approach to structuring the sentencing discretion.

This problem clearly falls within the domain of law and psychology (behavioral science) and, accordingly, I turned to these two disciplines in search of potentially useful conceptual frameworks. Two frameworks were selected. One was a legal model of the structure of the sentencing judgment and the tariff sentence, developed by the academic lawyer David Thomas (1979); the other was from a family of models of decision making, falling within the field of decision analysis or multiattribute utility measurement, together with its associated measurement techniques, and commonly associated with the names of Ward Edwards (Edwards, 1977; Edwards & Newman, 1982) and Ralph Keeney (Keeney, 1977; Keeney & Raiffa, 1976). This project, then, involves the application of psychology (behavioral science) to law in a way that takes legal concepts, thought, and expertise seriously. Although, clearly, sentencing is a criminological issue, the present project should not be regarded as a criminological study, because the analysis is restricted to problems directly related to introducing greater precision into the sentencing judgment and does not canvass broader issues associated with the development and implementation of schemes for structuring the judicial sentencing discretion (e.g., whether the description of sentencing policy should be advisory or presumptive, the appropriate aims of sentence, the extent to which the structuring of discretion should be legislatively based, the proper limits and most effective controls of the judges' sentencing discretion, the role of the prosecutor, the effects on plea bargaining, the coherence of the legislative framework, the quality of the information before the court, and the like (Blumstein, Cohen, Martin, & Tonry, 1983a, 1983b; Chan, 1987; Galegher & Carroll, 1983; Galligan, 1981; Shapland, 1987; Thomas, 1987; Tonry & Zimring, 1983).

As a result of the current disenchantment with traditional approaches to sentencing, significant programs have been proposed and introduced. Notable sentencing reforms germane to the present study are John Hogarth's (1986a, 1986b) proposal for the detailed description of current practice, Leslie Wilkins's descriptive guidelines (Wilkins, Kress, Gottfredson, Calpin, & Gelman, 1978), Anthony Doob's sentencing data base (Doob, 1986; Doob & Park, 1987), the United States Sentencing Commission's (1987) presumptive guidelines, the Minnesota Sentencing Guidelines Commission's (1984) prescriptive guidelines, and the guideline judgments of the Court of Appeal (Criminal Division) in England (see Ashworth, 1984). All of these approaches seek to provide a more rigorous description of sentencing policy in a way that provides the judge with greater guidance, especially regarding the classification and combination of information. Each of these reforms is reviewed regarding this goal to assess its potential. It is concluded that each reform has significant limitations, and on this basis an alternative solution to the problem is developed and presented. This alternative approach is based on the assumption that to describe sentencing policy accurately it is necessary to fit case data to a model faithful to the structure of judicial decision making. The purpose of the model is to provide a framework for the scaling of the seriousness of any case in relation to the facts of the case and for relating this assessment of seriousness to the appropriate quantum of sentence.

This model was developed after a review and synthesis of the relevant legal and psychological literature. To give detail to the model, I relied on legal analyses of sentencing judgments to determine which case factors are material to sentence and how these factors are related to sentence. It was then possible to test tentatively the model's potential. This was done by taking 100 cases of burglary that had been previously determined in the higher courts, construing the case facts (offense and offender characteristics) of these cases in terms of the model, and then examining whether this construction of the seriousness of the cases was systematically related to the actual sentences imposed in the courts. The initial study affirmed the validity of the model, and a cross-validation study on a second sample of 100 cases confirmed that result. In the light of this conclusion, judicial input was introduced in the development of the model.

A small sample of judges participated in a series of scaling exercises. In the first task, the judges developed four scales, one for each of four offense factors of burglary, showing the relationship between various levels on an offense factor and seriousness (e.g., how seriousness is related to changes in the total amount of money stolen). In a second task, the judges made numerical assessments of the relative weights of the four offense factors in the assessment of the overall seriousness of cases of burglary. A third scaling exercise demonstrated that the judges' assessments of the relationship between the facts of a case and seriousness were coherent. In the fourth and final task, the judges set the quanta of sentence appropriate for the various levels of case seriousness. As a result of these analyses, it was concluded that the conceptual framework and the empirical techniques introduced in this study of sentencing could be used, first, to improve the description of sentencing policy to facilitate the judges' determination of appropriate sentences for particular cases according to that policy and, second, to facilitate judicial input into the development of a more precise and comprehensive sentencing policy. This second aspect is critical. A precise description of sentencing policy presumes that in the mind of the judiciary there is a comprehensive and rigorously articulated policy; because such a policy does not exist, the judiciary should be provided with a means of declaring their views in a way that would facilitate the development of policy. Each of these analyses is described in turn in subsequent chapters. In the remainder of this chapter, four issues are addressed: the structure and nature of the sentencing judgment; imprecision in the sentencing judgment; legal perspectives of the problem of imprecision; the goals of the study and their relation to the notion of disparity and the role of discretion in sentencing. Such matters are of primary importance, because they define the problem and set constraints on any potential solution.

The Structure and Nature of the Sentencing Judgment

Appellate courts are responsible for monitoring sentencing practices in the courts of first instance and for developing sentencing policy for those courts. These twin roles are performed by the appellate courts in the course of their determining appeals. Some reported appellate judgments and unreported decisions present comprehensive analyses of the court's deliberations and, accordingly, offer insight into the court's exercising of the sentencing discretion. Australia, Canada, England, and Scotland have active appellate courts, and as a matter of course they hear and determine appeals against sentence. Sometimes these judgments declare principles expressly; often the policy is implicit and ripe for discovery. In any case it is there, as works by Fox and Freiberg (1985), Victoria, Australia; Ruby (1980, 1986), Canada; Thomas (1979), England; and Nicholson (1981, 1985), Scotland testify, although often it is necessary to study a series of decisions to identify a pattern and from that a policy, notwithstanding the imprecision and instances of inconsistency and unprincipled (impressionistic) reasoning in appellate decisions (Ashworth, 1984; Rinaldi, 1980; Thomas, 1983). The following picture therefore presents what might be described as an ideal structure or model of the sentencing judgment.

One can discern two elements in traditional judicial judgments about what is an appropriate sentence for a particular case (see Lovegrove, 1984b). First, there is discussion about the principles of sentencing to be applied in particular cases. Do the facts of the case warrant a sentence grounded on the principle of retribution or deterrence or denunciation or rehabilitation, or perhaps a mix of aims, say retribution moderated by rehabilitation? Then there is the matter of selecting the disposition that would give best effect to the chosen aim in the circumstances of the case. Second, there is reference to the court's view of the types and quanta of sentence that similar cases have attracted in recent years within the jurisdiction. Through the former component the appellate courts interpret and develop the law of sentencing and provide reasoned decisions to guide judges sentencing in the first instance. This component of the judgment is the heart of the process of the court's individualizing sentence, and in it one may observe the court meeting the Victorian (Australia) Chief Justice's requirement that judges must hold the scales of justice between the offender and the community (Young, 1979). The second dimension, generally referred to as the "tariff" (or, colloquially, by expressions like the "going rate") provides a standard of the quantum of sentence against which the court may weigh its present response. Together these two aspects of the judgment provide for principled uniformity.

Members of the Victorian Court of Criminal Appeal have attested to the salience of the former component. Adam and Crockett, JJ., said, "The purposes of punishment are manifold and each element will assume a different significance not only in different crimes but in the individual commission of each crime." They added that one matter to be considered is whether the crime's contemporary prevalence is a source of considerable disquiet in the community (*Williscroft & others*, 1975, p. 299). Clearly, an appellate court's resolutions of these questions are not immutable over time. In a judgment (*Adams & others*, 1972, unreported) delivered by Jacobs, P., the New South Wales (Australia) Court of Criminal Appeal emphasized the significance of the tariff, "The duty of this Court is to see that there is a consistency in the sentences and it is the duty of all courts to see that some scale is observed. The scale is basically the product of the day to day experience of the many judges. . ." (cited by Rinaldi, 1979, p. 120).

To understand why some have argued that sentencing cannot be reduced to the mechanical application of a table (Young, 1979), one must appreciate the significance of the former element of the judgment. Tonry and Morris (1978) succinctly state the position of those who subscribe to this view, "Equality in punishment is not an absolute principle. It is a value to be weighed and considered among others. There can be just sentences in which like offenders are not treated alike. . ." (p. 445). They cite the use of exemplary sentences as instances of principled sentencing disparity. Similarly, Thomas (1977) concluded that "(t)he concept of equity in sentencing means more than mechanical quantification of punishment. Equity requires the consistent application of a recognizable and articulated body of principle" (p. 13).

Such considerations ought not to be taken as undermining the significance of the tariff as a determinant of sentence. Cross and Ashworth (1981), speaking of judges who reject the notion of tariff, stated, "It cannot be said that they exclude altogether the notion of the appropriate range of sentence, although it may well play its part in determining the final sentence at a later stage in their case than in that of some other judges" (p. 169). McKenna (1969), in the course of a lecture delivered while he was a member of the English High Court, imputed a critical role to the tariff in the determination of sentence. After deliberating on the purposes of punishment, he commented as follows:

In practice the judge escapes from these perplexities by pursuing the ideal of equal punishment. If he has no certainty about the right sentence to deter or punish, he can at least try to give the kind of sentence recently given by others for the offence in question, . . . In the exercise of trying to give the same sentence as others have given he has the help of the criminal statistics. (p. 610)

Sentencing judges, then, in exercising their discretion, must deliberate on three interrelated matters: (1) the appropriate goals of sentencing and their relative weights in view of the particular facts of the case; (2) how to give effect to these aims in the circumstances of the case; (3) the specific sentence that this particular set of case facts ought to attract. The first two points relate to the former element of the sentencing judgment, whereas the third point underlies the latter element. These first two points may be viewed as the raison d'être for the outcome observed under the third point. This approach shares common elements with the model of sentencing proposed by Hood and Sparks (1970). (See Lovegrove, 1986.)

Academic lawyers have sought solutions to the problem of structuring the judicial sentencing discretion where justice is individualized. The directions in which they would set reform dovetail with the analysis of the sentencing judgment in the preceding paragraphs. Galligan (1981), focusing on penal aims, argued that to develop the law of sentencing and to apply it correctly and consistently it is necessary to establish relationships between sets of case facts and appropriate mixes of sentencing aims and to systematize links between these policies and consequent penalties. As Galligan says, one must examine and set standards for the policies that the penalties are to based on and determine how best the policies might be achieved by way of penalties for particular types of cases. Ashworth's (1983a) agenda for his proposed sentencing council in England covers the relationship between case facts and sentence, and complements Galligan's strategy. Consider the tasks he would set for the council: (1) distinguish within types of offenses according to prominent factors and patterns of offending; (2) declare penalty ceilings for the various classifications in relation to their seriousness; (3) lay down principles for calculating the precise sentence beneath the ceiling in terms of critical offense and offender characteristics.

This analysis of the structure of the sentencing judgment provides a context for examining the nature of the decisions required in each of the two previously identified elements. According to Thomas (1979), on the basis of his analysis of appellate judgments in England, the judge must first decide whether the sentence should emphasize the seriousness of the offense or whether the rehabilitation prospects of the offender should be the salient determinant of sentence. (Thomas used the terms *tariff sentence* and *individualized measure* to denote these respective approaches. This use of the word *tariff* differs from the notion of *tariff*, previously mentioned, that is colloquially termed *the going rate*.) This is the primary sentencing decision. In practice, a tariff sentence usually is an amalgam of the aims of retribution, deterrence, and denunciation. Although a court occasionally will distinguish between these various penal goals in terms of their effect on the determination of sentence, typically, the guiding principle is that of proportionality between the culpability of the offender and the quantum of sentence. The primary decision normally turns, it is said, on the seriousness of the statutory classification of the offense and the strength of the offender's rehabilitation prospects. When a tariff sentence is determined to be appropriate, the judge's task then is to fix a term of imprisonment proportional to the culpability of the offender: this depends on the seriousness of the circumstances of the offense and, normally, any factors acting by way of mitigation to reduce the offender's culpability. Where a judge opts for an individualized measure, it is a matter of selecting from among the noncustodial sentences the disposition most likely to maximize the offender's chances of rehabilitation. These are the secondary decisions.

There are two problematic points, germane to the present discussion, in Thomas's (1979) analysis. Apparently, in practice, at least in Australia and Canada, there may be considerable overlap between the tariff and the individualized approaches, such that not infrequently regard to an offender's rehabilitation may significantly moderate the quantum of sentence that otherwise would have been deemed appropriate on the grounds of culpability. See, for example, the previously cited quotation from the decision of the Victorian Court of Criminal Appeal in *Williscroft and others* (1975); also, the Canadian Sentencing Commission (1987) referred to the practice of Canada's Courts of Appeal of blending and balancing the aims of sentencing. There is a second difficulty in the analysis. For Thomas, tariff sentences are sentences of imprisonment and individualized measures are the noncustodial dispositions; moreover, it will be remembered that the seriousness of the legal category of the offense is a determinant of the primary decision. Taken together, these two points render his analysis of the sentencing decision problematic in respect of the many statutory offense categories for which both custodial and noncustodial sentences are not infrequently imposed (see, e.g., the sentencing statistics compiled by the Law Department–Victoria, Management Information Section, 1985). Now, if it is assumed that the seriousness of the offense is considered together with the circumstances of the offense in the particular case, then the problem disappears. Indeed, the Canadian Sentencing Commission (1987), in discussing the "in/out" decision, similarly concluded that for many statutory offense categories in the midrange of seriousness the use of "in" and "out" presumptions was an inappropriate form of guidance, and the Commission therefore introduced qualified presumptions for these offenses. Let it be clear, these qualifications are not in any way inconsistent with Thomas's analysis; it is rather a matter of emphasis.

One can discern in this analysis of sentencing decisions two types of decision making. One type is quantitative, where the sentencer must develop and refer to an implicit *scale* of seriousness based on the relevant offense and offender characteristics of the case. This scale is used as part of the determination of whether a tariff sentence is appropriate and, if it is, it acts as a basis for the judge's fixing the quantum of sentence. The second type of decision involves qualitative assessments in which case characteristics, either singly or in combination, are used as *indicators* of the appropriateness of a tariff sentence or an individualized measure and, if the latter, the measure most appropriate to the offender's rehabilitative needs. On this point it is worth noting that evidence from a pilot survey of a small sample of English circuit judges conducted by Ashworth, Genders, Mansfield, Peay, and Player (1984) supports the notion that judges perceive the sentencing task as involving both scaling seriousness and matching individualized measures to offenders in relation to the facts of cases.

This discussion has explained the nature of the decisions in determining appropriate sentences for particular cases, and these two types of decision cover both elements identified in the preceding analysis of the structure of judicial thought, that is, (1) the interrelation of case fact, policy, and penalty and (2) the relation between case fact and penalty. It was necessary to engage in this exposition because the purpose of the present study is to develop a more precise means of representing the relationship between the offense and offender characteristics of a case and the type and quantum of sentence deemed appropriate by the court in accordance with the judicial approach to the exercise of the sentencing discretion. The point will be developed later that, unless such an analysis is so grounded, there would be three important undesirable consequences: (1) the demonstrated relationship between case fact and penalty would confound the tariff and individualized approaches and as a consequence would be unnecessarily imprecise, perhaps unintelligible; (2) the analysis could not be used as a basis for the development of sentencing policy, because it would not be linked to a relevant conceptual framework; and (3) the analysis would not be readily understood by judges and could not be related by them to their own decision schemas and, accordingly, it would not provide a suitable basis for the guidance of sentencers in the exercise of their discretion.

The present study is restricted to the decision whether to impose a sentence of imprisonment and the determination of the length of imprisonment. Accordingly, the present study, with its quantitative and numerical orientation, covers the development of the scale of offender culpability and of the indicator of an offender's rehabilitation prospects, based on the offense and offender characteristics considered relevant to these assessments by the courts. This analysis is developed later.

Imprecision in the Sentencing Judgment

In the introductory section the traditional sentencing judgment was characterized as subjective, qualitative, and intuitive. This section expands on these notions. What more appropriate way to begin an examination of the nature of imprecision in the sentencing judgment than to refer to an appellate court's view of this aspect of its work? Adam and Crockett, JJ., speaking as members of the Court of Criminal Appeal in Victoria, made the following—now much-quoted— observation on this matter:

Now, ultimately every sentence imposed represents the sentencing judges's instinctive synthesis of all the various aspects involved in the punitive process. . . it is profitless. . .to attempt to allot to the various considerations their proper part in the assessment of the particular punishments presently under examination. It is sufficient to say that in our opinion the learned Judge did not in the cases before him give to the aspects other than reformation the weight that ought to have been allotted to them. . . .

We are aware that such a conclusion rests upon what is essentially a subjective judgment largely intuitively reached by an appellate judge as to what punishment is appropriate. (*Williscroft & others*, 1975, p. 300)

It should be noted that the Court, in reaching its decision, also examined data on the sentences previously imposed in the jurisdiction for the type of offense before it, to get a feel for the current standard, but noted the imprecision attending such an evaluation.

Here, the Court has made a significant statement about its view of the nature of the sentencing decision and, more importantly, has implicitly drawn attention to the consequence of this position: at this time the process of sentencing cannot be objective, quantitative, and deliberative. It should be emphasized that this is not the sentencing nihilism found in the doctrine that "each case turns on its own facts," for the Court in reaching its decision examined principles governing the choice of appropriate penal goals and studied the quanta of sentence imposed in this type of case. Rather, it is a statement about the way in which the Court evaluates information about the facts of a case in arriving at an appropriate sentence, that is, the process by which it assesses facts to determine the seriousness of the case and the offender's rehabilitation prospects, as well as the appropriate aim(s) and the type and level of sentence, in view of its past decisions. The intuition is, therefore, not unprincipled.

Nevertheless, there are instances of sentencing nihilism. In *Sawyer* (1985) the Court of Appeal (Criminal Division) in England declared that it was not appropriate for counsel to seek to draw the Court's attention to its earlier decisions on what appeared to counsel to be similar cases. The Court offered two interdependent reasons for its approach. First, what is an appropriate sentence for a particular case depends wholly on the facts and circumstances of that case. This is the argument that cases are not comparable because of their uniqueness. Second, reports of earlier cases, on which any comparison must rest, may not refer to all of the critical case characteristics underlying the Court's decisions. The latter reason must be regarded as spurious, for surely the Court would have otherwise made a plea for sentencing judgments to provide a full statement of the Court's reasons for its decisions? Not surprisingly, Thomas (1985) took issue with the Court on the soundness of the attitude it expressed in *Sawyer*, but noted that this approach appeared to run counter to the general practice of the Court in recent years. To Thomas, the Court's approach in *de Havilland* (1983) was standard and to be encouraged. There the Court took the view that previous decisions on sentencing may be cited as examples of how the Court has dealt with a particular offender in relation to a particular offense, on the ground that this may aid uniformity in sentencing. The Court warned, however, that previous decisions could not be regarded as binding, because the circumstances of the offense and the offender present almost infinite variety from case to case. The position in England, then, is akin to the approach in Australia.

From the discussion of the sentencing judgment in the Report of the Canadian Sentencing Commission (1987) and the analyses of appellate sentencing judgments in Ruby (1980), the nature of the exercise of the sentencing discretion by Canadian judges is similar to the courts' approach to sentencing in Australia and England. The following extracts from the Commission's Report paint a vivid picture of how the courts typically consider the aims and quantum of sentence.

> It is not that Courts of Appeal, or trial courts, never state the principles underlying their approach to sentencing, it is that they do it infrequently and when they state these aims, the practice of blending and balancing results more in obscuring their approach than developing a uniform approach to sentencing aims. (Canadian Sentencing Commission, 1987, p. 80)

The Commission explained how descriptions in the appellate judgments of this process of blending and balancing, like ". . . using our best judgment as to what is in the interest of society, we will change the two year sentence. . ." (Canadian Sentencing Commission, 1987, p. 80), lie at the heart of the problem. The Commission further observed that the Courts' consideration of how particular factors affect the quantum of sentence similarly is obscure: "A vast majority of appeal court decisions lists a catalogue of factors present in a case. . . (t)he court then throws the factors into a melting pot and, ". . .taking into account all the circumstances" arrives at a final disposition. . ." (p. 84). Moreover, still, it would appear, the view that each case turns on its own facts dies hard. The Canadian Sentencing Commission (1987) noted a reluctance among appeal courts to seek uniformity through detailed guidance; the fear on the part of the appellate courts is that with such guidance the unique characteristics of cases might not be given sufficient weight in the determination of sentences. In his discussion of the concept of the tariff, Ruby (1986) noted that "(t)he range of sentence reflects individual cases, but does not govern them" (p. 449).

The limitations of principled intuition as a means of determining the appropriate sentence can be made no more clear than through direct references to the reasoning of an appellate court. The following examples are taken from separate decisions of the Court of Criminal Appeal of Victoria in cases of appeals against sentence.

First, extracts from a judgment delivered by Young, C.J., in *Bateman* (1977). It should be noted that these extracts focus on aspects of the decision dealing with the evaluation of facts of the case and were made in the context of a factual summary of the case.

> Fifteen years is a very long time and, notwithstanding the serious nature of the offences, I doubt whether I should have imposed so long an effective term. However I am not able to say that the sentence is so manifestly excessive that the Court should conclude that there must have been some unidentifiable error in the sentencing process.

It was submitted that His Honour had given insufficient weight to the rehabilitation aspect of punishment, and whilst I think there is some difficulty in establishing that ground when expressed in those terms, I have been troubled by a doubt whether His Honour concentrated so much upon the prevalence of armed robbery at the present time that he gave insufficient consideration to the other aspects of sentencing. (p. 3)

Nor do I wish to be taken as indicating that it is incumbent upon a sentencing Judge to elaborate upon all the matters which he takes into account in passing sentence. But when, as here, the sentencing Judge's remarks are couched in strong terms and those remarks are all adverse to the prisoner— or at least such observations as are made in his favour are not in equally strong terms—and a high effective sentence is imposed, one is apt to doubt whether all the matters that should have been taken into account have been given appropriate weight. (p. 4)

This second (following) series of extracts draws attention to the problem associated with the Court's using previous decisions as a standard for its present response. Again, the judgment was delivered in the Court of Criminal Appeal of Victoria by Young, C.J., and Kaye and McGarvie, JJ., in the case of *McCormack and others* (1981).

The perils of seeking to make a logical progression from the sentence in one case to the sentence in another are well illustrated by Crisp, J. in *Wise v. R.*, (1965) Tas. S.R. 196, at pp. 200–201. He said: "Sentencing is an art and not a science. By that I mean that if in any given case it were possible to arrive at the exact measure of the punishment to be awarded by the application of logical rules which proceeded with mathematical inevitability to a determinate conclusion, then indeed the judge's responsibility would be a different one from that which we know. Notwithstanding this fundamental fact, this court is constantly faced with attempts, based on some system of analysis, to expound principles of precision in relation to punishments awarded from time to time by different judges in respect of crimes of the same generic character no doubt, but which differ individually and infinitely both in degree and circumstance. . . ." (p. 111)

An example of the variety of sentences imposed in England for the comparable offence involving danger to the public, affray, appears in Thomas, *Principles of Sentencing*, 2nd ed., pp. 110–2. But although it is not possible to make a logical progression from the sentences passed in *Caird's Case*, *supra*, to the appropriate sentences in the present case, there remains the question whether the sentences imposed by the learned Judge went beyond the range of sentences open to him. (pp. 111–112)

One cannot help but sense the Court's struggle as it seeks to do justice and apprehend its dissatisfaction with the process. But what faults lie at the heart of principled intuition? Simply, they are that decisions regarding the selection, classification, and aggregation of facts about a case in the course of determining an appropriate sentence, and the reporting of those decisions, are unnecessarily subjective and qualitative. Each aspect will be illustrated in turn.

Selection

Undoubtedly, the general significance of major case factors like the level of organization, degree of violence, and the value of the theft in the assessment of seriousness and, then, in the determination of sentence for a common offense like robbery is well settled. That this is so is clear from analyses of sentencing judgments, such as Thomas's (1979) *Principles of Sentencing*. Moreover, such factors more likely than not are mentioned in the judgment or are discernible from a reading of the facts of the case. Nevertheless, this is not always so, particularly where an individual case, rather than a class of cases, is being examined. But there are factors that may weigh heavily in the final decision in the minds of some judges and yet whose significance is an open issue among others. Personal experience suggests that certain factors taken by some judges as indicative of an offender's rehabilitation prospects illustrate this point, for example, the offender's employment status and demeanor in court. (See also, Ashworth et al., 1984, for a survey of English judges with an anecdotal account of possible idiosyncratic usage and interpretation of particular case facts.) Certainly, there is reason for alarm when these considerations do not find their way into sentencing judgments, and this is probably the rule rather than the exception. Indeed, one of the main reasons why an appellate court is reluctant to interfere with the sentencing judge's discretion is that the court of first instance may have had additional relevant information about the case, especially about the offender, before it. The problem is that this additional information is unspecified and perhaps should not have been considered relevant. One reaches the extremes of despair on this matter over the admission by a small minority of English judges in Ashworth's pilot survey that they usually avoided giving an explanation of the sentence because they sometimes felt that they reached the right conclusion for the wrong reasons (Ashworth et al., 1984).

As a result of this state of affairs, a shroud partially covers some of the case factors taken into account by sentencing judges and there is ambiguity over the legitimacy of certain offense and offender characteristics considered in the determination of sentence. Without doubt, greater clarity is required on the identification of the relevant as well as the illegitimate decision factors, together with a more certain knowledge of the types of case characteristics underlying the courts' decisions.

Classification

Typically, appellate court judgments involve an outline of the facts of the case together with a catalog of the more extreme aggravating and extenuating features, accompanied by descriptions like "horrendous violence" or "pathetic organization." There are two problems with this approach. First, the contribution of circumstances of moderate seriousness surrounding an offense could be easily overlooked in the assessment of the overall seriousness of the case. Second, and more important, this approach provides no basis for drawing comparisons across cases and makes for crude assessments of seriousness in particular cases. For example, both the violence in one case where a person is shot and sustains a minor injury and in another case in which a gun is held at the victim's head in a threatening manner could be described fairly as "grave," and yet it would not be unreasonable to regard the first instance of violence as significantly more serious. But what is the basis for an assessment of differential seriousness? And what is the relative difference in seriousness? And how do these examples of violence compare in terms of seriousness with other manifestations of violence? Simply, terms like *grave* ensure that this type of question draws a blank. The antidote is to provide, for each major case factor, descriptions in concrete, case-specific terms of the various levels across the range of seriousness, together with a numerical indication of the relative seriousness of each of the levels on the factor. For example, if $100,000 is a realistic upper limit of the amounts stolen in cases of burglary, the question is, then, what is the relative seriousness of amounts such as $5,000 and $50,000, and so on?

Combination

The term *combination* covers the aggregation of the assessments of each of the individual offense and offender factors to arrive at a view of the overall seriousness of the case, the rehabilitation prospects of the offender, and the effect on the type and quantum of sentence of these two assessments. It involves two components. One concerns the relative importance or contribution (generally referred to as the weight) of each of the factors in the assessment of case seriousness. The operational significance of this concept can be illustrated simply. Consider the determination of seriousness for two cases of robbery. One case is marked by very serious violence but negligible organization; the other is characterized by a professional level of planning with minimal violence. If the cases are similar in all other aspects, then the first case would be more serious if violence was weighted more heavily, whereas the second case would be regarded as more serious if organization was the more important factor. The second component embodied in the notion of combination is the rules governing the combination of the individual assessments. In nontechnical terms the essential concern here is whether overall case seriousness is determined by, as it were, simply adding (or subtracting) the effects of the aggravating (or extenuating) case factors, allowing for their relative weights, or whether for certain combinations of factors the presence of one factor may enhance the effect of another.

Appellate judgments have least to say on this aspect of the sentencing process; indeed they are virtually silent, and where rules are set down (e.g., on the effect of prior convictions on the determination of sentence) they are poorly specified (see Chapter 4). Indeed, it would be fair to say that to the mind of the lawyer it is impossible to describe precisely how the facts of a case relate to the quantum of sentence because of the large range of variation in the circumstances of the offense and the offender. However, this view fails to appreciate the following points. If judges are determining sentences reliably, then they must be consistently applying a common set of rules for combining information; moreover, if these judgments were made explicit, then techniques of behavioral science could be used to represent them. It is ironic that this should be the least developed aspect of the sentencing judgment, not only because it probably provides, in the absence of guidance, the greatest scope for idiosyncratic sentencing, but perhaps more so, because even if there were clearly enunciated policies (sets of rules) they would be so complex as to exceed the limits of human information-processing skills, with inevitable error in the determination of case seriousness and sentence. Ashworth (1983a) directed attention to the heart of the matter in his succinct observation, "It takes little imagination to envisage the difficult problems which can arise when cases involve cross-currents of mitigating and aggravating factors" (p. 3). Diamond (1981) investigated this matter empirically. In a study of actual sentencing decisions in the United States, Diamond found that cases involving disagreement over the appropriateness of a custodial sentence were characterized by the presence of both strong aggravating and strong mitigating factors. This finding is consistent with conclusions drawn from the general literature on human information processing—that as decisions increase in complexity (a greater number of factors and more conflict among the factors) the less humans are able to allow accurately for the combined effects of those factors (Einhorn & Hogarth, 1981; Pitz & Sachs, 1984; Saks & Kidd, 1980; Slovic, Fischhoff, & Lichtenstein, 1977).

Of course, the preceding criticisms of the traditional sentencing judgment are not original and have been cataloged by other writers, such as Ashworth (1984) in his review of sentencing guidance in England. What I have tried to do in this section is to detail and present the problems in a form that anticipates a possible solution.

Never has anyone been more scathing about the Victorian Court of Criminal Appeal's use of the term *instinctive synthesis* to describe the sentencing process than Rinaldi (1980) in his commentary on *Kellow and Townsend*. In that case one of the appellate judges delivered a dissenting judgment, to which Rinaldi made the cutting comment, "The Court's "instinctive synthesis" did not bless one of the members who was not able to see anything wrong with the trial judge's sentences" (p. 56). There can be no doubt that the means of significantly improving the precision of the sentencing judgment in relation to the issues raised under "selection" and "classification" lie within the scope of judicial skills; the technique of guideline judgments, developed over the last decade by the Court of Appeal (Criminal Division) in England bears testament to that. But the matters considered under "combination" are in a different bag. On this aspect of the sentencing process, I prefer to treat the Victorian Court of Criminal Appeal's description of sentencing as an "instinctive synthesis" as a frank (and if I may say respectfully) correct statement of the present state of the art of sentencing (Lovegrove, 1984b). Moreover, I would suggest that commentators like Rinaldi, who study appellate court judgments in an attempt to distil and catalog the principles of sentencing to promote consistency, are deceiving themselves if they believe that their efforts are qualitatively different. For their descriptions of the effects on sentence of the various aspects and elements of cases are similarly qualitative, subjective, and intuitive; yet it is these very characteristics of their approach that place severe limitations on the degree of precision their strategy can achieve.

Unless this problem of imprecision in the sentencing process can be solved, critical aspects of sentencing policy will remain largely veiled. As a consequence, debates about penal policy will remain shallow, judges sentencing in the first instance will be given little guidance, and the imposition of punishment will continue to be unhealthily idiosyncratic. The purpose of the present project is to offer a numerical strategy addressing the problems of imprecision associated with the selection, classification, and combination of information for scaling offender culpability and deriving indicators of an offender's rehabilitation prospects. The present discussion has deliberately centered around appellate judgments, since they act as a model for the reasoning required from the sentencing judge.

Legal Perspectives on the Problem of Imprecision in the Sentencing Judgment

Now, the nature of imprecision in the sentencing judgment having been examined, it is appropriate to review practices and proposals, initiated by the judiciary, academic lawyers, and law reform commissions, which seek to address this problem. In line with the orientation of this present project, the discussion is limited to those practices and proposals of relevance to a numerical solution. It is convenient to consider this matter under four headings: statistics describing practice and numerical guidelines prescribing policy, differentiated according to whether the source is the judiciary or law reformers.

Descriptive Statistics: Judiciary

It is clear that in Victoria the courts want detailed statistical information on their current sentencing practices (Lovegrove, 1984b); these would show the relationship between the types and levels of sentence and various combinations of the more common offense and offender characteristics for cases determined in the recent past, differentiated according to statutory offense classifications. Reference to these statistics when determining sentence has been viewed favorably by members of the Victorian Court of Criminal Appeal. Adam and Crockett, JJ., upon calling for statistical data relating to sentences imposed in the State for the type of offense before them, said, "... a judgment as to what is appropriate by way of sentence must depend upon knowledge of sentences for the same or similar offences..." (*Williscroft & others*, 1975, p. 301). However, Young, C.J., in delivering a judgment of the same Court, reacted to the present statistical data with greater caution. He commented that statistics not differentiated according to certain offense and offender characteristics are of little if any use to the courts in their task of determining the quantum of sentence (*Yuill & Besson*, 1975). The significance of sentencing statistics is that in Victoria an appeal may be allowed if the sentence imposed in the case is deemed by the appellate court to be manifestly, not merely arguably, excessive or lenient, and in reaching this decision the Court not infrequently considers sentencing statistics.

In Victoria the Law Department prepares annual statistics of sentencing practices in the courts of first instance. The data for the higher courts are classified by principal offense into well over 100 categories and show the numbers of persons on whom each of the possible penalties was imposed; sentences of imprisonment are subdivided according to length (Law Department–Victoria, Management Information Section, 1985). So now when judges refer to these statistics, they can ascertain the precise range of the sentences imposed for any particular principal offense, but they are left to guess where a particular case lies in relation to that distribution. The Court therefore treats these statistics as but a rough guide and, accordingly, of limited usefulness.

Despite the Court's repeatedly declared healthy skepticism of simple (cf. detailed) sentencing statistics, the observation has been made that there appears to be an increasing trend for members of Counsel to place a great deal of weight on the figures contained in the Law Department's official sentencing statistics and in other statistical material, prepared by counsel, in the course of addressing the Court on sentence (T. Gyorffy, personal communication, April 19, 1985). Indeed, the reasons in the judgment in *Zouras* (1984) comprised largely an analysis of the sentences imposed in 45 similar cases heard in recent years within the jurisdiction, together with very brief summaries of the associated facts of the cases, including the offender's age and prior convictions, the charge(s), general nature of the offense, and the quantity of the drug. (This was a case of trafficking in cannabis, and the sole ground of the appeal was that the sentence was manifestly excessive.)

Nor can it be said that this open attitude to sentencing statistics is characteristic of the Victorian Court of Criminal Appeal alone. Similar attitudes appear to exist in other appellate courts and among nonappellate judges in Australia. Indeed, the Law Reform Commission–Australia (1980) observed that Australian appeal courts are increasingly adopting the practice of requesting the prosecution to produce such statistics to help secure uniformity in sentencing. Similarly, Rinaldi (1979) cited instances when such statistical schedules have attracted laudatory comments from appellate courts in Australia. In a survey of Australian (Federal and State) judges, 83% of the respondents favored the provision of detailed sentencing statistics as a means of promoting uniformity; indeed, this was the most popular of the innovative measures canvassed in the survey (Law Reform Commission– Australia, 1980).

In England the position appears not totally dissimilar. In the review in the preceding section of this chapter, it was noted that in general the English Court of Appeal is prepared to consider its earlier decisions when determining an appeal, although apparently not to cases previously decided at first instance and not at the level of statistical detail as in the previously mentioned case of *Zouras* (1984) in Victoria. Nevertheless, it is said that the Court of Appeal (Criminal Division) regarded sentencing practices in the Crown Court when formulating some of its guideline judgments.

The official criminal statistics for England are published annually by the Home Office (*Criminal Statistics: England and Wales 1985*), but these provide the sentencer with little by way of detailed guidance on current practice. Walker (1985) in his discussion on information for the sentencing judge reached the same conclusion.

The only empirical data on the attitudes of English judges concerning statistical data on sentencing are in the pilot survey of Ashworth et al. (1984). The judges were asked how useful they thought they would find tables setting out the normal range of sentence (type and length) for each legal category of offense, differentiated in terms of the number of previous convictions, over the last 3 years. A majority responded unfavorably on the ground that such statistics would fail to allow for the extent to which sentences must be individualized. Among the minority who were not opposed to the idea there, nevertheless, ran a feeling that the tables could act as no more than a rough guide. These judges were an experienced group; however, on a positive note, a number indicated that the suggested table might be of assistance to some other judges, for example, those sitting at small court centers. At first thought, this response may seem to be more conservative than the Australian reaction, but one must remember that the positive response in Australia was to detailed sentencing statistics, whereas the English judges in the sample were offered only crude statistics, differentiated at a level at which Australian appellate courts tread warily. Indeed, presumably, the apparent acceptance of Thomas's *Principles of Sentencing* (1979) and *Current Sentencing Practice* (1982), which set out for the various offense categories the effects on the determination of the quantum of sentence of a wide range of case facts and patterns of case factors, indicates that at least under certain circumstances significant numbers of judges value detailed guidance on the current practices of the appellate courts (see Skinner, 1984). Also encouraging was the finding of Ashworth et al. (1984) that a majority of the judges valued consistency in sentencing and many would be prepared to modify their own approaches if that were necessary to achieve consistency.

The Canadian Sentencing Commission (1987) reported that sentencing takes place in a virtual statistical vacuum: there is almost no systematic, up-to-date and readily accessible information, provided on a continuing basis, about the types and quanta of sentence being imposed in the courts for the various legal offense categories. In a survey of judges, conducted as part of the Commission's work, 79% of respondents favored information about current sentencing practices of the courts; presumably, this would include numerical information, differentiated according to offense and offender factors.

In the United States the co-operation given by the judiciary in several jurisdictions to Wilkins and his associates (1978) for the development of descriptive sentencing statistics is evidence that some North American judges saw potential value in this approach (see Kress, 1980).

Clearly, in Australia, the time is ripe for detailed sentencing statistics for the information of sentencing judges. In England, the United States, and, in particular, Canada, many judges might find value in appropriately differentiated statistics on current sentencing practices. One of the main tasks of the present study is to address the problem of introducing detail into sentencing statistics so the data show the relationship between combinations of offense and offender characteristics and sentence.

Numerical Guidelines: Judiciary

In England the Court of Appeal (Criminal Division) has recognized and is now addressing the problem of unnecessary imprecision in the sentencing judgment (see Lovegrove, 1987). Lord Lane, C.J., highlighted the need for continuing policy development very clearly in his now famous judgment in *Bibi* (1980) when he stated that "(w)e are not aiming at uniformity of sentence. . . (w)e are aiming at uniformity of approach" (p. 179). This declaration is important not only because it confirms the need for more detailed guidance for sentencers to promote consistency but also because it sets the standard by which consistency in sentencing may be judged. An implication of this position is that consistency of sentence is an undesirable criterion because there is an inherent danger, arising from the failure to define *like*, that material differences between cases may be ignored, and, thereby, disparity in sentencing may be fostered. Rather, a safer criterion for consistency is being offered – sentences would be acceptably consistent if there were consistency of approach. And what is required for "consistency of approach"? Surely, it means that there must be agreement on the determination of material case factors, classification of case facts in relation to these factors, weighting of case factors, rules for combining case factors, and the appropriate types and levels of sentence for various combinations of case factors. It should be said parenthetically that the preceding points are a behavioral scientist's interpretation of the grounds on which appellate intervention is allowed, as they were set out by the Victorian Court of Criminal Appeal in the majority judgment of Lowe and Gavan Duffy, JJ., in *Taylor and O'Meally* (1958): these include, inter alia, taking into account matters that are not relevant, failing to take into account relevant matters, giving excessive or insufficient weight to a matter taken into account, or imposing a sentence that is obviously – not merely arguably – too severe or too lenient.

The guideline judgments of the Court of Appeal (Criminal Division) are the means by which the Court is addressing the problem of imprecision. In some of these judgments, the Court, when determining an appeal against sentence, takes the opportunity to set out some of the patterns of offending for that particular legal category of offense and then to lay down an appropriate range of sentence for each of the patterns. In this way the Court shows the joint effects on the quantum of sentence of *particular* combinations of *several* case factors. This is numerical guidance. Apparently, many sentencing judges find these decisions helpful. The point of introducing the notion of guideline judgments at this stage of the discussion is not to evaluate the extent to which they further the cause of precision; that is done in the next chapter. Rather, it is to draw attention to the fact that the Court of Appeal (Criminal Division) in England has sanctioned a form of numerical guidance. Moreover, the Court's attitude to consistency reveals that proposals for improving guidance in sentencing policy must incorporate methods for facilitating the Court's development of sentencing policy and not merely seek to describe the Court's current practice. The Court's expression "aiming at uniformity of approach" implies development.

This innovation has been introduced recently into some appellate courts in Canada, according to the Canadian Sentencing Commission (1987). These have taken various forms, including differentiating offenses within broad statutory offense classifications, setting starting points for tariffs, and listing material offense and offender characteristics. One appellate court has echoed the "uniformity of approach" sentiment. Nevertheless, there are few such cases. In the survey of Canadian judges, 59% thought that appellate guideline judgments would reduce disparity (Canadian Sentencing Commission, 1987).

Descriptive Statistics: Reform

In its Interim Report the Law Reform Commission—Australia (1980) recommended the collection of detailed data on current sentencing practices, with a view to developing a set of guidelines indicating the ranges of penalty for specific categories of offenses and offenders. In doing so, they drew attention to the work in the United States of Wilkins and his associates (1978) and asserted that these researchers had developed a reliable set of methods. It was stated expressly that the guidelines should be advisory only, designed to assist in general terms. An important question is whether Wilkins's strategy is valid—this matter is taken up in the next chapter.

In England the Advisory Council on the Penal System (1978) viewed Wilkins's guidelines approach favorably because its aim was in sympathy with the Council's own goal, namely, to describe and give greater weight to what the courts are now practicing. However, they doubted whether "such a sophisticated formalisation of the "tariff" would be acceptable in the English context" (p. 167), at least at this time.

The Canadian Sentencing Commission (1987), too, was favorably disposed to readily accessible, detailed information on current sentencing practices of the trial courts and decisions of the appellate courts being made available to sentencing judges. Indeed, the Commission proposed that the data describing current practice (and information on case law) should appear as advisory information on their proposed "guideline sheets" carrying the presumptive dispositions and quanta of sentence for the various offense categories. On the sheets included for illustrative purposes, this statistical information comprised simply the lengths of imprisonment for several percentile points. The Commission made it clear that they were fully seized of the need for more detailed information on current practice and drew attention to a pilot project investigating this matter. Presumably, the reference is to the work of Doob and Park (1987) who aim to show for each legal offense category the relationship between the type and quantum of sentence and various combinations of offense and offender characteristics for cases determined in the courts. However, the proposals of Hogarth (1986a), who is also working in Canada, deserve close attention and should not be forgotten. Both these projects are reviewed in the next chapter. Clearly, the desirability of developing and providing judges with detailed sentencing statistics is a live issue in the minds of academics and law reformers.

Numerical Guidelines: Reform

The Canadian Sentencing Commission (1987) has presented a major proposal aimed at structuring the decision whether imprisonment is appropriate in a particular case and, if it is, the quantum. It is a response to what the Commission perceived as an unhealthy vagueness and open-endness in current sentencing policy. The guidance is both quantitative and qualitative and is presented in the form of "guidelines sheets." For each legal category of offense, there is either a qualified or unqualified "in" or "out" presumption and, where appropriate, a (relatively) narrow presumptive range for the length of imprisonment. (To provide guidance on quantum, it was necessary for some broadly defined offenses to be subdivided.) For offenses with a qualified presumption, the sentencer must assess the seriousness of the offense, including the offender's culpability, and the extent of the offender's criminal record to determine the presumption in particular cases. These two factors are also germane to fixing the length of sentence within the guidelines, as well as determining departures from the guidelines. Finally, a nonexhaustive list of aggravating and mitigating factors is provided to guide sentencers in their assessment of the seriousness of the offense and the culpability of the offender. It is not relevant here to evaluate this proposal comprehensively. But it is appropriate to make and illustrate the point that this proposal leaves the sentencing judges with a wide discretion and offers only limited and imprecise guidance in their exercise of this discretion, especially regarding the classification and combination of information. This point is acknowledged frankly in the Report and an example is given there. The Commission asked, ". . .what is the threshold of seriousness beyond which a thief should be incarcerated if he has a relevant record?" (p. 327). The suggested answer is that it may be related to specific sums of money. This is the problem of classification. And, one may ask, how does the amount of money relate to the influence of other factors, such as the extent of the organization of the offense, in the determination of this threshold? In relation to this matter, consider the vagueness of the Commission's reference to one instance of weighting, "Nothing in the guidelines precludes a judge from giving greater weight to the absence of a criminal record in mitigation than the presence of a record as aggravating" (p. 322). This is the problem of combination. The Commission's approach is to hand the problem over to the appellate courts for guideline judgments. This proposal, then, leaves largely unsolved the problems of interest in this project: classification and combination as a source of imprecision.

Of course, in the United States there has been enthusiasm for prescriptive numerical guidelines, and several States have embraced or attempted to embrace them. Perhaps the best known example, the guidelines produced by the Minnesota Sentencing Guidelines Commission (1984), will be evaluated in the next chapter.

In a recent article Ashworth (1987) discussed the problems of devising guidance for sentencers and the nature of possible solutions in the English context. Accordingly, the analysis does not offer a clear and consistent set of proposals; indeed, it is possible to discern an ideal and an actual solution.

Ashworth's (1987) ideal system would seem to include a list of aggravating and mitigating offense and offender factors as well as the importance (weight) of each factor in the determination of the quantum of sentence; there would be ceilings and/or recommended sentences for specific statutory offense categories or subcategories, and these would act as reference points for determining the effect on sentence of the various case factors. Ashworth recognizes that the representation of this sort of guidance would require a complex numerical framework. Clearly, this scheme would require agreement on the material case factors and the starting points. That would be relatively easy. Ashworth acknowledges that the problematic element is determining the weights of the case factors, a process requiring complex and awkward decisions, but he notes reassuringly, "...in an evolving process of guidance that should not give rise to embarrassment" (p. 86). His illustration of the weighting problem explains the matter succinctly. Assume a theft of \$10 involving a breach of trust is more serious than a theft of \$100 where there has been no trust, at what value of theft would the second case be regarded as more serious? This proposal has much to commend it, but unfortunately Ashworth does not deal with the conceptual and empirical problems that would attend its development.

Ashworth's (1987) actual proposal is less sophisticated, in that the guidance it offers does not include factor weights derived through trade-offs; broadly, it contains the following five elements. (1) Differentiate offenses within legal offense categories according to the nature of the offending. (2) Divide each of these groups into six to represent offenders with zero to five or more prior convictions. (3) Set a ceiling or recommended sentence for each of the cells. (4) List the material aggravating and mitigating offense and offender characteristics. (5) Provide a qualitative indication of their normal effects on the quantum of sentence; for example, there might be a rule stating that less weight should be accorded to convictions for relatively minor offenses than to offenses similar in character to the present offense.

The positive feature of the preceding proposal is that it introduces greater precision in relation to ceilings/starting points and relevant factors. But on the effects of factors or combinations of factors on sentence it offers little, particularly for offenses of medium (e.g., burglary) and high (e.g., robbery) seriousness. In such offenses the aggravating and mitigating factors may have a dramatic effect on sentence. In the higher courts in Victoria, for approximately a half to a third of the cases of burglary, the disposition is by way of a noncustodial sentence and yet the normal upper limit is about 7 years, and in robbery approximately a quarter of the offenders receive noncustodial dispositions, with the upper limit around 16 years (Law Department–Victoria, Management Information Section, 1985). Of course, the use of statutory offense subcategories may ameliorate this problem in some cases, but it is not an efficient solution. Indeed, at a relatively high level of detail it would become impracticable. Clearly, the use of subdivisions within offense and offender characteristics is a means of allowing for the differential effects of various factors on sentence, but it is an inferior procedure to the trade-off.

In summary the bête noire of these ideal and actual solutions is Ashworth's failure to deal adequately with the numerical side of the classification and combination of case factors. A particularly noteworthy feature of Ashworth's proposal should be mentioned. It concerns his treatment of the problem of assessing the relative weights of factors by means of trade-offs between the factors in the process of comparing the seriousness of cases. His example of this process is outlined above; it is also worth adding his insightful comment on the possible legal view of the feasibility of determining weights through this process as a means of developing guidance.

> The great temptation. . . is to say: 'It depends'. And so it does. But it does *not* depend on an infinite number of factors, and in effect the question *is* answered every day by the courts all over the country. (Ashworth, 1987, p. 86)

The present study may be seen as building on this approach to the weighting of case factors.

Recently, von Hirsch (1987), in addressing the matter of providing the courts with more detailed guidance, compared and contrasted quantitative and qualitative guidelines. On this issue he stressed the potential contribution of the legislature in providing guidance to the courts on matters such as the primary rationale for sentencing, the major case factors that should determine sentence, with a general indication of their weight, and circumstances under which prison may or may not be a suitable sanction. It would fall to the appellate courts to decide cases according to these principles and in doing so to develop more detailed and precise rules as well as a tariff. Clearly, this proposal would leave the courts with the sort of decisions to which Ashworth's contribution is directed. Indeed, Ashworth (1987) noted that the practical difficulties associated with developing the elaborate framework required for numerical precision led von Hirsch (1981), in his attempt to translate aspects of penal policy into penalty, to propose (or at least apparently approve of) a rather crude weighting to take some account of variation in the seriousness of various prior convictions.

Nevertheless, numerical guidance should not take place in a jurisprudential vacuum, and in developing this link von Hirsch's (1985) analysis has made and will continue to make a valuable contribution. It is beyond the scope of the present study to say whether these broad underlying principles should be drawn up by parliament, a sentencing commission, or the appellate courts.

This section has examined the judiciary's attitude to structuring the sentencing discretion as it relates to the precision afforded by numbers. Additionally, the proposals of law reformers on this score have been examined. First, it appears reasonable to conclude that there is an increasing awareness among the judiciary that detailed sentencing statistics and numerical guidelines may be of some assistance in providing guidance to sentencers. Nevertheless, the curial innovations and the proposals of law reformers do not appear to deal adequately with the major problems associated with the imprecision in the traditional sentencing judgment.

The Study: Challenge and Constraints

The present study is concerned with the description and development of sentencing policy. It covers those aspects of policy concerned with the scale of offender culpability and the indicators of an offender's rehabilitation prospects. Currently, policy and practice relating to these decisions is characterized by imprecision associated with the selection, classification, and combination of relevant case information. In the present study a quantitative solution to this problem is developed and its feasibility explored.

Describing sentencing policy involves showing separately for the various statutory offense categories the relationship between the offense and offender characteristics of cases and the types and quanta of sentence imposed in the courts for those cases in the recent past. In this study the product is referred to as *detailed sentencing statistics*. This policy is found not only in the appellate courts but also in the decisions of judges sentencing in the first instance, since appellate courts deal with general principles and, with the exception of guideline judgments, determine only issues raised in the (biased) selection of cases with which these courts are required to deal; accordingly, much of sentencing policy can be discovered only in the courts of first instance, which necessarily are left with the task of giving detail to the broad appellate policies. It should be remembered that it is only the principles, enunciated in the appellate courts, which must be followed.

There are two reasons why it is important to attempt to describe current policy. First, debating sentencing policy with a view to reform is rather difficult when there is doubt over the content of current policy. The task of research on this matter then is to describe systematically those elements of policy already enunciated by the courts and to discover other aspects of policy yet to be declared publicly by the courts but on which there is agreement across the judiciary. Ideally, research should seek to identify policy directly, rather than indirectly through an analysis of actual court sentences, because the latter are noisy as a result of limitations in the information processing capabilities of judges. Moreover, policy considerations relating penal aims, case facts, and penalty are not available from an empirical analysis of sentencing practice. Of course, the belief that the task of comprehensively describing policy is achievable currently is naive, for there are matters that appellate courts and sentencing judges have yet to address and other matters about which the courts do not speak with one voice (Ashworth, 1984; Ashworth et al., 1984).

The second reason for attempting to describe sentencing policy is to ensure that all members of the judiciary are informed. To the extent that sentencers are uninformed or misinformed on particular matters they are forced to develop their own policies, and these inevitably will show idiosyncratic features. A functionally related notion is the concept of guidance. This refers to a device of some sort whose function is to assist the judge in classifying and aggregating information as part of the determination of the sentence; such an aid is necessary because humans' capacity for processing complex information without error is quite limited. Again, the effect of error will be idiosyncratic sentencing. Clearly, guidance cannot be introduced unless there is an articulated policy. In this context *idiosyncratic* is a synonym for disparity.

Disparity is a more complex notion than would first appear in its definition according to the maxim, "Like cases should be treated alike." In fact it is helpful to distinguish four forms of disparity. *Actual* disparity covers instances when significantly different sentences have been imposed in cases not differing in terms of case factors considered relevant in current sentencing policy, and vice versa, and that are similar in all other respects of possible consequence. This latter qualification acts to limit the usefulness of this face of disparity as an operational concept. Such disparity may be due to a judge's ignorance of sentencing policy, deliberate flouting of policy, or error in applying the policy. Description and guidance as remedies are directed primarily at the first and third wrongs. *Potential* disparity refers to instances when two similar sentences have been imposed in cases that do not differ in terms of case factors considered relevant in current sentencing policy but that differ in terms of case factors bearing on current policy. Such a situation would arise when two cases differed in terms of the offender's employment status and rehabilitation had been deemed by the appellate court to be a legitimate goal of sentence, and yet the court had not specifically addressed the effect of employment status on sentence. (This situation would also arise when different sentences had been imposed and the cases were similar in relation to employment status.) The source of this sort of disparity is an absence of a comprehensive sentencing policy. The appropriate course of remedial action is the further development of policy. It serves as a useful introduction to the third notion of disparity to note that the discussion to this point has been set in the context of policy covered or yet to be addressed by the legislature and the courts (as well as a sentencing commission/council, if one had been established).

Of course, the policy considerations acting as the standard here may be in the mind of the reformer, who may be the sentencing judge. In these circumstances it is convenient to apply the closely related but distinguishable notion of *hypothetical* disparity. It follows that those who are responsible for policy should be ever alert to the views of those who have the responsibility of administering punishment in individual cases.

Finally, *immaterial* disparity refers to instances where similar sentences have been imposed on cases that differ only on characteristics obviously immaterial to policy considerations. Clearly, this aspect of disparity is of no consequence.

Actual disparity is always unfair, if the validity of current policy is accepted; potential disparity may be unfair and can be determined only by those bodies responsible for policy; hypothetical disparity may be unfair, and is by its nature an open question and, again, it can be resolved only by the appropriate authority; immaterial disparity is never unfair.

What are the consequences of these deliberations? The discussion under actual and potential disparity predicates the moral necessity of attempting to describe and develop sentencing policy and to implement a system of guidance. Of course, it is impossible to describe or to develop policy fully. Indeed, it would be undesirable. The considerations relating to potential and hypothetical disparity caution one against any attempt to implement a system of comprehensive guidance in which the sentencer is not left with room to maneuver. There should always be an opportunity for novel factors, novel variations of common factors, or novel policies to influence sentencers in their determination of what are appropriate sentences for particular cases. This, of course, introduces the notion of discretion (see Davis, 1969). To the extent that sentencing policy has been articulated and there is guidance, the determination of sentence can be said to have been structured, and to the extent that it has been structured, there is less incentive or opportunity for the sentencing judge to exercise a personal discretion.

Discretion serves two important functions. First, it is widely acknowledged that the courts administer punishment as though with a blunt instrument. To say, as is commonly said, that discretion permits punishments to be fine-tuned is fanciful when the term *fine-tuned* is used to convey the notion of increased validity in the absence of any guidance, but discretion certainly permits differentiation. It would exceed, if not human wit then certainly human patience, to set down the effect on sentence of every imaginable variation in the patterns of offending and the characteristics of offenders. Indeed, the framework for providing guidance on more than the more common case factors would be unwieldy. Nevertheless, if judges are permitted a discretion, then less common case factors or less common variations or patterns of common case factors can play their part in the determination of sentence, as justice would require them to be considered. Unless a discretion resides with the judge sentencing in the first instance, such circumstances would be ignored or unnecessarily give rise to appeals. Second, when discretion resides with sentencing judges it is open to them to be creative. A sentencer may vary the aim or mix of aims of sentence normally associated with a particular set of common case factors or attempt to give effect to those aims with a penalty seemingly at variance with policy or current practice, because the sentencer believes that there are facts about the offense or circumstances relating to the offender that are not covered under current policy and yet appear to warrant a novel approach. And then there are changes in community attitudes to be reckoned with over time. This creative and innovative use of discretion requires the sentencer to exercise judgment outside the bounds of policy but not in disregard of policy. Nevertheless, the discretion must be exercised in a principled manner. It is important to recall Galligan's (1981) warning on this matter:

> . . . the distinction between policies and factors individual to the offender is misleading. If the factor is so personal to the offender that it is incapable of being generalised and related to broader sentencing policies, then it is hard to see why it should be allowed to form part of the sentencing decision. If on the other hand the factor is individual only in

the sense that the existing policies do not but should take account of it, then the question is one of sentencing policy and should be discussed by the sentencer in those terms. (p. 310)

If either the prosecution or defense feel that the sentencing judge in the course of exercising this discretion has failed to do justice, then it is for the appellate court to decide the issue. Of course, the potential danger associated with sentencing discretion is idiosyncratic sentencing practices, and this danger is greater where the influence of policy is diminished, and may reach a point where sentencing is open to charges of lawlessness, as it occurred in the United States in the 1970s and was captured poignantly by Frankel (1973) in the title of his book *Criminal Sentences: Law without Order.* There should be a balance between policy and discretion (see Davis, 1969; and also, Baldwin & Hawkins, 1984). Indeed, the balance to be struck between the control of disparity and the encouragement of individualization and imaginative responses to crime is no doubt a fine one. This principle is easily stated, but the determination of the balance has yet to be analyzed rigorously. In any case it is not germane to the task of the present analysis although it is of critical import in implementing a system of guidance. A second danger arises from the fact that in the discretionary component of a judgment the information must be processed unaided and is open to information-processing errors.

In view of the foregoing discussion, it is possible to formulate a role and place for particularized statistics describing judges' sentencing policies, namely, to quantify the tariff to reduce the degree to which judges must exercise their sentencing discretion intuitively and without knowledge of how their colleagues have acted or would act in similar cases (Lovegrove, 1984b). The detailed statistics would show the combined effects on sentence of common case characteristics, and these net sentences would act as precise reference points against which judges could individualize sentences further. The aim is deliberately couched in this qualified form so that judicial discretion is left unfettered in relation to the consideration of the uniqueness of the case. This standard against which judges would exercise discretion would also assist the appellate courts in their task of reviewing the exercise of the sentencing discretion in the courts of first instance. If this view of the role of sentencing statistics is accepted, then the representation (model) of the relationship between case facts and sentence must be intelligible to judges and compatible with the way in which they structure their sentencing decisions.

To explain this point clearly, it is necessary to digress. I discussed the development of detailed sentencing statistics with a lawyer. He queried the apparent complexity of it all. Lawyers were not interested in an academic's model describing how judges determine sentence; all they wanted were statistics simply showing what really happens now in the determination of sentence—how various combinations of case factors really affect sentence. Behavioral scientists will realize, of course, that there is no scientific answer to his deceptively simple request. Knowledge of what really happens is but a forlorn hope. All that we can continue to do is to develop models of (in this case) decision making that represent increasingly closer approximations to reality; without a model we would not know what information to select or how to construe it. This leads now to the point. On the ground that a model must be developed to interpret the data, and then to represent them, the contention here is that the model must be faithful to the structure of judicial thought (Lovegrove, 1984b). For if judges were not able to understand the basis of the reference point (the way in which the common case facts—the factors incorporated in the guidance—were related to sentence in the guidance, i.e., the means of deriving the factor weights and the rules for combining the individual case factors), and this framework was not congruent with their own approach, then it would be difficult for the judges to determine precisely the effect on sentence of unique case facts (the factors not incorporated in the guidance) in relation to the reference point provided by the guidance. Moreover, there are the related dangers that judges might be less inclined to individualize sentences in the face of incomprehensible guidance or, perhaps, ignore the guidance altogether. The challenge here is to develop an appropriate conceptual framework.

This discussion, having covered the description of sentencing policy, now turns to consider the second facet—development. The development of sentencing policy involves filling in the gaps in current sentencing policy, and may include formulating policy on matters previously untouched or declaring present policies in greater detail. The purpose of developing policy is to promote consistency of approach and thereby provide greater guidance to reduce disparity. Accordingly, the considerations raised previously are germane here. In the context of this study, this product is referred to as *numerical guidelines*. Clearly, to provide for development it is necessary to adopt or develop empirical techniques designed to facilitate judicial input in relation to both the structure and substance of sentencing policy. It follows from the discussion on discretion that the method must have the facility of permitting the ready incorporation of additions and changes in sentencing policy, because policies would otherwise be static. Here, again, there are similarities with the description of sentencing policy, because to describe policy one must discover it, and it will be seen later, this requires judicial input. Then there is the notion of reform. This is closely allied to the concept of development, but involves more, namely, changes to sentencing policy such as the reweighting of offense factors.

This chapter has concerned setting the idea of a quantitative approach to sentencing in its legal context and delineating the associated issues and problems. The next chapter turns to a description and evaluation of several proposed solutions to this problem.

2
Approaches to the Development of Detailed Sentencing Statistics and Numerical Guidelines

This chapter comprises a review of attempts to introduce greater precision and structure into the sentencing judgment through quantitative guidance showing the relationship between various combinations of case factors and the associated types and quanta of sentence; this review includes both descriptively and prescriptively oriented approaches. Specifically, the evaluation covers the guideline judgments of the Court of Appeal (Criminal Division) in England (see Ashworth, 1984); Wilkins et al.'s (1978) empirically based descriptive guidelines; Hogarth's (1986a, 1986b) sentencing data base; Doob's sentencing data base (Doob, 1986; Doob & Park, 1987); the Minnesota Sentencing Guidelines Commission's (1984) policy-based prescriptive guidelines; and the United States Sentencing Commission's (1987) presumptive guidelines. The following evaluations are not general but are confined within the framework of the present study; they are specifically concerned with the potential contribution of each of the approaches, where appropriate, to the development of detailed sentencing statistics describing current practice and to greater uniformity of approach in sentencing through the development of sentencing policy as a basis for guidance.

Guideline Judgments of the Court of Appeal (Criminal Division) in England

Guideline judgments take various forms and cover a range of matters, including general policy, recommended and forbidden patterns of reasoning and the listing of relevant case factors (Ashworth, 1984). This discussion centers on those judgments offering numerical guidance. In these judgments the Court, when determining an appeal against sentence, takes the opportunity to set out some of the patterns of offending for that particular legal category of offense and then to lay down an appropriate range of sentence for each of the patterns. Or the Court may identify some of the major case factors for a particular offense type and then provide guidance on how each of these factors or certain combinations of these factors affect the quantum of sentence. In this way the Court is able to show the joint effects on sentence of *particular* combinations of *several* case factors. The case of *Aramah* (1982), which deals with the importation and distribution of drugs, illustrates this approach well. The Court's strategy was to subdivide this class of offense into type of drug (Class A– particularly heroin and morphine, and Class B–particularly cannabis) and within each type according to whether the offense involved importing, supplying, or possessing the drug. In dealing with Class A drugs, Lord Lane, C.J., declared that deterrent sentences were appropriate here and then set about formulating a tariff. For large-scale importation, that is, where the street value is at least £100,000, 7 years may be regarded as a minimum; where the value reaches £1,000,000, sentences of 12 to 14 years are in order. And rarely should an importer of an appreciable amount receive less than 4 years. However, a confession of guilt together with considerable assistance to the police may properly be considered as a significant mitigating factor. For supplying the drug, the sentence depends on the degree of involvement of the offender, the amount of trafficking, the value of the drug being handled, and the nearness to the source of supply: 3 years may be considered a normal minimum, and the sentences within the range for large-scale importation may be appropriate in some cases.

The judgment continues, but the preceding coverage is sufficient for illustrating the point. A judgment in this form is an important step toward consistency of approach and the provision of detailed guidance to judges sentencing in the first instance. Material case factors are identified; reference is made to the relationship between levels on a factor and quantum of sentence; and direction is given on the effects of various combinations of factors on sentence. This is a move in the right direction, but it represents little more than a few faltering steps. The limitations in this guidance are obvious. Only a small number of factors are covered; the relationship between sentence and levels on a factor is delineated for only one factor and then only crudely–one is left to guess how the intermediate levels relate to the ends of the scale; the effects on sentence of combinations of factors is confined to no more than a few factors and combinations of factors. Nevertheless, Lord Lane, C.J., recognized the limitation of these judgments in his observation that it is difficult to give a precise indication of the appropriate sentence for a particular offense in advance, because there are so many possible variations in the commission of an offense (see the judgment in *Gould and others*, 1983). This is a correct and important observation. The reason for this limitation is that there is no rule specifying how the various elements should be combined to arrive at an overall assessment. This is the Achilles' heel of the guideline judgments. Unless such a rule is formulated, guidance must of necessity be limited and crude. Of course, the absence of a rule does not prevent relevant factors from being identified and weighted, nor does it prevent the delineation of the relationship between the levels on a case factor and sentence for the relevant case factors. Moves on these fronts should be encouraged strongly. However, unless there is a rule covering the aggregation of this information, then the sentencer is without guidance on how to apply each of the aspects of the guidance in particular cases.

And without guidance on combination, there is a danger that the detailed guidance on the individual elements will come to naught or even add to the sentencer's confusion. Now, when there is a rule covering the combination of case information, it is possible to show the effects on sentence of *any* combination of a *substantial* number of case factors.

The absence of an aggregation rule has consequences in addition to limiting the guidance to several combinations of a few case factors. First, the guideline sentences for the various combinations of case facts within each legal category are intuitively determined, and this entails the implicit application of factor weights and aggregation rules. Now, there is no way of checking whether the guideline sentences have been determined according to a coherent set of principles, unless they can be compared against sentences determined according to an explicit set of rules governing the combination of case information. The second point is not unrelated. It should be remembered that, even where guideline judgments apply to actual cases in the courts of first instance, sentencing judges retain a discretion to individualize the sentence within the guidelines according to case factors additional to the guidelines, or even to depart from the guidelines if the circumstances of a case justify such a course (see the judgment of the Court in *de Havilland*, 1983). Clearly, it may be difficult for a judge to make proper allowance for the less common case factors where the effects on sentence of the guideline factors are not explicit or, perhaps, even coherent.

Wilkins's Empirically Based Descriptive Guidelines

Wilkins and his associates' (1978) research is an original attempt to provide detailed statistics identifying the major offense and offender characteristics, together with their weights, associated with the quantum of sentence. These statistics are compiled by predicting actual sentencing decisions from the information before judges for cases determined in the courts. The resulting equations are said to represent a mathematical description of sentencing policy. The system proposed by Wilkins et al. is not only descriptive but it has a prescriptive component. To use this system for a particular case, the judge must allot points in terms of the extent to which it is characterized by the offense and offender characteristics identified in the statistical analyses. The scores on the two dimensions are used to identify the appropriate cell in the table and this provides sentencing data for particular combinations of offense and offender characteristics. Typically, the statistics cover the percentage imprisoned and, for those imprisoned, an estimate of the length of imprisonment.

This information comprises the guidelines. Judges are expected to impose sentences within the guidelines in about 85% of cases. The prescriptive element of this approach rests on the assumption that like-offenders committing like-offenses ought to be treated alike. Expressed from another perspective, this system requires the assumption that as a matter of course the major determinant in a judgment as to the appropriate sentence for a particular case is the quantum of sentence similar cases have attracted over recent years within the jurisdiction. And there's the rub.

In the United States the National Institute of Law Enforcement and Criminal Justice (1978) has produced what amounts to a manual to be followed by those implementing guidelines systems. For the purpose of later evaluation in this section, it is appropriate to outline some of the major steps in the procedure.

1. List the variables in the information available to the judge about the offenses and the offenders: Wilkins et al. (1978) used about 200 items.
2. Use stepwise multiple regression to identify a relatively small set of variables (and their weights) that together give the best prediction of actual sentencing decisions.
3. Establish categories and associated points for each of the variables found to be related to sentence, such that each category marks a substantially different sentence. The most complex variable in Wilkins et al.'s system has six divisions, but binary classifications are not uncommon.
4. Develop models showing the relationship between the sum of the scores on the offense and offender dimensions and the sentence. The classification of Wilkins et al. on the dimension covering offender characteristics used six items of information relating to past criminal record and employment history.

To differentiate offense, a separate guideline table was required for each of eight State statutory classes of offense. For the six tables presented, offenses were divided according to seriousness into three or four groups and assigned seriousness rankings determined by project staff members. Further differentiation was achieved by adding points to this rank according to the degree of harm or loss suffered by the victim. Each table comprised a two-dimensional grid, one axis for the offense and the second for the offender characteristics. The most complex table comprised 30 (6×5) cells.

McCarthy's (1978) guidelines were slightly more complex, including a set of variables tapping the offender's actions since last arrest and as well separate tables for specific offenses (cf. classes of offense). The presentation of his models also was more detailed. Each table had five dimensions; the most complex table comprised 48 cells. Another significant difference between the two approaches was that McCarthy's choice of variables for the assessment of offense characteristics was more closely based on the results of the regression analysis. Nevertheless, it is fundamental to the development of guidelines that an advisory board comprising judges has the final say on the structure and composition of the model where the board's view on the salience of factors differs from the empirical results.

Limitations of Wilkins's Approach

Describing Current Sentencing Practice: Developing Detailed Sentencing Statistics

In the first chapter a section was devoted to an analysis of the structure of the sentencing judgment and judicial thought as it bears on the determination of sentence. There, the view was taken that the traditional sentencing judgment comprises two elements: discussion about the principles of sentencing to be applied in particular cases and reference to the quanta of sentence similar cases have attracted in recent years. It is contended here that the source of all the difficulties associated with Wilkins et al.'s (1978) approach to the description of sentencing is his failure to take account of the nature and structure of the sentencing judgment in the development of his strategy. The point should be made parenthetically, however, that this omission is understandable, perhaps it was unavoidable, in the United States, where there is no strong tradition of an active appellate court determining appeals against sentence and, in performing that function, developing a body of policy. Wilkins's disregard of the significance of the first element of the sentencing judgment is one manifestation of this omission; a second is his adoption of inappropriate modeling techniques to represent the relationship between the facts of a case and sentence. Alternatively, it may be said Wilkins saw the problem of describing sentencing policy as involving no more than accounting for, in terms of a correlational (predictive) paradigm, the relationship between case facts and sentence.

If the first element of the sentencing judgment—deliberations about the punitive process—is ignored, then the sentencing process will become impoverished in a number of significant ways. First, by way of illustration, consider a hypothetical cell offering the following guidance: 50% of cases falling within the cell received a noncustodial sentence and of the remainder, 80% were imprisoned for a period of up to 2 years. In the light of the earlier analysis of the sentencing judgment one would be prompted to ask whether the justification for all or some of the noncustodial sentences was in terms of tariff principles (i.e., the offenders' culpability was not regarded as very serious and, therefore, on the principle of proportionality, a custodial sentence was not deserved) or on the basis of an individualized measure justified on the ground of rehabilitation, independent of considerations of proportionality. Clearly, in Wilkins's scheme the number of factors is too few, and the distinctions on the offense and offender factors are too crude to provide guidance on this point.

Moreover, judges would be expected to be discouraged from individualizing sentences and from pursuing creativity in sentencing in response to novel case characteristics, changes in the nature of offending, and changes in the circumstances of offenders and community attitudes. Such pressure might be based on a fear of exceeding the guidelines, might result from a perceived inferiority of personal judgment against a supposed scientific assessment, or simply might have roots in laziness or expediency. How can one therefore agree with Wilkins et al. (1978) that one advantage of guidelines is that they speed up sentencing? At this point the term "robot sentencing" (Zalman, 1978) strikes a chord. As a consequence, there would be a danger of the appellate court being effectively downgraded to little more than a board of clerks, whose duty then would be merely to check the additions of the sentencing judges; there would be no grist for the mill. Clearly, at the very least, the significance of the appellate court as a source of sentencing policy would be diminished. One therefore might expect little or no policy development and associated guidance on the circumstances of cases under which particular penal goals are most appropriate and the dispositions that would see justice done in various circumstances.

Because Wilkins's approach (Wilkins et al., 1978) does not appreciate the active and continuing role of the appellate court in the development of sentencing policy, it is not surprising that his system does not have the facility for readily and coherently incorporating the effects of new appellate court decisions. The reason for this is that his guidelines are formulated from a sample of actual sentencing decisions; so before reformulating the guidelines, one should wait until a large number of cases have been sentenced by judges cognizant of the appellate court's new rulings. It is to be expected that there would be many periods during which the guidelines would lag behind current sentencing practice. Clearly, this possibility makes actual sentencing practice an unattractive basis for the guidelines. Wilkins et al. (1978) suggest that the judges in a jurisdiction should meet regularly to review those decisions falling outside the guidelines and, if any of the departures indicate the need for policy revision, then the guidelines should be modified accordingly. One cannot but wonder why, then, the guidelines could not be constructed similarly. Indeed, surely there is the risk of introducing incoherence into the system when such ad hoc changes are introduced without regard to the logic underlying the construction of the guidelines. (See also, Wilkins, 1980, for his discussion on policy revision.)

Another consequence of Wilkins's orientation to the problem is that the researcher's mind is blinkered to the possibility of identifying sentencing policy directly rather than indirectly through an analysis of the relationship between case facts and sentence. This is responsible for the problematic nature of the process of updating the guidelines. It is also unfortunate because the sentence imposed in court (i.e., sentencing practice) is a noisy criterion: indeed, this is a raison d'être for guidelines. This latter point is developed later.

Finally, because Wilkins focuses on the second element of the sentencing judgment—the relationship between the facts of the case and sentence—rather than the first element—individualized justice in the light of sentencing policy—it is not surprising that the guidance provided by the sentences in the cells of the tables does not lend itself to being treated as a reference point against which judges can exercise their discretion. This is because the developers of these guidelines relied on sophisticated statistical techniques to identify and weight salient variables. They also used complex models to relate sentences to facts about cases, although the two-dimensional model of Wilkins et al. (1978) is simpler than some, for example, McCarthy's (1978) model with its five dimensions and 48 cells. To be sure, these guidelines models are easy to follow in the cookbook mode, where the judges' task is little more than to score the case according to the guidelines and then impose the guideline sentence. The point is that the representation of the relationship between specific combinations of case variables and the current types and quanta of sentence would not be comprehensible to judges and barristers without statistical training. This being so, there is the danger of the table becoming a master to be followed blindly, rather than one of a number of reference points against which the judges could exercise their discretion. And if judges did attempt to individualize further the punishment and yet did not understand how the case factors were related to sentence in the model, it is doubtful whether they could properly allow for the effects on sentence of the unique elements in relation to the common elements. Clearly, sentencing would be in danger of becoming mechanical and mathematical rather than deliberative and policy based.

This discussion now turns to the modeling techniques adopted by Wilkins et al. (1978) to show the relationship between the facts of the case and sentence. Stepwise multiple regression yields the average effect of the minimum number of case variables together providing the best linear and additive prediction of sentence. With this developmental strategy underlying the guidance, the product must necessarily be a nonveridical system incorporating only a few of the material case factors. Such analyses would be expected to omit and distort the effects of some of the variables that are material to sentence. This consequence might occur for variables that (1) are colinearly related to a second case variable and sentence, where this second variable is more strongly related to sentence; (2) are not linearly related to sentence; (3) only affect sentence in interaction with certain values of other variables; (4) have values that are uncommon features of cases and yet exert a salient effect when present. For each of these reasons one would not be surprised if the statistical analysis failed to identify age, for example, as material to sentence. Moreover, case factors not appropriate to the determination of sentence might nevertheless surreptitiously influence sentencing decisions based on the guidelines. Where detailed archival data bases were used, the method would not prevent certain variables that should be immaterial to sentence from being incorporated indirectly in the guidelines, even though these variables were omitted from the analysis. If race, for example, is in fact a determinant of sentence, then factors deliberately included in the data base and correlated with race, such as unemployment, for this reason alone would be found to be significantly associated with sentence. This does not appear as a problem in the context of Wilkins's strategy because his criterion for the inclusion or noninclusion of variables was statistical not jurisprudential. Now, in prediction one seeks a parsimonious solution, that is, the minimum number of variables together providing a substantial correlation with the outcome. Accordingly, case facts inappropriate to sentence on jurisprudential grounds will be included where they make a substantial independent contribution to the prediction, whereas case factors for which guidance may be desired will be omitted nevertheless, where they do not contribute significantly to the prediction. This situation arises because Wilkins did not take the sentencing judgment seriously in planning the strategy for the development of the guidelines. Of course, at one level Wilkins took the judges' views on sentencing seriously. After the completion of the mathematical analyses and before drawing up the final guidelines, the judges were shown the results and permitted to add or remove any case factors. This is taking the sentencing judgment seriously in a trite sense and in a way that risks introducing incoherence into the guidelines. Indeed, it again leads one to wonder whether the statistical analyses were necessary. No, the proper way of taking the sentencing judgment seriously is for the sentencing judgment to act as a framework for the analysis.

Wilkins et al. (1978) have argued that the relatively few variables (6 to 12) required to predict sentence attest to the simplicity of judicial decision making. The preceding deliberations point to another explanation. Indeed, it appears that Wilkins et al. may have deceived themselves in their conclusion that they had accounted for the sentencing decisions in 80% of cases (on cross-validation), because their criterion of a correct prediction of length of incarceration was indeed generous. For Felony-4 offenses (10 years' maximum), a hit was defined as within 1 year of the specified guideline ranges of between 1 and 2 years. This outcome is not unexpected in the light of the pilot analysis by Wilkins et al. using multiple regression. For one sample they found that the six significant offense–offender variables accounted for only 50% of the sentencing variance. On increasing the number of variables to 14, they accounted for only another 3%. A reanalysis of the data of Wilkins et al. by Hewitt and Little (1981) confirmed two of the original findings, namely, only a small number of variables were significantly associated with past sentencing practice and this set left much of the variance unexplained. Of course, it must be remembered that these estimates are in relation to total variance not reliable variance, which would be expected to be considerably lower, and no predictive system can account for error variance. This is, however, a two-edged sword. It follows that Wilkins might have accounted for substantially more of the reliable variance than his results at first indicate. As the error variance increases as a proportion of the total variance, however, one is led to question the value of sentences imposed in the courts as a criterion for the identification of sentencing policy.

The preceding discussion has been concerned with taking the content of sentencing policy seriously (i.e., the inclusion or noninclusion of case factors). The structure of the sentencing judgment is also vital (i.e., the rules covering the combination of the individual elements in reaching a global assessment of the case). The statistical model adopted by Wilkins et al. (1978) represents the combination of individual case information by, as it were, adding the average effects of each element on sentence. Although this may be appropriate for describing the combined effect of various offense elements on the seriousness of the offense, it is clearly inappropriate for representing the effects on sentence of those factors (e.g., remorse) which may underlie the determination of a tariff sentence in some cases (as an element mitigating an offender's culpability) and the choice of an individualized measure in other cases (as an element indicative of an offender's rehabilitation prospects). Nor would it be appropriate for allowing for the rather complex role of the offender's criminal history in determining the sentence (see Chapter 4). The problem here is that the multiple regression model is incompatible with the structure of judicial thought and, consequently, some of the complexities of judicial thought processes cannot be adequately represented. In discussing their approach to the modeling of decision processes, Gottfredson, Wilkins, and Hoffman (1978) declare a preference for solutions molded by the data. One is left with the impression that the use of a statistical analysis is atheoretical in the sense that it allows the researcher to find the structure of the decision maker's thought in the data. This is not correct; it belies the fact that in such an analysis the data are organized around the structure of the statistical model. Now, a researcher cannot analyze data in a vacuum; data must be interpreted in relation to some sort of model. Accordingly, I believe that a model faithful to the structure of judicial decision making has the potential to provide lawyers with the most accurate, comprehensive, and comprehensible representation of the determination of sentence. The last criterion is vital for judges to allow properly for the unique case factors in relation to the common elements when individualizing sentence—a point raised earlier.

The valid application of the Wilkins et al. (1978) system rests on the assumption that averages can be used to represent sentencing policy. This assumption would be invalid if a significant number of cells in the table comprised some sentences determined on tariff principles and other sentences imposed on rehabilitative grounds. It would also be somewhat problematic if the judges were adopting significantly different approaches in determining the appropriateness of, and in applying, tariff sentences and individualized measures. Unfortunately, studies of disparity suggest that this is so (Diamond, 1981; Palys & Divorski, 1984). (There would be no modeling problem if the interjudge disparity was due to variation around an essentially common approach.)

The effect of these problems associated with construing case data according to the mathematical model of multiple regression is that the quantification of sentencing policy would be imprecise; there would not be a high correspondence between actual sentencing policy and the policy as quantified from the multiple regression equation. The mathematical equation would not be an explicit statement of current judicial sentencing policy, despite claims to the contrary by Wilkins and his associates (1978). What would be the practical manifestations of this? First, the guidelines would unintentionally lead to the creation of new sentencing policies. In these circumstances judges following the guidelines would fail to allow for variables relevant to sentence or would take account of irrelevant case factors, or would give insufficient or excessive weight to factors. Second, the guidelines would be based on an impoverished set of offense and offender characteristics, and accordingly offer unnecessarily limited guidance. One need only compare the limited range of factors found in the guidelines solutions outlined previously with the wide variety of case factors held significant in the traditional common law approach, as presented in Thomas's (1979) analysis in England of the substance of the tariff, to appreciate this point; see, also, the range of case factors listed in the proposed Model Penal Code (American Law Institute, 1962) and the factors considered by the Twentieth Century Fund Task Force on Criminal Sentencing (1976). Vining and Dean (1980) in Canada were also struck by the contrast between legal and empirical analyses.

Morris (1979) criticized the empirical approach to guidelines on the ground that it gives a "false precision" (p. 13). Morris therefore rejected the empirical approach in favor of the traditional common law form as a basis for guidance. The alternative empirical solution, presented in this study, rests on the assumption that the empirical and common law approaches are not necessarily incompatible and that it is possible to develop a numerical aid to the common law approach.

There have been a number of reviews of the Wilkins et al. (1978) approach to guidelines (Blumstein et al., 1983a; Fisher & Kadane, 1983; Galegher & Carroll, 1983; Galligan, 1981; Lovegrove, 1984b, 1987; Rich, Sutton, Clear & Saks, 1982; Sparks, 1983). Some of the preceding points have been made by these writers, but the point of this evaluation has been to discuss Wilkins's strategy in relation to the present project.

Moving Toward Uniformity of Approach in Sentencing

To have uniformity of approach there must be agreement on, inter alia, which case factors are relevant to sentence, the weighting of these factors, and the rules for combining this information to arrive at a global assessment. To achieve this requires a comprehensive and accurate description of current sentencing policy, as a basis for considering an appropriate approach to determining a just sentence. Because sentencing policy is not applied consistently and, in any case, is not yet fully developed, it is also necessary to develop a means of directly eliciting judicial views on elements of sentencing policy (e.g., weighting of factors), rather than indirectly through a holistic analysis of sentences for cases. In any case a holistic analysis cannot provide information on the links between penal goals and the other elements of policy. From the preceding discussion it is clear that Wilkins's strategy (Wilkins et al., 1978) cannot meet these needs.

In summary, the fundamental flaw in Wilkins's approach is that he investigated sentencing practice to identify judicial policy, rather than describing practice in the light of an understanding of sentencing policy. More specifically, he adopted an inappropriate model in attempting to deal with the problem of combining information to show the relationship between case fact and sentence. What is required for the purpose of guidance and policy development is a model describing the legal considerations more or less consciously exercising the minds of judges as they apply sentencing policy in particular cases. Alternatively, it may be said, Wilkins sought consistency of sentence without regard to, and without attempting to develop, consistency of the judicial approach (see also, Lovegrove, 1987).

Hogarth's Sentencing Data Base

Hogarth (1986a, 1986b) in British Columbia is developing a multifaceted information system as an aid for sentencing judges. This brief exposition and critique of Hogarth's approach is confined to those aspects bearing on the quantification of the relationship between case fact and sentence.

The purpose of the system is to identify and record the ranges of sentence for various combinations of offense and offender characteristics of the cases determined in a particular jurisdiction. To implement this system, it is first necessary to establish the material offense and offender characteristics on which the determination of sentence is based. These factors are not identified empirically, but by lawyers on the basis of their understanding of current sentencing policy. In principle, the list of factors should be comprehensive, although in practice one would be satisfied with the inclusion of the more common case factors. The factors and the associated categories (e.g., "weapon used or possessed: yes/no") comprise the classificatory scheme. Each legal offense category, or at least each group of closely related legal offense categories, has its own classification. Once the case factors have been agreed on, it is necessary to compile a large data base of cases for each of the classificatory schemes and to file each case according to its appropriate scheme. For example, for the offense of robbery, the description of one case might be in terms of categories such as "weapon used," "no past record of violence," and "age 41–50 years"; for another robbery case the categories might include "no weapon used," "past record of violence" and "age 18–24 years." These two cases are instances of two different offense–offender patterns. (Actual descriptions of cases would, presumably, comprise more than three case factors.) The data base comprises the range of sentence for each of the patterns established after cases determined in the jurisdiction have been classified according to the offense and offender factors in the scheme. The system is computer based. To use Hogarth's sentencing data base for a particular case, the sentencer enters the case description in terms of the classificatory scheme, and the output is the sentences that have been imposed in the jurisdiction for cases with that particular combination of offense and offender characteristics. This system is still very much in the developmental stage, so that it is possible to describe it in general terms only.

Limitations of Hogarth's Approach

Describing Current Sentencing Practice: Developing Detailed Sentencing Statistics

For reasonably detailed guidance, Hogarth's (1986a, 1986b) system would require a substantial number of case factors, each of several categories. With such a structure there would be potentially a very large number of offense–offender combinations and, accordingly, cells in the classificatory scheme for each offense. For example, a scheme comprising four offense factors, each of four levels, could produce up to 256 cells. This is about the level of detail one might require for an adequate description of the patterns of offending for a particular legal category of offense, let alone the incorporation of prior criminal history and considerations of mitigation relating to the offender. Indeed, in the judicial model of sentencing, which was developed in this study for the offense of burglary, the description of each offense comprised four factors, each of four levels, covering the total value of the theft associated with the burglary(ies), the number of counts of burglary, and the degrees of organization and of violence (see Chapter 6); and it is apposite to mention here that in this study criminal history was characterized by eight elements and the average (mean) number of offender categories considered material to sentence for each principal offender was nine (see Chapter 8). This figure of 256 cells for the comprehensive classification of offense is, of course, an upper limit, and would be reduced to the extent that a particular legal offense category (e.g., burglary) is characterized by a discrete number of patterns of offending (i.e., there is a tendency for particular levels across the various factors to occur together).

The archival burglary study described later (see Part Two) provides some guidance here. On the basis of data collected for that study, it was found that for a representative sample of 100 cases of burglary determined in the County Court—cases in which burglary was the principal offense—there were 57 different offense patterns on these four factors among the 100 principal offenders. When this sample of cases was further differentiated according to three types of premises, the number of distinct offense patterns rose to 67. And in the cross-validation sample, again of 100 cases, differentiated in relation to premises, an additional 44 novel offense patterns were identified. Of course, these figures should be regarded as no more than an approximate estimate on which to assess the utility of Hogarth's system, for undoubtedly other patterns of offending would be expected to occur, even if only rarely. Taken together, these two figures show great variation in the commission of burglaries, and when allowance is made for the variation in factors relating to the offender, clearly one is forced to the conclusion that cases of burglary are characterized by diversity.

Hogarth's (1986a, 1986b) scheme would not be practicable unless each cell were represented by a reasonable number of cases—the guidance would be otherwise unreliable. Two factors must be borne in mind here. First, it is acknowledged that there is disparity in sentencing, and it is important that a few disparate cases should not appear to be the norm. Second, because any classificatory scheme could not cover all the relevant case factors and their variations, the sentences for the cases falling within any one particular cell would cover a range. But where there were only a few cases representing a cell, one would have little idea where the cases lay in that range. Moreover, the data base should not comprise cases that have been determined in the distant past, because the effects on the sentence of changes in sentencing legislation, policy, and practice would be unknown.

The point is that Hogarth's (1986a, 1986b) scheme has a thirst for cases. In a jurisdiction like Victoria, Australia, where there are not large numbers of cases in the various offense categories, this is its fatal flaw. In 1984 only 1,100 (approximately) persons were sentenced in the higher courts. Consider the figures for offenses relating to burglary and rape—in the order of 120 and 30, respectively (Law Department–Victoria, Management Information Section, 1985). Little analysis and imagination are needed to realize that over a 5-year period the system might be just able to offer a rough guide for the offense characteristics of an offense like burglary, one of the more numerous offenses, but that no account could be taken of the less common offenses or the offender characteristics of the more numerous offenses. The measure of the system's breakdown would be the presence of empty cells or cells in which there were too few cases to provide reliable guidance, and there would be plenty of empty or sparse cells in any operational system. This problem is further exacerbated by another consideration. For those many offenses for which mitigating offender factors may exert substantial weight in the determination of sentence (for example, burglary), the distributions of sentence across the cells in a scheme differentiated solely according to offense characteristics would show considerable overlap and, consequently, offer little by way of guidance.

The structural basis of Hogarth's (1986a, 1986b) classificatory scheme would not allow judges to estimate reliably the appropriate quantum of sentence for an empty or sparse cell by their making reference to the adjacent cells for which there were sufficient data. Coherent extrapolation would not be possible, because in the development of the system there is no attempt to interrelate with an appropriate logic the various offense–offender patterns in relation to the quanta of sentence. To achieve this would require a system describing how judges weight each case factor and the rules that they follow to combine this information. In summary, Hogarth's system is impracticable in a relatively small jurisdiction. The problem arises principally because there is no rule covering how the various case facts are combined to determine an overall assessment of the case. With an aggregation rule it is not necessary to have separate cells for each offense–offender pattern to represent the relationship between the quantum of sentence and the facts of the case.

A brief comment should be made about the accuracy of the guidance given. It must be assumed that the mean sentence for each cell indicates the average effect on sentence of the pattern of offending the cell represents. Accordingly, the seemingly appropriate course would be to allow for the effects of the uncommon case factors not included in the guidance in relation to the mean for the cell. However, if some of these unique case factors were correlated with that offense pattern, then the average guideline sentence for the cell would already incorporate their effects. Accordingly, these (correlated) unique factors would be overweighted, and the consideration of other (uncorrelated) unique factors would not necessarily be made in relation to an average case for that cell. With a greater number of case factors and categories in the system, so the errors associated with this problem would be expected to be less significant.

There are four further problems associated with Hogarth's (1986a, 1986b) approach to the provision of detailed sentencing statistics. These are discussed in the analysis of the Wilkins et al. (1978) empirically based descriptive guidelines and for this reason are referred to only briefly here. They, too, arise from Hogarth's failure to take cognizance of the nature and structure of the sentencing judgment in developing his system of guidance. First, Hogarth's system rests on the assumption that judges consistently apply a known sentencing policy regarding the scaling, weighting, and combining of the case factors. Evidence and experience, however, indicate that this proposition is not valid. The approach is also problematic in relation to the guidance provided by those cells comprising both tariff and individualized sentences. Accordingly, averages cannot be used to represent accurately sentencing policy and practice. Second, this approach to quantifying the sentence could not readily incorporate appellate court decisions effecting changes to sentencing policy, because it would be necessary to wait until a large number of cases had been sentenced by judges cognizant of the new ruling. Clearly, there would be periods when the statistics lagged behind current sentencing practice. Third, Hogarth's system, like Wilkins's guidelines, is vulnerable to the surreptitious influence of immaterial case factors. Consider a descriptive system including unemployment as a case factor but excluding race. Now, if a particular racial group was more likely to receive harsher sentences due to prejudice, and if this group had a higher level of unemployment, then the sentences for the offense–offender patterns of which unemployment was a component would be inflated due to the effects of race. This was alluded to previously. Finally, there is the problem of applying these statistics as a means of guidance in the courts. The quantification of the tariff must of necessity be limited to showing the combined effects on sentence of the more common case characteristics. Its function, then, is merely to provide a reference point against which judges can then exercise their discretion in allowing for the effects on sentence of any unusual case characteristics. In Hogarth's scheme it would be difficult for judges to estimate the effects on sentence of the unique elements in relation to the common case factors because the various combinations of case characteristics are not systematically related and in a way consistent with the judges' approach to determining an appropriate sentence. One would not be surprised then if judges were to apply the guideline sentences slavishly. In these circumstances many sentences would not be appropriately individualized for justice to be done, and the role of the appellate courts in policy development would be diminished.

Moving Toward Uniformity of Approach in Sentencing

To be regarded as a basis for a move toward uniformity of approach, an information system must show the effects on sentence of any combination of a reasonable number of common case factors. This can be achieved only if the weighting and combination of case factors has been specified. Without such an explicit statement of sentencing policy, it is not possible to identify points of disagreement between judges and those matters to which only scant attention has been paid.

Unfortunately, Hogarth (1986a, 1986b) has not tackled this problem. Indeed, he has expressly eschewed this course on what would appear to be false grounds (Hogarth, 1986a). Hogarth correctly acknowledged that such a course requires a rule-based expert system, which generates answers, but argued that the optimal conditions for a rule-based system do not exist. He set down two preconditions, and I shall discuss each one in turn.

1. It is possible to reach agreement on what is a "good" decision. In relation to the development of detailed sentencing statistics, surely this must be seen in terms of everyday curial decision making, and accordingly, this entails no more than agreement on what is appropriate by way of approach (and, hence, sentence) for particular types of cases. It is true this necessary knowledge on the way judges combine case information in arriving at a sentence is not currently available. Nevertheless, giant strides have been taken to this end. The principal contributor here is David Thomas (1979, 1982), who in England has distilled and cataloged many of the principles and much of the practice of sentencing and also has identified the judicial approach to the determination of sentence. The present study builds on the contribution of Thomas to the development of detailed sentencing statistics by applying standard strategies of behavioral science to his analysis of the principles and structure of sentencing decisions. Clearly, to ascertain this information it is necessary to develop a means of facilitating judicial input into policy development. Nevertheless, decision analysis (Edwards & Newman, 1982; Keeney & Raiffa, 1976) offers a relatively simple technology for this purpose, and this has been used here.

2. The decision task is a relatively simple one, for example, selecting the most appropriate alternative. This is not so. Modern decision theory can accommodate more complex thinking relating to the combining of case information. Consider an aspect of decision making that Hogarth (1986a, 1986b) regards as evidence of a lack of agreement on the correct approach to decision making and as indicative of the complexity of decision making in sentencing. In the sentencing process, he argued, a judge must choose among various penal objectives, and case data germane to one goal may be immaterial to another. This statement is true, but it is not an obstacle to the development of a rule-based system. It follows that the analysis must allow for the role and effect on decision making of these multiple objectives, and it must facilitate judges' attempts to identify and reconcile their different approaches.

Hogarth (1986a, 1986b) has ignored these issues, but not with impunity. For even in the deceptively simple task of describing sentencing practice, the considerations associated with these underlying problems are not rendered irrelevant when they are ignored. Indeed, these considerations led to the earlier conclusion that the average is not a valid index of sentencing policy and that Hogarth's system would make it difficult for judges to allow for the effects of unique elements in relation to the common case factors. Moreover, Hogarth's ignoring of the judges' approach to combining case information lay at the heart of his adopting an impracticable solution to the problem of representing the relationship between case fact and sentence.

In summary Hogarth's sentencing data base system cannot be used to quantify sentencing policy and practice, because it ignores the problem of how case information should be combined to show the relationship between case fact and sentence in accordance with the structure of the sentencing judgment. Again, Hogarth seeks consistency of sentence, without regard to, and without attempting to develop, a consistent judicial approach.

Doob's Sentencing Data Base

Doob's approach to the statistical description of current sentencing practice is conceptually similar to Hogarth's (1986a, 1986b) system (see Doob, 1986; Doob & Park, 1987). The evaluation of Hogarth's approach therefore is similarly applicable here and need not be repeated. However, one significant difference is worthy of comment and analysis.

Doob and Park (1987) recognized that the approach Hogarth (1986a, 1986b) appeared to be taking was impracticable. They emphasized the extraordinary number of cells that would be required to describe sentencing practice in terms of even a relatively small number of objectively defined case factors, each of several categories. Nevertheless, they realized that any description of sentencing practice would be of limited use unless it captured the complexity associated with the variations in the patterns of offending and circumstances of offenders. Their solution to this problem involved identifying six broad case characteristics as a basis for the classificatory scheme, each with three general categories. For example, one dimension is "previous criminal record of the accused," comprising the categories "none, inconsequential, or unrelated," "some, but not serious," and "substantial." Another characteristic is "relative severity of this particular offense as compared to other instances of the same offense," and includes the categories "less severe than most," "about the same as most," and "more severe than most." It is left to the judge to assess intuitively all the relevant information about a case to place it in the appropriate category on each of the six dimensions within the classificatory system. (A judge is not necessarily required to use the six characteristics, only the factor[s] that the judge considers to be the most important.) Herein lies the system's weakness. One of the requirements of uniformity of approach is that each of the material offense and offender characteristics should be defined objectively in relation to seriousness. For example, agreement is needed on the relative seriousness of various amounts of money taken in burglaries. However, the system provides no guidance here. Another requirement is that the components and the part played by those components in defining a dimension such as offense seriousness should be made explicit. Remember the illustrative weighting problem, posed by Ashworth (1987), regarding the relative contributions of the amount stolen and breach of trust to offense seriousness (Chapter 1)? Doob's system is silent on such matters; it has no answer and does not offer a means of providing an answer. Now, Doob and Park acknowledge that judges might differ about the objective criteria they would use to define the various dimensions and categories. How, then, Doob and Park can conclude that a judge is better off knowing the sentences imposed on offenders, where the seriousness of the offense is subjectively defined in relation to general categories rather than in terms of objective and specific factors such as the value of the theft, is difficult to comprehend. Is this not the recipe for a system designed to foster and hide inconsistency of approach?

Moreover, a close examination of the example Doob and Park (1987) used to illustrate their approach as an operational system leads one to doubt whether in fact their use of subjectively defined dimensions has overcome the problem rendering the Hogarth (1986a, 1986b) system impracticable. Their example was for the offense category "Assault bodily harm," for which there were 153 cases in the data base. When describing the case in terms of only two of their six dimensions ("aggravating and mitigating circumstances"–"aggravating," and "previous criminal record of the accused"–"substantial") there apparently were only 12 remaining cases on which the guidance could be based.

Minnesota Sentencing Guidelines Commission's Policy-Based Prescriptive Guidelines

The guidelines of the Minnesota Sentencing Guidelines Commission (1984) are in the form of a two-dimensional grid. One dimension represents the seriousness of the offense and the other defines the extent of the offender's criminal record. The scale of offense seriousness has 10 levels (groups), each of the groups comprising a substantial number of legal categories of offense. For example, level 4 includes, inter alia, offenses relating to "bribery," "false imprisonment," "use of drugs to injure or facilitate crime." However, some offenses have been subdivided and in this way are included in more than one level. For example "theft crimes—over $2,500" are in level 4, whereas "theft crimes—$250-2,500" are in level 3. Criminal history is defined by 4 elements. Points are allotted to a case, regarding the offender's number of prior felonies, juvenile offenses, and nontraffic misdemeanors and the offender's custodial status at the time of the current offense; some of the elements are differentially weighted according to a crude scheme. The dimension representing criminal record comprises 7 levels. Each cell in the table shows whether a sentence of imprisonment is appropriate for that particular combination of offense seriousness and criminal history and, if so, the length (presented as a relatively narrow range).

In the construction of the table, empirical or other analyses of past sentencing practices played a minimal role. Rather, after debate, a policy was adopted. It was determined that the dominant goal of the penal system should be retribution and that the severity of the sanction should be proportional to the seriousness of the offense and, to a lesser degree, the extent of an offender's criminal history. The setting of the sanctions was treated primarily as a normative problem; consequently, it was necessary to determine an appropriate sentence according to the policy for each particular combination of offense seriousness and criminal history.

Although judges may impose penalties that fall outside the presumptive ranges, this course generally is permitted only when the reasons are compelling and substantial, and such departures should occur only rarely (Minnesota Sentencing Guidelines Commission, 1984; von Hirsch, Knapp, & Tonry, 1987).

Limitations of the Minnesota Sentencing Guidelines Commission's Approach

Moving Toward Uniformity of Approach in Sentencing

First, use of the Minnesota guidelines (Minnesota Sentencing Guidelines Commission, 1984) would entail gross changes to current sentencing policy and practice in Australia, Canada, England, and Scotland, because various combinations of common case factors that now not infrequently may have a substantial effect on what is considered an appropriate sentence would, under this system, rarely exert more than a minimal impact. This can be deduced from the fact that, even though the guidelines recognize only coarse distinctions between cases (7 categories of prior record for each of the 10 broad groupings of legal offense category), the ranges of sentence considered appropriate for the various cells are quite narrow. For example for residential burglary (level 5), there is a presumptive sentence of imprisonment for offenders whose criminal history score places them at the 4th to the 7th levels, and the presumptive range within each level is 2, 4, 6, and 8 months, respectively. It will be shown later that, in Victoria, Australia, offense variations in residential burglary, covering organization, number of counts, value of the theft, and violence (not including physical injury), and for an offender with an extensive criminal history and little by way of mitigation, can be responsible for sentences being well distributed over a range covering approximately 1 to 7 years' imprisonment (see Table 16.12). The associated problem is not merely that judicial discretion would be reduced; rather, it is that the extent to which a sentence could be individualized to allow for the variation in case characteristics would be dramatically curtailed.

I said quite deliberately that the Minnesota system (Minnesota Sentencing Guidelines Commission, 1984) entails this problem. The solution does not lie in widening the presumptive ranges of sentence or in permitting frequent departures from them, because specific guidance would no longer characterize the statistics and there would be no point to them. The source of this dilemma leads me to the second objection. This is that this system seeks uniformity of sentence not through uniformity of approach but at the expense of it. Alternatively, it may be said that the Minnesota system does not solve the problem of how information should be combined to determine sentence, rather it largely avoids the issue.

Current sentencing statistics in Victoria (Law Department– Victoria, Management Information Section, 1985) readily tell us the precise range and distribution of the sentences imposed for each legal offense category—but no more.

Accordingly, what is required for numerical guidance is a framework to which the sentencer can refer to determine the relevant features of a particular case, the weight that should be attached to each feature, as well as how this information should be combined, so the sentencer is not left to guess where particular cases lie in the distributions of offense by sentence.

The importance of the rules for combining elements of information cannot be overemphasized, because without them an information system cannot be used to estimate the effects on sentence of any combination of a substantial number of case characteristics. Now, the alternative—the direct representation of the effects on sentence of particular combinations of case factors—becomes more and more unwieldy as the number of case factors increases. Consequently, the system adopted by Minnesota cannot provide guidance for more than a small number of case factors.

Moreover, even if it was practicable to represent the effects on sentence of any combination of a substantial number of case factors, there would remain a problem concerning the way in which sentences for the various combinations would be determined. The Minnesota Sentencing Guidelines Commission (1984) determined the presumptive sentences intuitively, and each represents what was thought to be an appropriate sentence based on a retributive philosophy for that particular combination of offense seriousness and criminal history. Now, the intuitive determination of each sentence still entails applying weights and rules for combining information, even though they are not stated explicitly. The critical question is whether these intuitive judgments are internally consistent. This can be checked rigorously only if the means of combining the information is specified so that quanta of sentence determined according to the rules can be compared with the quanta of sentence determined intuitively. However, in the Minnesota system, the means of combining case information is not dealt with adequately, and so it is not possible to test the internal consistency of the intuitions. Furthermore, an additional consequence is that the sentencer is given no quantitative guidance on how to allow for the effects of case factors warranting departures from the guidelines.

Sparks (1983) was aware of the problem of testing the coherence of an intuitively developed set of quantitative guidelines. To meet this problem he offered a set of illustrative critical question such as, "Do these ranges "step up" in a reasonably orderly fashion?" (p. 240). The task of those involved in setting the guidelines is to determine then whether any apparent anomalies are in fact justifiable. In the absence of an aggregation rule, there is no alternative to this piecemeal approach. However, it begs the question whether the answers to the individual questions used to assess coherence are themselves coherent.

Finally, the current Minnesota system (1984) was developed without detailed reference to the previous sentencing system—a system in which a large number of case factors had potential significance in the determination of sentence. There was no serious attempt to use the earlier system as a basis for reform, and the present system does not provide a structure that can be employed to make this comparison. Again, this resulted because the Commission did not develop a means of representing the effects on sentence of any combination of a substantial number of case factors. Although this was not a significant problem in Minnesota, because their system of sentencing underwent a radical change, it would be a problem if reform entailed not abandoning a system of individualized justice but strengthening and refining it, that is, reweighting factors and the like. Clearly, a description of such a sentencing system in terms of Minnesota's 70-cell table would be so crude as to be meaningless. The distributions of sentence in the various cells would be characterized by substantial overlap.

In summary the Minnesota Sentencing Guidelines Commission's (1984) approach is an unsatisfactory basis for quantifying the tariff for the system of individualized justice in Australia, and in Canada, England, and Scotland, because it does not deal with the problem of describing how information about cases should be combined (see also, Lovegrove, 1987).

United States Sentencing Commission's Presumptive Guidelines

The United States Sentencing Commission's (1987) numerical guidelines are presented in the form of a two-dimensional grid. One dimension represents the seriousness of the legal category of the offense and incorporates the circumstances of the actual offense, and the other dimension covers the offender's criminal history. The guidelines provide for fine discriminations within and between offense categories. There are over 50 offense categories, and most comprise several subcategories. Each subcategory offers specific guidance on one offense in regard to the offense's base severity level together with its associated aggravating specific offense characteristics. By way of illustration, there are two subcategories for burglary ("residence" and "other structures"), and the specific factors cover whether the offense involved more than minimal planning; property taken or destroyed in excess of $2,500 (6 levels); theft of a firearm, destructive device, or controlled substance; and an offender carrying a firearm or other dangerous weapon. Offense seriousness is further differentiated according to non–offense-specific factors: the victim (vulnerable, official, restrained by offender); the offender's role in the offense (significant organizer, secondary role, position of trust, use of special skill); the obstruction of justice by the offender as defendant; multiple counts; the offender's acceptance of responsibility; and the offender as a career or professional criminal. The seriousness of each offense's base level is quantified by a score. Also, the seriousness of each of these offense-specific and non–offense-specific factors is quantified by a score, and the scores for the applicable factors in a particular case are incorporated as adjustments to the base-level score to determine a score for the offense characteristics of the case. At this stage the case can be placed in one of the 43 levels on the dimension representing offense seriousness. The criminal history score allows for the length of prior sentences of imprisonment (2 levels), the number of prior sentences, whether the present offense was committed while the offender was under sentence, and time since the last serious offense (1 level). In the grid there are 6 levels on the dimension representing the seriousness of the offender's criminal history. Each cell in the table shows whether a sentence of imprisonment is appropriate and, if so, the length (presented as a range of approximately 25%). Under certain circumstances the judge retains a discretion to impose probation in place of a guideline sentence of imprisonment. The guidelines also provide for what would appear to be liberal departures. The sentencing judge may further differentiate the effects of factors quantified in the guidelines, and there are unquantified factors to which the judge also may give effect. Finally, consideration may be given to other factors not incorporated in the guidelines or the accompanying policy statements and commentaries; for example, the court may consider departing from the guideline sentence if the criminal history score does not adequately reflect the seriousness of the offender's past criminal conduct or likelihood of recidivism.

The guidelines were developed on the basis of an analysis of past sentencing practice, although some modifications were introduced on the basis of policy considerations. The rationale for this approach is that the accumulated wisdom of the legislature and the judiciary is the most appropriate point of departure for the development of a coherent sentencing system as a basis for guidance (United States Sentencing Commission, 1987).

Limitations of the United States Sentencing Commission's Approach

Moving Toward Uniformity of Approach in Sentencing

In the context of the present project, two problems beset the United States Sentencing Commission's (1987) guidelines. The first matter relates to the way in which the guidelines were developed. The numerical guidance was substantially based on a description of past sentencing practice. Accordingly, to give substance to the grid, the Commission had to ascertain the case factors underlying the determination of sentence, the importance attached to these factors in this decision, and the quanta of sentence deemed appropriate for the various combinations of these factors. The Commission's assessments concerning these matters were based on what appeared to be in effect an intuitive synthesis of the results of statistical analyses of various sets of relevant archival data, including conviction and presentence reports and the United States Parole Commission's guidelines and associated statistics, together with the Commission's own policy judgments.

For the reasons adduced in the preceding evaluation of the Wilkins et al. (1978) approach, the Commission, in eschewing a description of sentencing practice in terms of a mathematical model, was well placed for providing a description of sentencing policy that was accurate, comprehensive, and had the potential to act as a sound basis for the development of sentencing policy. The Commission, however, failed to capitalize on this move; it made two errors of omission. First, the Commission failed to interrelate penal aims, case factors, and sentence–

probably the most critical distinction here is between tariff sentences and individualized measures (see Thomas, 1979). A consequence of the Commission's not linking penal policy and sentencing practice is that the representation of the relationship between the facts of a case and sentence must necessarily be less precise. Another consequence is that the Commission has not established a basis for the development of a rational and coherent system of punishment. The second error of omission concerns the Commission's reliance on an intuitive assessment of its data bases as a means of ascertaining the way in which courts determine sentence. This is a problematic strategy for several reasons. It is an extraordinarily imprecise technique in which there can be no estimate of the error. Furthermore, the Commission, in the course of developing and finalizing its representation of the sentencing process, would have been forced to resolve apparent conflicts and fill in gaps in the data base. (The Commission also quite deliberately modified some aspects of current practice on the basis of its own views on appropriate sentencing policy.) The problem here is that the conflicts and gaps in sentencing policy and practice and the Commission's resolution of them remain hidden. What is required for the development of sentencing policy is a means of identifying and representing the conflicts and gaps in policy in a way that will facilitate a coherent resolution of these matters. Of course, it is possible to analyze the Commission's scoring system and sentencing table and in this way determine the relative weights accorded to the component offense and offender factors. It is unfortunate that these aspects of policy are not explicit, because sentencing policy cannot be soundly based in the absence of a means of tapping and representing the views about each component of policy of those who are responsible for its development. This point complements the preceding conclusion. Indeed, it is impossible to test adequately the coherence of intuitive determinations of appropriate sentences for particular sets of case facts unless the rules governing the aggregation of the component information have been independently specified. (This point was made regarding the guidance in the grid developed by the Minnesota Sentencing Guidelines Commission, 1984.)

The other problem associated with these guidelines relates to their level of detail. The United States Sentencing Commission (1987) initially sought to describe case characteristics in a significantly greater level of detail than is found in its final product. However, the Commission abandoned this attempt at developing what it described as a "pure real offense system" on two grounds: (1) it would have had to decide precisely what factors are relevant to sentence and how the courts aggregate this information; (2) it found no practical way of allowing for the large number of potentially relevant case factors across a range of circumstances—the proposed solution was so complex that it was impracticable. Nevertheless, the Commission's final solution does provide considerable differentiation within offense categories, but this is limited by the constraints imposed by the use of a two-dimensional grid as a means of representing the diversity among offenses and offenders. However, the Commission took the view that its guidelines did not sufficiently provide for the degree of individuation necessary for just sentencing and, apparently, for this reason accorded judges considerable discretion within and outside the guidelines. Indeed, Robinson (1987), in his dissenting opinion on a draft of the Commission's proposed guidelines, expressed the view that the guidelines represented in effect a failed attempt at capturing the complexity of the sentencing process; accordingly, the guidelines were characterized by complexity and yet failed to overcome the necessity for the sentencing judge to retain considerable discretion—the source of disparity and the sentencing system's need of guidelines.

In summary the United States Sentencing Commission's (1987) approach to guidelines does not provide a sound basis for the move toward uniformity of approach in sentencing, because it does not deal adequately with the problem of representing the aggregation of information about cases and does not provide a means of facilitating input in relation to the elements of sentencing policy by those who are responsible for policy development. The present project attempts to develop solutions to these two problems.

3
Toward a Model of Judicial Decision Making: An Unproductive Review of Psychological Research*

In Chapter 2 through the separate evaluations of current approaches to the development of detailed sentencing statistics and numerical guidelines there ran a common thread of criticism; namely, the modeling techniques were inadequate for representing the relationship between the facts of a case and sentence and, in particular, the aggregation of individual case elements in arriving at an overall assessment of the case.

To be veridical and relevant, a model must relate to the decisions required of judges in the course of their determining appropriate sentences for particular cases. These decisions were identified in the first chapter as (1) the appropriate aim or mix of penal aims in the light of the facts of the case and (2) the penalty most likely to give effect to the aim in the circumstances of the case. If a tariff sentence is chosen, then the judge's task is to fix a quantum of sentence proportional to the seriousness of the case. In cases for which an individualized measure is deemed appropriate, the judge chooses the sanction most suited to the offender's rehabilitative needs. In reaching these decisions the judge uses information quantitatively and qualitatively; the question is how? To answer this question, the model must incorporate the judiciary's view of (1) case factors relevant to determining sentence; (2) operational definitions of case factors (e.g., the definition of violence to the victims) and the levels on each case factor (e.g., no violence, threat of violence, minor personal injury, serious personal injury); (3) weighting of case factors; (4) rules for combining case factors; (5) the appropriate types and levels of sentence for the various combinations of case factors.

The purpose of this chapter is to review psychological research in judicial decision making and sentencing. What is sought is a conceptual framework, an empirical strategy, or research findings that may facilitate the development of a relevant model, faithful to the structure of judicial thought. Because the appellate courts have yet to develop a comprehensive sentencing policy, it follows, then, that one is also looking for empirical methods designed to facilitate the develop-

*This chapter is based on material that was reviewed from another perspective in Lovegrove (1986).

ment of sentencing policy through direct judicial input on the various elements of the sentencing decision. Clearly, these matters fall within the domain of psychology, and so various theoretical and empirical contributions are examined and assessed with regard to their potential contribution here.

Atheoretical Approaches to the Study of Sentencing

Atheoretical approaches to the study of sentencing are characterized by empirical analyses conducted in the absence of a theoretical framework drawn from psychology. In these studies the sentence of the court is the dependent variable; however, they may be usefully distinguished in terms of whether the independent variable covers offense and offender factors or personal characteristics of judges.

Case Oriented

Although empirical studies of sentencing are numerous, two researchers who have developed a substantial raison d'être for their approach are Konečni and Ebbesen (Ebbesen & Konečni, 1981; Konečni & Ebbesen, 1981, 1982). Because judges exercise wide discretionary powers in sentencing and yet are given little guidance for this task, Konečni and Ebbesen argue that the first aim of research should be to understand the causal case elements accounting for most of the variation in the decisions. They hope decision makers themselves will then compare how the system is operating with how it should function with respect to the use, weighting, and combination of information available to them. So the goal of description is to set the scene for informed discussion on policy issues. This position is taken also by Gottfredson and Gottfredson (1980).

A major problem with Ebbesen and Konečni (1981) and Konečni and Ebbesen's (1981, 1982) approach is that it ignores the judges' reasoning processes. Konečni and Ebbesen's reliance on archival information starkly contrasts with the classic work of Hogarth (1971), who gave emphasis to subjective interpretations of sentencing. One can readily agree with Konečni and Ebbesen that empirically derived decision strategies might not bear any resemblance to those claimed to be used by the decision makers themselves, because judges might not be aware of the determinants of their decisions, at least not with the desired degree of precision, or they might not apply the policy truly. The danger of ignoring the sentencing judgment's structure and the judges' considerations of sentencing policy is that the decision model might not be usable in the task of understanding sentencing—an aim with which Konečni and Ebbesen concur. In terms of the analysis of the sentencing judgment presented earlier (see Chapter 1), their work links case facts and penalty, but ignores the ties between case facts and sentencing aims as well as penal goals and penalty. Yet these latter two components of the sentencing judgment are the raison d'être for the nature of the relationship between the facts of the case and the sentence. Consequently, Konečni and Ebbesen's research cannot be used to account for variance in jurisprudential terms, and so it is of limited use as a basis for policy. As Fuller (1966) would say, they have emphasized signpost-setting at the expense of road building; in terms of what the Lord Chief Justice of England has said, they have sought consistency of sentence instead of consistency of approach (see the judgment in *Bibi*, 1980).

This point leads to a second source of concern. The way certain case factors (e.g., the degree of contrition shown by the offender) contribute to sentence determination may vary depending on whether the judge is considering a tariff sentence or an individualized measure. Clearly, these two effects could not be teased out of data comprising sentencing decisions, in the absence of an understanding of sentencing policy as it guides judges in the exercise of this discretion.

Then there are the patently false assumptions underlying Konečni and Ebbesen's work, namely, sentencing policy is fully formulated, all judges share this policy, and they apply it reliably. This and the preceding point were canvassed in the discussion of the work of Wilkins and his associates (1978) and do not require elaboration here, save to say that they lead one to question the primacy given by Ebbesen and Konečni (1981) and Konečni and Ebbesen (1981, 1982) to description in the sequence of the research problems within their research program. This is not to deny the importance of description, but merely to point out that such an orientation would tend to blinker researchers to disparity and incline them to favor conclusions of uniformity. Rather, it is suggested that in the application of the techniques of behavioral science to the study of sentencing greater emphasis should be given to the task of helping judges to identify gaps in sentencing policy and to resolve policy differences, and in this way to develop sentencing policy. This reorientation would not require researchers to abandon the goal of description, because differences in policy must be identified, preparatory to resolution, and other matters of policy can be developed in the course of seeking description. Rather, it is necessary to collect additional information—data on how judges select the appropriate aim or mix of aims in the light of the facts of the case and, then, how they determine a quantum of sentence proportional to the seriousness of the case or select an individualized measure appropriate to the offender's rehabilitative needs; moreover, the unit of analysis must be the individual judge. So one's hope is that behavioral science offers concepts and methods for analyzing individual judicial decision making in this way. Studies allowing for differential approaches to sentencing therefore have more to commend them. Indeed, this is one of the positive aspects of disparity; it acts as a catalyst for policy development.

There are studies illustrating this approach. Palys and Divorski (1984) asked judges to impose sentences for several cases and then (1) indicate the facts that the judges perceived to be relevant, (2) rank these facts in relation to importance, and (3) specify the legal objectives that the judges were trying to maximize. The authors' results showed, in a diagram, first, the relationship between the disposition (noncustodial, short-custodial, and long-custodial) and the percentage of judges, within each disposition, who cited each case fact as one of the three most important and, second, the relationship between the legal objectives and disposition. They found that case facts, legal objectives, and sentences tended to be packaged into a cohesive and rational unit. For example judges who imposed long terms of imprisonment emphasized the goal of deterrence and gave weight to lack of remorse and violence but ignored favorable aspects of character, social background, and prior record. The purpose of this research was to help judges explore the links between their preferred policies and their sentencing practices. Clearly, this research addressed relevant issues, although the analyses would have been rounded off if the authors had linked case fact and legal objective directly. The second limitation of this research, as it relates to the present study, is that the authors did not satisfactorily quantify the link between case fact and sentence.

A similar type of approach has been developed by Lawrence (Lawrence, 1984; Lawrence & Homel, 1987). In her technique cases were presented to magistrates, who were asked to verbalize their thought processes as they determined sentence. In this study the unit of analysis was the individual magistrate's decision making in respect of a particular case, and the results showed in the form of a diagram the links between sentencing objective, perceived offense seriousness, critical case facts, and penalty. This is a neat means of explicating magistrates' personal applications of sentencing policy as they determine appropriate sentences for particular cases but, again, it is not quantitative.

Diamond (1981) also predicated the value of her analysis on the assumption that disparity can be used to identify issues requiring resolution. This study is divided into two parts. First, a multivariate analysis of case characteristics (offense and offender variables) associated with cases for which judges tended to disagree on disposition; for example, there was a comparatively high level of disparity associated with the use a custodial sentence in cases where both aggravating and mitigating factors were present. The second part of the study offered a structural model on which the issues of disparity could be analyzed. The data analysis provided evidence of four sources of disparity (1) evaluation of offense severity; (2) selection of material case factors; (3) weighting (magnitude, but not direction) of material case factors; and (4) within-judge inconsistency in the combining of case factors, especially for certain combinations of mitigating and aggravating factors. The value of this type of analysis is that it can be used to point to some of those aspects of judicial decision making and discretion in need of policy development and structuring, but it is not sufficiently specific to go any further. Moreover, because the analysis relied solely on case data, it could not be used to differentiate tariff and individualized sentencing nor identify the ties between penal goals, case facts, and sentence. Clearly, this research would have been more valuable if it had examined policy considerations at the root of these differences.

Judge Oriented

Numerous studies are judge oriented, and all of these seek to find correlations between personal characteristics of judges, their environments, and sentence. Personal characteristics refer to attitudes (general and legal) and background, whereas the notion of environment covers the circumstances in which judges find themselves. Factors that have been examined include, for example, questionnaire responses to measures of liberalism (Nagel, 1962) and general punitiveness (Lemon, 1974), religious affiliation (Barber, 1974), having sons eligible for military service in cases relating to draft offenses (Cook, 1973), and public opinion (Gibson, 1980).

What are the criminological difficulties associated with this research into judicial correlates of sentence? Grossman (1966) noted that these studies show evidence of a "more-likely" relationship, typically accounting for only a small percentage of the variance (see also, Champagne & Nagel, 1982; Konečni & Ebbesen, 1981, 1982). Moreover, they do not adequately examine the question of conversion: how these personal factors are translated into sentencing policy (Grossman, 1967).

Even if the preceding problems were overcome, however, a more fundamental and damning question would still lurk unresolved. Apart from perhaps satisfying our curiosity, what is the usefulness of such information? Researchers who have incorporated this type of analysis into their studies have proposed that judges should be selected and trained on the basis of such personal qualities (e.g., Hogarth, 1971). However, there appear to be insurmountable constitutional, jurisprudential, and practical problems associated with these proposals. Take selection. First, it would be unconstitutional for the executive arm of government to stack the bench with judges of a certain persuasion (Ashworth, 1983b). Second, in any case the measures do not have a sufficiently high degree of validity to differentiate judges sharply. Third, there is a positive point against selection. It is that the law will be developed most creatively if the appellate court is given the opportunity to rule on a diversity of judicial interpretations. This will be achieved only if the judiciary represents a wide range of community attitudes and backgrounds so that these views can find expression through judges' exercising discretion within the law as they determine particular cases. Programs directed at training or educating judges with a view to changing the approach to sentencing of some judges and in that way overcoming perceived undesirable effects of certain personal characteristics would undoubtedly be unconstitutional, striking at the heart of judicial independence. Ashworth (1983b) has succinctly summarized his understanding of both the ambit and effects of what he has called a taboo:

> There is a principle of judicial independence; attempts by the executive arm of government to influence sentencing policy are unconstitutional; attempts by the legislature to interfere with the sentencing discretion of the courts are, even if not strictly unconstitutional, bound to result in both practical confusion and injustice to defendants; the development of sentencing policy should therefore be left to the wisdom of the courts, under the guidance of the Court of Appeal, and intervention by other bodies can only worsen the situation. (p. 59)

The point of these arguments is to show that the application of psychological research on personal judicial characteristics to the problem of the determination by judges of appropriate sentences is unsound. This type of study is commendably concerned with uniformity in sentencing, but the price of this strategy might be the stagnation of sentencing policy. There is a fine balance to be struck between the control of disparity and the encouragement of imaginative responses to crime.

In any case legal and empirical analyses have revealed apparent sources of disparity for which relatively simple remedial measures would be expected to be effective. Sources of disparity of significance here include limitations of human information processing and lack of a fully articulated sentencing policy. Not until measures directed at these matters have been shown to be unsuccessful would it seem appropriate to explore the problem in greater depth. Haney (1980), too, has pointed with favor to the ergonomic solution relating to the application of psychology to legal change. His review showed that the value of much legal reform is predicated on the assumption that if more suitable personnel were selected then the quality of justice would inevitably be improved. Citing the work of Mischel (1968), he argued that this person-centered strategy ignores the importance of the situation in controlling behavior and concluded that legal reform manipulating personnel but not structural aspects of legal settings is not likely to produce substantial benefits. Haney's approach also has a pragmatic basis. The person-centered strategy would almost certainly be perceived by the practical mind of the lawyer (Haney, 1980) as esoteric and as treating the judiciary as an object of curiosity. To the extent that these feelings were engendered, co-operation would not be forthcoming. Finally, in the situational approach, focusing directly as it does on the sentencing judgment, the consequent remedial measures would assist judges in the development, communication, and application of sentencing policy.

In view of the preceding deliberations, one cannot help but be surprised at the conclusions drawn by some commentators when reviewing research reporting the correlates of sentence and judicial characteristics. Champagne and Nagel (1982) viewed it as valuable. Saks and Hastie (1978) also noted with apparent regret the judges' lack of co-operation. To me it is clear why the judiciary has not responded with enthusiasm.

Theoretical Approaches to the Study of Sentencing

The common feature of theoretical research on sentencing is that the empirical analyses are based on formal psychological theory.

Decision Making

McKnight (1981) adapted two psychological theories and applied them in a complementary way to predict sentence. The two theories, multiattribute utility theory and personal construct theory, were used to identify and link sentencing objectives, their importance, and the extent to which a particular sentence would achieve an aim.

First, the quantitative relationship between the sentence and how a case is construed was established through multiattribute utility theory. Second, the relevant constructs, the possible aims of sentencing, and their assessment in regard to a case, were elicited according to personal construct theory. It was predicted that judges would impose the sentence with the highest subjective expected utility. The utility of a sentence was defined as the rating of a sentence in relation to a goal of sentence (i.e., the extent to which a sentence would achieve a goal for the case under consideration) multipled by the weight assigned to that construct (i.e., the importance of that goal for that case). This product was added to similarly derived products for each goal of possible significance, and the utility of a sentence was the sum of these products. This calculation was repeated for each of the sentences. McKnight (1981) elicited this information from the sentencers in a simulation exercise and found that he was able to predict the sentences imposed there with a high degree of accuracy. One clear advantage of quantification based on a model of judicial decision making is that it is a move toward the precise description of the judicial determination of sentence, with the consequent potential for developing guidance for sentencers in the form of either detailed sentencing statistics or numerical guidelines. For this potential to be realized, the model must be able to predict sentences with a high degree of accuracy and the judiciary must accept that the structure of the model is compatible with their approach to the determination of sentence. There is evidence suggesting that McKnight's model may satisfy both of these conditions. There is another consideration, however, and in relation to the purpose of the present project, this is where the approach founders. To be a useful basis for guidance, it would be necessary to (1) establish the grounds relied on by judges in their assessment of the extent to which a sentence would achieve a particular goal for a given set of case facts and their assessment of the importance of that goal for that case and (2) quantify these assessments in relation to the facts of the offense and circumstances of the offender in a particular case.

A related use of decision theory has been introduced by Nagel and Neef (1979). They used decision theory as a mathematical model for determining which of the available options should or would be used to maximize benefits, after allowing for the costs, and regarding the probable occurrence of uncertain events. In this way one could analyze decisions regarding the choice between the options of a custodial sentence and a noncustodial sentence, with the uncertain event being whether or not the person would reoffend. According to this theory the judge should select the option with the highest expected value; expected value was defined as the sum of the products of the benefits (and the costs) and the probabilities of occurrence of the associated events.

There are several obvious limitations to this approach. First, although this analysis may provide a meaningful framework when incapacitation is the overwhelming aim of sentence, clearly, to the extent that certain other aims are relevant to sentence (e.g., retribution), this approach breaks down. Moreover, it offers no basis for determining when incapacitation as an aim should be the major consideration. An additional matter bearing on the utility of Nagel and Neef's analysis is that incapacitation would appear generally not to be a primary determinant of sentence in the courts in Austrailia, Canada, England, Scotland, or the United States.

Psychophysical Scaling

The preceding theoretical analyses were concerned with combining information. A related issue concerns the scaling of seriousness in relation to the case facts. An approach to the solution of this problem has been offered by Fitzmaurice and Pease (1982, 1986), who attempted to standardize retributive sentencing. The operational goal of retributive sentencing is to ensure that length of imprisonment is proportional to offender culpability. To quantify this proportionality, Fitzmaurice and Pease turned to psychophysics and Stevens's (1975) power function. In the context of sentencing, the power function states that psychological sensation (prison length) grows as a power function of the stimulus magnitude (seriousness of crime). The power (β) is the relative rate of increase along the two scales and defines the proportionality. To find the numerical value of the rate, judges are required to assign seriousness scores and set penalties (lengths of prison terms) for a series of cases. With this information the equation can be solved for β. Unless β can be standardized across judges, sentence length cannot be used as a valid comparative measure of judges' perceptions of the seriousness of offenses.

The major problem with Fitzmaurice and Pease's (1982, 1986) analysis is that it does not explicate the link between the facts of a case and the assessment of seriousness. The seriousness of a case is a multifaceted concept comprising an aggregation of separate assessments of a case in relation to offense components (e.g., the degree of organization, value of the thefts, etc.) and offender components (e.g., the degree of remorse). In the context of the present study, the use of an overall assessment of seriousness hides more than it reveals. Rather, one requires assessments of seriousness in regard to each of the components of a case (e.g., organization), together with an understanding of how these component assessments are aggregated in arriving at an overall assessment of the seriousness of a case.

Personality

An example of the use of personality theory is Lemon's (1974) relating of the variable of concreteness/abstractness to sentence. It is postulated that this dimension bears on how well a person can weigh and aggregate a mass of information, a fundamental task in sentencing. The earlier evaluation of research into judicial correlates of sentence is equally germane here, at least to the extent that the variable of concreteness/abstractness is tied to attitudinal variables such as religiosity and conventionality, and selection and training are seen as possible remedial measures. Nevertheless, there is no constitutional problem where this variable is the basis for predicating the value of a training program aimed at developing the skills of sentencers, independently of particular sentencing policies, in assessing and combining information, or the value of using decision aids as a means of overcoming human information-processing limitations. The question is whether it is worthwhile or possible to distinguish between individuals in regard to this skill. Little would appear to be gained and much to be lost.

The Role of Theory in Sentencing

Konečni and Ebbesen (Ebbesen & Konečni, 1981; Konečni & Ebbesen, 1981, 1982) discussed the role of sociopsychological theories used to explain the behavior of participants in the criminal justice system. These authors believe that frequently these concepts are selected merely because they are currently of interest in psychology, rather than on the grounds of their relevance to the law. Consequently, they said, many significant variables in the decision making of criminal justice system participants are omitted because they are not of theoretical interest to psychologists. Undoubtedly this is so, but it is not a fault of the use of theory per se but the use of theory in the absence of a relevant legal framework. In any case, this was the reason for Konečni and Ebbesen's favoring an atheoretical, descriptive approach to sentencing in the first instance or, at least, before later theoretical development. Their failure however, to collect and analyze their data in accordance with the nature and structure of the sentencing judgment was responsible for their overlooking legally significant aspects of sentencing policy, because they were forced to rely on a statistical criterion. Accordingly, Konečni and Ebbesen argued that when describing the criminal justice system one's task should be to account for as much of the predictive variance as possible. To accomplish this, it is necessary, they said, to select from a large set of variables, those accounting for the largest percentage of the variance in the decisions and yet not explainable by other known factors or combinations of factors. This line of reasoning led Konečni and Ebbesen to castigate psychologists who pursue the study of concepts accounting for only a small percentage of the variance, because they believe this undermines the efforts of researchers in the task of describing (predicting) the operation of the system.

There are a number of reasons for rejecting this statistical criterion. If one's aim is to understand how judges determine appropriate sentences for particular cases, then the percentage of variance criterion is irrelevant. Rather, the significant criterion should be whether the variable is legally significant. The jurisprudential bankruptcy of Ebbesen and Konečni (1981) and Konečni and Ebbesen's (1981, 1982) argument is revealed in their rejecting (individual differences in) philosophies of sentencing (penal goals) as a variable worthy of study on the grounds that it accounts for only a small percentage of the variance. Now, if the authors had considered the nature of the sentencing judgment, they would have realized that a possible explanation of this apparent negligible effect of sentencing philosophies, apart from the effect of disparity, is that a particular sentence may reflect a mix of aims and, in any case, particular sentencing goals are not directly related to quantum of sentence; they would not have concluded that penal goals are an insignificant element in the sentencing process. Clearly, one could not claim an understanding of sentencing before documenting the relationship between the facts of the case and the determination of the aims of sentence. Bray and Kerr (1979) also have wisely observed the dangers of adhering to a criterion of predictive significance in applied research.

A second undesirable consequence of the percentage of variance criterion is that researchers are left without a framework for explaining the significance of relationships observed between particular case variables and sentence or the possible significance of the lack of a relationship between other variables in their data; observations themselves are unsatisfying, meaningless, and provide no basis for future research (Monahan & Loftus, 1982). Say, for example, age was not found to be a correlate of sentence in a particular jurisdiction. One would not be moved to ask whether this relationship was expected, whether age is or should be material to the determination of sentence, and if it is, or should be, whether the legislature or the appellate court should provide greater guidance on how it is to be taken into account. Moreover, there would be no basis for querying whether the failure to identify this relationship could be attributed to the analysis; whether one had missed detecting its effect because the analysis was inappropriately structured. Indeed, it was the stark contrast between the numerous case factors in Thomas's (1979) legal description of sentencing and the few case factors in the Wilkins et al. (1978) guidelines model and Konečni and Ebbesen's account of sentencing that led one to suspect the validity of a (correlational) prediction paradigm. See also, Vining and Dean (1980) for a similar conclusion.

Finally, the inadequacy of this criterion can be demonstrated in another way. Consider an offense (e.g., minor theft) for which almost all offenders receive a noncustodial sentence and another (e.g., rape) for which imprisonment is imposed in most cases. Clearly, such an analysis would provide an almost perfect prediction of sentence but would be of no use to the practitioner. Variance as an index of explanation is not a satisfactory criterion; the law looks for explanation in terms of legally relevant variables and classifications.

This is a convenient introduction to a discussion of the way that case variables are inappropriately operationalized in many empirical studies. Again, this fault can be traced to researchers' failing to take the nature of the sentencing judgment seriously. By way of illustration, again consider the work of Ebbesen and Konečni (1981) and Konečni and Ebbesen (1981, 1982). They argued that in an analysis the case variables (and the associated categories) acting as predictors of decision making should be consonant with terms as they are typically used and understood by participants in the criminal justice system and should not be operationalized to accord with sociopsychological theory. One cannot dispute this principle.. However, Konečni and Ebbesen can be criticized for the way they operationalized some of their case variables. First, consider the seriousness of the crime. They classified this into offense-specific categories such as theft, burglary, and so on. Finding, however, that severity of crime, as defined, is related to sentence is merely to discover the obvious. Rather, the problem lawyers address is the effect on sentence of differences in seriousness within (cf. between) categories of offense, that is, the effect of particular offense characteristics (e.g., presence of a loaded gun) on severity of penalty (Ashworth, 1987; Canadian Sentencing Commission, 1987; Galligan, 1981; Tonry & Morris, 1978). This approach has the potential for a more precise description of sentencing, because although the average penalty for convicted robbers is more severe than for burglars, some burglars receive harsher penalties than some robbers (Law Department–Victoria, Management Information Section, 1985), and the reason for this is to be found in the circumstances of the offense, differentiated in terms of factors such as presence of a weapon and the like.

This is a characteristic fault of studies in this area and, undoubtedly, is one reason why empirical research has not been fruitful. For example Gottfredson and Gottfredson (1980), after reviewing research on the relationship between case characteristics and sentence, concluded confidently that a connection had been found only between seriousness of crime, prior record, and sentence. Happily, some researchers are conscious of this problem. Sutton (1978) reported that in his multivariate analysis of the relationship between several case characteristics and sentence approximately half of the variance was unexplained and then concluded that researchers must incorporate additional variables into their analyses and refine the definitions of case factors to reflect subtle and yet important aspects of relevant variables. Similarly, Vining and Dean (1980), after observing that empirical studies typically account for only a relatively small percentage of the sentencing variance, suggested that this is because empiricists have ignored appellate judgments as a rich source of variables for inclusion in statistical analyses.

Moreover, although Ebbesen and Konečni (1981) and Konečni and Ebbesen (1981, 1982) did not base their categories on psychological concepts, they did code certain case factors in terms of mediating constructs. For example the case factor "degree of premeditation" was coded on a dimension whose poles were defined by the terms "a lot" and "none," rather than in terms of concrete, case-specific factors such as the presence of a getaway vehicle. This is particularly salient where differential classification of material case factors is a source of disparity. Contrast this with Thomas's (1979) analysis of appellate court judgments. There he differentiates offenses in terms of such factors as amount of money stolen, factors that are concrete, case-specific, and found in the judgments of appellate courts as relevant to sentence.

Psychological Contributions to the Study of Sentencing: An Overview

This chapter reports a search through the psychological literature for a model describing how judges select, classify, and combine information about the facts of an offense and the circumstances of an offender in the course of determining the aim(s) of sentence in a case and then an appropriate sentence for that case to achieve those aims; the role of the model would be to facilitate the task of quantifying the links between the facts of the case and the penalty. Unfortunately, the search was in vain.

Of some of the research reviewed, such as the work of Ebbesen and Konečni (1981) and Konečni and Ebbesen (1981, 1982) and the previously mentioned judge-oriented investigations (pp. 57–59), it would seem none too harsh to conclude that these studies appear to have been conducted in spite of the nature of the sentencing judgment and therefore have little to offer. A plethora of these types of study exist, and indeed, they represent the traditional contribution of empirical psychology to sentencing.

A review of research into judicial sentencing is timely, because state-of-the-art reviews in law and psychology have typically addressed general issues or directed their attention to topics other than sentencing (e.g., Elwork, Sales, & Suggs, 1981; Farrington & Hawkins, 1979; Lloyd-Bostock, 1981a, 1981b; Monahan & Loftus, 1982; Tapp, 1976). Further, those reviews focusing on the judge and sentencing (Champagne & Nagel, 1982; Gottfredson & Gottfredson, 1980; Saks & Hastie, 1978) have paid scant attention to the issues arising directly from the interface of psychology and law, although Diamond (1983) is an exception to this. So we should urgently develop a position on the problematic issues in this field to promote the acceptance of the role of psychological enquiry in sentencing and through it move closer to a just and efficient sentencing system. The present review is, of course, not comprehensive, because it has been undertaken with a specific purpose in mind. In the light of the dearth of review material, it is appropriate to digress to extend the scope of this review and to offer some general observations on the application of psychology to this aspect of the legal system. The work of Ebbesen and Konečni (1981) and Konečni and Ebbesen (1981, 1982) is particularly apposite to the present discussion because they concluded one of their reports with a series of recommendations based heavily on their analyses.

Konečni and Ebbesen (1982) wrote an emotional and loosely argued diatribe as a finale to their book on the criminal justice system. They commenced the chapter in a confident tone and asserted that their research was ready to be applied. In contrast the mood of their ultimate paragraph was somber and pessimistic. The two psychologists confessed that they did not expect that legal practitioners would implement their recommendations or indeed that this and similar volumes would have much impact on legal circles. Legal inertia and the unchallenged authority of the judiciary, harnessed to maintain the vested interests of the judges, were perceived by the authors as the forces shaping this scenario. On a related, although more basic matter, other psychologists have complained of the difficulty (e.g., Elwork et al., 1981) and, more often than not, of the futility of attempting to persuade judges to participate in psychological research.

Frequently, researchers lay the blame for this state of affairs at the feet of the judiciary. This is one possible explanation. An alternative view is that most psychological research relating to sentencing is so lacking in legal and jurisprudential relevance and validity that the judiciary could not responsibly introduce consequent policy changes confident in the knowledge that the quality of justice would be improved. Many psychologists incline themselves to the former view; this is unfortunate because this position harbors rationalization and inhibits self-criticism. More importantly, perhaps the latter view is correct. Indeed, the problems associated with the work of Ebbesen and Konečni (1981) and Konečni and Ebbesen (1981, 1982) lead one to favor the latter explanation. Perhaps, therefore, the blame should lie with the psychologists. Perhaps, what may be described as commendable enthusiasm is clouding the professional judgment of some psychologists as they attempt to apply the results of their research to improve the quality of sentencing. An unintended effect may be a lowering of lawyers' and judges' respect for psychologists, thereby hindering further cooperation (Johnson, 1980).

Problems Associated With the Application of Psychological Research to Sentencing

Quality of Research Findings

Konečni and Ebbesen (1982) asserted that their research findings were ready to be applied and on this basis made specific recommendations. The issue is whether the quality of these findings is sufficiently high that these data could be reasonably regarded as a sound base for remedial measures. There are two criteria bearing on this assessment, and when measured against these criteria, Konečni and Ebbesen's work is not ready to be applied. These criteria are (1) the conclusions should follow logically from the findings; (2) the findings should have been cross-validated or substantiated across studies—where inconsistency is found across studies, it is incumbent on the researchers to account for the differences in favor of their own study before proceeding.

Consider, for example, Konečni and Ebbesen's (1982) conclusion that judicial sentencing decisions are based on only a few (four) variables. This type of research study has typically accounted for between 35% and 50% of the variance (e.g., Sutton, 1978; Wilkins et al., 1978). Although to some extent this low figure may be attributable to inconsistency in judicial sentencing practices, a plausible alternative is that researchers have not incorporated relevant variables and in an appropriate manner in their analyses (Sutton, 1978; Vining & Dean, 1980; see also, the analysis of Wilkins et al.'s work in the previous chapter). Until this issue has been resolved, one cannot conclude that judicial sentencing is not complex. Moreover, one of Konečni and Ebbesen's (1982) significant conclusions runs counter to the main body of research findings. These authors concluded that sentencing strategies are largely uniform across judges, whereas Diamond's (1981) conclusion, in line with the overwhelming weight of research studies (Forst, 1982; Kapardis, 1985; Lovegrove, 1984a) is contrary to this. At this point one is reminded of Meehl's (1971) warning, "... when a fireside induction is held nearly *semper, ubique, et ab omnibus* a similar skepticism should be maintained toward experimental research purporting, as generalized, to overthrow it" (p. 97).

Nature of the Recommendations

When authors write a recommendation on the basis of their research in relation to sentencing, they should demonstrate an understanding of the nature of sentencing, appreciate the principles and conventions associated with the judiciary and the courts, be alert to the possibility of unintended consequences, and have pretested, as far as is practicable, their product. We should not forget Lloyd-Bostock's (1981b) warning against the tendency of some psychologists to make critical judgments about the operation of the legal system without apparently understanding the complexity of the issues. The following discussion shows that this warning is timely.

Konečni and Ebbesen (1982) recommended that probation officers should replace judges as the sentencers (because they believe judges merely follow probation officers' recommendations) and concluded that if decision making in sentencing were computerized then penalties would be fairer and more certain. To illustrate the inherent problems, aspects of these recommendations will be considered in regard to each of the preceding criteria.

First, the law of sentencing will be developed most creatively if an appellate court is given the opportunity of ruling on a diversity of judicial interpretations of sentencing law in relation to particular cases. Computer sentencing would prevent this. Konečni and Ebbesen (1982) would have been wise to have considered, as an alternative remedial measure, Thomas's (1977) case for the appellate courts in the United States to take an active role in sentencing.

Second, the proposal that probation officers determine the sentence is inconsistent with the adversary nature of the criminal trial. The role of the probation officer is to put facts about the offender to the court so it can individualize the sentence (Cross & Ashworth, 1981). Clearly, the position of the prosecution would be seen to be prejudiced if there were no independent party to arbitrate the conflict.

Third, undoubtedly, computerized decision making would eliminate sentencing discretion and so ensure certainty in sentencing. Almost certainly, however, it would not remove the impact of human judgment on the determination of the penalty. Rather, the exercise of discretion might then be displaced to the prosecution or enforcement agencies (Tonry, 1982). So, instead of an improvement in the quality of justice, the outcome might be less desirable, for the discretion might be hidden and, accordingly, unchecked, and no longer under the control of an independent body of individuals, experienced in arbitrating between opposing cases.

Fourth, Konečni and Ebbesen (1982) did not evaluate what may be regarded as pretests of their product. Wilkins et al. (1978) also concluded that relatively few variables are required to predict sentence. Yet a close analysis of their data suggests that they might have deceived themselves in their conclusion that they had accounted for the sentencing decisions in approximately 80% of cases, for their criterion of a correct prediction of length of incarceration was indeed generous: for Felony-4 offenses (10 years' maximum) a hit was defined as within 1 year of the specified guideline ranges of between 1 and 2 years. Clearly, this evidence is against the view that a computer program incorporating a small number of variables could be written to account accurately for sentence. In any case at about the time of Konečni and Ebbesen's report, academics (e.g., Tonry, 1982) were aware of a report (Rich et al., 1982) in which Wilkins's sentencing guidelines as an operational system was evaluated unfavorably.

Attitudes of Researchers to Criminal Justice Personnel

There are good reasons for treating the subjects in one's study with respect. Courtesy demands it, and criminal justice professionals who were treated contemptuously would understandably be inclined to mistrust the objectivity of researchers and would be less open to future cooperation. One therefore was surprised at Konečni and Ebbesen's (1982) vitriolic and largely unfounded attack on the competence and integrity of criminal justice personnel and the judiciary in particular. One example will suffice to illustrate this point:

> Judges attend one hearing after another, believing (or pretending?) that they are making decisions, when, in fact, they often merely rubber-stamp the decisions made by others—the prosecutors (for the amount of bail), the probation officers (for the sentence), or the psychiatrists (for the disposition of mentally disordered sex offenders). Meanwhile, at public expense, they surround themselves with pomp and circumstance, with flags and gavels, presumably "to instill respect" . . . . (p. 400)

This is an apposite example of Lloyd-Bostock's (1981b) observation that there has been a rather arrogant tone to some of the attempts of psychologists to get lawyers to take notice of their work. Yet we have been wisely counseled by Kalven (1968) against viewing the law as a museum of irrational procedures and brushing aside the shortcomings of science.

Konečni and Ebbesen (1982) frankly admitted that their editorial would have been less emotional had it not been for the closed-door policy adopted by some personnel in the system. Of course, the legal system, like all systems, is most refractory to change in areas bearing on self-maintenance (Haney, 1980). Nevertheless, I believe that many judges are open to innovations that might be reasonably expected to improve the quality of justice (see also, Saks, 1982), and they do not veto research proposals for self-serving reasons or from a lack of concern for justice and efficiency in the courts. If judges were to countenance research that in their opinion was not soundly based, then they would be abrogating their responsibility. Winning the hearts and minds of the judiciary is part of the research challenge in the field of judicial sentencing and empirical psychology, and it may sometimes require both social (Mungham & Thomas, 1981) as well as legal and political (Haney, 1980) skills, with no small measure of luck thrown in. One must be prepared to go forward slowly and graciously, but as Mungham and Thomas (1981) have written in the context of their study in another area of the legal system, "(t)hose researchers who can manage these transactions will yield rich rewards; those that cannot will glean little" (p. 91).

What are the reasons for psychologists experiencing difficulties in conducting and applying research in this field? Perhaps it is that psychologists generally are not trained to study human behavior in an applied area, especially where it is characterized by complex social situations, where the behavior occurs within a framework of complex and authoritative (nonpsychological) rules, where the subjects are intelligent and socially powerful so that they are capable of critically evaluating the research and of controlling its future, and where the research is to be the basis of public policy with significant social consequences. Such is the domain of sentencing. Moreover, the standard approaches of empirical psychology (hypothesis testing in specific situations; traditional empirical techniques, e.g., simulation; and routine analyses, e.g., prediction and correlation) exacerbate some of these problems, for they predispose the researcher to concepts and strategies that are not consonant with the nature of sentencing; the consequence is that research findings cannot be critically related to legal and jurisprudential issues. Simply, traditional research orientations blinker the psychologist to the subtleties of sentencing.

In any psychological study the researcher must solve the traditional sorts of problems associated with conceptual and empirical validity; for example, the derivation of hypotheses from theory and the experimental manipulation and control of variables. In applied sociopsychological research, however, that is, research used to comment on a social process with a view to modifying it, there is a second set of deliberations confronting the researcher. These are the constraints and demands that the field of enquiry imposes on the theoretical and empirical aspects of the study; in this case the considerations are jurisprudential and legal. Moreover, one cannot treat these legal considerations as an additional problem, in the sense that one can plan a study and then modify it to accommodate them. Rather, the legal considerations are the problem, and so are inextricably linked to the theory and method of the psychological study. Clearly, the traditional standards of valid psychological research, although necessary, are not sufficient.

Tapp (1976) adopted a musical metaphor to express her hope for the future success of research at the psychology–law interface—that we compose in concert. Alas, all too often psychological studies of judges and sentencing appear to have been planned and conducted despite the law and reported without regard to the legal milieu. If psychological research is to be taken up by the law, then its legal and jurisprudential basis must be relevant and sound (Elwork et al., 1981); it must be anchored in the legal literature (Lloyd-Bostock, 1981b). To meet these requirements the research must be faithful to the structure of legal thought, examine legally salient issues, and not be at variance with the conventions of the legal system. As Elwork et al. (1981) remarked in their review, psychologists have often failed to learn and take heed of the realities and the requirements of the law and the legal system, with the consequence that their research has answered legally irrelevant questions. Indeed, this is one reason why practitioners ignore research findings (Johnson, 1980). In a similar vein Lloyd-Bostock (1981b) and Tanke and Tanke (1979) emphasized that the legal literature is an invaluable resource. Kalven's (1968) plea succinctly expresses the tenor of my argument:

> The millennium will come sooner when the cause of science is embraced by those with a respect for the wisdom of durable institutions and procedures and a respect for seasoned experience; in brief, a respect for what the law already knows. (p. 59)

Happily times change. Now, one can clearly discern what may come to be regarded as a new generation of psychological research in sentencing. The direction taken by Palys and Divorski (1984), Lawrence and Homel (1987), and Hogarth (1971) in their analyses of the qualitative relationship between the facts of the case, the goals of sentence, and the penalty imposed; together with Fitzmaurice and Pease's (1982, 1986) venture into scaling seriousness in relation to the description of a case and the sentence imposed; and finally, McKnight's (1981) adoption of decision theory as a means of quantifying the aggregation of the various elements of a sentencing decision in the course of determining a penalty for a case—all of these and other studies suggest a new level of sophistication exists among psychologists and behavioral scientists at the psychology–law interface, at least in the area of sentencing. (Indeed, Diamond, 1982, in her review of the application of psychology to other aspects of the legal system similarly noted that the field is maturing.) Unfortunately, not one of these studies dealt adequately with the problem of quantifying the relationship between case fact, penal objective, and penalty—at least, that is, not in relation to the purposes of the present study. But they certainly contained the seeds of a few ideas.

Judge Bazelon of the United States, when addressing a conference of psychologists on the topic of corrections, made the following very thoughtful observation (quoted by Tapp, 1976), "The critical issue . . . is whether the fundamental postulates of your discipline make it impossible for you to reach the central problem . . . " (p. 371). At least regarding the present search for an appropriate model of judicial decision making in relation to the determination of appropriate sentences, the answer must favor the negative. Fortunately, an academic lawyer, David Thomas (1979), has developed a model describing in general terms the structure and elements of the judicial determination of sentence and including an account of the more or less conscious thought processes of judges as they reconcile the facts of a case, the penal goals, and the penalty. His model may accordingly not inappropriately be described as a psycholegal model, and it forms the foundation of the present study.

Part Two An Archival Study of a Legal Model of Judicial Decision Making in Sentencing

4
A Legal Model of Judicial Decision Making

The task of this chapter is to develop a legal model of judicial decision making describing, first, how judges decide whether a tariff sentence or an individualized measure is the more appropriate disposition in a particular case and, second, for tariff sentences, how judges determine the appropriate quantum of sentence (see Chapter 1). This discussion initially turns to the problem of scaling culpability in the course of determining a tariff sentence and then considers the choice between a tariff sentence and an individualized measure. The model is developed and particularized in relation to cases in which the legal offense category of burglary is the principal offense. Burglary is an apposite offense because it is an offense for which both offense and offender characteristics are ordinarily given substantial weight in the determination of sentence (Thomas, 1979).

In Chapter 2 it was argued that what is required is a model that, in representing the relationship between the facts of the case and sentence, is faithful to the structure of judicial decision making. To my knowledge, David Thomas's (1979) analysis of the nature and the structure of the judicial determination of sentence is the only analysis offering an account of the legal considerations more or less consciously exercising the minds of judges as they apply sentencing policy in individual cases. Accordingly, it was adopted as a basis for the present model and developed for the task of construing the relationship between case fact and sentence. The model is, of course, a model of ideal decision making in the light of current sentencing policy, because it neither takes account of the limitations of human information processing nor allows for the possible effects of immaterial case factors.

The purpose of the model is to act as a basis for the description of sentencing policy and practice (detailed sentencing statistics) and for the development of sentencing policy (prescriptive numerical guidelines). This will be achieved when a relationship has been established between various combinations of objectively defined offense and offender characteristics of cases and the appropriate quanta of sentence.

In the development of detailed sentencing statistics, the model is used to represent the variations between offenses and offenders and their relationship to the sentence. First, actual case data are fitted to this model, and then this representation of seriousness is used to show the relationship between this construction of the facts for a set of cases and the sentences imposed in the courts for these cases. This would provide a description of current sentencing policy and practice, and the information could be used by the courts as a guide to appropriate sentences for particular cases.

The model could also be used to develop new sentencing policies. In applying the model in this second role, changes could be contemplated to the existing model. Case factors could be added or removed or redefined, weights could be modified, and the rules for combining the information could be reformulated, and changes could be approved respecting the types and levels of sentence for the various patterns of offending and offenders. This product would be numerical guidelines. In this way the model would be acting as no more than a conceptual framework for a guideline judgment.

In moving along the path toward a uniform approach to sentencing, the uses of legal analysis and behavioral science are interdependent. For example, the definition of a case characteristic covering the value of money and goods stolen requires an appreciation of how this characteristic is distributed across cases of burglary. Moreover, the detailed sentencing statistics could not be finalized until matters such as the weightings given to the various case factors had been settled as a matter of law. This second matter, of course, raises a dilemma for the present analysis, particularly in relation to the task of applying the decision model to a specific offense (in this case burglary), because appellate court judgments are silent on many issues and in any case lack specificity. Furthermore, senior judges would understandably not want to give the guidance necessary for the development of these detailed sentencing statistics until they had an opportunity to examine a prototype. This left me with the unenviable task of intuiting the definitions, weightings and rules that most nearly captured the general trends in sentencing policy in the courts of first instance. It is possible that many of these decisions might be seriously in error and, as a consequence, the types and levels of sentence determined appropriate by the model might not match the actual sentences. The danger inherent in this approach is that the strategy for developing detailed statistics might be rejected on the basis of these results when, in fact, the fault could lie with my decisions rather than the strategy per se.

Scaling Culpability

The purpose of this section is to develop a model describing how judges scale culpability in terms of offense and offender characteristics (see also, Lovegrove, 1984b, 1987).

Offense Characteristics

In his analysis Thomas (1979) adopted the concept of the tariff, defining this as a framework to which a sentencer can refer to determine which factors in a particular case are relevant and the weight that should be attached to each factor. Clearly, Thomas's analysis has both descriptive and quantitative elements. For these reasons it seemed appropriate to adopt his model of judicial thought as a basis for collecting, analyzing, and interpreting the sentencing statistics in the present study. Moreover, in sympathy with the position of Thomas, the present attempt to quantify some of the principles underlying what he has called "the substance of the tariff" is presented as no more than a numerical aid to the common law approach.

First, it is appropriate to outline Thomas's (1979) approach. He proposed that judges follow three steps to determine the quantum of sentence:

1. Defining the range.The assumption behind the tariff is that within any legal definition a variety of factual situations relating to the offense will recur and that within each set of factual situations there are upper and lower limits within which the sentence is presumed to fall in the absence of exceptional circumstances relating to the offense and without regard to mitigating circumstances relating to the offender.
2. Determining the ceiling. Typically, the judge's task is to relate the facts of the case (offense) to one of the established patterns for that type of offense and then to locate the established range of sentence in relation to the particular set of facts. The upper limit of the range is the ceiling.
3. Reducing the sentence to allow for the effects of mitigating factors.

Now consider how Thomas structured the representation of offense characteristics. To present his sentencing data, Thomas identified groups representing patterns of offending within fairly specific legal offense categories. He then set out the range of the sentences allowed by the English Court of Appeal (Criminal Division) for each of the identified groups. The appropriate sentence for any particular offense is determined by adding (or subtracting) the effects of aggravating (or extenuating) factors in relation to the quantum of sentence within the range for the group in which the particular offense is most appropriately placed. Although the specification of the range of sentence for each group is stated quite precisely (although biased toward the more serious cases, see Ashworth, 1983b), the effect of material factors on sentence within a range is presented only qualitatively. The only guidance for this latter aspect of the determination of sentence is to be found in his brief descriptions of the critical elements of selected cases (offender characteristics are largely ignored) together with an indication of where each case fell within the range of sentence for that type.

It has already been pointed out that this type of analysis is unnecessarily subjective, qualitative, and intuitive; as well it is not based on a representative sample of cases. Another point, however, requires further discussion; it concerns the use of groups as a primary means of characterizing the variation in offenses.

Consider how Thomas classified varieties of robbery. Thomas divided robbery into four groups (large-scale organized robbery, violent robbery, robberies of tradespeople and small business premises, and mugging), and he then cited the typical characteristics of each group. The basis of this classification is principally in terms of the value of the money and property sought, in association with factors indicative of scale; for example, a high degree of organization is assumed to characterize robberies in which the target is a very large sum of money.

Now, experience indicates that many of the characteristics comprising Thomas's groups are imperfectly correlated. Indeed, past research has demonstrated that such inconsistency is a significant feature of these groups for armed robbery (Lovegrove, 1983). Unless sentencing statistics incorporate such distinctions, allowance for these variations is left to the judge's discretion, and there is a potential source of disparity. For example presumably the sentences for mugging reflect the fact that most offenses in this category are poorly organized. A longer sentence, however, may be more appropriate where the degree of organization aggravates the offense.

The limitation of Thomas's (1979) analysis in this regard is clearly illustrated in his analysis of burglary. For this offense Thomas did not delineate patterns of offending; one reason for this was that burglary covers such a wide range of factual situations. Rather, he merely characterized burglary according to one or more case factors in an unsystematic fashion and, accordingly, failed to provide a logical structure in which combinations of case characteristics were systematically and precisely related to sentence.

There is another problem with Thomas's approach. His analysis of appellate court judgments shows that when judges determine sentence not only do they refer to the range of sentence appropriate for the particular group of offenses but they also distinguish between cases within the group by, as it were, adding (or subtracting) time for aggravating (or extenuating) factors. Now, a representation of the tariff founded on groups cannot adequately incorporate this second element of decision making.

One way of overcoming these problems would be to classify offenses not according to groups but in relation to a set of dimensions and defining categories (e.g., a dimension of financial loss, the categories being specified by monetary limits). Indeed, the use of dimensions and categories seems implicit in judicial thinking. One can discern from Thomas's descriptions of various patterns of offending that many of the defining characteristics (e.g., violence) or their contrasts (no violence) recur across groups. A further advantage of a dimensional solution is that it would provide a common descriptive base and, consequently, a more elegant solution.

There are three reasons why the group solution should not be completely abandoned. First, it appears to be consistent with the structure of judicial thinking. Experience suggests that sentence lengths for the various types of offense within a legal offense category tend to cluster around substantially different averages. Indeed, an analysis of sentence lengths for types of armed robbery supported this view (Lovegrove, 1983). Now, it may be that the absolute effect of any particular aggravating or extenuating factor varies across types. If this is so, then the examination of such factors within groups would increase the precision of the analysis. Second, it would be expected that the significance of the categories on the dimensions describing offenses would be maximized if they were defined in relation to the distributions of the cases in terms of the dimensions for the population under study. This is a useful way to establish categories to draw distinctions between offenses in terms of the amount of property seized in a robbery, for example. If one did not separate these distributions, however, for banks and individuals in armed robbery for example, then significant distinctions might be overlooked. Third, if the different types of offense within a legal offense category vary in their degree of seriousness, then the use of groups would provide for the possible differential weighting of mitigating offender characteristics across these groups.

The preceding discussion points to a possible strategy for presenting more detailed sentencing statistics. First, for each legal offense category (e.g., armed robbery or burglary), define a small number of groups describing patterns of offending for that offence. Second, differentiate offenses within each of the groups according to a set of dimensions and categories that is common to all groups.

From Thomas's (1979) analysis it appeared that the type of premises would be related to the factors used to describe variations in the offenses within a legal offense category in which theft was an element of the offense. The type of premises therefore was used to define the groups describing the patterns of offending for the earlier study of armed robbery, and the data supported this assumption (Lovegrove, 1983).

Representing the Seriousness of Burglary

When this conceptual framework was employed to construe offenses of armed robbery according to seriousness, a high degree of association was found between seriousness and severity of the actual sentence (Lovegrove, 1983). Accordingly, the same approach was adopted for the study of burglary.

The first step, then, was to identify groups representing patterns of offending. Intuitively, it seemed that commercial premises, dwelling houses, and public buildings may define critical groups. One distinction concerns the sanctity of the premises, and the courts have clearly ruled that particular gravity attends the violation of a citizen's home (see Fox & Freiberg, 1985, for relevant appellate decisions in Victoria, Australia, and also, the judgment of Lawton, L.J., in the English Court of Appeal – Criminal Division – in *Smith and Woollard*, 1978). A second classification is suggested by the results of empirical studies of burglary (Clarke, 1978; Maguire, 1982; Scarr, 1973). One would not be surprised if a not-uncommon feature of the burglaries of public buildings (e.g., school, football club pavilion) was vandalism, whereas theft of money and goods would seem to be the predominant motive behind burglaries of nonpublic premises (i.e., commercial premises such as a doctor's surgery, factory canteen, private club, shop). It was not possible , however, to discriminate between premises in terms of the amount of money or goods that the offender(s) hoped to seize, because in most cases this could not be intuited from a description of the premises. This classification of burglary can be contrasted with the one adopted for armed robbery. Armed robberies are qualitatively similar across types of premises, in that they are characterized by theft associated with actual or threatened violence. Salient distinctions can be made, however, in terms of the amount of money or property the offenders hoped to seize, and generally it is possible to estimate this if one knows the types of premises that were the target of the attacks.

In the next step, a set of dimensions (and associated categories) that it seemed would comprehensively describe offenses of burglary was identified and defined. Source material for this analysis was provided principally by legal analyses of sentencing judgments in England (Thomas, 1979, 1982), Canada (Ruby, 1980), and in several Australian states (Daunton-Fear, 1977, 1980; Newton, 1979), as well as case factors that were found in the data collected for the present study. On the basis of this review, it was decided that cases of burglary could be comprehensively described according to the following general dimensions: the total value of the money and property stolen (*total value of the theft*); the number of counts of burglary (*counts of burglary*); the degree of organization characterizing the count(s) (*organization*); and the amount of violence and property damage associated with the counts (*violence to the victims*). Notice was also taken of the numbers of attempted burglaries, offenses connected with the execution of the burglaries, unconnected offenses, and pending charges taken into account in the sentence. These latter factors were not incorporated in the calculation of the tariff but were noted in the final statistical tables. A detailed description and specification of these case characteristics is presented in Chapter 6; there the constituent categories of each dimension are defined. Fox and Freiberg's (1985) subsequent analysis of sentencing judgments in Victoria confirms the validity of these four offense factors of burglary.

In developing a conceptual framework for describing phenomena, it is necessary to strike a balance between simplicity and precision. It appeared that the preceding four general dimensions covering the value of the theft, number of counts, organization, and violence represented the minimum number of conceptually distinct descriptors incorporating the material features of burglaries and to which reference is most commonly made in the courts. Four similar dimensions had been found to represent armed robbery well (Lovegrove, 1983). Therefore, it was decided to adopt this classification, at least in the first instance. Of course, this does not preclude allowances being made by a judge in the exercise of the sentencing discretion for other factors and for significant variations in offense characteristics relating to these general dimensions.

The third step in representing the seriousness of offenses involved the process of assigning numbers to case characteristics in accordance with the degree to which these factors may aggravate the offense, a process consistent with Thomas's account of judicial thinking. Benjamin Franklin, in a much-quoted letter to the British scientist Joseph Priestly in 1772, documented his arguments for preferring systematic and numerical methods to intuition. Franklin wrote:

> In the affair of so much importance to you, wherein you ask my advice, I cannot, for want of sufficient premises, advise you what to determine, but if you please I will tell you how. When these difficult cases occur, they are difficult, chiefly because while we have them

under consideration, all the reasons pro and con are not present to the mind at the same time; but sometimes one set present themselves, and at other times another, the first being out of sight. Hence the various purposes or inclinations that alternatively prevail, and the uncertainty that perplexes us. To get over this, my way is to divide half a sheet of paper by a line into two columns; writing over the one Pro, and over the other Con. Then, during three or four days consideration, I put down under the different heads short hints of the different motives, that at different times occur to me, for or against the measure. When I have thus got them all together in one view, I endeavor to estimate their respective weights; and where I find two, one on each side, that seem equal, I strike them both out. If I find a reason pro equal to some two reasons con, I strike out the three. If I judge some two reasons con, equal to some three reasons pro, I strike out the five; and thus proceeding I find at length where the balance lies; and if, after a day or two of further consideration, nothing new that is of importance occurs on either side, I come to a determination accordingly. And, though the weight of reasons cannot be taken with the precision of algebraic quantities, yet when each is thus considered, separately and comparatively, and the whole lies before me, I think I can judge better, and am less liable to make a rash step, and in fact I have found great advantage from this kind of equation, in what may be called moral or prudential algebra. (quoted in Hogarth, 1980, p. 142)

The strategy adopted for the present study is in sympathy with Franklin's approach to decision making. In the first part of this process of representing the seriousness of the offense characteristics of individual burglaries, each dimension was divided into four categories (as for armed robbery), each category within each dimension marking a different level of seriousness. For each dimension the category defining the most aggravating behavior was assigned a code (score) of 4, and for the least aggravating category the code was 1, the intermediate categories being 3 and 2. In determining the characteristics that defined each of the categories on the dimensions, the underlying aim (and assumption) was that the differences in the characteristics between pairs of adjacent categories (on a particular dimension) should represent equal degrees of aggravation (or extenuation) on an interval scale. These decisions necessarily had a substantial intuitive component, but empirically based criteria (e.g., frequency distributions) and nonempirical criteria (e.g., common sense and criminological considerations) were applied to guide this process (see Chapter 6 for details). To classify a particular burglary in terms of this scheme, it was necessary to identify one category (the category whose defining content most closely matched that aspect of the facts of the offense) for each of the four dimensions. In this way the offense characteristics of a case were described in terms of four codes (one for each of the dimensions), and each code acted as a score quantifying seriousness in accordance with the degree of aggravation associated with that aspect of the offense.

The second part of this process required the formulation of rules for combining this information so that the degree of seriousness of the various combinations of offense characteristics could be represented by a single score. Before this could be done, a decision had to be made on the weight that was to be assigned to each dimension. The crucial question regarding this point concerns the relative aggravating effects of behaviors classified in the top categories on the dimensions covering the value of the theft, number of counts, degree of organization, and amount of violence. One must determine whether serious violence is more, or less, or equally aggravating as a high degree of organization, and so on. It appeared from analyses of appellate court judgments in Australia and England that these issues have not been addressed directly. Nevertheless, it was possible to discern some guidance on these matters. The courts have drawn individual attention to extreme forms of each of these four offense characteristics when commenting on the seriousness of various cases. Consequently, there seemed to be no grounds for discriminating between the potential importance of these four offense characteristics, and therefore the four dimensions were weighted equally. Accordingly, the score representing the seriousness of the offense characteristics of a particular case was derived simply by adding the four codes for that case together. (This procedure requires that the previously mentioned assumption is valid and that the categories on the four dimensions cover the same range of gravity.)

In assessing the validity of these assumptions, it must be remembered that they refer to equal aggravation or extenuation. These assumptions are probably more soundly based than if they referred to seriousness, because aggravating (or extenuating) factors exert a fractional increase (or decrease) on seriousness. Accordingly, the effects of errors associated with these assumptions would be minimized because they would operate in the context of a case. Moreover, the actual effects of such errors might be further lessened by the fact that the aggravating (or extenuating) effects of the factors are considered within type of premises and, consequently, within common distributions of sentence that were expected to be narrower than if burglary had not been differentiated. Also relevant to this argument is that the representation of the relationship between offense and sentence is intended as no more than a guide and, accordingly, the sentencer may allow for offense characteristics that are not captured adequately by the descriptive categories. A final justification for this strategy is that it was found to produce a valid representation for armed robbery.

A comment should be made on the use of the dimension of counts of burglary as a characteristic of cases in which burglary is the principal offense. Clearly, this dimension is not a characteristic of individual burglaries, in the sense that the other three dimensions can be applied to compare and contrast various types of burglary. Nevertheless, the dimension of counts of burglary is a relevant case factor of cases in which burglary is the principal offense. Indeed, multiple counts of burglary is a common characteristic of such cases. It is clear from Thomas's (1979) and Fox and Freiberg's (1985) analyses of appellate decisions in cases of burglary that the presence of numerous counts of burglary is a factor that may lead the court to approve a substantial sentence of imprisonment, just as professional planning may underlie a severe sentence. The point is, how does a judge take the number of counts into account in arriving at an effective sentence for a case characterized by multiple counts of a particular offense?

The court is required to determine an appropriate sentence for each count as well as a total effective sentence for the case. In arriving at the effective sentence, the court may make the sentences for the individual counts cumulative, partially concurrent, or concurrent. The sentence for each count should properly reflect the gravity of the particular count, and the total effective sentence should be appropriate for the criminal conduct viewed as a whole. This is the totality principle (Fox & Freiberg, 1985; Thomas, 1979). In Victoria, the judgment of the Victorian Court of Criminal Appeal in *Tutchell* (1979) sets out the approach to sentencing in cases comprising multiple counts.

> One of the first decisions in a case such as this is whether to impose sentences of imprisonment or noncustodial sentences: . . . (a)n important consideration in making this decision is the seriousness of the ten offences considered separately and in the aggregate. If imprisonment is decided to be the appropriate form of sentence, the judge would then impose a sentence on each count. In considering the orders of concurrency to be made and the effective sentence to result from those orders, the judge would consider the individual offences and sentences and also the offences and sentences in the aggregate. Similarly in deciding on the minimum period to be served before becoming eligible for parole the judge would consider the individual offences and sentences and also consider them as a whole. At each of the stages of deciding whether to impose custodial sentences or not, what concurrency orders are to be made, and what minimum sentence is to be imposed, the weighting given to each offence is most important. (pp. 252–253)

Thomas (1979) expressed the import of the totality principle from a different perspective and concluded:

> (t)his formulation would allow an aggregate sentence longer than the sentence which would be passed for the most serious offence if it stood alone, but would ensure that the sentence bore some recognizable relationship to the gravity of that offence. (p. 59)

On the basis of these considerations it seemed that a proper approach in arriving at an appropriate effective sentence for a case was to consider the seriousness of the case as the unit of the analysis and, accordingly, use counts of burglary as one of the dimensions in the determination of the effective sentence. Nevertheless, Thomas's view perhaps represents a different approach in that sentencers who follow this approach may not acknowledge that counts of burglary can be incorporated into the decision in this way or, if they do acknowledge it as a factor, their perception of its weight relative to the other offense factors may differ from what may be considered appropriate by those who follow the former approach.

Finally, in cases with multiple counts of burglary, the use of the dimension of total value of the theft is somewhat problematic, because sometimes the court in giving reasons for sentence refers to the total value of the amount stolen, all counts considered, whereas on other occasions the court appears to concentrate on the (typical) value of the amount stolen in each of the counts. Again, this is a matter requiring judicial resolution. Nevertheless, it can be concluded that both these aspects of value are of relevance to the approach expressed in *Tutchell* (1979), whereas a consideration of only the latter aspect is consistent with the view expressed by Thomas (1979).

TABLE 4.1. Material offender characteristics

Type	Specific factors
Exculpatory	Age, previous good character, reason for the offense, role in the offense, remorse (confession, reconciliation, current character, rehabilitation prospects, action taken for rehabilitation)
Aggravation	Prior convictions, breach of trust
Mercy	Suffering the offender has already undergone because of the offense, deprived family background, personal and family suffering that might be caused by imprisonment, potentially debilitating effects of imprisonment on rehabilitation

Offender Characteristics

In terms of Thomas's (1979) analysis, the offense score representing seriousness marks the ceiling for a particular offense. In determining a sentence so that it is proportional to an offender's culpability, a sentencer also may consider characteristics relating to the offender and, if the net effect of these factors is mitigating, then the sentencer may reduce the offender's culpability (offense seriousness score) accordingly. This problem of mitigation is now addressed; the aim and strategy are the same as the approach for the offense, namely, the derivation of a score representing the extent of mitigation for each case by combining the scores on the constituent elements of mitigation. There are four aspects to this problem.

1. Identification and weighting of material offender characteristics
2. Prior convictions and their role in mitigation
3. Combination of offender characteristics
4. Relationship between offense and offender characteristics

Identification and Weighting of Material Offender Characteristics

There are three types of offender characteristics. Some are exculpatory, others are aggravating, whereas the third group relate to mercy rather than culpability but are significant because their presence requires that an otherwise appropriate sentence should be reduced in severity. Table 4.1 lists these offender characteristics. Again, it was felt that these characteristics adequately represent the factors that are found in the previously mentioned (p. 78) analyses of sentencing judgments (see also, Wasik, 1987), general analyses of mitigating factors (Hampel, 1978), empirical studies (Shapland, 1981), and the data in the present study. A detailed description and specification of these factors is presented in Chapter 8, where the constituent categories of each factor are defined and then weighted by being assigned single codes (scores) that mark the extent of their mitigating effects.

Analyses of sentencing judgments provided minimal guidance for the weighting of offender characteristics, and so heavy reliance was placed on the contents of the pleas and judgments in the present sample. One could not help but feel, after perusing the records of the pleas and judgments, that mitigating factors are not of equal importance. Consequently, it was decided to weight offender characteristics differentially to attempt to reflect these trends in the judges' views. Of course, in view of the intuitive and unsystematic nature of this analysis, the assigned weights are but a rough approximation to the true weights. One could have sought some empirical support for the analysis, such as examining the relative emphasis given to particular mitigating factors where they were mentioned in the judgments. Because, however, data in the pleas and judgments do not directly bear on this issue (e.g., many first-instance judgments make little more than an incidental reference to the range of material factors apparently weighed in mitigation by the judge), it is doubtful whether these references could be used to improve the estimates. In any case in view of the strategy underlying the development of the model, precision at this point is not critical. As long as these decisions are a reasonable approximation to judicial decision making, the initial model will provide an adequate base for the subsequent process of fine tuning.

Prior Convictions and Their Role in Mitigation

Of all the material case factors, it is an offender's record of prior convictions for which most guidance has been given by the courts. Yet much has been left unsaid. It is clear that offenders cannot be sentenced on their records. Even despite an extensive past record, the characteristics of the present offense set the ceiling for the appropriate quantum of sentence. The consequence of this is that an offender's score for prior convictions could not be simply added as a negative quantity to the other case characteristics to determine culpability.

In determining the effect of prior convictions, it appears that the courts have regard to the number, frequency, seriousness, and recency of the counts, especially those similar in kind to the present offense. Accordingly, in determining a score to represent the extent of an offender's past record, these aspects of past record were represented by separate dimensions for offenses involving dishonesty as well as by dimensions not involving dishonesty. There were categories with associated codes for each dimension, and for each case the appropriate codes (one per dimension) were summed. Convictions for trivial offenses not having an element of dishonesty were ignored, and the set of dimensions covering prior convictions relating to dishonesty was assigned twice the weight of the set covering nondishonest offenses. Again, one cannot look to appellate judgments for precise specification of the elements of this factor (see Chapter 8).

As an offender's past record increases in seriousness, there is a corresponding decrease in the allowance for the effect of mitigating offender characteristics until a point is reached where the mitigating characteristics can have no effect on determining culpability. Actually, it is not clear from the reviews of the authorities by Fox and O'Brien (1975), Fox and Freiberg (1985), and Thomas (1979) whether past record may override the effects of all the mitigating factors or just those bearing on good character. Now, *previous good character* and *remorse* would seem to be the only offender characteristics conceptually linked to good character (see Table 4.1). Moreover, *prior convictions* is used as a measure of an offender's prospects of reform and, in this way, seems to be tied to previous good character and remorse. One can use this view to derive a weight for prior convictions. If prior convictions are conceptually linked to previous good character and remorse, then the highest actual score for the former in a representative sample of cases should be adjusted so that it is equal to the sum of the highest actual scores for the latter two, that is, the weight of prior convictions should be equal to the combined effect of previous good character and remorse. In this way an offender's claim to mitigation arising from a very commendable previous good character together with extreme remorse would be just negatived by an extensive past record.

To give effect to this position, the offenders' scores on previous good character and remorse were totaled, and the distribution of the offenders' scores measuring prior convictions was transformed so that the highest observed score for this dimension was set at the highest (negative) observed combined score for the other two dimensions, the rest of the scores being transformed on the basis of the similarity of their positions within their respective cumulative percentage frequency distributions. (This analysis illustrates how the mathematical model of Wilkins et al., 1978, is incompatible with the structure of the sentencing judgment.)

Two further matters of policy arise from this position. One concerns offenders whose score for the past record is greater than their score for good character. Under such circumstances should the past record merely negative good character or may the remainder continue to exert an effect? It appears that some judges' policy is consistent with an affirmative answer to the latter question. The advantage of this construction is that for offenders with an extensive past record it is possible to differentiate in terms of culpability between those for whom there is evidence of substantial current good character and remorse and those without such mitigating claims. Of course, the one qualification to this position must be that the residual can be effective only to the extent that there are other mitigating factors to be negatived, because past record cannot aggravate culpability beyond the level set by the offense. The second matter of policy concerns an implication of the proposed construction of past record. Consider an offender whose strong claims to mitigation arising from previous good character and remorse are exactly negatived by an extensive prior record but who has additional claims to mitigation (say, a strong reason for the offense). Under the procedure adopted here, the offender would receive credit for these other mitigating factors because the effects of past record would have been exhausted by remorse and previous good character.

It must be stressed that there are other ways to construe past record and its effects and yet not flout current sentencing policy, such is the vagueness of current authority on many points. For example the weight of prior convictions could be equated with the combined weight of all other mitigating factors rather than just previous good character and remorse. More importantly, perhaps an absence of prior convictions should be mitigating even when in the offender's background and present circumstances and conduct there are no features indicative of previous good character and remorse. Certainly, this appears to be Ashworth's (1983a, 1987) position. The advantage of attempting to develop a model of judicial thinking is that these issues are clearly identified and the implications of the various constructions of culpability are clarified. Clearly, these points must be resolved before there can be uniformity of approach. This point, although made in relation to past record, applies to the whole of this analysis.

Combination of Offender Characteristics

To classify the offender factors in a plea in terms of this scheme, it was necessary to identify the categories (on the offender factors) whose defining content most closely matched the facts. Each category has an associated code (score), which marks the importance (weight) of the category in mitigation, and so at this point each plea was represented by a series of scores. (Because the number of potentially material offender factors is much greater than the actual number found in any one plea, not all the mitigating categories are used for each case.) Next, the codes for the dimensions relating to prior convictions were weighted and added together, and the total score for prior convictions was transformed to be appropriately weighted relative to the combined effects of remorse and previous good character. Then, the codes for the offender factors (not including prior convictions) were added together (the codes are negative except for *breach of trust*). (For some of these factors a case may receive a score on none or more than one category.) Finally, the score (zero or positive) for prior convictions was added to the (usually) negative score for the other offender factors, and the final score represented the extent of the mitigation (high negative scores represent substantial mitigation).

Thomas (1979) argued that it is not possible to construct a "negative tariff" for mitigation, because for certain combinations of factors the presence of one factor may enhance the effect of another (i.e., the joint effect of certain combinations of mitigating factors is greater than the sum of their individual effects). This is known technically as interaction. Unfortunately, however, Thomas did not explicate this aspect of mitigation, and indeed, on can find only scant reference to mitigating combinations in his analysis. Moreover, he offered no systemic evidence for interactive effects over and above simple cumulative effects. In the absence of such evidence it seems hazardous to conclude that interaction is a feature of the effects of mitigating factors.

Nevertheless, three types of conditional mitigating effects can be discerned and should be considered here. First, Thomas (1979) identified factors that are likely to have a greater effect if certain conditions prevail; for example, the loss of an offender's employment where the offense was not committed by the offender as an employee. However, this does not involve two independently mitigating factors, and so the condition for the greater effect is properly considered as part of the definition of the one factor. Second, there are some examples of apparent interaction, although they appear to relate to the one class, namely, a person whose offenses can be attributed to an exculpatory factor and who has been otherwise of good character. In this case there are two potentially mitigating factors – good character and reason for the offense. For example, drunkenness is a factor identified in connection with this argument and yet, even here, Thomas merely claimed that alcohol has little or no independent mitigating effect but may add some marginal weight to a more substantial mitigating factor. This is hardly a strong case for interaction. Indeed, there is a hint that Thomas may sometimes have equated a factor's likelihood of being effective with interaction. This would be a mistake because the two concepts are quite different. It may be that a court is more likely to accept a reason as exculpatory if it is combined with good character, but this is different from giving the reason greater mitigating effect because it occurs with good character. Third, one can discern within Thomas's analysis two classes of factor that the court may be tempted to combine interactively, although it is not construed in this way by Thomas. This point requires a detailed examination.

References to the strong mitigating effects of an offender's favorable rehabilitation prospects, especially where the offender has taken steps to improve his chances of reform since the offense, are commonplace in sentencing judgments; the courts always deliberate with an eye to the rehabilitation of offenders. For the purpose of this analysis, an offender's rehabilitation prospects were considered to be favorable if an offender met the following conditions: plea of guilty; no admitted or proven offense committed since the current offense; offender not in possession of any profits from the offense; offender is not now subject to the influence of significant criminogenic factors (see Chapter 10 for a detailed specification of these factors). Moreover, it has been well settled by authority that young offenders, first offenders (in this case in respect of dishonesty), offenders who have a strong exculpatory reason for their behavior, and offenders whose previous offenses of (in this case) dishonesty are in the distant past, have special claims to mitigation. (Precise definitions of these factors are given in Chapter 10.) Although, of course, both classes of factor carry weight in a plea, one feels that the mitigating claims of an offender who fell in one of these special categories of offender and whose rehabilitation prospects were favorable might be enhanced over and above the simple sum of the mitigating effects of category of offender and rehabilitation prospects. If this analysis is a correct interpretation, then it would be an instance of interaction between mitigating factors and it should be represented accordingly. Thomas is incorrect when he says that interactive effects preclude the scaling of mitigation. Such effects can be accommodated simply by defining a category covering this condition and weighting it accordingly. The appropriate cases thereby would be scored for favorable rehabilitation prospects, special category of offender (e.g., youth), *and* a category covering rehabilitation in association with the special offender category. This approach is demonstrated in this study.

Relationship Between Offense and Offender Characteristics

The final step in determining a score representing an offender's culpability involved reducing the offense seriousness score by the score for mitigating offender characteristics. It is quite clear from Thomas's (1979) discussion of the totality principle that the effect of mitigating factors is properly considered in relation to the overall seriousness of the offense including the consideration of multiple counts. For most cases these mitigation scores would be expected to be negative (or zero), however, a small percentage might be positive, due to the effects of prior convictions and breach of trust; because offense seriousness sets a ceiling for culpability and so cannot be aggravated by prior convictions, any positive scores arising from the effects of prior convictions must be reduced to zero. The offender's culpability, then, is defined as the offence seriousness score plus the (usually negative) mitigation score.

Before this step could be taken, it was necessary to weight mitigation in relation to offense seriousness. For the more serious armed robberies, the courts in Victoria, Australia, have clearly stated that mitigating offender characteristics normally carry less weight than offense characteristics (see Fox & Freiberg, 1985). Although imprecise, it is some guidance. Unfortunately, neither the Full Court in Victoria nor the Court of Appeal (Criminal Division) in England appear to have spoken to this matter for the offense of burglary, although it is clear that greater allowance may be generally made for mitigating factors in cases of burglary than in cases of armed robbery (Thomas, 1979). Accordingly, offense and offender characteristics were weighted equally. To give effect to this position, the distribution of the offenders' scores measuring offense seriousness was transformed so that the highest observed score for seriousness was set at the highest (negative) observed score for mitigation, the rest of the scores being transformed on the basis of the similarity of their positions within their respective cumulative percentage frequency distributions (for this transformation, the offenders' mitigation scores did not include interaction effects).

Credit for mitigation is not an entitlement of the offender because the sentencer is permitted to refrain from allowing for mitigating factors to achieve a recognized penal objective such as deterrence or incapacitation (Fox & Freiberg, 1985). In these instances the punishment is matched to the seriousness of the offense rather than to the culpability of the offender (Thomas, 1979). (Although, it would appear to be unreasonable to disallow credit for any mitigation that might arise from the factor *role in the offense*.) Such a course appears to be reserved for grave cases. The judgment delivered in the English Court of Appeal (Criminal Division) in *Brewster* (1980) appears to illustrate this course. Lawton, L.J. referred to " . . . professional criminals, who have long records, great skill as criminals and who from time to time make very valuable hauls . . . " and concluded that "(a)ll that the courts can do with . . . his like is to ensure that they do not carry out raids on other people's houses for very substantial periods" (pp. 191–192). This approach was operationally defined in terms of this study's classificatory scheme as an offender whose appropriate placement is in the highest category on total value of the theft and in the highest category of either or both organization and appearances involving dishonesty (see Chapter 10). Clearly, the Court's concept of professionalism could have been operationalized differently, but this demonstrates how indicators of the various decisions in sentencing can be included in this system of detailed statistics. (One should note here Ashworth's, 1983b, warning about the difficulties of defining "professional criminal.")

Primary and Secondary Decisions in the Sentencing Judgment

The primary decision (Thomas, 1979) concerns whether it is more appropriate to impose a tariff sentence (emphasizing the culpability of the offender or emphasizing, if mitigation is withheld, the seriousness of the offense) or an individualized measure (meeting the rehabilitative needs of the offender).

According to Thomas, a tariff sentence should be imposed (1) if the offense is serious or (2) if the history and attitude of the offender suggest that the response to an appropriate individualized measure would not be positive, whereas an appropriate individualized measure should be preferred (1) for cases in which the offense is not serious and there is no reason to believe that the offender would not respond favorably to an individualized measure or (2) for offenders who are young, or who are first offenders (in this case a first offense of dishonesty), or who have a strong exculpatory reason for their behavior, or whose previous offenses of dishonesty are in the distant past, and whose rehabilitation prospects appear to be favorable, except cases in which the offense is extremely serious. The sentencer, having resolved this matter, then turns to the secondary decision. If a tariff measure is to be imposed, then the level of sentence must be made proportional to the culpability of the offender (or to the seriousness of the offense). In cases in which an individualized measure is to be imposed, the judge's task is to select the measure that would be most likely to facilitate reform in the light of the offender's needs. This latter aspect of the secondary decision is not considered in this present analysis.

It was argued that not infrequently a court's regard to an offender's rehabilitation may significantly moderate the quantum of sentence that would otherwise have been deemed appropriate on the grounds of culpability. In such instances weight is given to the goal of rehabilitation as well as to the aims of sentence normally associated with tariff sentencing (retribution, deterrence and denunciation; see Chapter 1). The construction of culpability in the present study, incorporating as it does the factor of remorse, ensures that weight is given to the goal of rehabilitation for cases in which the offender can demonstrate evidence of reform.

The Construction of the Sentencing Statistics

The primary and secondary decisions are represented by using both scales and indicators in the detailed sentencing statistics developed in this study. Because the seriousness of the offense appeared to be central to the primary decision, the sentencing statistics were developed around a scale measuring the culpability of the offender. The actual sentences imposed for the sample of cases were placed on the scale according to the calculated scores for the offenders' culpability (or gravity of the offense where credit for mitigation was withdrawn). (Actually, Thomas, 1979, referred to the seriousness of the legal category of offense as the critical determinant, rather than the culpability of the offender. As it was discussed in Chapter 1, this is not appropriate for those many legal offense categories, like burglary, for which both tariff and individualized measures are not infrequently imposed. In such cases offender culpability, determined by the circumstances of the offense and the offender's claim to mitigation, would appear to be the appropriate critical determinant of the primary decision. This approach was followed here.) After the cases had been scaled according to culpability, those cases having the previously mentioned features defining a preference for an individualized measure were noted by the use of indicators against the entry.

With the sentencing statistics so constructed, it is possible to show the type (custodial/noncustodial) and level (length of custody) of sentence considered appropriate for any combination of the offense and offender characteristics of burglary incorporated in the classificatory scheme. If a close relationship is found between the type and level of sentence and the characteristics of the case, then the data could be regarded as supporting the validity of the model of judicial decision making developed in this analysis. It may be regarded as self-evident that imprisonment is purely a tariff sentence and that the length of imprisonment should be proportional to severity. Of the available alternatives to imprisonment in Victoria (Fox, 1983), the fine is clearly a tariff measure only, although sentences of youth training, and attendance center, community service, and probation orders, and bonds may be imposed as a punishment (tariff sentence) in some instances and yet used as a means of facilitating rehabilitation in other cases (individualized measure). This view is more in sympathy with Ashworth's (1983b) interpretation. Ashworth rejected Thomas's (1979) equating of individualized measures with noncustodial sentences. However, the number of judges who would accept that there is a tariff element in noncustodial measures other than the fine and the rankings in terms of severity that they would assign to these measures is not known. Indeed, the law on this matter is not clear in Victoria (Freiberg & Fox, 1986), although my view from personal experience is that Victorian judges differ on this issue. The position among English judges would appear to require clarification also (see Ashworth et al., 1984). The consequence of this is that some judges may impose some of the so-called individualized measures as a tariff sentence and without regarding the offenders' rehabilitation prospects. Finally, in Victoria, there are statutory provisions that ought to be mentioned here. For instance a person sentenced to a term of imprisonment for more than 1 month and less than 12 months may be permitted to attend an attendance center as an alternative. Another legislative provision worthy of particular mention concerns cases of drunkenness or drug addiction contributing to an offense for which the offender is sentenced to prison and the offender is an alcoholic or drug-dependent person; such offenders may be released on a bond conditional on their seeking treatment (Fox, 1983). These, then, are qualifications to Thomas's analysis, although they have not been incorporated in the empirical analysis. (Since the completion of this study there have been changes in the sentencing options available to the courts. On June 1, 1986, the courts were given the power, under certain conditions, to suspend or partly suspend a sentence of imprisonment and a power to make a community-based order. The community-based order replaces attendance center, community service, and probation orders. See the Supplement to Fox & Freiberg, 1985.)

The remaining chapters in Part Two report an empirical, archival study in which the validity of this model is tested for cases of burglary determined in the higher courts. Burglary was chosen because it is an offense for which both offense and offender characteristics are ordinarily given substantial weight (Thomas, 1979); moreover, higher courts are provided with more information and would be expected to give greater consideration to the principles of sentencing.

Before turning to the account of this study, may I be permitted the personal indulgence of paying a brief tribute to the man whose ideas underlie the model adopted for this project. I do this because I believe that his academic contribution to the understanding of common law sentencing is unparalleled and yet not properly recognized.

David Thomas: An Overdue Tribute

In the review by Blumstein et al. (1983a) of the state of the art of research in sentencing there is, as it were, a clarion call for a model of the sentencing decision incorporating the logic of the decision maker, the judge; it should be a model relating penal policy to sentence (Sparks, 1983). In making this call it was assumed that there is no theory about how judges decide cases.

It would appear that these reviewers in the United States may (understandably) have overlooked the substantive and heuristic value of Thomas's (1979) model for researchers, at least for students of the English and similarly based sentencing systems. My hope is that the present chapter has realized the potential of this aspect of Thomas's contribution to the sentencing literature. For years Thomas's *Principles of Sentencing* has provided a guiding light to judges sentencing in the first instance and to judges determining appeals against sentence (see, e.g., the judgment of the Victorian Court of Criminal Appeal in *McCormack and others*, 1981). This practical role of Thomas's analysis is most valuable in the fight against arbitrariness in sentencing, but it is not one that I intend to elaborate on here. Rather, I should like stress its value as a conceptual analysis in the move toward uniformity of approach in sentencing. The model developed in this study is clearly founded on Thomas's conception of the structure of the sentencing judgment. I should also venture to suggest that the source of the idea for what I believe will prove to be one of the most significant curial developments in the move toward uniformity of approach in sentencing, the guideline judgment, pioneered in the 1970s by Lawton, L.J. (see Ashworth, 1984), is at least in part a product of Thomas's search for uniformity in judicial sentencing—a search that began in 1962 (Thomas, 1983), became a matter of public record in Thomas's truly seminal article, "Sentencing—The case for reasoned decisions," published in 1963 and brought to fruition in 1970 with the publication of the first edition of *Principles of Sentencing*. The similarities between the goals and formats of the guideline judgments and Thomas's analysis of the substance of the tariff and other sentencing principles, together with the acceptance, indeed the high professional profile of Thomas's work, would appear to make this conclusion inescapable.

Perhaps the most enduring and unfailing test of intellectual achievement in the field of academic endeavor is whether a researcher can be said to have identified and described uniformity in phenomena or events hitherto without apparent system even to the professional observer. It is a rare attainment, and much more productive and attractive than the more common higher scholarly criticism. In view of Thomas's attainment in distilling and cataloging the principles of sentencing from the apparent diversity in the daily decisions of the Court of Appeal (Criminal Division) in England, the epithet "intellectual achievement" is properly stamped across the works of David Thomas. Clues to the daunting task that faced him are found in many places in his discussion of the principles of sentencing; for example, "A tariff sentence will normally be upheld . . . in some cases with a degree of consistency which suggests the existence of a firm policy" (Thomas, 1979, p. 15). This is illustrated more clearly in Thomas's own account of his early progress.

> Few principles were articulated in general terms, but like cases were dealt with alike, and as the cards went into the index a pattern of decisions began to become apparent. It became clear that the court was acting on principle, even though those principles were not necessarily stated. (1983, p. 61)

Walker (1985), in reflecting on a passage from *Principles of Sentencing* on the structure of the sentencing judgment, aptly points to Thomas's contribution:

> The 'primary decision' is between 'individualised' and 'tariff' sentencing. When this passage was first published, in 1970, it was not so much a description as a rationalisation: few sentencers thought so clearly. Read as a description, however, it was very persuasive, and within a few years had become a fair account of the way in which many—even most—judges reasoned. (p. 118)

To my mind Thomas is an unsung hero of common law sentencing. Why then is there this apparent lack of recognition of the real significance of his work?

Perhaps the clue is in Walker's analysis: Thomas's theory became orthodoxy in a few short years and without much fuss. Under such circumstances it is probably all too easy for academics to see Thomas's analysis of the sentencing judgment as descriptive rather than theoretical, as a statement of the obvious rather than as insightful and, for the academic socialist revolutionaries (some of whom appear to believe only they carry a torch) as conservative not radical.

The point of this tribute to David Thomas is to say "1963 is a year to remember in sentencing."

5
The Data Base and Data Collection

The Principal Offense

This analysis comprised 100 persons who were sentenced in the County Court, Victoria, Australia, and who were the principal offenders in a sample of 100 cases in which the principal offense was burglary. This definition of principal offense did not include the common law offense of attempted burglary or the statutory offense of aggravated burglary.

The offense of burglary is created by s.76 of the *Crimes Act* 1958 (as amended). For this offense the maximum term of imprisonment, fixed by statute, is 14 years; there is no prescribed minimum period. As a principal offense, burglary is one of the most common offenses for which persons are sentenced in the higher (Supreme and County) courts. In 1981 burglary was the principal offense of 9.4% of persons sentenced in these courts (Law Department–Victoria, Research Section, 1982); the corresponding figure for 1982 and 1983 was 10.0% (Law Department–Victoria, Management Information Section, 1983, 1984). The vast majority of cases of burglary are determined in the Magistrates' Courts, and normally the Supreme Court (the superior court of record in the State) does not determine cases of burglary.

The Sample of Cases

Burglary was considered to be the principal offense of an offender with multiple offenses if the count for which the most severe penalty was fixed was a burglary. For this purpose penalties were ranked, from the most severe, as follows: imprisonment (including youth training center), attendance center, community service, probation, bond (including alcoholic and drug-dependent person bond), and fine. Where the same type of sentence or order was imposed, the principal offense was determined by introducing, in order, the following criteria: length of sentence or order or bond, amount of fine, maximum prescribed penalty under the Act, and number of counts. (These rules are similar although not identical to those adopted by the Law Department–Victoria for its statistics on sentencing.)

In those cases in which there were multiple offenders and all the offenders participated in all of the counts, burglary was considered to be the principal offense of the case if an offense of burglary attracted the severest penalty when the counts of all the offenders were considered together. In those cases in which not all the offenders participated in all of the counts, there was considered to be a principal offense of burglary if for at least one of the offenders a count of burglary attracted the severest penalty when those counts in which that offender participated singly and jointly were considered together.

Cases were defined by presentment number. Separately numbered presentments were treated as separate cases, and similarly numbered and joint presentments were considered as single cases. An exception to the former part of the rule was made for co-offenders who were tried separately for offenses relating to the same incident(s). They were included with the other offenders as a single case. A joint presentment was defined as the joining of two or more separately numbered presentments for hearing and determination at a single trial and could relate to one or more accused persons.

Cases comprising joint presentments for single individuals were included in the sample only if a burglary was the principal count when the individual presentments were considered together.

Where there were multiple offenders in a case, only those offenders who had been already sentenced in the County Court were included in the sample (although the other offenders were considered for the purposes of describing the characteristics of an offense, for example, the number of offenders).

On May 20, 1980, certain amendments to the jurisdiction of the Magistrates' Courts were proclaimed, and from this date offenses of burglary involving amounts up to $10,000 could then be dealt with summarily (see s.69 of the *Magistrates' Courts Act* 1971, as amended). Since it was desirable that the jurisdiction of the Magistrates' Courts should remain constant over the period of the study, only cases committed for trial on or after this date were included in the sample.

To select cases for the sample, reference was made to cards held in the Office of the Director of Public Prosecutions. There is a card for every offender, and each case is assigned a presentment number and filed sequentially according to the date of the preliminary hearing. Of those cases heard and sentenced in the 1st year following the date of the change in the jurisdiction, there was a gradual increase over time in the number that were committed on or after May 20, 1980; it was not until May 1981 that almost all of the cases determined and sentenced after that date were also committed on or after May 20, 1980. To avoid biasing the sample in favor of those offense and offender characteristics associated with an early hearing, cases were not included in the sample if they had been determined and sentenced before June 1981. Consequently, the initial sample comprised cases meeting these two criteria.

Practical considerations forced additional restrictions on the selection of cases for the sample. Verbatim records of pleas in mitigation and sentencing judgments are made for all the cases. For some cases the record is taken in shorthand whereas others are tape-recorded (of the cases satisfying the criteria for inclusion in the present sample, approximately one third of those heard in Melbourne were tape-recorded, and all the cases determined in rural areas were on tape). These records are transcribed, however, only when the court requires a written record, for example, for a presentence report, breach of probation, or for an appeal; these constitute only a minority of cases. Because it was not practicable to have the shorthand records transcribed, the sample was restricted to cases for which there was a record on tape (n = 71) or cases for which the shorthand record had been transcribed (n = 29).

The sample comprised the first 100 cases, according to presentment number, satisfying all the preceding criteria. These cases were determined and sentenced between June 1981 and November 1983. In this sample there were 131 offenders who participated in a principal offense of burglary, and these offenders were presented on 381 counts of burglary. (There were, of course, other offenders involved in these counts, but they were not presented for trial during the period of the study.) The 100 principal offenders were a subgroup of these 131 offenders.

There are several potential sources of bias in this sample. First, cases for which there was an existing transcript might have covered a disproportionate number of offenders for whom an individualized measure was considered more appropriate. Second, because all of the trials in rural areas are tape-recorded, these were overrepresented in the sample (approximately 15% of the sample). Such cases may differ from those heard in the city in terms of the type of offender and the availability of appropriate correctional facilities. The biases were not expected to be significant, however, because these types of cases constituted a comparatively small percentage of the initial sample. Finally, it seemed unlikely that use or not of a tape recorder would be related to case characteristics.

To check whether there was any evidence of significant biases in the type and length of the sentences, Table 5.1 was constructed. It compares the total effective sentences fixed for offenders in the present sample with those imposed on all burglary offenders (principal offense) sentenced in the higher courts in 1981. This latter set of figures is taken from the sentencing statistics published by the Victoria Law Department. Clearly, the two distributions are almost congruous, and consequently, this justifies the conclusion that the analysis was based on a representative set of sentences. Unfortunately, the Victoria Law Department's sentencing statistics for 1982 and 1983 do not include total effective sentences (Law Department–Victoria, Management Information Section, 1983, 1984). Nevertheless, it was possible to determine that in 1982 and 1983 the percentage of burglary offenders (principal offense) imprisoned was approximately 51% and 55%, respectively, and that compared with 1981 there was similar use of the various noncustodial measures and terms of imprisonment for the offenders' principal count of burglary. Consequently, these data do not cast doubts on the representativeness of the sentences in the present study.

TABLE 5.1. Comparison of percentages for total effective sentences for burglary offenders in the current study (n = 131) with burglary offenders before the higher courts in Victoria in 1981 (n = 108)

	Penalty													
	Noncustodial						Imprisonment (years)							
Sample	Fine	Bond[a]	ADDP Bond	Probation	Attendance Center	Total	<1	1–<2	2–<3	3–<4	4–<5	5–<10	Total	Total
Current sample	3.8	22.9	3.1	19.1	3.8	52.7	10.7	12.2	7.6	7.6	4.6	4.6	47.3	100.0
Higher courts, 1981	4.6	20.3	2.8	19.4	7.4	54.5	10.2	10.2	10.2	7.4	3.7	3.7	45.4	99.9

Note. The source of the figures for the higher courts, 1981, was Law Department–Victoria, Research Section (1982).
[a] This category includes a bond and fine.

Sentences and Orders of the Court

For this analysis of sentences and orders of the court, penalties were classified according to whether they were custodial or noncustodial. (See Fox, 1983, for an overview of sentencing law in Victoria at the time of this archival study.) Of the 100 principal offenders, 49 received noncustodial effective sentences.

Custodial Sentences

The custodial sentences category includes imprisonment and detention in a youth training center. Where an accused person is convicted on a number of counts and more than one sentence of imprisonment is imposed, the sentences are usually served concurrently or partially concurrently but may be fixed cumulatively. In any case the resultant sentence is referred to as the total effective sentence. Where a court imposes an effective sentence of more than 12 months' imprisonment, it almost invariably sets a minimum term. The minimum term must be at least 6 months less than the maximum term. The minimum term is fixed in relation to the maximum term, and normally the (proportional) gap between the two should not be substantial. Minimum terms cannot be set for prison sentences of less than 12 months' duration or for persons detained in youth training centers. The minimum term is the period, minus one-third remissions, that prisoners must serve before they are eligible for release on parole. Concurrency orders made in relation to a sentence of imprisonment that an offender might have been currently serving were not taken account of in this analysis. One final point, time spent in custody awaiting trial is deducted from the term of imprisonment. In all cases in this sample, this was left to the prison authorities rather than taken account of by the judge.

Noncustodial Sentences

The noncustodial sentences category includes attendance center, community service and probation orders, fines, good behavior, and alcoholic and drug-dependent person bonds.

Appeals

The sentences for the cases in the data base comprised the sentences imposed by the judges sentencing in the first instance. No account was taken of the results of appeals.

Data Sources

Information relating to the facts of the offenses, the characteristics of the offenders, and the sentencing judgments was taken from the files held in the Office of the Director of Public Prosecutions and the tape recordings and transcripts held by the Victorian Government Reporting Service (known at the time of the study as the Court Reporting Branch). (Klarion Enterprises Pty. Ltd. was paid to transcribe the tape recordings for the rural cases in the sample.) In 32 of the cases presentence reports were put before the court. Permission was sought from the trial judges for access to these reports, and the requests were granted for 12 of the cases. The principal sources of information were as follows:

1. The sentencing judgment delivered by the Full Court (if an appeal had been heard)
2. The sentencing judgment delivered in the court of first instance
3. Comments by the judge during the plea (comments appearing to convey conclusions)
4. Determinations of guilt by the court in relation to the charges on the presentment for connected and unconnected offenses and for prior convictions
5. Evidence given under oath at the plea in support of the defense
6. Evidence given under oath at the plea in support of the prosecution
7. Evidence given under oath by the accused and defense witnesses at the preliminary hearing
8. Evidence given under oath by the witnesses for the prosecution at the preliminary hearing
9. Information and presentment
10. Unsworn evidence put before the court at the plea, including statements made by the defense counsel, accused, and prosecution; presentence reports, covering social, medical, psychological, and character reports; assessment of damage and loss and medical reports on injuries to victims
11. Evidence presented at the preliminary hearing, including statements and records of interview of the accused (excluding allegations made by the police during questioning) and depositions of the witnesses.

Where there was inconsistency over alleged facts about the offense or the offender between two of the sources of information, precedence was given to the information in the more highly ranked source. Moreover, if there was inconsistency or uncertainty within one of the sources of information and this was not resolved or clarified by one of the higher sources, then the offender was given the benefit of the doubt. Account was taken of offense factors implied in "guilty" verdicts; also noted were alleged facts negatived by "not guilty" verdicts, by the failure of the prosecution to lead evidence, or by the withdrawal of charges in relation to the connected or more serious offenses covering the same incident.

The presentence reports that were examined did not contain any salient information not available from the other sources. It is possible, of course, that the withheld reports did contain sensitive and material information that would have influenced how those cases were classified.

Procedure

Initially, information was extracted from the files, transcripts, and tapes, and these data, together with their sources, were recorded in detail. At this point all information about a case (covering the offense, offender, and other case characteristics put before the court—and only information put before the court—together with the judge's comments and judgment) was noted. The point of this step was to compile complete, written records of all the cases so that the information was compact and concise and yet minimally distorted by this reduction. During this process no regard was paid to the dimensions and categories that were used to code these data because one of the determinants of these descriptors was the material in this data base.

I then read the records for 20 cases and, together with the research assistant, formulated a set of dimensions and associated categories that appeared to describe comprehensively the material case factors. In determining which case factors were to be regarded as material, legal analyses of appellate court judgments (Daunton-Fear, 1977, 1980; Newton, 1979; Ruby, 1980; Thomas, 1979, 1982) were considered, and the case factors that appeared to exercise the minds of the judges in determining sentences for the cases in the present sample were also considered. Of course, in identifying and defining the material case factors, one was searching for apparent trends in the data. This process of identifying and defining material case factors was aided by my referring to other analyses of case factors thought material to the determination of culpability; they included the American Law Institute's *Model Penal Code* (1962) and the works of Hampel (1978), Shapland (1981), Twentieth Century Fund Task Force on Criminal Sentencing (1976), and Vining and Dean (1980).

To increase the precision of the coding system, the categories were defined in terms of concrete and specific case factors. All the cases were then coded in relation to these dimensions. During the coding of the remaining 80 cases, other apparently material case factors were identified. In addition, different manifestations of some of the initial case factors were observed. As a result of this experience, some of the dimensions were redefined to incorporate the additional factors and to accommodate other variations in the patterns of offending and the characteristics of the offenders. After this process was complete, it was necessary to recode all the cases in terms of this final set of dimensions and categories. The coding was done by the research assistant in consultation with the author.

The Cross-Validation Study

The cross-validation sample of cases was selected according to the previously mentioned definitions of principal offense of burglary and principal offender, together with the other practical considerations that governed the selection of cases in the original study. It comprised the next 100 cases, according to presentment number, satisfying all these criteria; these cases were determined and sentenced between March 1983 and August 1986. In this sample there were 132 offenders, all of whom participated in a principal offense of burglary, and these offenders were presented on 436 counts of burglary. The 100 principal offenders were a subgroup of these 132 offenders.

For 53% of these cases the record of the plea in mitigation was on tape; 11% of the cases were tried in rural areas. (Approximately one quarter of the burglary cases heard in Melbourne over this period were tape-recorded and all the cases from rural areas were on tape.)

The same sources of information provided the data base for this supplementary analysis. Presentence reports, however, were not examined, because in the original study the reports that were examined did not contain any significant information not available from the other sources.

In this analysis the definitions of the case factors and their categories; the rules governing the coding, classification, and combination of this information; and the definitions of principal count and offender were unchanged from the original study. Moreover, the scores for offense seriousness and criminal history were transformed according to the distributions established for this purpose in the original study. Finally, the definitions of the categories on the dimensions representing offense seriousness, mitigation and case seriousness, in the tables showing the relationship between these dimensions and sentence (see Chapters 7, 9, and 10), were taken directly from the analyses of these relationships in the original study. No new case factors (or categories) or rules were introduced in the cross-validation study, and all coding decisions were left to the coder.

The collection and analysis of the data in the cross-validation study did not begin until the data in the original study had been analyzed.

Of the 100 principal offenders, 51 received noncustodial effective sentences.

6
Offense Characteristics of Burglary

In Chapter 4 it was decided that the offense of burglary should be differentiated in terms of three groups describing different types of offending, and particular offenses should be described according to a common set of dimensions and associated categories and in relation to one or other of these groups. The type of premises burgled appeared to offer a means of distinguishing between burglaries in regard to patterns of offending and the nature of the offense. For this purpose three types of premises were identified, namely, dwelling houses, commercial premises, and public buildings. This chapter defines the dimensions and categories describing burglary. The four principal dimensions are amount of violence, degree of organization, value of the theft, and number of counts of burglary; the four supplementary characteristics cover connected offenses, unconnected offenses, attempted burglaries, and charges pending. These descriptors are defined in detail here, together with an account of the rationale of their development. Furthermore, the code (score) quantifying the level of aggravation associated with each category is presented. At this early stage in the development of these dimensions, it is impossible to define the categories comprehensively. One reason for this is that 100 cases is an insufficient number for representing adequately many of the possible variations in the offense. The second reason relates to the quality of the depositions. Not infrequently the witnesses' reports and the offenders' statements were found to be indefinite, imprecise, and incomplete. Consequently, the qualitatively defined categories should be regarded as illustrative rather than definitive, and the quantitative categories considered tentative. In any case it is not necessary at this stage to catalog every nuance in the patterns of offending.

Violence to the Victims (Nonoffenders)

The categories on this dimension are intended to mark qualitatively different levels of violence in relation to seriousness; here, violence covers personal injury and property damage perpetrated deliberately or accidently during the burglary or in association with it (such as during the getaway). The categories on the dimension of violence, together with their codes, are shown in Table 6.1.

TABLE 6.1. Definitions of the categories on violence to the victims for the offense of burglary

Code	Category
4	Assault or attempted assault on the victim (even if victim initiated) Accidental injury to victim Injury to a domestic animal to an extent that specialized treatment was required Wanton damage, not confined to a small section of the building or otherwise substantial; major fire damage
3	Threat to assault victim Wanton damage, confined to a small section of the building or otherwise not very substantial; valuable document or irreplaceable item destroyed Minor fire damage Significant damage to the contents of the building during the search, e.g., safe cut open, valuable document or irreplaceable item destroyed Massive damage to the building associated with the entry or exit
2	Victim in the building during burglary but ignored by offender Wanton damage to a few inexpensive and replaceable items only Property strewn around the search area or damage to property greater than necessary during entry, search, or exit, e.g., door smashed rather than lock forced or hole made through the floor, wall or roof by elaborate means; replaceable items damaged during the search
1	Victim not on the property during the burglary or, if on the property, offender fled or attempted to legitimize his or her presence Minor damage and disturbance associated with entering, searching, or leaving the building, e.g., window broken, locks forced

As a guide to the coding of damage associated with the theft (entry, search, and exit) and wanton damage, the following guidelines were set: entry and exit were coded 1 or 2, but if extraordinary, were coded 3; search was coded 2 or 3, but if minimal, was coded 1; wanton damage was coded as 3 or 4, but if minimal, was coded 2. On applying these rules, it was found empirically that the typical ranges (actual ranges in parentheses) of the value of the damage per count for categories 1 to 4 was under \$50 (\$25 to \$300), \$150 to \$200 (\$80 to \$200), \$200 to \$300 (\$120 to \$300), and \$900 to \$8,000 (\$600 to \$20,000), respectively. It should be stressed, however, that not infrequently the value of the damage was not specified or was of doubtful validity.

Organization

The 12 components used to define this dimension all appear to be indicative generally of preparation, organization, and a sophisticated approach, and it seemed reasonable to assume that normally the number of these criteria characterizing a count of burglary would be related directly to the degree of organization

TABLE 6.2. Components comprising organization

Offender (or at least one offender where there were multiple offenders) found guilty on the current presentment (or joint presentment) of multiple counts of burglary or attempted burglary committed since the date of his or her last conviction
Two offenders involved in the actual commission (cf. planning) of the offense (including those persons acting as drivers, watchmen, etc.)
Three or more offenders involved in the actual commission (cf. planning) of the offense (including those persons acting as drivers, watchmen, etc.)[a]
Use of breaking implements or other mechanical aids (carried by the offender) to effect the burglary
Evidence of elaborate measures in thwarting security–protection, e.g., use of safe-cutting equipment, or use of skeleton keys, or access to the building/safe or storeroom arranged beforehand through an insider (self or others)[a,c]
Observer stationed to keep watch at the scene of the burglary
Evidence of elaborate measures in thwarting security–detection, e.g., one of the offenders actually disconnected (i.e., not merely damaged) the alarm or deliberately avoided activating the alarm, or made deliberate plans to facilitate a speedy escape[a]
Evidence of elaborate measures for removing or disposing of the goods, e.g., offender arranged for a commercial vehicle to remove the goods, or took the goods straight to the fence or final purchaser
Burglary committed at night (i.e., between 8:00 p.m. and 7:00 a.m.)
Another offense was committed to facilitate the burglary, e.g., use of another person's license to hire the vehicle, or theft of a vehicle for use in the burglary[b]
Premises placed under surveillance beforehand, e.g., one of the offenders telephoned or called at the premises, or determined the occupier's movements, or prepared a list of potential properties, or had burgled the same property on more than one occasion
Evidence of elaborate measures in selecting the particular premises, e.g., contact with an insider (self, others, or owner known to offender)[a,c]

[a] This criterion is not an alternative to the preceding item (i.e., an offense may be scored on both); a score on the second item entailed a score for the offender on the preceding item, even if that item did not apply directly.
[b] This criterion was accepted as a characteristic of the burglary if there appeared to be clear evidence for the connected offense, unless the offender was charged but found not guilty of the apparent offense.
[c] These (the 5th and the 12th) criteria were considered mutually exclusive if the element of "insider" was the sole reason for regarding them as relevant.

behind the offense and, consequently, the degree of seriousness. Of course, there are other elements material to the determination of the level of organization, for example, certain aspects of preparation before the burglary. Some of these aspects of organization, however, were not included as criteria, because the relevant information was frequently unavailable or appeared to be unreliable. The 12 components are presented in Table 6.2.

Using these criteria, the score (cumulative) for the degree of organization for a count could range from 0 to 12. Accordingly, it was necessary to determine cut-off points and thereby define categories for this dimension. This was done by

TABLE 6.3. Frequencies for the components of organization: All counts of burglary

Score	0	1	2	3	4	5	6	7	8	9	10	11	12	Total
Frequency	2	99	89	84	50	27	11	9	7	2	1			381
	(2)	(107)	(141)	(85)	(52)	(35)	(8)	(5)	(1)					(436)

Note. The data for the cross-validation study are presented in parentheses.

TABLE 6.4. Definitions of the categories on organization for the offense of burglary

Code	Score on the components of organization
4	7–10
3	5–6
2	3–4
1	0–2

constructing and then inspecting the distribution of these scores for all counts of burglary (see Table 6.3); these distributions were not differentiated in relation to the type of premises, because the significance of a score on organization should not depend on the type of premises.

When inspecting this distribution to set the values defining the categories, account was taken of three factors: (1) natural discontinuities in the distribution; (2) the desirability of the four dimensions each having the same number of categories, so that the use of respective categories on different dimensions could be compared readily; (3) the desirability of having reasonable numbers in each category so that all of the categories would have utility (of course, one would not aim for numerically equal categories within a dimension, because particularly serious behaviors generally would be less frequent). The results of these deliberations are shown in Table 6.4.

The structure of the categories on this scale was designed to reflect the fact that almost all the burglaries were characterized by at least one of the criteria, and a burglary for which there is evidence of 7 of the 12 criteria may be very well planned. A rough-and-ready check on the validity of this scale was made by comparing several apparently well-planned counts with several poorly organized offenses; the scale was found to differentiate these cases. However, there were several burglaries in the sample for which this scale did not appear to capture the element of professionalism.

Total Value of the Theft

The dimension entitled total value of the theft covers the total value of the cash and property taken for all the counts of burglary constituting a case. In this study, assessment of the value of goods did not include motor cars or taxis, unless these

TABLE 6.5. Frequencies for total value of the theft in relation to the type of premises: All cases of burglary (n = 100)

Value ($)	Type of premises: Dwelling houses (n = 46) (53)	Commercial premises (n = 47) (38)	Public buildings (n = 7) (9)
0–99	2 (13)	10 (6)	3 (2)
100–199	3	1 (1)	(1)
200–299	1	(1)	
300–399	1	(2)	
400–499	1	2 (1)	2
500–999	3 (3)	4 (4)	(2)
1,000–1,499	2 (3)	2 (2)	
1,500–1,999	2 (1)		1 (2)
2,000–2,499	2 (1)	(2)	
2,500–2,999	(1)	3 (1)	(1)
3,000–3,499	(2)	2 (2)	
3,500–3,999	1	1	
4,000–4,499	3 (2)	2	
4,500–4,999	2 (1)		
5,000–5,499	(1)	2	
5,500–5,999	1		
6,000–6,499	3	(1)	
6,500–6,999		1	
7,000–7,499	1		
7,500–7,999	1 (1)	1 (1)	
8,000–8,499		1	
8,500–8,999	2	1	
9,000–9,499	1		
9,500–9,999	(1)		
10,000–14,999	(6)	2 (1)	1 (1)
15,000–19,999	3 (2)	2 (6)	
20,000–24,999	(3)	1 (2)	
25,000–29,999	3 (2)	(2)	
30,000–34,999	3 (1)	2	
35,000–39,999	1 (2)	2	
40,000–44,999	(2)	1	
45,000–49,999	2 (2)		
50,000–69,999	1 (1)	(1)	
70,000–89,999	(1)	1 (1)	
90,000–119,999	1 (1)	1	
(120,000)		(1)	
(156,900)		1	
(250,000)		1	

Note. The data for the cross-validation study are presented in parentheses.

items were taken with the intention of permanently depriving the victims of them; nor did it include items of low value (including drugs), because they would not have significantly altered the value of the property stolen and, in any case, the value of such goods rarely was stated; moreover, checks were not included in

TABLE 6.6. Definitions of the categories on total value of the theft for cases of burglary

Code	Value ($)
4	≥40,000
3	15,000–39,999
2	2,000–14,999
1	<2,000

these assessments. In several of the cases with multiple counts, the value of the theft was unavailable for at least one of the counts; in such cases the value of the theft for the count was set at the average of the other counts, unless it appeared that the actual amount would have been substantially different (in such cases a conservative estimate was made).

To define total value of the theft in relation to the type of premises, it was necessary to select a representative count for each of the cases in which there were multiple counts. For this purpose, cases in which there were multiple

TABLE 6.7. Frequencies for counts of burglary in regard to type of premises: All cases of burglary (n = 100)

	Type of premises		
Number of counts	Dwelling houses (n = 46) (53)	Commercial premises (n = 47) (38)	Public buildings (n = 7) (9)
1	17 (17)	27 (24)	3 (3)
2	8 (10)	5 (3)	1 (2)
3	5 (4)	5 (4)	1 (3)
4	7 (3)	3 (3)	
5	(2)	1	(1)
6	1 (3)	1 (1)	
7	(2)		
8		(1)	
9	2 (2)	(1)	1
10	(1)	2	
11	2 (1)	1	
12			
13	(1)	1 (1)	
14	(1)		1
15	1		
16	(2)		
17	1 (1)	1	
(24)	(1)		
(26)	1		
(34)	1		
(39)	(1)		
(44)	(1)		

Note. The data for the cross-validation study are presented in parentheses.

counts were classified according to the principal count of burglary. This was defined as the count for which the most severe sentence was imposed. Where two or more counts within a case were sentenced similarly, the following criteria were introduced, in the order shown here, to determine the principal offense: count for which the sum of the codes on violence to the victims and organization was the highest (i.e., the most serious combination); offense for which the code on violence to the victims was highest (if one of the codes was 4 or 3); offense for which the value of the theft (as defined previously) was highest. Each case then was assigned to one of the three types of premises, according to the type of premises in the principal count. The number of cases assigned to dwelling houses, commercial premises, and public buildings was 46, 47, and 7, respectively.

To determine cut-off points defining the categories on this dimension, distributions for the total value of the theft in relation to the type of premises were constructed for all the cases (see Table 6.5).

The purpose of the categories was to differentiate cases to mark different degrees of seriousness associated with the total value of the theft. When inspecting these distributions to set the values defining the categories, account was taken of the three criteria adopted to interpret Table 6.3. The results of these deliberations are shown in Table 6.6.

It did not seem necessary to differentiate the type of premises in the coding scheme for the total value of the theft, because the distributions for both dwelling houses and commercial premises, which together covered almost all of the cases, were similar regarding the range and the position of the discontinuities.

Counts of Burglary

A similar process of decision making was followed to develop the coding scheme for the dimension scaling seriousness for the number of counts of burglary associated with a case. The distributions for counts of burglary in regard to the type of premises are shown in Table 6.7.

The definitions of the categories on counts of burglary are presented in Table 6.8. Again, it did not seem necessary to differentiate the type of premises in the coding scheme for counts of burglary.

TABLE 6.8. Definitions of the categories on counts of burglary for cases of burglary

Code	Number of counts
4	>14
3	5–14
2	2–4
1	1

TABLE 6.9. Frequencies for use of the codes on the dimensions describing cases of burglary: All cases ($n = 100$)

Code	Dimension			
	Violence to the victims	Organization	Total value of the theft	Counts of burglary
4	13 (14)	7 (5)	9 (10)	5 (6)
3	8 (8)	16 (16)	17 (20)	13 (18)
2	30 (30)	44 (33)	34 (26)	35 (32)
1	49 (48)	33 (46)	40 (44)	47 (44)

Note. The data for the cross-validation study are presented in parentheses.

Comparison of the Frequency of the Use of the Categories Across Dimensions

The frequency with which cases fell within each of the categories (codes) on each of the dimensions used to describe cases of burglary was examined. The results are shown in Table 6.9. (For a case with multiple counts of burglary, the code for violence to the victims was taken as the highest code on this dimension among the counts of burglary, and the code for organization was the code for the principal count; see Chapter 7.)

The data in Table 6.9 demonstrate that all of the categories were well used. This result is, of course, a consequence of the method of constructing the dimensions of total value of the theft and counts of burglary and, to some extent, organization. It was important, however, to check whether the categories on violence to the victims appropriately captured the variation in offending in relation to this characteristic of cases of burglary.

It is also worth noting that in general across the four dimensions the higher codes (marking the more serious aspects of the dimensions) apply less frequently to cases of burglary. One would expect that the more serious aspects of burglaries would be less common.

Supplementary Categories

In addition to the burglaries associated with a case, account was also taken of the number of counts of attempted burglary and the number of connected and unconnected offenses for which the principal offender was sentenced on the presentment (or joint presentment) with the count(s) of burglary. Here, attempted burglary was defined as on the presentment, whereas a connected offense was defined either as an offense committed at the time of the burglary and as part of the same incident (e.g., criminal damage in the building or a theft outside the building) or as an offense committed to execute the burglary (e.g., theft of a vehicle to carry the stolen property) but excluding separate counts of burglary. An unconnected offense was defined as an offense that was not connected with the burglary. Occasionally, it was unclear whether a count was connected with a burglary. Note also was taken of any pending charges that were taken account of when the sentence was determined by the court.

Cross-Validation Study

Clearly, there is a high degree of similarity in the way in which the cases in the original and cross-validation samples are distributed in relation to the offense factors and their categories. This indicates that the definitions of the categories on the offense factors are based on a reliable data base.

7
The Relationship Between Offense Characteristics of Burglary and Sentence

The previous chapter was concerned with the development and description of the four dimensions (and their associated categories) used to describe burglary; namely, amount of violence, degree of organization, value of the theft, and number of counts of burglary. To classify a particular burglary in terms of this scheme, it was necessary to identify one category—the category whose defining content most closely matched the facts of the offense—for each of the four dimensions. At this point the case was described in terms of four codes, one for each of the dimensions, and each code being a score quantifying seriousness according to the degree of aggravation of the associated behavior. These descriptions of burglary were differentiated in terms of the type of premises: dwelling houses, commercial premises, and public buildings. Cases for which there were multiple counts were classified under the type of premises for the principal count.

This method of describing a case raised potential problems for those cases with multiple counts. The first problem arose because the code assigned to violence to the victims or organization for the principal count may be lower than for the other counts of burglary in the case. (Such instances were not common; $n = 7$ for violence to the victims and $n = 2$ for organization, and the difference between the codes was never greater than one. The corresponding figures for the cross-validation study were 6 and 4, respectively.) This was seen as a problem, particularly concerning violence to the victims, rather than organization, because a case would seem better represented by the most serious violence inflicted on the victims but would seem adequately characterized by the level of organization for the principal count. A case with multiple counts therefore was coded on violence to the victims according to the code for the count with the most serious violence.

A second potential problem concerns lack of uniformity among the premises in cases with multiple counts. This was found not to be a problem, however. The codes for the type of premises were uniform for 44 (50) of the 53 (56) cases with multiple counts, and for 5 (1) of the remaining 9 (6) such cases, the premises in the principal count were the same in a majority of the constituent counts. (The figures in parentheses are from the cross-validation study.)

After the means of describing the cases of burglary in terms of the four codes had been developed, it was then necessary to combine this information for each case to represent the degree of seriousness of each of the cases with a single score. In Chapter 4 it was concluded that, when determining the seriousness of a crime, judges appear to add (or subtract) time for aggravating (or extenuating) factors and, in combining the various case factors in this way, appear to treat each dimension as equally important. The point also was made that this process could be represented numerically by the simple addition of the four codes describing the case in terms of the four dimensions (violence, organization, value of the theft, counts of burglary).

At this stage in the commentary, it is necessary to digress to make two points regarding the weighting of the dimensions. First, the simple addition of the codes across the dimensions is a means of unit weighting that treats the dimensions as equally important and yet does not guarantee equal weighting, because it permits one dimension to be weighted more heavily in the combined score where the standard deviations are unequal. (Actually, the data in Table 6.9 suggest numerically similar standard deviations across the four dimensions.) The validity of this procedure rests on the assumption that the behavioral differences between pairs of adjacent categories (on a particular dimension) represent equal degrees of aggravation (or extenuation) on an interval scale and requires that the categories on the four dimensions cover the same range of scores and the same range of gravity. Second, it has been argued that scores on correlated dimensions should not be combined by simple addition, because these dimensions would represent the same construct and, consequently, simple addition would result in the double weighting of that construct compared with the uncorrelated dimensions (Hogarth, 1980). This argument is acceptable if there are no grounds for treating the empirically correlated factors as independent. In this study, however, although correlations between the dimensions would be expected to arise from patterns of offending, this should have no bearing on whether these case factors are considered to be independently material to the determination of culpability. The reason for this is that in this study the aggregation rule could be based on a model describing judicial decision making, and it appears that judges regard these four dimensions as independent matters in determining the seriousness of a case. Nevertheless, Hogarth's argument would have substance in a predictive analysis where there was a necessary relationship between case factors, for example, total value of the theft and the number of counts of burglary.

The relationship between the offense characteristics of cases of burglary and sentence was determined for the 100 principal offenders in the sample. Where there were multiple offenders in a case, the principal offender was selected by introducing the following criteria in the order shown here: the offender participating in the principal count; the person on whom the most severe effective sentence was imposed; the offender participating in the most counts; the offender with the most connected offenses; the offender with the most attempted burglaries; the offender first mentioned. As explained previously, not all the persons participating in the burglaries on which this study is based are in the sample and some of these other persons may have been regarded as principal offenders.

TABLE 7.1. Relationship between offense seriousness scores and length of effective sentence (years) for principal offenders in burglary cases: Dwelling houses

Offense seriousness score	Original study (n = 46)				Cross-validation study (n = 53)			
	n	Mean	SD	Custody (%)	n	Mean	SD	Custody (%)
12–13	3	2.0	2.8	33	3	3.0	0	100
10–11	4	1.3	1.5	50	7	2.8	2.9	57
8–9	15	2.4	2.1	73	19	1.7	2.3	53
6–7	19	0.7	0.8	47	16	1.5	1.8	63
4–5	5	0.7	0.9	60	8	0.3	0.5	25

A problem arises for cases in which the principal offender did not participate in all the counts ($n = 2$). (This figure for the cross-validation sample was 9.) This was solved by adjusting the codes for these offenders on the dimensions covering the total value of the theft, violence, and the number of counts of burglary; organization for the principal count was again treated as characteristic for the case and so was not adjusted.

An offense seriousness score was calculated for each principal offender by summing the codes for total value of the theft, violence to the victims, organization, and counts of burglary; these scores (adjusted where necessary according to the preceding rules) then were related to the lengths of the custodial sentences imposed on these offenders (a noncustodial sentence was treated as 0 length). The results of these analyses are shown in Tables 7.1 to 7.5. There is a clear, direct relationship between offense seriousness score and length of effective sentence as well as percentage of custodial sentences for the principal offenders in burglaries of commercial premises (Table 7.2). The representation of the same data, however, in Table 7.5 reveals a considerable degree of overlap in the ranges of the sentences for all except the highest level of offense seriousness scores. By way of contrast, no clear relationship exists between offense seriousness score and length of effective sentence for principal offenders in burglaries of dwelling houses; this is apparent in Table 7.1 but is demonstrated

TABLE 7.2. Relationship between offense seriousness scores and length of effective sentence (years) for principal offenders in burglary cases: Commercial premises

Offense seriousness score	Original study (n = 47)				Cross-validation study (n = 38)			
	n	Mean	SD	Custody (%)	n	Mean	SD	Custody (%)
12–13	4	4.3	1.3	100	3	1.5	1.8	67
10–11	5	1.7	1.4	60	2	1.5	1.5	50
8–9	13	0.9	1.0	54	9	0.5	1.0	22
6–7	13	0.4	0.6	46	12	1.3	1.5	58
4–5	12	0.2	0.4	25	12	1.0	1.4	42

TABLE 7.3. Relationship between offense seriousness scores and length of effective sentence (years) for principal offenders in burglary cases: Public buildings

Offense seriousness score	Original study (n = 7)				Cross-validation study (n = 9)			
	n	Mean	SD	Custody (%)	n	Mean	SD	Custody (%)
10–11	2	2.6	2.6	50	2	1.9	1.9	50
8–9	3	0.3	0.5	33	2	0.8	0.8	50
6–7	2	0	0	0	4	0.3	0.4	25
4–5	–	–	–	–	1	0	0	0

dramatically in Table 7.4. (Generally there were too few offenders within each of the offense-seriousness-score levels to have much confidence in the reliability of the averages. Consequently, offense-seriousness-score levels were paired to form five subgroups. This had the effect of increasing the numbers of cases in each of the subgroups. Averages, means, then were calculated for the sentences of the principal offenders within each subgroup.)

Validity of the Assumptions Underlying the Use of Groups for Differentiating Offenses Across Premises Types and the Use of Dimensions to Differentiate Offenses Within Premises Types

The value of the strategy of differentiating offenses across premises types and using dimensions to differentiate offenses with premises types was predicated intuitively on three assumptions (see Chapter 4).

1. The dimensions used to describe burglary would be correlated with type of premises (i.e., cases would be differentially distributed in relation to the categories on each dimension across the three types of premises).

2. The correlations between the type of premises and the dimensions used to describe burglary would not be very strong, that is, most of the categories (codes) on each of the dimensions would be required to describe the cases, and this would hold for the three types of premises.

Table 7.6 shows the distribution of cases in relation to the categories (codes) on each dimension within each type of premises for the cases of burglary. (For a case with multiple counts of burglary, the code for violence to the victims was taken as the highest code on this dimension among the counts of burglary, and the code for organization was the code for the principal count.) It is readily apparent that there are no clear and systematic differences within the distributions across type of premises. Possible differences between dwelling houses and commercial premises tend to be limited to adjacent codes within the higher (3 and 4) or lower (1 and 2) pairs of codes. An exception to this conclusion may be public buildings within violence to the victims; however, the frequencies are too low to place

TABLE 7.4. Frequencies of effective sentences in relation to offense seriousness scores for principal offenders in burglary cases: Dwelling houses

Offense seriousness score	Effective sentences (years)								
	0	≤1	≤2	≤3	≤4	≤5	≤6	≤7	≤8
Original study (n = 46)									
12–13	11						1		
10–11	11		1		1				
8–9	1111	11	1	11	111	11	1		
6–7	11111	1111	1111	1					
	11111								
4–5	11	11		1					
Cross-validation study (n = 53)									
12–13				111					
10–11	111			11			1		1
8–9	11111	1	1111	11			11		1
	1111								
6–7	11111	111	1111		1	1	1		
	1								
4–5	11111	1	1						
	1								

TABLE 7.5. Frequencies of effective sentences in relation to offense seriousness scores for principal offenders in burglary cases: Commercial premises

Offense seriousness score	Effective sentences (years)								
	0	≤1	≤2	≤3	≤4	≤5	≤6	≤7	≤8
Original study (n = 47)									
12–13				1	1	1		1	
10–11	11		1	1	1				
8–9	11111	11	1111	1					
	1								
6–7	11111	1111	11						
	11								
4–5	11111	11	1						
	1111								
Cross-validation study (n = 38)									
12–13	1	1			1				
10–11	1			1					
8–9	11111		1	1					
	11								
6–7	11111	1	111	11		1			
4–5	11111	1	1	11	1				
	11								

TABLE 7.6. Frequencies for use of the codes on violence to the victims, organization, total value of the theft, and counts of burglary in relation to type of premises: All cases of burglary (n = 100)

	Violence to the victims			Organization			Total value of the theft			Counts of burglary		
Code	Dwelling houses	Commercial premises	Public buildings	Dwelling houses	Commercial premises	Public buildings	Dwelling houses	Commercial premises	Public buildings	Dwelling houses	Commercial premises	Public buildings
1	19 (23)	29 (22)	1 (3)	25 (27)	8 (17)	0 (2)	15 (20)	19 (17)	6 (7)	17 (17)	27 (24)	3 (3)
2	19 (21)	9 (9)	2 (0)	15 (17)	24 (10)	5 (6)	17 (16)	16 (8)	1 (2)	20 (17)	13 (10)	2 (5)
3	2 (3)	6 (3)	0 (2)	6 (8)	8 (8)	2 (0)	10 (10)	7 (10)	0 (0)	5 (13)	6 (4)	2 (1)
4	6 (6)	3 (4)	4 (4)	0 (1)	7 (3)	0 (1)	4 (7)	5 (3)	0 (0)	4 (6)	1 (0)	0 (0)

Note. In Table 6.9 the distributions for each dimension are the same as the distributions of the row totals for each of the corresponding dimensions in this table. The data for the cross-validation study are presented in parentheses.

TABLE 7.7. Frequencies of the sentences for the principal counts of burglary ($n = 100$) in relation to type of premises

Sentence (months)	Type of premises: Dwelling houses ($n = 46$) (53)	Commercial premises ($n = 47$) (38)	Public buildings ($n = 7$) (9)
0	20 (24)	24 (23)	5 (6)
≤6	6 (2)	3 (3)	
≤12	9 (12)	6 (2)	2 (1)
≤18	5 (6)	5 (2)	(2)
≤24	2 (5)	5 (2)	
≤30	1 (1)		
≤36	2 (3)	2 (4)	
≤42		2	
≤48		(1)	
≤54			
≤60		(1)	
≤66			
≤72	1		

Note. For those cases in which multiple offenders participated in the principal count, the most severe sentence imposed for the count was used in this table.
The data for the cross-validation study are presented in parentheses.

much reliance on their stability. One can conclude that the cases generally are well distributed across the categories on each of the dimensions, although the lower (less serious) codes clearly tend to be used more frequently.

3. The sentence lengths for each type of premises would tend to cluster around different averages. This assumption was tested by examining the relationship between the sentences for the principal count of burglary—most severe sentence for cases with multiple offenders—and the type of premises (Table 7.7). This seemed the most appropriate sentence for testing the assumption that sentences for different types of premises would tend to cluster around different averages, because the sentence for the principal count is least contaminated by the effects on sentence of other counts and offender characteristics. Clearly, the distributions of sentences for dwelling houses and commercial premises are very similar; again the frequencies for public buildings are too low for one to conclude confidently that these sentences were distributed differently.

The following conclusions can be drawn from the preceding analyses. First, there was no evidence indicating that patterns of offending and the distributions of sentences were related differentially to dwelling houses and commercial premises and, consequently, it is unnecessary to distinguish between these two groups on these grounds to increase the precision of the analysis. Second, differentiation according to the type of premises (dwelling houses, commercial premises, and public buildings) alone certainly could not be used as a basis for providing detailed sentencing statistics. Rather, the only means of structuring detailed statistics to capture the diversity of offending is through the use of descriptive dimensions and their associated categories.

Cross-Validation Study

Whereas in the original study a clear and direct relationship exists between offense seriousness score and length of the effective sentence as well as the percentage of custodial sentences for burglaries of commercial premises but not for dwelling houses, in the cross-validation study there is evidence of a relationship for dwelling houses but not for commercial premises. Nevertheless, in both the original study and the cross-validation study, the representations in Tables 7.4 and 7.5 show considerable overlap in the ranges of the sentences across the levels of offense seriousness.

It should be noted that a high degree of similarity exists in the way in which the cases in the original and cross-validation samples are distributed on offense seriousness. This suggests that the levels of seriousness associated with the offense characteristics for the cases in the two samples are similar. It should be noted, however, that the effective sentences are not stable across the original and cross-validation study within levels on offense seriousness.

Finally, similar conclusions can be drawn from the cross-validation study regarding the validity of the strategy of using groups (type of premises) and dimensions (offense factors) to represent the seriousness of burglaries.

8
Offender Characteristics and Prior Convictions in Cases of Burglary

This chapter defines the offender characteristics bearing on culpability, rehabilitation prospects, and mercy in cases of burglary. The particular factors considered are age, previous good character, reason for the offense, role in the offense, remorse (confession, reconciliation, current character, rehabilitation prospects, action taken for rehabilitation), breach of trust, suffering the offender has already undergone because of the offense, deprived family background, personal and family suffering that might be caused by imprisonment, potentially debilitating effects of imprisonment on rehabilitation, and prior convictions. The categories associated with these factors are defined in detail and presented together with the codes quantifying the level of exculpation (mitigation) or, for breach of trust and prior convictions, the level of aggravation associated with each category (see Table 4.1). I and the research assistant made decisions about the relative weights of the categories within the mitigation, with one exception; in making these judgments we considered general trends in the courts' views on the significance of the factors. The exception to this process was for the factor of prior convictions; here the justification for the weights of its components had a substantial empirical basis. It should be stressed that some of these offender characteristics cannot be regarded as dimensions (all four offense characteristics were treated as dimensions). Rather, the nondimensional offender characteristics should be seen as factors comprising groupings of conceptually linked categories; it follows that for some of these factors more than one of their constituent categories may relate to a case and that for some cases none of the categories associated with a factor may be relevant. One final general point: the qualitatively defined categories should be regarded as illustrative rather than definitive, and the quantitative categories considered tentative. The definitions of the offender categories (and their associated weights), with the exception of prior convictions, are presented in Table 8.1.

Use of Offender Categories

Table 8.2 shows for each offender category the number of principal offenders to whom the category was considered applicable by the coder. The data are self-

TABLE 8.1. Characteristics of burglars bearing on culpability

Factor	Code
Age	
17–18	−4
19–20	−3
21–22	−2
23–24	−1
Comment: Age in years was taken as at the time of the offense (first offense for cases with multiple counts)	
Previous good character (up to the time of the offense)	
Specific act of bravery (in civilian life or during war service), or substantial commitment to community service (e.g., organized a youth club)	−4
OR	
General war service, or minor community service (e.g., regular participation in a sports or service club), or instances of considerable kindness or generosity	−2
No prior or subsequent convictions or admitted pending charges and no evidence of associations with known criminals	−4
History of steady employment or study or earnest and sustained attempts to obtain employment (having lost the previous job through retrenchment or being yet to obtain employment), or being enrolled in a formal course of study, or having a good reason, such as illness, for not meeting this criterion	−4
OR	
Substantial (reasonably continuous) periods of employment/study or, for alcoholics and drug addicts, a stable employment/study history up to the time of the addiction	−2
Comment: An offender could score on all these categories "No prior convictions" included convictions for major and minor offenses	
Reason for the offense (significant contributory factor)	
Offender in financial difficulties (inability to meet existing financial demands and commitments arising from his or her need to provide food and shelter for a sick spouse or dependent child, or to pay debts to support a drug habit, or to meet mortgage commitments for the family's principal residence or a business that is the family's principal source of income)	−6
AND	
The financial difficulties were beyond the offender's control (e.g., drug addiction, unemployment, low income, misjudgment, or misfortune despite earnest endeavor, cf. gambling)	
The misappropriated money was used to this end	
The offender was not gambling or otherwise living extravagantly after the onset of the financial difficulties	
OR	
The offender (with no significant debts or financial demands) had insufficient means to meet his or her own and/or family's needs for reasonable food, shelter, and entertainment because of unemployment or low income and despite earnest endeavor to find adequate work	−2

TABLE 8.1. (*Continued*)

Factor	Code
The offender clearly was under the influence of drink or drugs at the time of the offense to such an extent that his or her self-control or judgment of the propriety of the behavior was significantly impaired, or the offender was an alcoholic or drug-dependent person	−6
OR	
Evidence that the offender had been drinking or on drugs just before the offense to such an extent that it might have been sufficient to have influenced his or her behavior	−2
The offender genuinely and reasonably believed that he or she had a right to the money/property in the victim's possession	−6
OR	
The offender's belief in his or her right to the property was genuine but not reasonable	−2
Other individuals had exerted a significant degree of coercion (including extreme threats such as violence) on the offender so as to force him or her to commit the offense (excluding cases where the coercion related to the offender's debts from gambling or other extravagant living or normal peer-group pressure)	−6
OR	
Coercion on the offender, which did not involve violence or threats of violence or other extreme threats and excluding normal peer-group pressure	−2
The offender was suffering from intellectual impairment or a medical or psychiatric illness or emotional distress (e.g., depression, whether or not it was due to identifiable environmental causes such as unemployment) at the time of the offense and to such an extent that his or her self-control or judgment of the propriety of the behavior was significantly impaired	−6
OR	
No expert or other substantial evidence that the impairment, illness, or distress was very significant, but it appeared to be a possible and reasonable explanation	−2
Comment: The maximum allowable score for this factor was 8 Related causes were classified under one category only (e.g., debts from a drug habit caused by emotional distress were classified as financial difficulties), whereas unrelated causes were classified independently (e.g., intellectual retardation and excessive drinking were classified separately)	
Offender's role in the offense	
The offender did not know or appreciate the amount and value of the money/merchandise stolen—where the value attributed by the offender would have placed it in a lower category on total value of the theft	−2
The offender did not participate in the offense until after the general plan had been formulated or participated in the offense only after being subjected to normal peer-group pressure (i.e., offender was a follower, cf. a leader)	−2
The offender did not act violently toward the victim(s) in an offense characterized by violence (i.e., in an offense coded as 3 or 4 on violence to the victims, the offender did not show behavior characteristic of these categories)	−3
The offender actively made a sustained attempt to prevent his or her co-offender from acting violently (as defined previously)	−4

TABLE 8.1. (*Continued*)

Factor	Code
The offender played a secondary role in the offense (e.g., drove the vehicle or acted as an observer during the offense, and did not enter the premises)	−3
The planned offense subsequently was modified to one of lesser heinousness by the offender(s)	−3
Comment: An offender could score on all these categories	
Remorse—confession	
The offender confessed before being suspected by the police	−4
OR	
During the police interview the offender confessed to counts that the police had not put to him or her (e.g., indicated the burgled premises to the police) or handed self over to the police after being suspected by the police	−3
OR	
The offender admitted his or her role in all the offenses put by the police (and on which he or she was presented) during the first set of interviews and signed the interviews (even if the incident(s) were denied initially) and pleaded guilty at the preliminary hearing	−2
OR	
The offender pleaded guilty before the prosecution had led any evidence at the trial	−1
Comment: A score on the higher categories required that the lower categories were satisfied	
Remorse—reconciliation	
The offender assisted the police, and as a result the co-offenders were arrested	−4
OR	
The offender assisted the police and as a result the money and property stolen by the co-offenders was recovered (where the co-offenders had not yet been apprehended by the police and had their share of the proceeds in their possession)	−3
At the time of the plea, the offender actually had repaid a substantial proportion of the proceeds from the burglary or series of burglaries involving a not insignificant financial gain and had demonstrated the capacity and willingness to compensate the victim(s) totally	−4
OR	
The offender had demonstrated the capacity and willingness to compensate the victim(s) totally	−3
OR	
A substantial amount of the stolen property and money had been recovered on the offender's initiative	−2
OR	
A substantial amount of the stolen property and money had been recovered	−1
Comment: An offender could score on both these categories "Substantial" in the last two elements of the second category was defined as at least 75% (approx.) of the amount accepted by the court as having been stolen *or* as the court deeming that a substantial amount had been recovered and it appeared to be about 75%	

TABLE 8.1. (*Continued*)

Factor	Code
Remorse – Current character	
The offender had not been convicted of an offense (but not including a minor nondishonest offense) committed since the date of the current offense(s) and had no admitted pending charges for subsequent offenses	−3
OR	
The offender had not been convicted of an offense of dishonesty committed since the date of the current offense(s) and had no admitted pending charges for subsequent offenses of dishonesty	−2
Specific act of bravery, or substantial commitment to community service (e.g., organized a youth club) since the commission of the current offense(s)	−4
OR	
Minor community service (e.g., regular participation in a sports or service club) or instances of considerable kindness or generosity since the commission of the current offense(s)	−2
Remorse – Rehabilitation prospects	
The offender at the time of the plea was not subject to the influence of any significant criminogenic factors (offender had relatively permanent employment or was enrolled in a formal course of study or had a substantial and continuing voluntary commitment to a legitimate community organization while actively seeking work or waiting to begin a formal course of study; the offender had successfully completed or was participating successfully in an appropriate program of treatment for the medical or psychological problem underlying his or her offending, or the offender did not require treatment; the offender was not associating with known criminals or the co-offenders; the offender had stable accommodation and a stable and close relationship with a person who had offered support and could exercise control, or the offender lived with his or her family	+4– (−4)
Comment: This category comprises four elements – employment/study, treatment, criminal disassociation, stable accommodation and close relationships; an offender would obtain full credit (i.e., −4 points) for this category if the four elements were satisfied or if he or she made arrangements to satisfy them but had been prevented from so doing, for example, the offender was in custody; credit for an element was not given if the offender had not attempted to take action but was prepared to do so, or if the offender had made an unsuccessful attempt, or if the matter was not mentioned in the plea; where an offender refused assistance or did not avail him or herself of a clear opportunity, a point was lost for that element (i.e., +1); actually, the scoring for criminal disassociation was somewhat different from the other three – credit was given if the offender had severed links with criminal associates or if the offender was trying to avoid known criminals or if the matter was not mentioned, even if there was suspicion (cf. evidence) that the offender still had criminal associations (i.e., −1); credit was not given (i.e., 0) if this matter was not mentioned but there was evidence (cf. suspicion) that the offender had criminal connections in the past; credit was lost for this matter if the offender was still associating with known criminals (i.e., +1)	

TABLE 8.1. (*Continued*)

Factor	Code
Remorse–Action taken by the offender to facilitate rehabilitation	
The offender had taken positive action to remove the influence of significant criminogenic factors by:	
Obtaining employment or enrolling in a course of study	−2
Successfully completing or participating in an appropriate treatment program	−2
Severing links with criminal associates	−2
Arranging stable accommodation or developing a relationship which had stabilized his or her behavior	−1
Comment: To satisfy each of these criteria, the offender must have taken the appropriate action since the offense and not have satisfied the criterion at the time of the offense	
Each of these criteria would be satisfied if the offender made the appropriate arrangements to satisfy it but had been prevented from doing so, for example, the offender was in custody	
An offender satisfying any one of these criteria automatically qualified for the corresponding criterion in "Remorse–rehabilitation prospects"	
The maximum allowable score on this category was 7	
Personal loss caused by the offense	
Any very significant personal suffering that the offender experienced as a result of having committed the offense: e.g., a serious, long-term physical injury; loss of career prospects or loss of employment where there was difficulty in getting another position of similar standing; loss of substantial accrued pension benefits; significant loss of community standing; breakdown of a personal relationship over which the offender was very depressed	−4
Comment: To satisfy this criterion the loss must have been very significant and defense counsel must have put this argument to the court (and the court not have expressly rejected it) or the sentencer must have indicated that it was material	
Deprived family background	
The offender suffered very severe psychological or physical neglect or abuse as a child (<17 years)	−3
OR	
There were significant disturbances to the offender's early development in relation to affection and discipline	−2
OR	
The offender spent a significant period (<4 years) as a child in an institution for care	−2
At least one of the offender's parents or older siblings with whom he or she spent much time had at least one custodial sentence and the family member's criminality appeared to be linked to the offender's present offense	−2
Comment: An offender could score on both categories	
If the deprived family background related to one of the reasons for the offense (see "Reason for the offense," preceding) then it scored in that category only	

TABLE 8.1. (*Continued*)

Factor	Code
Personal suffering (offender)	
Physical or mental illness or behavioral disorder or domestic instability (e.g., marriage instability) that would have been seriously aggravated if a custodial sentence had been imposed; or an additional and extreme hardship that the offender almost certainly would have suffered in prison because of his or her position (e.g., police officer), nature of the present offense (e.g., offense against a child) or past behavior (e.g., police informant)	−4
Comment: To satisfy this criterion the anticipated additional suffering must have been extreme and defense counsel must have put this argument to the court (and the court not have expressly rejected it) or the sentencer must have indicated that it was material	
Family suffering	
The offender's family would have had exceptional strains placed on them if a custodial sentence had been imposed: e.g., the offender was required to assist a child or spouse because of one of the latter's chronic illness, disablement, etc.; the offender was the sole parent in a single-parent family comprising at least one dependent child and there were no other members of the extended family who could have cared for the child; the reduced income would have ensured that the family could not have maintained loan repayments for essential items (where there was at least one dependent child); the offender's spouse was unemployed or unable (because of illness or a young family) to work and so his or her income was essential to sustain the family (where there was at least one dependent child); the spouse or child was suffering from a psychiatric illness that would have been seriously aggravated by the offender's imprisonment; the offender's imprisonment would have ensured that a family business that was the principal source of family income would have been closed permanently or have been set back seriously	−4
Comment: To satisfy this criterion the anticipated additional suffering must have been extreme and defense counsel must have put this argument to the court (and the court not have expressly rejected it) or the sentencer must have indicated that it was material	
Potentially debilitating effects of a custodial sentence	
The notional length of the custodial sentence would have seriously lessened the offender's chances of rehabilitation, in that, e.g., it would have caused the offender to have lost relatively permanent employment; placed the offender in a position of severe financial hardship; caused the breakdown of a potentially stabilizing relationship; seriously interrupted a course of study, especially for a young offender; been the offender's first time in prison (excluding remand) and his or her first opportunity to learn from and associate with experienced criminals; imposed a crushing sentence on the prisoner because he or she was then undergoing or had just completed a custodial sentence; prevented the offender from being treated adequately for a condition that contributed to his or her offending, or otherwise inhibited his or her rehabilitation	−4
Comment: To satisfy this criterion the anticipated debilitating effects must have been severe and defense counsel must have put this argument to the court (and the court not have expressly rejected it) or the sentencer must have indicated that it was material	

TABLE 8.1. (*Continued*)

Factor	Code
Breach of trust	
The offender used a position of trust as an insider to create an opportunity to commit the offense or to gain knowledge vital to committing the offense	+3
Comment: Friendship or acquaintanceship was not sufficient to qualify for a position of trust	

TABLE 8.2. Frequencies of the use of the offender categories for the principal offenders ($n = 100$)

Category	Frequency of use
Age <25 years	65 (62)
Specific bravery/substantial community service	2 (3)
Minor community service	3 (1)
No prior convictions	9 (17)
Excellent employment/study history	15 (20)
Very good employment/study history	28 (21)
Financial difficulties, severe	4 (5)
Financial difficulties, moderate	2 (5)
Alcohol/drug influence, severe	29 (36)
Alcohol/drug influence, moderate	8 (11)
Right to money/property, genuine and reasonable	1 (0)
Right to money/property, genuine	0 (0)
Coercion, extreme threats	2 (0)
Coercion, no extreme threats	1 (2)
Medical disorder, severe	9 (12)
Medical disorder, moderate	9 (6)
Underestimated value of merchandise	8 (1)
Follower	8 (9)
No violence in a violent offense	1 (2)
Attempted to prevent violence	0 (0)
Secondary role in offense	7 (3)
Modified plans so offense less heinous	2 (1)
Confessed before suspected by police	2 (3)
Confessed to additional offenses during questioning	16 (14)
Admitted all the offenses alleged by the police	56 (62)
Pleaded guilty before the trial	12 (8)
Assisted in arrest of co-offenders	2 (3)
Assisted in recovery of money/goods stolen by co-offenders	0 (0)
Repaid a substantial proportion of the proceeds	1 (0)
Intention to repay proceeds	2 (1)
Proceeds recovered on offender's initiative	5 (1)
Proceeds recovered	36 (21)
No subsequent convictions	76 (70)
No subsequent convictions for dishonesty	6 (5)

TABLE 8.2. (*Continued*)

Category	Frequency of use
Subsequent substantial community service	6 (0)
Subsequent minor community service	7 (4)
Employed/student currently	49 (40)
Employment/study rejected	0 (0)
Sought treatment/treatment unnecessary	84 (78)
Treatment rejected	1 (0)
No criminal associations	89 (96)
Associations with criminals	2 (2)
Accommodation and stable relationship	79 (78)
Accommodation/stable relationship rejected	1 (0)
Obtained employment/enrolled in study course since offense	29 (30)
Sought treatment	27 (30)
Severed criminal links	12 (9)
Obtained accommodation or developed a stable relationship	30 (24)
Significant personal suffering due to offense	1 (0)
Severe neglect as a child	0 (4)
Disturbances in early development	3 (11)
Substantial period of institutionalization as a child	2 (6)
Criminality of guardian	1 (2)
Personal suffering aggravated by prison	3 (3)
Family suffering aggravated by prison	5 (4)
Debilitating effects of prison	44 (14)
Breach of trust	7 (1)

Note. The data for the cross-validation study are presented in parentheses.

TABLE 8.3. Dimensions of prior convictions

Dimension
1. Number of counts of offenses involving dishonesty
2. Number of appearances in which at least one count involved an offense of dishonesty
3. Time since the last offense of dishonesty (from date of current offense to date of conviction for earlier offense)
4. Average (mean) time between the appearances involving counts of dishonesty (excluding current offenses)
5. Sum of the effective lengths of the custodial sentences for appearances in which the principal count involved dishonesty
6. Number of appearances in which none of the counts involved an offense of dishonesty and excluding those appearances in which the counts comprised solely minor offenses
7. Number of counts not involving an offense of dishonesty and excluding counts of minor offenses
8. Sum of the effective lengths of the custodial sentences for the appearances in which the principal count did not involve an offense of dishonesty and excluding appearances in which the counts comprised solely minor offenses

Note. For dimensions 5 and 8 no account was taken of concurrency orders between sentences imposed in separate appearances.

Where the current appearance comprised multiple offenses, a conviction recorded after the date of the first offense was not considered to be a prior conviction.

explanatory. A majority of the categories were well used, and almost all of the categories were required to describe the material personal characteristics of the principal offenders in the sample. Given these data, it is not surprising that the mean number of categories considered material to sentence for each principal offender was 9.1 (standard deviation = 2.9). (The corresponding data for the cross-validation study were 8.4 and 2.3.) The important point to note here is the substantial number of offender characteristics incorporated in the present model

TABLE 8.4. Distribution of counts of dishonesty for the principal offenders ($n = 100$)

Counts of dishonesty	Frequency
0	16 (7)
1	9 (4)
2	9 (8)
3	1 (2)
4	4 (6)
5	5 (2)
6	3 (1)
7	3 (4)
8	2 (5)
9	1 (2)
10	2
11	1 (3)
12	1 (3)
13	1
14	2 (2)
15	2 (1)
16	3 (4)
17	1
18	3 (1)
19	1 (1)
20	2 (2)
21–25	5 (5)
26–30	4 (5)
31–35	6 (1)
36–40	1 (3)
(52)	(1)
(56)	(1)
(60)	(1)
(64)	(1)
(65)	(2)
(74)	1
(85)	(1)
(86)	1
(88)	(1)

Note. There were 10 (20) offenders with no prior convictions.
The data for the cross-validation study are presented in parentheses.

TABLE 8.5. Distribution of appearances involving dishonesty for the principal offenders ($n = 100$)

Appearances involving dishonesty	Frequency
0	16 (7)
1	15 (10)
2	10 (12)
3	11 (11)
4	8 (4)
5	6 (3)
6	6 (9)
7	2 (8)
8	3 (3)
9	2 (4)
10	2 (2)
11	3
12	2 (2)
13	1
14	1 (1)
15	(1)
16	(1)
(19)	(2)
(24)	1
(37)	1

Note: There were 10 (20) offenders with no prior convictions.
The data for the cross-validation study are presented in parentheses.

TABLE 8.6. Distribution of the time since the last offense of dishonesty for the principal offenders ($n = 100$)

Time (months)	Frequency
≤1	10 (8)
2	6 (1)
3	1 (3)
4	(3)
5	1 (4)
6	1 (2)
7	3 (1)
8	2
9	2 (4)
10	5 (5)
11	2 (1)
12	2 (4)
13–18	12 (10)
19–24	5 (9)
25–30	3 (4)
31–36	5 (5)
37–42	2 (2)
43–48	(3)
49–54	
55–60	4
>60	8 (4)

Note. There were 10 (20) offenders with no prior convictions and 16 (7) offenders with no prior convictions for dishonesty.
The data for the cross-validation study are presented in parentheses.

of judicial decision making in contrast with the paucity of factors found in the descriptive sentencing guidelines based on predictive techniques (Kress, 1980; Wilkins et al., 1978). In Chapter 3 it was argued that these sentencing guidelines models comprise relatively few variables because the correlational analyses are inappropriate and, consequently, distort and fail to capture the effects of material case factors. Of course, the reposte of Wilkins and his associates is that judges in fact take few factors into account and would delude themselves if they believed otherwise (see also, Konečni & Ebbesen, 1982). This response, however, misses the critical issue: whether or not a substantial number of factors actually are determinants of sentence in any one case is a secondary consideration. Rather, the point is that a substantial number of factors should be considered at any one time. Clearly then, what is needed is a model of decision making with the potential to incorporate most of the material factors and also to offer a framework that the judiciary could use to define, weight, and combine the information. Given the range of material case factors mentioned in pleas (Table 8.2; see also, Shapland, 1981), the approach of Wilkins and his associates to the problem must be regarded as simplistic.

TABLE 8.7. Distribution of average time between appearances involving counts of dishonesty for the principal offenders ($n = 100$)

Time (months)	Frequency
≤1	1 (2)
2	(4)
3	2 (3)
4	1 (4)
5	2 (3)
6	2 (3)
7	3 (4)
8	4
9	1 (2)
10	2 (4)
11	2 (1)
12	4 (3)
13–18	19 (10)
19–24	6 (4)
25–30	5 (3)
31–36	1 (4)
37–42	1 (2)
43–48	1 (1)
49–54	1 (3)
55–60	1
>60	(3)

Note. There were 10 (20) offenders with no prior convictions and 31 (17) offenders with fewer than two prior appearances for counts involving dishonesty.

The data for the cross-validation study are presented in parentheses.

TABLE 8.8. Distribution of the sum of the lengths of the effective (custodial) sentences for appearances in which the principal count involved dishonesty: Principal offenders ($n = 100$)

Time	Frequency
≤6 months	8 (5)
7–12	5 (4)
13–18	6 (6)
19–24	3 (6)
25–30	(2)
31–36	5 (3)
37–42	6 (1)
43–48	4 (1)
49–54	3 (4)
55–60	2 (1)
≤6 years	3 (6)
7	2 (1)
8	1
9	1 (4)
10	1 (1)
11	1
12	(1)
13	
14	
15	1
16	
17	
18	2 (1)
19	1 (1)
20	(1)
(33)	1

Note. There were 10 (20) offenders with no prior convictions and 34 (31) offenders who had no prior convictions for counts involving dishonesty or who had not been given a custodial sentence for an offense of dishonesty.

No account was taken of concurrency orders between sentences imposed in separate appearances.

The data for the cross-validation study are presented in parentheses.

TABLE 8.9. Distribution of the number of appearances in which none of the counts involved an offense of dishonesty: Principal offenders ($n = 100$)

Appearances	Frequency
0	38 (27)
1	23 (28)
2	12 (12)
3	11 (5)
4	1 (2)
5	1 (2)
6	2 (3)
7	1 (1)
(22)	1

Note. Appearances comprised solely of minor offenses were not counted for this table.

There were 10 (20) offenders with no prior convictions.

The data for the cross-validation study are presented in parentheses.

TABLE 8.10. Distribution of counts that did not involve dishonesty: Principal offenders ($n = 100$)

Counts	Frequency
0	30 (24)
1	17 (8)
2	5 (9)
3	8 (12)
4	4 (5)
5	9 (4)
6	5 (7)
7	4 (3)
8	1 (1)
9	2 (4)
10	(1)
11	1
12	3
13	(1)
14	(1)
(22)	1

Note. There were 10 (20) offenders with no prior convictions.

Counts involving minor offenses were not counted for this table.

The data for the cross-validation study are presented in parentheses.

TABLE 8.11. Distribution of the sum of the lengths of the effective (custodial) sentences for appearances in which the principal count did not involve an offense of dishonesty: Principal offenders (n = 100)

Time (months)	Frequency
≤6	20 (18)
7–12	5 (7)
13–18	3
19–24	3 (2)
25–30	2 (1)
31–36	2
37–42	
43–48	
49–54	
55–60	1
(78)	1
(122)	(1)
(125)	1
(130)	(1)
(144)	1
(191)	(1)

Note. Appearances comprised solely of minor offenses were excluded.

There were 10 (20) offenders with no prior convictions and 51 (49) offenders who had no prior convictions for counts not involving dishonesty or who had not been given a custodial sentence for such offenses.

No account was taken of concurrency orders between sentences imposed in separate appearances.

The data for the cross-validation study are presented in parentheses.

Prior Convictions

As described in Chapter 4, prior convictions were defined in terms of the number, frequency, seriousness, recency, and type of offense (dishonest, major nondishonest, and minor nondishonest). Accordingly, the following aspects of an offender's prior record were formulated to describe this factor (Table 8.3). Prior convictions covered convictions recorded before the date of the current offenses. Minor nondishonest offenses included offenses such as failure to appear on bail, unlicensed driving, resisting a member of the police force, possession of an offensive weapon; major nondishonest offenses included offenses such as attempted escape, assaulting a member of the police force, possession of a firearm without a license. To a large degree, decisions relating to this distinction were governed by the circumstances of the offense rather than its legal category.

To identify cut-off points defining the categories on these dimensions, it was necessary to construct and then inspect the distributions for these dimensions for the principal offenders (see Tables 8.4 to 8.11); in these tables the definition of no prior convictions covered only offenders who had neither dishonest, nor major nor minor nondishonest offenses. When inspecting these distributions to

TABLE 8.12. Definitions of the categories for the dimensions describing prior convictions

Counts: dishonesty		Appearances: dishonesty		Time since last count: dishonesty (months)		Average time between appearances: dishonesty (months)		Sum of custodial sentences: dishonesty (months)		Appearances: nondishonesty		Counts: nondishonesty		Sum of custodial sentences: nondishonesty (months)	
Code	No.	Code	No.	Code	Time	Code	Time	Code	Time	Code	No.	Code	No.	Code	Time
1	1–3	1	1	1	≥49	1	≥37	1	≤12	1	1	1	1–2	1	≤6
2	4–8	2	2–3	2	25–48	2	19–36	2	13–24	2	2	2	3–4	2	7–12
3	9–16	3	4–6	3	13–24	3	13–18	3	25–48	3	3	3	5–7	3	13–24
4	17–30	4	7–10	4	7–12	4	7–12	4	49–84	4	4–5	4	8–10	4	25–48
5	≥31	5	≥11	5	≤6	5	≤6	5	≥85	5	≥6	5	≥11	5	≥49

TABLE 8.13. Percentage use of the codes in relation to the dimensions describing prior convictions for the principal offenders ($n = 100$)

Code	Counts: dishonesty $n = 74$ (73)	Appearances: dishonesty $n = 74$ (73)	Time since last count: dishonesty $n = 74$ (73)	Average time between appearances: dishonesty $n = 59$ (63)	Sum of custodial sentences: dishonesty $n = 56$ (49)	Appearances: nondishonesty $n = 52$ (53)	Counts: nondishonesty $n = 60$ (56)	Sum of custodial sentences: nondishonesty $n = 39$ (31)
1	26 (19)	20 (14)	16 (5)	7 (14)	23 (18)	44 (53)	37 (30)	51 (58)
2	23 (25)	28 (32)	14 (19)	20 (17)	16 (24)	23 (23)	20 (29)	13 (23)
3	18 (21)	27 (22)	23 (26)	32 (16)	27 (14)	21 (9)	30 (25)	15 (6)
4	22 (19)	12 (23)	22 (21)	27 (22)	18 (24)	4 (8)	5 (13)	10 (3)
5	12 (16)	12 (10)	26 (29)	14 (30)	16 (18)	8 (8)	8 (4)	10 (10)

Note. The data for the cross-validation study are presented in parentheses.

set values and thereby define the categories, account was taken of four factors: (1) natural discontinuities in the distributions; (2) the desirability of the dimensions each having the same number of categories, so that the use of respective categories on different dimensions could be compared readily; (3) the desirability of having reasonable numbers in each category so that all of the categories would have utility (of course, one would not aim for numerically equal categories within a dimension, because particularly serious behaviors generally would be less frequent); (4) legally significant distinctions, for example, the distinction between no and one prior appearance. The results of these deliberations are shown in Table 8.12.

Comparison of the Frequency of the Use of the Categories Across the Dimensions of Prior Convictions

Table 8.13 shows the frequency distributions for the codes in relation to the eight dimensions describing the prior convictions of the principal offenders. These data clearly show that all the categories were well used and that the categories marking the more serious aspects of the dimensions of prior criminal behavior tended to apply to fewer offenders.

Cross-Validation Study

Clearly, there is a high degree of similarity in the way in which the cases in the original and cross-validation samples are distributed in relation to the offender categories and the factors comprising criminal history.

9
The Relationship Between Offender Characteristics of Burglary and Sentence

The previous chapter concerned the development and description of offender characteristics bearing on culpability in cases of burglary. To classify a particular burglary in terms in this scheme, it was necessary to identify the categories whose defining content most closely matched the facts about the offender. (It should be remembered that some of the offender characteristics are not dimensional and, accordingly, for these characteristics none, one, or more than one of the constituent categories may apply to a particular case.) At this point the cases were described in terms of a series of codes – the number of relevant categories varied across cases – each code being a score quantifying the level of exculpation associated with its category (except for breach of trust and prior convictions; these characteristics aggravate culpability). This chapter explains how these scores were combined to derive a single score quantifying mitigation for the 100 principal offenders and then examines the relationship between these scores and sentence. This analysis first concerns the scoring and weighting of prior convictions, after which the other offender characteristics are incorporated in the analysis.

The Scoring and Weighting of Prior Convictions

Prior convictions comprised eight dimensions, five covering dishonesty and the remaining three relating to aspects of offenses not involving dishonesty. The scores for each offender were summed separately for these two sets of dimensions, and the two subtotals were then combined algebraically so that the set of dimensions covering dishonesty was given twice the weight of the other set. (The raw scores on each dimension were not standardized in order to derive the combined scores on prior convictions; see Chapter 7.) The distribution of these combined scores on prior convictions for the principal offenders is shown in Table 9.1 (these combined scores in Table 9.1 were uniformly adjusted so that the maximum possible score was 42; see the following discussion).

TABLE 9.1. Distribution of adjusted scores and transformed scores on prior convictions for the principal offenders ($n = 100$)

Adjusted score	Frequency	Equivalent transformed score	Adjusted score	Frequency	Equivalent transformed score
0	20 (24)	0	17	6 (5)	11
1			18	3	12
2	1	3	19	(1)	
3	2 (1)	3	20	4 (3)	13
4	(3)		21	2 (2)	13
5	1	4	22	6 (5)	14
6	3 (1)	5	23	4 (5)	15
7	(1)		24	2 (2)	15
8	7 (1)	6	25	3 (2)	16
9	1 (3)	7	26	4 (5)	17
10	1 (1)	7	27	2 (4)	18
11	2 (1)	7	28	1 (3)	18
12	5 (3)	8	29	2 (3)	19
13	5 (4)	9	30	2 (1)	19
14	1 (3)	9	31	3 (2)	21
15	5 (4)	9	32	1	24
16	1 (7)	10			

Note. The maximum possible adjusted score on prior convictions was 42.

The 0 score comprised 10 (20) offenders with no prior convictions and 10 (4) offenders whose prior convictions were for minor offenses only.

The data for the cross-validation study are presented in parentheses.

After the scores for prior convictions were derived, it was then possible to consider their weighting in the total mitigation. In Chapter 4 it was argued that the weighting of prior convictions should be equal to the combined effect of previous good character and remorse. To give effect to this, each principal offender's codes (scores) on the relevant categories comprising these two offender characteristics were summed (the maximum possible score for each offender was -42), and a cumulative percentage frequency distribution was constructed for these scores. A comparison of this distribution with a cumulative percentage frequency distribution based on the distribution of adjusted scores in Table 9.1 for the 80 principal offenders with a non-0 score (i.e., with a nonminor offense) showed that the two distributions covered a substantially different range. The purpose of adjusting the scores on prior convictions was to ensure that a claim to mitigation arising from a very commendable previous good character together with extreme remorse could be just negatived by an extensive past record; clearly, this initial transformation was too crude. To increase the degree of precision, the distribution of the non-0 scores on prior convictions was transformed using common percentile points so that it corresponded to the distribution of the combined scores for previous good character and remorse. That is, the highest observed score for prior convictions (extensive record) was set, regarding the sign, at about the lowest observed combined score for previous good character and remorse (strong mitigation), the rest of the scores being transformed on the basis of the similarity

TABLE 9.2. Distribution of scores showing the mitigating effects of offender characteristics (excluding prior convictions) for the principal offenders (n = 100)

Score	Frequency	Score	Frequency	Score	Frequency
0		−14	6 (4)	−28	4
−1		−15	3 (6)	−29	1 (2)
−2	(1)	−16	2 (8)	−30	2
−3		−17	6 (7)	−31	1 (1)
−4		−18	5 (3)	−32	2
−5	2	−19	8 (7)	−33	1 (1)
−6	1	−20	5 (8)	−34	
−7	4 (1)	−21	3 (2)	−35	1
−8	2 (2)	−22	5 (7)	−36	(1)
−9	4 (1)	−23	5 (9)	−37	
−10	1 (7)	−24	6 (3)	−38	
−11	4 (3)	−25	4 (1)	−39	1
−12	3 (6)	−26	2 (4)	−40	
−13	3 (4)	−27	3 (1)		

Note. The data for the cross-validation study are presented in parentheses.

of their positions within their respective cumulative percentage frequency distributions. This distribution of transformed scores on prior convictions for the principal offenders is shown in Table 9.1.

For both of the distributions involved in the transformation, cases were well distributed across their range but tended to cluster around the middle. It follows that there was an adequate data base for the transformation and that the data

TABLE 9.3. Distribution of total mitigation scores for the principal offenders (n = 100)

Score	Frequency	Score	Frequency	Score	Frequency
+13	(1)	−3	4 (3)	−19	2 (2)
+12		−4	3 (4)	−20	1 (3)
+11	2 (1)	−5	3 (4)	−21	2 (1)
+10	4	−6	2 (5)	−22	1 (4)
+9	1	−7	6 (1)	−23	5 (4)
+8	1 (1)	−8	5 (2)	−24	1 (1)
+7	1 (3)	−9	1 (5)	−25	2
+6	1 (1)	−10	2 (8)	−26	1 (2)
+5	1 (3)	−11	3 (2)	−27	1
+4	1 (2)	−12	2 (1)	−28	2
+3	4 (2)	−13	3 (2)	−29	2 (1)
+2	2 (4)	−14	3 (3)	−30	
+1	2 (4)	−15	2 (2)	−31	
0	2 (2)	−16	3 (2)	−32	2
−1	4 (4)	−17	4 (2)	−33	1 (1)
−2	2 (2)	−18	3 (4)	(−36)	(1)

Note. The data for the cross-validation study are presented in parentheses.

TABLE 9.4. Relationship between total mitigation scores and length of effective sentence (years) for principal offenders in burglary cases: Dwelling houses

	Original study (n = 46)				Cross-validation study (n = 53)			
Total mitigation score	n	Mean	SD	Custody (%)	n	Mean	SD	Custody (%)
≥ +9	3	3.4	2.0	100	1	1.5	0	100
+4-(+8)	3	3.8	1.0	100	5	2.0	0.7	100
−7-(+3)	16	1.6	1.7	81	19	2.4	2.5	68
−23-(−8)	19	0.8	1.4	37	27	1.1	2.0	37
≤ −24	5	0	0	0	1	0	0	0

Note. A high negative score indicates substantial mitigation.

would have been distorted if the process had been based on ranks. Moreover, if the distributions had been normalized then, again, they would have been distorted and, consequently, might have misrepresented judicial decision making. The present approach obviated both these undesirable outcomes. There is one problematic point—the omission of the 0-score cases from the analysis. However, if such cases were included in this type of transformation, then this might produce anomalous outcomes. A linear transformation of the form ($y = bx + c$) would seem to have been equally appropriate as the procedure adopted here. The former procedure preserves the relative seriousness of the cases on an interval scale across the transformation; however, the general shape of the transformed distribution remains unchanged and, accordingly, would differ from the criterion distribution where the untransformed and criterion distributions differ in shape. Alternatively, the procedure adopted here ensures that the shapes of the transformed and criterion distributions are somewhat similar but, as a consequence, under certain circumstances (when the distribution that is to be transformed and the criterion distribution differ in shape), the relative seriousness of the cases on an interval scale would not be maintained across the transformation.

TABLE 9.5. Relationship between total mitigation scores and length of effective sentence (years) for principal offenders in burglary cases: Commercial premises

	Original study (n = 47)				Cross-validation study (n = 38)			
Total mitigation score	n	Mean	SD	Custody (%)	n	Mean	SD	Custody (%)
≥ +9	4	3.1	2.1	100				
+1-(+8)	5	1.3	1.2	100	9	2.2	1.8	78
−6-0	12	1.0	1.2	58	8	1.0	1.0	63
−17-(−7)	14	0.9	1.3	43	10	0.6	1.2	20
≤ −18	12	0.2	0.6	8	11	0.5	0.9	27

Note. A high negative score indicates substantial mitigation.

TABLE 9.6. Relationship between total mitigation scores and length of effective sentence (years) for principal offenders in burglary cases: Public buildings

Total mitigation score	Original study (n = 7)				Cross-validation study (n = 9)			
	n	Mean	SD	Custody (%)	n	Mean	SD	Custody (%)
≥ −12					6	0.8	1.4	33
−15–(−13)	2	0.5	0.5	50				
−24–(−16)	3	1.8	2.5	33	1	1.5	0	100
≤ −25	2	0	0	0	2	0	0	0

Note. A high negative score indicates substantial mitigation.

TABLE 9.7. Frequencies of effective sentences in relation to total mitigation scores for principal offenders in burglary cases: Dwelling houses

Total mitigation score	Effective sentences (years)								
	0	≤1	≤2	≤3	≤4	≤5	≤6	≤7	≤8
Original study (n = 46)									
≥ +9			1	1			1		
+4–(+8)				1	1	1			
−7–(+3)	111	11111 1	111	1	11		1		
−23–(−8)	11111 11111 11	11	11	1	1	1			
≤ −24	11111								
Cross-validation study (n = 53)									
≥ +9			1						
+4–(+8)		1	11	11					
−7–(+3)	11111 1	11	1111	11		1	111		1
−23–(−8)	11111 11111 11111 11	11	11	111	1		1		1
≤ −24	1								

TABLE 9.8. Frequencies of effective sentences in relation to total mitigation scores for principal offenders in burglary cases: Commercial premises

Total mitigation score	Effective sentences (years)								
	0	≤1	≤2	≤3	≤4	≤5	≤6	≤7	≤8
Original study (n = 47)									
≥+9			11	1				1	
+1-(+8)		111	1		1				
−6-0	11111	111	11	1	1				
−17-(−7)	11111 111	11	11	1		1			
≤−18	11111 11111 1		1						
Cross-validation study (n = 38)									
≥+9									
+1-(+8)	11	1	1	11	11	1			
−6-0	111	11	11	1					
−17-(−7)	11111 111			11					
≤−18	11111 111		11	1					

In instances where the distribution that is to be transformed and the criterion distribution are similar, as was the case here, the outcomes of these two procedures would be similar.

Offender Characteristics (Excluding Prior Convictions)

Each principal offender's combined score on previous good character and remorse was added to his or her codes (scores) on the relevant categories comprising the other offender characteristics (excluding prior convictions). The distribution of these scores quantifying the levels of exculpation associated with the personal characteristics of the principal offenders (excluding prior convictions) is shown in Table 9.2.

Total Mitigation Scores

The (negative) scores for the offender characteristics were added to the (zero or positive) scores for the prior convictions to provide a total mitigation score for

TABLE 9.9. Relationship between total mitigation scores and type of premises for the principal offenders ($n = 100$)

	Type of premises		
Total mitigation score	Dwelling houses ($n = 46$) (53)	Commercial premises ($n = 47$) (38)	Public buildings ($n = 7$) (9)
≤ −25	4 (1)	5 (2)	2 (2)
−16–(−24)	8 (12)	11 (10)	3 (1)
−7–(−15)	15 (15)	10 (9)	2 (2)
+2–(−6)	9 (18)	15 (12)	(2)
≥ +3	10 (7)	6 (5)	(2)

Note. The data from the cross-validation study are presented in parentheses.

each principal offender (see Table 9.3), and these scores were then related to the lengths of the custodial sentences imposed on these offenders (a noncustodial sentence was treated as 0 length). The results of these analyses are shown in Tables 9.4 to 9.8. There is a direct relationship between the total mitigation score and the percentage of custodial sentences for dwelling houses and commercial premises and between mitigation and the length of the effective sentence for commercial premises. However, the representations of these relationships in Tables 9.7 and 9.8 reveal a considerable degree of overlap in the ranges of the sentences between most of the total-mitigation-score levels both for dwelling houses and commercial premises.

Because the principal offenders fell right across the range of total mitigation scores, it was necessary to form subgroups across the range to increase the numbers in each category and thereby improve the reliability of the estimates. To make the relationship between offense seriousness score and sentence comparable to the relationship between total mitigation score and sentence, the cut-off scores for the categories on total mitigation were set so that each category had, as nearly as possible, the same number of offenders as the corresponding category on offense seriousness; this was done separately for each type of premises.

A comparison of the respective tables (Tables 7.1 to 7.3 and Tables 9.4 to 9.6) suggests a tendency for the extent of mitigation to show a closer relationship than offense seriousness to effective sentence for dwelling houses, and perhaps a slight tendency for offense seriousness to be more closely related than mitigation to sentence for commercial premises; clearly, the differences are tenuous and, in any case, represent modest improvements on poor relationships.

Relationship Between Total Mitigation Scores and Type of Premises

It was noted in Chapter 7 that for cases with multiple counts there was a strong tendency for the same type of premises to be involved in all or most of the counts comprising a particular case. This suggested the possibility that offender characteristics may be related to the type of premises. If it was found that the offenders falling within one type of premises had greater claims to mitigation than those falling within another type, then the precision of the analysis might be increased by the distinctions between types of premises made in the analysis. To test whether this relationship existed in the data, Table 9.9 was constructed to show the relationship between the principal offenders' total mitigation scores and the type of premises. The data clearly show that the offenders' total mitigation scores are well distributed across the range of mitigation for each type of premises. It follows that distinctions in the type of premises would not increase the precision of the analysis regarding allowance for the effects of mitigation.

Cross-Validation Study

The analysis of the data in the cross-validation confirms the tenor of the conclusions from the original study on the relationship between total mitigation score and length of sentence as well as the percentage of custodial sentences. It should be noted that there is a high degree of similarity in the way the cases in the original and cross-validation samples are distributed on criminal history and total mitigation. This suggests that the levels of seriousness associated with the offender characteristics for the cases in the two samples are similar.

10 The Relationship Between Case (Offense and Offender) Characteristics of Burglary and Sentence

Up to this point, the analysis has provided two scores for each principal offender: one score quantifying the degree of aggravation associated with the offense, the other score representing the degree of exculpation by way of mitigation. The purpose of this chapter is to explain how these two scores were combined for each principal offender to derive a single score quantifying culpability and then to examine the relationship between these scores and sentence. Before this relationship is examined, some of the case scores representing culpability must be adjusted to allow for interaction between certain mitigating offender characteristics and to disallow credit for mitigation in particularly grave cases. Each of these four matters is considered in turn.

The Combination of Offense Seriousness and Total Mitigation

In Chapter 4 it was argued that offense and offender characteristics should be weighted equally and that offense seriousness sets a ceiling for culpability and so cannot be aggravated by offender factors. To give effect to these principles, any positive scores (arising from prior convictions) for total mitigation were reduced to zero ($n = 22$), and a cumulative percentage frequency distribution was constructed for the negative scores ($n = 78$). A comparison of this distribution with the cumulative percentage frequency distribution for the offense seriousness scores showed that the two distributions covered a substantially different range. Consequently, it was necessary to transform the distribution of scores for offense seriousness to ensure that an extreme score for offense seriousness could just be negatived by a very strong claim to mitigation. Accordingly, the scores measuring offense seriousness were transformed using common percentile points so that they corresponded to the distribution of the total mitigation scores, that is, the highest observed score for offense seriousness (serious offense) was set, regarding the sign, at the lowest observed score for total mitigation (strong mitigation); the rest of the scores were transformed on the basis of the similarity of their positions within their respective cumulative percentage frequency distributions.

TABLE 10.1. Distribution of original and transformed offense seriousness scores for the principal offenders ($n = 100$)

Original score	Frequency	Equivalent transformed score
4	9 (13)	3
5	8 (8)	5
6	21 (18)	9
7	13 (14)	13
8	21 (19)	19
9	10 (11)	23
10	7 (5)	26
11	4 (6)	28
12	4 (5)	31
13	3 (1)	33

Note. The data for the cross-validation study are presented in parentheses.

Table 10.1 shows the distribution of the original and the transformed offense seriousness scores for the principal offenders. Again, for both of the distributions involved in the transformation, cases were well distributed across the range but tended to cluster around the middle.

These transformed offense seriousness scores were added to the (zero or negative) total mitigation scores to derive a case score for each principal offender.

Adjustment of the Case Scores

Interaction

It was argued in Chapter 4 that the mitigating effects of an offender's youth, previous good character (in relation to prior convictions), or strong exculpatory reason for the offending may be greater than it would otherwise be, where the

TABLE 10.2. Criteria defining favorable rehabilitation prospects

Code of −1 on remorse–confession

AND

Code of −3 on remorse–current character (no reoffending)

AND

75% (approximately) of the money and property stolen was recovered (unless the money and proceeds had been already spent or disposed of), and the offender did not appear to be in possession of any profits from the offense

AND

For remorse–rehabilitation prospects, codes of −1 on treatment, criminal disassociation, stable accommodation/relationship and a code of −1 on employment or a code of 0 on employment but with at least one code of −1 or −2 on remorse–action taken by the offender to facilitate rehabilitation

Note. These criteria constitute the minimum requirement. For full definitions of these case factors, see Table 8.1.

TABLE 10.3. Definitions of the special categories of offender

Category of offender	Definition	Number with favorable rehabilitation prospects
First offense of dishonesty	No prior convictions or no prior convictions for offenses involving dishonesty	11 (11)
Last offense of dishonesty in the distant past	A code of 1 on time since the last offense of dishonesty (see Table 8.12), with the proviso that the offender had been out of custody for a period totaling at least 4 years since the last offense	5 (1)
Reason for the offense	A code of −6 on reason for the offense (see Table 8.1)	21 (16)
Youth	A code of −4 or −3 on age (see Table 8.1)	21 (11)

Note. The data from the cross-validation study are presented in parentheses.

offender's rehabilitation prospects are also favorable. These factors are defined in Tables 10.2 and 10.3.

When the criteria in Table 10.2 were applied, 42 principal offenders were deemed to have favorable rehabilitation prospects. When these offenders were considered in regard to the categories of offender defined in Table 10.3, it was found that 37 principal offenders fell within at least one of the categories of offender that may interact in mitigation and also were considered to have favorable rehabilitation prospects. (There were 33 and 26 such offenders, respectively, in the cross-validation study.) To allow for this category of interaction—rehabilitation in association with youth or previous good character (in relation to prior convictions) or strong exculpatory reason—the case score of each of these principal offenders was reduced by a further 4 points. The quantification of this category was to some extent arbitrary; nevertheless, this decision was taken in the light of the facts that 4 points was the most common mitigating effect for the offender characteristics and the average effect of one offense category after the transformation was between 3 and 4 points.

Withdrawal of Mitigation

In Chapter 4 it was concluded that an offender's credit for mitigating factors, other than the factor covering role in the offense, should be withdrawn for cases in which the characteristics of the offense (large haul of money and goods, high degree of organization) and the offender (long record of dishonesty) suggest professionalism. Criteria identifying cases for which mitigation should be disallowed on these grounds are defined in Table 10.4.

When the criteria in Table 10.4 were applied, three cases were characterized by professionalism. In two of these cases, the principal offenders did not have a net mitigation for which they could have received credit (i.e., their total mitiga-

TABLE 10.4. Criteria for the withholding of mitigation

Code of 4 on total value of the theft
AND
Code of 4 on organization or a code of 5 on appearances involving dishonesty

Note. For full definitions of these case factors, see Tables 6.4, 6.6, and 8.12.

tion scores were positive); in the third case the offender's total mitigation was −4, and so this offender's case score was increased by + 4.

In the cross-validation study, one case satisfied the criteria for professionalism.

Atypical Offense Characteristics

The two previous adjustments to the case scores were made to accommodate salient features of Thomas's (1979) model of the structure of judicial sentencing decisions; in that sense they were theoretically based. In contrast the following adjustments are not theoretically based but are properly characterized as fine-tuning. For violence to the victims there were three cases in which the violence perpetrated toward the victims seemed to be significantly more serious than in the other cases coded 4. In these three cases the principal offender assaulted the victim with a weapon, and the assault was either malicious and deliberate or the result of gross negligence with a weapon. To allow for this particularly serious violence in quantifying seriousness, the case scores of these three offenders were adjusted upward: the magnitude of the adjustment for each case was the increase in the transformed offense seriousness score that would result from an increase of one point in the original offense seriousness score for that case (see Table 10.1). Furthermore, for total value of the theft the top two cases appeared to involve significantly greater amounts than the other cases falling in the highest category on this dimension (see Tables 6.5 and 6.6); accordingly, their case scores were similarly adjusted. The magnitude of the increase in the case scores was no greater than 4 points for any one case; moreover, if an extra point had been added to the original offense seriousness scores of these cases, then they would have still fallen within the same subgroups in Tables 7.1 and 7.2.

In the cross-validation study there were three cases characterized by particularly serious violence. In two of these cases there was a minor sexual assault, one with the threat of violence, by a man on a woman in her home; in the other case a group of youths assaulted two men and the victims were injured physically.

Comment on the Adjustments to the Case Scores

The adjustments to the case scores on the preceding three grounds were minor. None of the cases was adjusted on more than one ground. Because the case scores were well distributed across a wide range of scores, these adjustments were indeed comparatively small.

TABLE 10.5. Relationship between adjusted case scores and length of sentence (years) for principal offenders in burglary cases: Dwelling houses

	Original study (n = 46)				Cross-validation study (n = 53)			
		Effective sentence	Minimum sentence[a]			Effective sentence	Minimum sentence[a]	
Adjusted case score	n	Mean[b]	Mean[b]	Custody (%)	n	Mean[b]	Mean[b]	Custody (%)
≥ +27	2	4.9 (1.1)	4.0 (1.0)	100	1	3.0 (0)	2.0 (0)	100
+23–(+26)	3	4.7 (0.9)	3.3 (0.3)	100	4	4.3 (3.0)	2.8 (2.4)	75
+14–(+22)	4	2.0 (2.1)	1.5 (1.7)	50	9	3.1 (2.2)	2.0 (1.4)	100
+6–(+13)	11	1.9 (1.2)	1.0 (0.5)	100	14	1.6 (1.9)	1.0 (1.1)	64
−9–(+5)	21	0.5 (0.8)	0.3 (0.5)	38	21	0.8 (1.4)	0.5 (0.9)	33
≤ −10	5	0 (0)	0 (0)	0	4	0 (0)	0 (0)	0

[a]For sentences of youth training, the minimum term was taken as the notional nonparole period, and where a minimum term was not set for sentences of imprisonment, the minimum term was considered to be equivalent to the effective sentence.
[b]The standard deviations are in parentheses.

Relationship Between Adjusted Case Scores for Burglary and Sentence

The adjusted case scores were related to the lengths of the custodial sentences imposed on the principal offenders (a noncustodial sentence was treated as 0 length). The results of these analyses are shown in Tables 10.5 to 10.10.

There is a clear, direct relationship between the adjusted case scores and the lengths of the effective and minimum sentences, as well as the percentage of custodial sentences, for the principal offenders in burglaries of commercial premises and public buildings, and between adjusted case scores and the lengths of the maximum and minimum sentences for dwelling houses. The representations of these data in Tables 10.8 to 10.10 reveal some overlap in the ranges of the sentences between the case-score levels. Within each level, however, the sentences tend to cluster in one or two cells, particularly for commercial premises, and when viewed in this light there is a very strong relationship between case score and sentence. Another feature of the relationship is the tendency toward a particularly sharp cut-off on the distribution of the adjusted case scores between custodial and noncustodial sentences, although this demarcation for dwelling houses is less marked.

Because the principal offenders fell right across the range of adjusted case scores, it was necessary to form subgroups across the range to increase the numbers in each category and thereby improve the reliability of the estimates. To make the relationship between adjusted case score and sentence comparable to the relationships between sentence and offense seriousness score and sentence and total mitigation score, the cut-off scores for the levels on adjusted case score were set so that each level had, as nearly as possible, the same number of

TABLE 10.6. Relationship between adjusted case scores and length of sentence (years) for principal offenders in burglary cases: Commercial premises

	Original study (n = 47)				Cross-validation study (n = 38)			
	Effective sentence		Minimum sentence[a]		Effective sentence		Minimum sentence[a]	
Adjusted case score	n	Mean[b]	Mean[b]	Custody (%)	n	Mean[b]	Mean[b]	Custody (%)
≥ +25	4	4.1 (1.4)	2.6 (1.4)	100	2	2.3 (1.8)	1.8 (1.3)	100
+18–(+24)	5	2.0 (0.9)	1.1 (0.5)	100	2	1.5 (1.5)	1.3 (1.3)	50
+10–(+17)	5	1.9 (1.2)	1.3 (0.8)	100	3	2.2 (2.1)	1.4 (1.5)	67
+3–(+9)	8	0.6 (0.6)	0.5 (0.3)	75	11	1.2 (1.4)	0.9 (1.0)	55
−4–(+2)	13	0.3 (0.7)	0.2 (0.4)	15	9	0.8 (1.2)	0.5 (0.7)	33
≤ −5	12	0.1 (0.2)	0.1 (0.2)	8	11	0.5 (0.9)	0.3 (0.6)	27

[a]For sentences of youth training, the minimum term was taken as the notional nonparole period, and where a minimum term was not set for sentences of imprisonment, the minimum term was considered to be equivalent to the effective sentence.
[b]The standard deviations are in parentheses.

offenders as the corresponding level on offense seriousness score (and, consequently, total mitigation score); this was done separately for each type of premises. A problematic feature of these sets of categories is that for dwelling houses and commercial premises, the category representing the third most serious level of case seriousness covered a very wide range of seriousness and in a section of this dimension for which the quantum of sentence might be expected to vary considerably; this category therefore was divided into two categories at its midpoint on the dimension representing case seriousness.

TABLE 10.7. Relationship between adjusted case scores and length of sentence (years) for principal offenders in burglary cases: Public buildings

	Original study (n = 7)				Cross-validation study (n = 9)			
	Effective sentence		Minimum sentence[a]		Effective sentence		Minimum sentence[a]	
Adjusted case score	n	Mean[b]	Mean[b]	Custody (%)	n	Mean[b]	Mean[b]	Custody (%)
≥ +18					1	3.8 (0)	2.5 (0)	100
+8–(+17)					3	0 (0)	0 (0)	0
0–(+7)	2	3.1 (2.1)	2.3 (1.7)	100	3	0.8 (0.6)	0.4 (0.3)	67
−7–(−1)	3	0 (0)	0 (0)	0				
≤ −8	2	0 (0)	0 (0)	0	2	0 (0)	0 (0)	0

[a]For sentences of youth training, the minimum term was taken as the notional nonparole period, and where a minimum term was not set for sentences of imprisonment, the minimum term was considered to be equivalent to the effective term.
[b]The standard deviations are in parentheses.

TABLE 10.8. Frequencies of effective sentences in relation to adjusted case scores for principal offenders in burglary cases: Dwelling houses

Adjusted case score	Effective sentences (years)								
	0	≤1	≤2	≤3	≤4	≤5	≤6	≤7	≤8
Original study (n = 46)									
≥ +27					1		1		
+23–(+26)					11		1		
+14–(+22)	**11**			1		i			
+6–(+13)		**1**11	**+**i+111	1	**1**	i			
−9–(+5)	**11111** **1**1111 111	**11**11i	1	+1					
≤ −10	**1111**1								
Cross-validation study (n = 53)									
≥ +27				i					
+23–(+26)	1			1			i		i
+14–(+22)		+	+11	i11			**i**		**1**
+6–(+13)	11111	11	i+1+1	**1**			11		
−9–(+5)	i1111 111**1** 11**1i**1	**1**i	1+	**+**	1	**1**			
≤ −10	**i11**1								

Note. A dot represents offenders who had three or more unconnected offenses or whose unconnected offenses resulted in an increase in sentence of more than 6 months.

Boldface represents offenders who fell in one of the categories of offender interacting in mitigation and who had favorable rehabilitation prospects.

A hyphen represents sentences of youth training.

A comparison of the indices of the relationship between adjusted case score and effective sentence with the indices of the relationship between effective sentence and offense seriousness score (Tables 7.1 to 7.5) and effective sentence and total mitigation score (Tables 9.4 to 9.8) shows that the combination of offense and offender characteristics provided a better account of the sentencing data than either offense or offender characteristics alone; Tables 7.4 to 7.5, 9.7 to 9.8, and 10.8 to 10.9. show this particularly clearly.

In Chapter 4 it was argued that an individualized measure is the preferred course (i.e., imprisonment should be avoided unless the offense is extremely serious) for young offenders, first offenders (in this case, a first offense of dishonesty), offenders who have a strong exculpatory reason for their behavior, or offenders whose previous offenses of dishonesty are in the distant past, *and* whose rehabilitation prospects are favorable (see Tables 10.2 and 10.3 for the

TABLE 10.9. Frequencies of effective sentences in relation to adjusted case scores for principal offenders in burglary cases: Commercial premises

Adjusted case score	Effective sentences (years) 0	≤1	≤2	≤3	≤4	≤5	≤6	≤7	≤8
Original study (n = 47)									
≥ +25				1	11			1	
+18–(+24)		1	1ł	1ł					
+10–(+17)		11	11			**1**			
+3–(+9)	11	1111	11						
−4–(+2)	**11111** 1111i i		**1ł**						
≤ −5	**11111** 11111 1	**1**							
Cross-validation study (n = 38)									
≥ +25		1			i				
+18–(+24)	**1**			1					
+10–(+17)	1		1			1			
+3–(+9)	11111	1	11	11	1				
−4–(+2)	1i111 **1**	1		i1					
≤ −5	**i1111** 111		**łł**	**1**					

Note. A dot represents offenders who had three or more unconnected offenses or whose unconnected offenses resulted in an increase in sentence of more than 6 months.

Boldface represents offenders who fell in one of the categories of offender interacting in mitigation and who had favorable rehabilitation prospects.

A hyphen represents sentences of youth training.

operational definitions of these criteria). Accordingly, offenders satisfying these requirements for an individualized measure are indicated in Tables 10.8 to 10.10.

Finally, unconnected offenses, attempted burglaries, and pending charges that were taken account of by the court are yet to be addressed in this analysis. These three types of associated offenses were all treated as unconnected offenses for the purpose of identifying the principal offenders convicted of such offenses. Table 10.11 gives the details for the principal offenders whose sentences were increased because they had unconnected offenses. Of the offenders with unconnected offenses whose sentences were not increased, the vast majority had fewer than three such offenses. The offenders with three or more unconnected offenses and the offenders whose sentences were increased by more than 6 months are identified in Tables 10.8 to 10.10.

TABLE 10.10. Frequencies of effective sentences in relation to adjusted case scores for principal offenders in burglary cases: Public buildings

Adjusted case score	Effective sentences (years)						
	0	≤1	≤2	≤3	≤4	≤5	≤6
Original study (n = 7)							
≥+10							
+8-(+17)							
0-(+7)		**1̶**					i
−7-(−1)	**111**						
≤−8	**11**						
Cross-validation study (n = 9)							
≥+18					1		
+8-(+17)	**111**						
0-(+7)	i	1	1̶				
−7-(−1)							
≤−8	**11**						

Note. A dot represents offenders who had three or more unconnected offenses or whose unconnected offenses resulted in an increase in sentence of more than 6 months.

Boldface represents offenders who fell in one of the categories of offender interacting in mitigation and who had favorable rehabilitation prospects.

A hyphen represents sentences of youth training.

An inspection of Tables 10.8 to 10.10 revealed that the identification of the offenders with unconnected offenses served to account, at least partially, for some of the sentences that had previously seemed particularly excessive, whereas the identification of the offenders for whom an individualized measure should have been preferred pointed out a number of apparently anomalous sentences.

The Sentencing Decision

It was predicted that the culpability of the offender as measured by the case score would be a major determinant of the decision to impose a custodial sentence and, if such a sentence was imposed, its length. The data support these predictions clearly, although it would appear that the relationship between case score and sentence is stronger for the use of a custodial sentence than for the length of the custodial sentence, because there is little overlap between the use of custodial and noncustodial sentences in relation to case score but considerable overlap in the ranges of the lengths of custody between case-score levels. It is interesting to note that the transition between the judges' preferences for custodial sentences over noncustodial sentences is around a case score of 0—the point where an offender's

TABLE 10.11. The effects on sentence of unconnected offenses

Study	Number of unconnected offenses	Increase in the effective sentence (months)	Resultant effective sentence (years)
Original[a]	1	3	1¼
	1	6	6½
	2	3	4¼
	2	6	3½
	3	24	5
	4	3	¾
	7	33	5¼
	7 (plus 8 pending charges)	15	4½
Cross-validation[b]	1	1	¾
	1	3	2¼
	1	6	1½
	1	18	3
	7	48	6
	8	48	8
	10	36	5¾

[a]There were 8 principal offenders whose sentences were increased because of the effect of unconnected offenses.
[b]There were 7 principal offenders whose sentences were increased because of the effect of unconnected offenses.

culpability arising from the offense is just mitigated by the exculpatory effects of the offender's personal characteristics; of course, the effect may be coincidental or otherwise of no theoretical significance. The prediction also was made that the relation between sentence and case score would be modified by the assessed rehabilitation prospects of an offender, as follows: (1) unless the offense was extremely serious, an individualized measure would be preferred (i.e., imprisonment would be avoided) for offenders who fell within one of the special mitigating categories (young, etc.) and whose rehabilitation prospects were favorable; (2) a tariff sentence would be imposed on offenders when there was reason to believe that the offender would not respond favorably to an individualized measure. This former position could not be rigorously tested, because the cases combining special category of offender and favorable rehabilitation prospects were predominantly associated with low case scores. There was, however, a sufficient number of exceptions to this prediction so that one was forced to conclude that the hypothesized modifying role of special category of offender in association with favorable rehabilitation prospects was not supported or, at least, that for most judges the offender's culpability is the dominant factor in determining sentence. The second proposition could not be tested, because the case records did not

TABLE 10.12. The relationship between type of premises and mean effective sentence (years) in relation to adjusted case score: Principal offenders (n = 100)

	Type of premises		
Adjusted case score	Dwelling houses (n = 46) (53)	Commercial premises (n = 47) (38)	Public buildings (n = 7) (9)
23–33	4.8 (4.0)	3.5 (2.3)	– (3.8)
12–22	1.7 (2.9)	1.9 (2.4)	– (0)
1–11	1.4 (1.3)	0.5 (1.0)	5.3 (0.6)
−10–0	0.2 (0.2)	0.4 (0.8)	0.2 (0)
≤ −11	0 (0)	0 (0.4)	0 (0)

Note. The data for the cross-validation study are presented in parentheses.

provide reliable information material to this matter, such as the response of offenders to previous noncustodial measures.

The Relationship Between the Type of Premises and the Length of the Effective Sentence

Clearly, if the judges tended to impose differential sentences across the three types of premises for cases with similar adjusted case scores, then it would be necessary to represent the relationship between culpability and effective sentence separately for each type of premises. To test this, a table showing this relationship was constructed. The dimension of adjusted case score was divided equally to form five levels (Table 10.12).

Clearly, no strong evidence is shown here of a clear relation between the type of premises and quantum of sentence for cases with similar adjusted case scores.

Cross-Validation Study

The analysis of the data in the cross-validation study confirms the tenor of the conclusions from the original study on the relationship between adjusted case score and quantum of sentence; nevertheless, it is clear that the degree of fit was appreciably tighter in the original study. (It should be remembered that the categories on the dimension of adjusted case score for Tables 10.5 to 10.10 [and Table 10.12] were established on the basis of the data in the original study and prior to the cross-validation study.)

Again, there is a high degree of similarity in the way in which the cases in the original and cross-validation samples are distributed on offense seriousness (Table 10.1), and concerning the adjustments to the case scores for interaction, withdrawal of mitigation, and atypical offense characteristics, and in relation to the distributions for adjusted case scores. This further supports the conclusion that the levels of seriousness associated with the cases in the two samples are similar.

11
Toward Detailed Sentencing Statistics

By way of introduction I shall summarize the aims and strategy underlying the present approach to the problem of structuring the sentencing discretion through detailed sentencing statistics.

1. Appellate courts have demonstrated clearly their belief that sentencing should be more structured. In England the Court of Appeal (Criminal Division) has delivered guideline judgments, and in Australia the appellate courts, including the Victorian Full Court, have called for and considered statistical information on past sentencing practices as part of their determination of appropriate sentences for particular cases. These moves are consistent with the writings of law reformers.

2. A review of the literature suggested that present curial approaches to sentencing are unnecessarily qualitative, subjective, and intuitive and that detailed sentencing statistics could ameliorate some of these problems inherent in the determination of sentence by providing greater precision in relation to the definition of material case factors, the weighting of these factors, and the rules for combining this information. A related problem is that the appellate courts have yet to establish a policy on many specific points relating to these three matters.

3. The problem of structuring the sentencing discretion is not seen merely as one of specifying the material factors, their weights, and the rules for combining the information; there also is the problem of providing an aid to judges in their task of balancing the competing effects of various combinations of aggravating and mitigating factors present in particular cases.

4. The aim of this present analysis is to develop detailed statistics that precisely define a fairly comprehensive set of material case facts and show the relation between various combinations of these factors and quantum of sentence. It is important that the general strategy is intelligible to judges so that the statistics would act as no more than a guide to the exercise of the judges' discretion. An argument was advanced that, to accomplish this, a legal model must be developed that describes how judges determine sentence, that is, a model that describes how judges give effect to sentencing policy when determining sentence in particular cases. Case facts would then be fitted to the model and related to the quantum of sentence. If a clear relationship were found between the facts of a case construed

according to this model and sentence, this would support the model's validity and its use as a basis for detailed sentencing statistics.

5. This model of judicial decision making could be used to structure the sentencing judgment in two ways: (1) show the relationship between various combinations of factors associated with actual cases and the sentences imposed in these cases and thereby describe current sentencing practice, and (2) provide a framework for representing judicial decision making to identify critical questions about sentencing policy and to present the answers with precision and, in this way, act as a basis for the development of sentencing policy.

With this background to the study, the discussion now turns to consider the findings regarding the specific tasks associated with the development of the statistics and then moves on to address more general issues.

The first task was to investigate whether the major variation in offense characteristics across cases for the legal offense category of burglary could be described by a manageable set of dimensions and categories. It was the coder's impression that the four dimensions, each of four categories, could be related readily to cases and indeed provided a wide coverage of the salient offense characteristics of almost all the cases. A similar conclusion was reached regarding the personal characteristics of the offenders. At this early state in the development of these dimensions, it was impossible to define the categories comprehensively and with an acceptable degree of precision. One reason for this is that 100 cases is an insufficient number to represent adequately many of the possible variations in the offense and offender characteristics. The second reason relates to the quality of the depositions of the witnesses and the statements and records of interview of the accused as well as to the nature of the pleas. Not infrequently, this information was found to be indefinite, imprecise, and incomplete. These problems appeared to characterize the mitigation more than the written records about the offense but, nevertheless, they were significant in both areas. If the system were to become operational then it would be necessary to provide more detailed definitions for each of the categories as well as examples of the variations in the case characteristics coded under each of the categories. The ultimate test of the adequacy of the dimensions and their associated categories would be the degree of reliability with which a representative group of judges could code a representative sample of cases. Such a test would be premature at this stage.

A related point bearing on the adequacy of the classificatory scheme concerns the degree of agreement judges would show over the identification of case factors that might be deemed to be material and yet not incorporated in the statistics. The attempt by a former English High Court judge to account for disparity provides a timely warning about the potential ineffectiveness of attempts to structure sentencing discretion:

> A judge . . . more imaginative than another about the pains of imprisonment . . . may find circumstances to justify a still lower sentence where another would not. A judge who . . . holds that the wickedness of the crime calls for severe punishment . . . will be less likely than the other to find mitigating circumstances. (McKenna, 1969, p. 610)

Therefore, in an operational system, it would be necessary to require the sentencing judge to list all the factors taken account of (including those factors in the classificatory scheme as well as any other factors deemed by the judge to be material) in determining a sentence.

The dimensions and categories on which the detailed sentencing statistics would be developed would offer a secondary benefit: they would specify and provide a framework for the basic information that the prosecution and defense counsel should put before the court at the time of sentencing. The coder felt that not infrequently material about the nature of the offenses and the backgrounds and circumstances of the offenders was not available in sufficient detail to permit the reliable classification of information according to the categories. If the quality of the information put before the courts were to be improved, this would permit fairer comparisons between cases and perhaps more appropriate and effective sentences in particular cases. This conclusion was also reached by Shapland (1981) on the basis of her study of mitigation. (See also, Shapland, 1987.)

Next, the analysis demonstrated that is possible to develop a relatively simple set of rules, based on a model of judicial decision making, for weighting and combining the specific offense and offender characteristics of individual cases of burglary to construe the facts of cases for the purpose of sentencing. Moreover, it was shown that this representation of case characteristics was related to the actual effective and minimum sentences imposed by the courts. This finding supports the validity of the model of judicial decision making, the use of the model as a basis for the development of detailed sentencing statistics and, indirectly, the validity of the classificatory scheme. Indeed, the degree of association for each of the three types of premises was quite remarkable considering the following limiting conditions: (1) undoubtedly, there were cases with uncommon offense and offender characteristics deemed to be material by judges and yet not incorporated in the classificatory scheme; (2) one would be surprised if there were not significant disparity between judges in the determination of sentence; (3) to proceed with this feasibility study, the coder and I had to intuit what definitions, weights, and rules most nearly captured sentencing policy; now, some of our judgments might have been seriously in error; (4) it was assumed that the offenders' culpability associated with the connected offenses was covered in the dimensions used to describe the offense characteristics, and yet this was not always so; (5) the effect on culpability of the unconnected offenses was handled crudely; (6) there would have been cases for which material information was known to the judge but was not on record.

It is possible that two factors acted to inflate the association between the representation of the seriousness of the case characteristics and sentence, namely, the method of identifying the material case characteristics and of defining the qualitative categories and setting cut-off points for the quantitative categories. The effects of these factors, however, are not likely to have been substantial; the coder and the author did not consciously look at the sentences when defining the dimensions and categories and coding the data in relation to them and, in any case, such is the level of the complexity of the classificatory and scoring system that the effect of a specific coding decision on the relationship between case fact and sentence would have been rarely apparent. Moreover, the vast majority of these decisions were clear-cut and left the coder and the author with little personal discretion. The appropriate way of investigating the magnitude of these effects is a cross-validation study.

Indeed, this supplementary analysis confirmed the relationship between case characteristics and sentence, although the degree of fit between the construction of case seriousness in terms of the model and sentence was not as tight. The evidence is against the view that the validity shrinkage was due to a significant extent to case factors, levels on case factors, or combinations of case factors not found in the sample of cases in the original study and, accordingly, not in the classificatory scheme; the conclusion regarding the first matter is based on the observations of the coder, and the evidence for the other two points is to be found in the high degree of similarity in the way in which the cases in the original and cross-validation samples were distributed in relation to the case characteristics and categories and in relation to the dimensions representing offense seriousness, criminal history, mitigation, and case seriousness. In the light of the similarity in the structure of the cases in the two samples, one is prompted to wonder whether in the cross-validation sample there was greater disparity among the judges in their determination of the appropriateness and length of custodial sentences.

It is reasonable to conclude that these analyses of offense and offender characteristics of burglary confirm the feasibility of this strategy for developing detailed sentencing statistics, and this finding complements the conclusion of the first feasibility study (and cross-validation) for offense characteristics of armed robbery (Lovegrove, 1983). Of course, the design of the analysis does not permit a conclusion about whether or not all of the factors in the model actually influenced the judges' determinations of sentence; rather, one can conclude only that when case facts were construed according to the model there was a clear, direct relationship between the characteristics of a case and the sentence imposed on the offender. Almost certainly, the degree of reliability of the dependent variable would not be sufficiently high to permit the individual effects of many of the case factors to be tested by investigating whether the appropriate changes to the model would affect the strength of the relationship. In any case this is not a problem for the present strategy, because the development of the statistics is not based solely on the data. I shall return to this matter later.

Finally, a comment should be made about the validity of the dimensions-within-groups solution to the problem of construing case facts as precisely as possible. The analysis of the data confirmed the assumptions underlying this approach for armed robbery (Lovegrove, 1983). The present analysis for burglary, however, showed no relationship between the type of premises and (1) the dimensions and categories used to describe burglary, (2) the (most severe) sentence on the principal count of burglary, (3) the distribution of total mitigation scores, or (4) the lengths of the effective sentences within each of the levels on adjusted case score. Consequently, it is unnecessary to classify cases of burglary according to the type of premises to maximize the precision of the analysis.

(There were too few cases for public buildings to draw firm conclusions on this matter regarding this category of premises.) Now that the specific tasks associated with the development of the statistics have been related to the analysis, the discussion turns to general issues.

Detailed Sentencing Statistics as an Operational System

It is now appropriate to consider how this model of judicial decision making could be applied to develop detailed sentencing statistics describing current sentencing practice. The present analysis has taken some steps toward achieving this goal for one offense (burglary) by demonstrating that it is feasible to develop a model that describes how judges classify and combine information to determine sentence; the model can be used to show the relationship between various combinations of factors associated with actual cases and the sentences imposed for these cases in the jurisdiction. There are both quantitative and qualitative components in the representation of this relationship. The former is a measure or scale of the seriousness of various combinations of offense and offender characteristics together with the degree of punishment appropriate for each level of seriousness; the latter are indicators defined by particular case characteristics and showing: (1) whether a tariff sentence or an individualized measure is more appropriate for the offender and (2) where a tariff sentence is appropriate, whether the quantum of sentence should reflect the culpability of the offender (i.e., relate to both offense and offender characteristics) or reflect only the gravity of the offense (i.e., credit for the available mitigation should be withdrawn).

Of course, it would be necessary to take several more steps before the system could become operational. First, to develop the representation of case characteristics in relation to penalty, I had to make decisions concerning the definitions of the dimensions and categories, the weights of these factors, the set of rules for combining case factors, and the nature of the representation. Now, these decisions are properly the province of the judiciary and, accordingly, it would be necessary for judges to study the model and, where necessary, to modify some of these decisions to preserve judicial independence and to ensure that existing sentencing law would be applied correctly. The case data then would be fitted to the revised model and re-related to the sentencing data. This refinement to the model would have the potential to provide a tighter relationship between the case facts and the sentence. Provided, however, my decisions did not vary substantially from the process of sentencing, this study may be regarded as a sound basis for evaluating the feasibility of detailed sentencing statistics. In fact the degree of improvement that could be obtained by using the revised model would depend on the extent to which judges are reliably giving effect to a common policy and the extent of the difference between the hypothesized and revised models; if some judges' current sentencing practices were inconsistent with the revised model or showed a significant degree of instability, then not much improvement could be expected.

As a second step, it would be necessary to include many more cases in the analysis to cover a wider range of offense and offender characteristics and to provide more data points for the less frequently occurring combinations of case characteristics (particularly at the higher levels of culpability), thereby increasing the reliability of the estimates.

Third, three aspects of sentencing policy were not included in this scheme and yet seem to be significant. One matter concerns an offender's response to previous noncustodial measures. This factor was not considered here, because frequently it was not mentioned even though the records revealed a breach and in other cases it was not possible to determine from the records how an offender had responded to such measures. A second matter concerns how unconnected offenses (including attempted burglaries, pending charges, and offenses other than burglary) should be treated. Finally, other sentencing principles, for example, parity between co-offenders sentenced in different courts, are yet to be incorporated in the scheme.

In presenting the relationship between the seriousness of a case and the quantum of sentence for the purpose of providing guidance to sentencers, it is necessary to make much finer discriminations (i.e., have more categories) in the scaling of case seriousness and length of sentence than are found in the tables used to test the validity of the model (Tables 10.5 to 10.7). To illustrate the representation of current sentencing practices, Figure 11.1 was constructed using the current data from the original study, showing adjusted case scores in relation to effective sentences. The dimension of adjusted case score was divided into units of two (27 levels), and length of sentence was divided into intervals of 3 months. The data for dwelling houses and commercial premises were combined because the distributions of sentence in relation to case score for these two types of premises were so similar (see Table 10.12). To simplify the representation no distinction was made between youth training and imprisonment, and offenders for whom an individualized measure was the preferred course were not indicated; furthermore, unconnected offenses were not distinguished. The mean lengths of the custodial sentences (0 for a noncustodial sentence) were calculated for each level above an adjusted case score of −3 (the level below which noncustodial sentences predominate over custodial sentences). The relationship between the adjusted case score and sentence was represented by drawing the line apparently providing the best fit to the (mean) sentences. Figure11.1 shows the notional quantum of sentence that would be appropriate where the sentence is to be made proportional to the culpability of the offender (i.e., a tariff sentence imposed): for offenders whose case score is above 3, it is a custodial sentence equal to the length marked by the line; below a score of −2 the notional tariff sentence does not require a custodial sentence; and between −2 and 3 there is not a clear demarcation between custody and noncustody, although the majority of sentences are noncustodial, particularly between −2 and 1. The quantum of sentence defined by the table must be regarded as no more than notional because (1) the judge is free to allow for the effects on culpability of material case factors that were not included in the classificatory system; (2) in certain cases the consideration of an offender's personal characteristics would dictate that an individual-

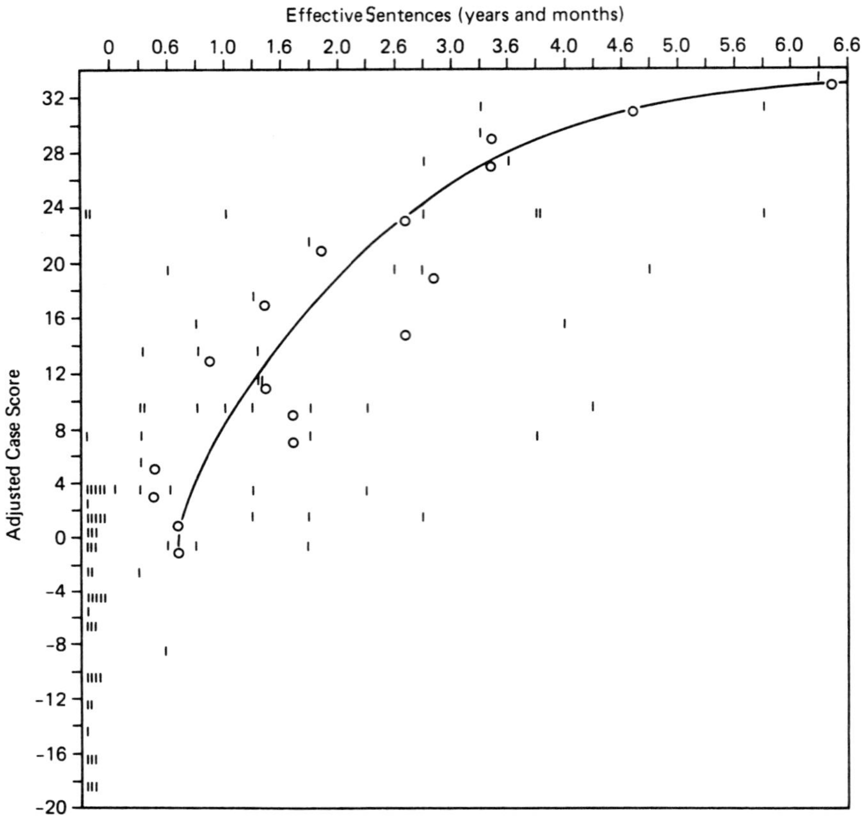

FIGURE 11.1. Relationship between adjusted case scores and effective sentences for burglaries of dwelling houses and commercial premises—principal offenders (n = 93). *Note.* The mean sentences for the various levels are indicated by the circles. The categories on effective sentences cover a range, with the upper limit of each category indicated. For example, the second category includes all custodial sentences up to and including a length of 3 months exactly. The categories on adjusted case scores cover a range, with the lower limit of each category indicated. For example, the top category includes case scores of 32 and 33. These data are from the original study.

ized measure was more appropriate; (3) there are other sentencing principles that a judge must regard, for example, parity between co-offenders sentenced in different courts. The decision to represent the data points (mean sentences) by way of a curve, rather than a straight line, was heavily influenced by the most serious case, and this case may be atypical; clearly, more data points at the higher levels of case seriousness are required before it could be concluded that a curve is more appropriate than a straight line.

Actually, the relationship between the adjusted case score and (mean) effective sentence as shown in Figure 11.1 is remarkably strong, considering the fineness of the discriminations along the dimension of culpability, the small numbers of cases in some of the levels and the other limiting conditions discussed previously. As already mentioned, one might expect that this relationship would be tighter after the model had been refined and the case data refitted to it. One should be careful before concluding that the data in Figure 11.1 demonstrate disparity between judges' sentencing practices, particularly for their determination of the length of custody, until the previously mentioned deficiencies have been rectified.

Following, the application of the system of detailed sentencing statistics is illustrated, using one of the cases from the sample. The purpose of this presentation is to demonstrate how to code and score a case in terms of the classificatory system. First, the research assistant's written record of all the information put before the court (excluding the offender's name and the presentment number) is presented for one of the cases in the current sample. Second, the information is coded in terms of the classificatory scheme. Third, the adjusted case score is calculated; in doing so, the case characteristics are assessed according to the relevant criteria for (1) the interaction between mitigating characteristics and (2) the withdrawal of the effects of mitigation. Fourth, this score is related to the notional tariff sentence. Finally, the case characteristics are related to the criteria defining favorable rehabilitation prospects and to the special categories of offender to determine whether an individualized measure might be an appropriate sentence for the offender.

The Written Case Record

General

Burglary, 1 count, plea of guilty
Handling, 1 count, plea of guilty
Sentence: Count 1: 18 months with a minimum of 9 months
Count 2: 6 months, concurrent with count 1
Date of birth: 4/4/55

Priors (All Admitted)

Court	Charges	Sentence
Children's Court 4/21/70	Housebreak and steal (11 charges) Illegal use of a motor car (7 charges)	1 month Youth Training Center on each charge—cumulative
Children's Court 5/18/70	Escape from legal custody Attempt illegal use of a motor car	3 months on each charge
Children's Court 10/9/70	Escape from Youth Training Center Loiter with intent	3 months Youth Training Center 3 months Youth Training Center

Children's Court 10/13/71	Housebreak and steal (5 charges) (6th charge dismissed)	First charge 2 months Youth Training Center, charges 2 to 5 – 1 month Youth Training Center on each charge Total: 6 months
Petty Sessions (N.S.W.) 11/14/73	Vagrancy	1 month hard labor
Magistrates' Court 12/9/74	Burglary (housebreak and steal) (4 charges)	1 month on each charge
Magistrates' Court 9/16/76	State false address	$30 default 3 days
Magistrates' Court 7/3/78	Burglary	6 months
Petty Sessions (W.A.) 9/6/78	Unlawfully drove motor vehicle	$300 with costs of $9.50
Magistrates' Court 10/9/78	Possess housebreaking implement	$200 default 20 days
	Unlicensed driver	$100 default 10 days
	State false name and address	Disqualified from obtaining license for 6 months
Magistrates' Court 9/25/79	Theft	3 months

CURRENT PRESENTMENT

First Count 5/6/1980, Burglary

Owner's Statement. Provided a list of the goods stolen:

1 clothes rack
119 leather suede coats
24 jackets
66 leather coats
49 battle jackets
Other leather, suede, and fabric jackets
Trousers and coats
Value approx. $38,000

Some recovered, found in accused's possession: a few leather coats (3), 1 suede coat, trousers, etc.

Statement of Victim. Partner in the clothing business and assistant manager for both their stores.

This store is a factory and showroom.
He left these premises 6:00 p.m., securely locked, and returned 3:30 a.m. (on advice), found place broken into and all stock in showroom stolen.

The lock on front sliding door had been "jimmied" open and bottom bolt on security door cut, padlock on top of security door was also cut, and all were lying on floor (front door and sliding door—inside door is metal security grill with padlocks in two places).

Noticed two large sheets of iron placed over gutter at front of shop.

Statement of Police.

They attended scene and found marks in timber beside lock, on door, and the lock forced open.

The bolts on bottom of security door cut off, and padlock off top cut.

Ten days later went to accused's residence, with other police; accused ran out to balcony. They arrested accused.

Found some coats branded with name of the victim company and found color T.V. (accused said he bought it in a pub, "it's hot").

The accused admitted the burglary and said that he had sold most of the clothing, had thrown some away, and kept some in apartment.

Used screwdriver on front door and bolt cutters on metal security door to gain entrance.

Record of Interview. With accused, signed.

Employed as an occasional salesman with a car firm.

Did the burglary at about 3:00 a.m.

Did it alone.

He was going to back the car through the window, got metal plates from "down the road," laid them across gutter, but then decided that he could open door with screwdriver and cut locks on security door.

Loaded everything into his station wagon.

He says he didn't take as much as claimed and no rack.

Did it because, "Just sick of the way I was living, that's all. Things were going bad, that's all. I owe the boss two thousand."

He knew shop had alarm system, but thought he would get a few coats, but alarm didn't go off, so he stayed. Got all the goods out of the front, then went to the back. That's when the alarm went off.

Took everything from front showroom because of fingerprints.

Sold most of it in pubs.

Second Count 5/8/1980, Receiving Stolen Goods

Record of Interview. With accused, signed.

Color T.V.

Said he bought it in a hotel, swapped it for leather coats.

Assumed it was stolen (knew its value, about $1,300, exclusive brand).

"Too good a bargain to pass up."

PLEA AND SENTENCE

Accused: I work as a laborer. I don't vote.

His Honor: What is the position here? Value of goods from the shop is substantial, that is, the amounts he's admitted. What's the value of what he did take?

Defense Counsel: I can only determine it as a proportion. The discrepancy is large. Police found 80 coat hangers—perhaps corresponding with the number of garments. The accused was surprised at the value. He hadn't thought the coats were worth that much. He was using a medium-to-large station wagon. I imagine that he would have had difficulty fitting 300 leather coats in the back. It's impossible to put a 6-foot rack in the back of a station wagon.

Crown Prosecutor: I can't add to the witness's statement about the value of the property. The accused admits to 60 items, 20 found in possession.

His Honor: Even that's substantial. What's the value? Say it's one quarter the $38,000 claimed, then one quarter would be about $9,000.

Defense Counsel: That accords with my client's own description. He says he got $2,500 from the sale of the coats.

My client has been married 8 years and has two children. He has had little education—left school at 15. On leaving school, he got in trouble almost immediately. [The Defense Counsel refers to the list of priors.] From 1970 to early 1974, my client was continually in trouble. But the interesting thing is that he was married in 1973, and between 1973 and July 1978, he had only one criminal conviction, if you exclude the conviction in 1976 for false name and address. After that, he took a 4-year break. Between July and December 1978, he had 3 criminal charges.

He doesn't drink, except on rare occasions. All previous offenses occurred when he drank and offended, that's why he doesn't drink; he knows when he does he gets involved in criminal activities.

About July 1978, that's how the burglary occurred. He was sentenced on that burglary. He lodged a notice of appeal—faced 6 months—and absconded to Western Australia. He said the charge in Western Australia was used as holding charge for extradition and was not in the nature of illegal use. Offenses in September to October 1978 all relate to the period of June to July 1978. He was going through a bad patch and was drinking. He says this offense is the first time he has ever committed a planned professional offense when stone, cold sober. His reason for the offense doesn't appear in the Record of Interview, which says that he was disenchanted with his life-style and was in debt to his boss. My instructions are that that wasn't the real reason.

History

The accused has a brother serving life imprisonment for murder. Over the years, the brother, who previously was not in trouble with police, would pitch in and help whenever the accused was in trouble with bail, and so on.

In 1979, Christmas Eve, his brother told him he had shot a man. Both the accused and his brother went into hiding until March, when the brother was arrested and convicted.

His parents are elderly. They decided to mortgage their house to finance private legal assistance for his brother. My client felt that this was not right; his brother had always looked after him, and my client thought that he should help his brother. Therefore, the reason for the crime was that my client wanted to save his parents the expense. I can't call evidence, because that may mean implicating another member of the family.

The case was set to come to court in September last year. Two nights before he was at the house of his surety. His surety and his wife told him how silly he was, chiding him for not being responsible about the way he was conducting his life. He got up and ran away.

He has been working as a car salesman and is in touch with his wife. Eight weeks ago he was arrested in the course of breaking and entering (sentenced to 3 months) and therefore currently is in prison.

Before Christmas Eve 1979, he worked for a clothing company for 6 to 8 months during the day and he also worked night shift (4 hours), that is, he held two jobs. Before this, for years, he was in and out of work (casual work, laboring mainly). At this stage, in 1979, he was getting along fairly well in the family environment and was out of trouble for some time. With the appearance of his brother, the structure that he'd built up started to decay and fall around him.

My client accepts that because of the nature of this crime and its professional nature, there is no alternative but to impose a term of imprisonment. He wants to serve his time and put it behind him.

He has a problem with his wife. Following his disappearance, his relationship was not particularly happy. She does visit him regularly in Pentridge and wants reconcilation but not if she would be subject to the type of pressures of the last year and a half. So she'll visit him, and she'll wait and see if he means to improve.

It's my submission that although your Honor is constrained to impose a term of imprisonment, impose the minimum.

His Honor: When is he due for release?

Defense Counsel: The accused is not sure. He thinks in the next 3 to 4 weeks.

His Honor: On the 19th of May he got 3 months. [Discussion between His Honor and the Defense Counsel about the prisoner's current sentences.] The best thing would be to sentence him now rather than await reports.

Defense Counsel: [Agrees, doesn't think reports would help.]

His Honor: (Judgment) I don't know how much to accept; the narrative simply explains why the crimes were committed. Most crimes are committed for reasons that seem to be sufficient to the person who commits the crime. This one involved a large amount of property, and if the prisoner didn't actually take the lot, then he probably facilitated someone else in taking the balance. It was also planned, and it also involved people who buy stolen property who might not otherwise deal with stolen property. Also, he has a record and it's therefore obvious that courts will treat such crimes quite seriously. You have pleaded guilty here, however, which shows tangible evidence of remorse. I'll take that into account.

In those circumstances and in view of your age: 18 months for the burglary and 6 months for the handling, concurrent with the first count, with a relatively low minimum of 9 months.

Coding the Case

Scoring of Offense Characteristics

Coding the case in relation to the offense characteristics in the classification scheme is demonstrated in Table 11.1. The table presents summary descriptions of the dimensions and their associated categories and the categories—one on each dimension—considered to match most closely the relevant facts of the offense. (Tables 6.1, 6.2, 6.4, 6.6, and 6.8 were consulted when coding these data.)

TABLE 11.1. The coding of offense characteristics

Dimension	Category		Code
Violence	Assault/injury/extensive wanton damage		
	Personal threat/some wanton damage/major damage associated with the search, etc.		
	Victim in building/minor wanton damage/significant damage or disturbance associated with the search, etc.		
	Victim absent/minor damage or disturbance associated with the search, etc.		1
Organization	Multiple counts of burglary on presentment		
	Two offenders		
	Three or more offenders		
	Breaking implements	X	
	Elaborate thwarting of security-protection		
	Observer		
	Elaborate thwarting of security-detection		
	Elaborate removal/disposal of goods		
	Night burglary	X	
	Connected count(s)		
	Previous surveillance		
	Elaborate selection of premises		
			1
Total value of the theft ($)	≥40,000		
	15,000–39,999		3
	2,000–14,999		
	<2,000		
Counts of burglary	>14		
	5–14		
	2–4		
	1		1

The principal count involved burglary of a clothing factory/showroom, and so this case was classified under commercial premises. The offense seriousness score for a case is the sum of 1 (violence), 1 (organization), 3 (value), and 1 (counts), and is therefore equal to 6. This score must be transformed so that offense seriousness is weighted properly. According to Table 10.1, the transformed score quantifying the offender's culpability associated with the offense characteristics is 9.

SCORING OF OFFENDER CHARACTERISTICS (EXCLUDING PRIOR CONVICTIONS)

The coding of the case in relation to the offender characteristics in the classificatory scheme is demonstrated in Table 11.2. The table presents summary descriptions of the categories and the categories considered to match most closely the relevant facts of the case (see Table 8.1).

The score representing the degree of exculpation associated with the offender characteristics (excluding prior convictions) is the sum of the codes on the salient offender characteristics and is therefore equal to −6.

TABLE 11.2. The coding of offender characteristics

Category	Code
Age 17–18	
Age 19–20	
Age 21–22	
Age 23–24	
Specific bravery/substantial community service	
Minor community service	
No prior convictions	
Excellent employment/study history	
Very good employment/study history	
Financial difficulties, severe	
Financial difficulties, moderate	
Alcohol/drug influence, severe	
Alcohol/drug influence, moderate	
Right to money/property, genuine and reasonable	
Right to money/property, genuine	
Coercion, extreme threats	
Coercion, no extreme threats	
Medical disorder, severe	
Medical disorder, moderate	
Underestimated value of merchandise	−2
Follower	
No violence in a violent offense	
Attempted to prevent violence	
Secondary role in offense	
Modified plans so offense less heinous	
Confessed before suspected by police	
Confessed to additional offenses during questioning	
Admitted all the offenses alleged by the police	−2
Pleaded guilty before the trial	
Assisted in arrest of co-offenders	
Assisted in recovery of money/goods stolen by co-offenders	
Repaid a substantial proportion of the proceeds	
Intention to repay proceeds	
Proceeds recovered on offender's initiative	
Proceeds recovered	
No subsequent convictions	
No subsequent convictions for dishonesty	
Subsequent substantial community service	
Subsequent minor community service	
Employed/student currently	
Employment/study rejected	
Sought treatment/treatment unnecessary	−1
Treatment rejected	
No criminal associations	−1
Associating with criminals	
Accommodation and stable relationship	
Accommodation/stable relationship rejected	
Obtained employment/enrolled in a study course since offense	
Sought treatment	
Severed criminal links	

TABLE 11.2. *Continued.*

Category	Code
Obtained accommodation or developed a stable relationship	
Significant personal suffering due to offense	
Severe neglect as a child	
Disturbances in early development	
Substantial period of institutionalization as a child	
Criminality of guardian	
Personal suffering aggravated by prison	
Family suffering aggravated by prison	
Debilitating effects of prison	
Breach of trust	

THE SCORING OF PRIOR CONVICTIONS

The coding of the case in relation to the offender's record of prior convictions according to the classificatory scheme is demonstrated in Table 11.3. The table presents summary descriptions of the dimensions and the associated categories and the categories considered to match most closely the relevant facts of the case (see Tables 8.3 and 8.12).

The score representing the degree of aggravation associated with the offender's prior convictions is determined according to the following steps:

1. Add the relevant codes relating to prior convictions for dishonesty (see Table 11.3): $5 + 4 + 4 + 3 + 3 = 19$
2. Multiply this total by 1.2: $19 \times 1.2 = 22.8$
3. Add this multiple to the sum of the relevant codes relating to prior convictions for the nondishonest offenses (see Table 11.3): $22.8 + 1 + 1 + 1 = 25.8$
4. Multiply this sum by 0.93: $25.8 \times 0.93 = 24$

This score must be transformed so that the prior convictions score is properly weighted; according to Table 9.1, the transformed score quantifying aggravation associated with the offender's prior convictions is 15.

SCORING OF TOTAL MITIGATION

The score quantifying the extent of the offender's total mitigation is calculated by adding the score for the offender characteristics excluding prior convictions (-6) and the transformed score for prior convictions ($+15$). Accordingly, the offender's total mitigation score is $+9$. (See Scoring of Offender Characteristics and Scoring of Prior Convictions, preceding.) However, because offender characteristics may not aggravate culpability, the total mitigation score was adjusted to 0.

TABLE 11.3. The coding of prior convictions

Counts: dishonesty	Appearances: dishonesty	Time since last count: dishonesty (months)	Average time between appearances: dishonesty (months)	Sum of custodial sentences: dishonesty (months)	Appearances: nondishonesty	Counts: nondishonesty	Sum of custodial sentences: nondishonesty (months)
1–3	1	≥49	≥37	≤12	1 1	1–2 1	≤6 1
4–8	2–3	25–48	19–36	13–24	2	3–4	7–12
9–16	4–6	13–24	13–18 3	25–48 3	3	5–7	13–24
17–30	7–10 4	7–12 4	7–12	49–84	4–5	8–10	25–48
≥31 5	≥11	≤6	≤6	≥85	≥6	≥11	≥49

TABLE 11.4. Criteria defining the preconditions for interaction/individualized measures

Factor	Criteria	Assessment (yes/no)
Favorable rehabilitation prospects	Guilty plea	Yes
	No subsequent offenses	No
	Money/property recovered or proceeds disposed of	Yes
	No salient criminogenic factors	No
Category of offender	Youth	No
	First offense of dishonesty	No
	Gap since previous dishonesty	No
	Exculpatory reason	No

CALCULATION OF THE OFFENDER'S CASE SCORE

The score quantifying the offender's culpability for this case is calculated by adding the transformed score for the offense characteristics (+9) and the score for total mitigation (0); accordingly, the offender's case score is equal to +9. (See Scoring of Offense Characteristics and Scoring of Total Mitigation, preceding.)

ADJUSTMENT OF THE CASE SCORE

Interaction

There is an interaction effect if the offender falls within one of the special categories of offender *and* has favorable rehabilitation prospects. The assessment of the case in relation to the criteria defining these conditions is demonstrated in Table 11.4. The table presents summary descriptions of the criteria and the assessment of the case in terms of these criteria (see Tables 10.2 and 10.3).

The offender satisfied only two of the criteria defining favorable rehabilitation prospects and did not fall in one of the special categories of offender. Consequently, the offender's mitigation did not qualify for an interaction effect and so his mitigation score was not reduced by 4 points.

Withdrawal of Mitigation

No allowance is made for mitigating factors where the case can be described as professional. The assessment of the case in relation to the criteria defining "professional" is demonstrated in Table 11.5. The table presents summary descriptions of the criteria and the assessment of the case in terms of these criteria (see Table 10.4).

The case did not satisfy any of the criteria defining professional. In any case the offender had no net mitigation (see Scoring of Total Mitigation, preceding).

ADJUSTED CASE SCORE

The case did not satisfy the criteria for interaction or for the withdrawal of mitigation. Consequently, the adjusted case score is the same as the case score of 9

TABLE 11.5. Criteria for the withholding of mitigation

Criteria	Assessment (yes/no)
Value of theft $40,000 or more (see Table 11.1)	No
At least 11 previous appearances involving counts of dishonesty (see Table 11.3)	No
OR	
Offense characterized by at least 7 of the criteria defining organization (see Table 11.1)	No

(see Calculation of the Offender's Case Score, preceding), and this score of 9 is the index of the offender's culpability.

Sentence

TARIFF SENTENCE

Figure 11.1 shows that for an adjusted case score of 9, the notional effective sentence is 1 year and 3 months.

APPROPRIATENESS OF AN INDIVIDUALIZED MEASURE

An individualized measure is preferred for offenders who fall within one of the special categories of offender *and* who have favorable rehabilitation prospects (see Table 11.4). An inspection of Table 11.4 shows that the offender satisfied only two of the four criteria required for favorable rehabilitation prospects and did not fall in one of the special categories of offender. Consequently, an individualized measure could not be considered appropriate.

The sentencer's final task is to consider whether there are any material case factors for which the classificatory or scoring system does not make adequate or proper allowance. Where there are unique case factors, the judge may allow for the effects of these factors in relation to the common factors and adjust the notional tariff sentence accordingly.

Detailed Sentencing Statistics: Problems and Prospects

There are two features of the present approach to the development of detailed sentencing statistics, which set it apart to advantage from the approaches of Hogarth (1968a, 1986b), Wilkins and his associates (1978) and Doob (Doob, 1986; Doob & Park, 1987) to the description of current sentencing practice. The characteristic that gives the model its special value is not that the salient elements of the sentencing decision are identified, defined, and weighted (although this feature sets it apart from curial intuition) but that these elements are interrelated quantitatively according to an aggregation rule. Consequently, the model can be used to grade an offender's culpability on a dimension for any combination of the offense and offender characteristics covered in the classificatory system and then to relate this grade to the appropriate quantum of sentence. The second critical characteristic is that the rules for combining case data in the course of determining an appropriate sentence are based on a model of decision making that is faithful to the structure of judicial thought. Accordingly, the model has the potential to provide not only an accurate and comprehensive account of the determination of sentence but also an account comprehensible to judges, thereby permitting them to use the statistics as a standard against which they can exercise discretion as justice requires in particular cases.

Nevertheless, problematic matters are associated with the present strategy; some of these are shared, but generally to a lesser degree, with the previously mentioned approaches.

First, these detailed sentencing statistics comprise averages taken directly from past sentencing practices and so require the assumption that an established sentencing policy exists and that judges follow this policy with a high degree of consistency. The evidence, however, does not favor this view; under such circumstances the use of averages to quantify sentencing policy is problematic.

Second, the test of the validity of the model is not rigorous, because it too requires this assumption. Indeed, the reason for proceeding with the development of sentencing guidance is that analysis and evidence firmly indicate that there is not a comprehensive and well-established sentencing policy and that existing policies are applied by judges somewhat inconsistently. It is therefore pointless to compare the validity of my model of judicial decision making with that of Wilkins et al. (1978) regarding the degree of fit between case seriousness, as it is construed according to each of these models, and sentence. Even if it were true that judges draw on and take account of only relatively few case factors in the determination of sentence and, accordingly, the Wilkins et al. model fitted the data as closely, his model would not be as valid in the context of this project, since legal analyses clearly reveal that such a simple model would misrepresent sentencing policy and, therefore, would not provide a sound basis for the development of guidance in sentencing.

Third, as an appellate court enunciated new policies their effects on the determination of sentence could not be incorporated readily in the statistics. With a data base of past sentencing practices, there would be a lag until a significant number of cases had been sentenced by judges cognizant of the new rulings.

Fourth, for most legal offense categories, the higher courts in Australia determine only a relatively small number of cases in a year; and so if these offense categories were differentiated in regard to the dimension of seriousness, then the spread of cases would be thin indeed. In terms of Figure 11.1, many of the seriousness levels would be empty and most of the remaining levels would have only small numbers of cases. Accordingly, if the statistics were based on past sentencing practices, then it would be impossible for most of the legal offense categories to present reliable estimates of the quanta of sentence for many of the combinations of the case characteristics associated with these offense categories. (It must be remembered that burglary is one of the more numerous offenses determined in the higher courts in Victoria.)

Finally, the guidance provided by this model of judicial decision making would incorporate the hidden effects of both material and immaterial case factors not included in the guidelines, as well as distortions associated with the limitations of human information processing. The operation of these factors leads one to question the validity of the reasons underlying Walker's (1985) proposal that detailed sentencing statistics should not simply comprise indicators of the average or typical sentences for the various combinations of case characteristics but rather should provide comprehensive data on the distributions of sentences regarding type and quantum for the divisions within the statistics. Now, although statistics in this form would encourage judges to individualize sentences further (the point of Walker's proposal), such sentencing statistics would not offer sound guidance for this exercise of discretion, because a not insignificant component of some of the distributions would represent the hidden effects of the previously mentioned factors. In any case, where the statistics were finely differentiated in terms of case characteristics, there would be insufficient numbers of cases in most of the divisions for providing a reliable indication of the possible distributions of sentence.

The consequences of the first, fourth and fifth problems would be somewhat lessened in the present statistics, because the various seriousness levels are logically interrelated and, consequently, the notional tariff sentences for the various levels of seriousness are not based solely on the sentences for the cases falling at those levels; rather, they are taken from a line of best fit.

On the basis of the preceding logical and empirical analyses, it is suggested that the feasibility of detailed sentencing statistics has been supported to the extent that the salient issues have been examined in this study. One necessary next step is that these analyses must be repeated for other legal offense categories; this has been done already for offense characteristics of armed robbery, and the results were found to support the validity of the present strategy (Lovegrove, 1983). Second, before this feasibility study of detailed sentencing statistics for burglary can proceed, an appropriate judicial body must determine as a matter of law whether the model of judicial decision making developed in this study is valid. In moving along the path toward a uniform approach to sentencing, legal analyses and the techniques of behavioral science are interdependent.

The third, and final, part of this work describes a study in which judges assessed the validity of that part of the model covering the determination of sentence in regard to the offense characteristics of burglary. After this study has been presented, it will be possible to give detail to the previously introduced notion of numerical guidelines and to consider solutions to these five problems besetting the current approach to the development of detailed sentencing statistics.

Part Three Sentencing Policy and Numerical Guidance as a Deliberative Process

12
Judicial Input Into the Model of Sentencing

In the early stages of this study, the argument was made that to develop detailed sentencing statistics it would be necessary to develop a model of judicial decision making for the purpose of construing the relationship between case facts and sentence. The preceding analyses in the archival burglary study were based on a model of judicial decision making that I developed. To construct this, I was forced to intuit the definitions, weights, and aggregation rules that judges apply to case factors as they determine the sentence for a case. I accomplished this principally by attempting to capture the general trends in sentencing policy found through reading sentencing judgments in the courts of first instance and the appellate courts, as well as systematic academic analyses of these judgments. When one attempts to use legal analyses to quantify decision making, one really comes to appreciate how vague they are in relation to quantitative standards. Indeed, they are characteristically imprecise or silent about the definition of material case factors, as well as their weights and the rules for combining them (see Ashworth, 1983a, 1984). For example, consider the matter of weighting the four offense characteristics in the burglary study. The only guidance that could be discerned from the appellate court judgments was that extreme forms of each of these offense characteristics have been mentioned where the courts have stressed the gravity of particular cases. Consequently, there seemed to be no grounds for discriminating between the potential importance of these four factors, and accordingly they were weighted equally. This line of reasoning is admittedly tenuous (see Chapter 4).

In the context of this study there are two immediate problems. First, some of my decisions may have been seriously in error in that the interpretation of sentencing policy may have been incorrect. Second, a quantitative analysis is so specific that it raises matters for which there is no explicit corporate judicial policy although, of course, individual judges in determining sentence in a particular case must form at least implicit views on matters such as the scaling of the seriousness of the value of the goods stolen; of course, it is another matter whether or not these policies are applied consistently by particular judges or, indeed, across the bench. Simply, of real concern is the fact that in the first stage of this study I was, in effect, not only interpreting current sentencing policy but also developing it. Clearly, these decisions are ultimately the exclusive province of the judiciary. Before the system could become operational, to preserve judicial independence (see Ashworth, 1983b), it would be necessary for an appropriate body of judges to check and, where necessary, modify my application of current sentencing policy and to determine as a matter of law those other matters that have risen through the precision of the quantitative analysis. As already explained, what is required is a model of the principles and rules judges attempt to follow as they determine sentence in accordance with sentencing policy, that is, a model of their more or less conscious thought processes, free from the distortions that may arise from information overload, personal prejudice, and the like. After the model had been modified to include judicial input, the seriousness of the cases in the data base would then be construed according to this revised model of judicial decision making and re-related to quanta of sentence. The detailed statistics that would be used by the courts would be based on this revised model. Of course, whether the effects of such changes could be detected empirically would depend on the magnitude of these modifications and the extent to which judges accurately and reliably give effect to sentencing policy.

The purpose of the following series of exercises is to develop a basis for judicial input into the model of decision making. Because this was a feasibility study, it was confined to the offense factors of one offense. Furthermore, the analyses were restricted to the scaling of seriousness as a basis for a tariff sentence, that is, a sentence proportional to the seriousness of the case. The previously developed model of judicial decision making for determining the seriousness of offenses of burglary (see Chapter 4) and the subsequent empirical analyses, in which this model was used to represent the relationship between actual cases of burglary and sentence, acted as the framework and reference for these current analyses (see Part Two). Specifically, the model incorporated the identification and the operational definitions (the description and scaling) of the material offense factors, as well as their weights and the aggregation rules, together with the quanta of sentence considered appropriate for the levels of seriousness of the various combinations of offense characteristics. It was on these matters that judicial input was sought.

The four offense factors identified in the archival burglary study formed the basis of the present analysis. The factors are total value of the theft, counts of burglary, violence to the victims, and organization. There is a quite extensive appellate and scholarly literature covering the identification of the major material offense factors and including, but to a lesser degree, descriptions of the contents of these factors; and it is a literature not marked by significant contention. Consequently, our understanding of these matters may be regarded as comparatively satisfactory. Judicial views on this aspect of policy therefore were not canvassed systematically. Points potentially at issue include whether other factors should be added to the list (it is unnecessary to explore whether any of the factors should be removed, because this is covered by the assessment of factor weights); whether the contents of the factors of violence to the victims and organization should be modified (the contents of counts of burglary and total value of the theft are obvious); and whether the factor set should be restructured, for example, substituting a factor covering the average value of the theft per count for total value of the theft. Although judicial views were not explored systematically, the judges were asked whether these four offense factors may be reasonably regarded as material and comprehensive and whether they felt, on these grounds, uncomfortable in assessing the seriousness of the offense of burglary in terms of them. It is fortunate that at this stage of the development of the model, one could proceed satisfactorily, despite the superficiality of this part of the analysis, because formal strategies for eliciting this sort of information are as yet not well developed; the danger is that the decision maker is under pressure to adopt for the purposes of the study what may be to him or her an invalid structure or perspective for the decision (see Slovic et al., 1977). (For an introduction to this topic in the decision-making literature see, e.g., Aschenbrenner, 1977; Beach, Townes, Campbell, & Keating, 1976; Einhorn, Kleinmuntz, & Kleinmuntz, 1979; Gardiner & Edwards, 1975; McKnight, 1981; Nisbett & Wilson, 1977; Payne, Braunstein, & Carroll, 1978; Pitz, Sachs, & Heerboth, 1980; Smith & Miller, 1978.) Nevertheless, it is recognized that this aspect of the model of judicial decision making requires more systematic attention.

Our real ignorance about judicial sentencing policy concerns the scaling of seriousness in regard to the individual case factors, the case factor weights, the rules for combining this information, and the relationship between the overall seriousness of the case and the appropriate quantum of sentence. Fortunately, there are formal and well-established methods for eliciting and handling this information. Actually, there are two diametrically opposed approaches to scaling—the decomposed and the holistic scaling procedures. Both strategies were considered for the present problem, although only the former was used here. I shall briefly describe each approach in turn, and then compare and contrast them in terms of their applicability in the context of this study.

Before this excursion into the area of scaling, a comment on a matter relating to the analysis of individual judges' responses to the information sought is in order. A degree of inconsistency is expected between judges in their responses made in terms of the elements of the sentencing model. One would be surprised if it were otherwise in view of the evidence in the literature for sentencing disparity (see, e.g., Diamond, 1981; Forst, 1982; Kapardis, 1985; Lovegrove, 1984a; Palys & Divorski, 1984), the fact of dissenting judgments delivered in the appellate courts and, indeed, judicial recognition of the need for greater uniformity in sentencing policy (see the already-quoted judgment of the Lord Chief Justice of England, Lord Lane, in *Bibi*, 1980 [p. 21]). Now, inconsistent responses between judges on matters such as the scaling and weighting of case factors would have to be averaged before these data could be fed into the model. The use of averages here, however, should be distinguished from Wilkins and associates' (1978), Hogarth's (1986a, 1986b) and Doob's (Doob, 1986; Doob & Park, 1987) reliance on averages of the sentences falling within a category or cell as a basis for guidelines. My objection there, voiced in Chapter 2, is that the average of a set of sentences is meaningless where the judges may have reached the decision on the basis of different case factors, different weights, different goals of sentence, and so on, and that the individual effects of the disparate assessments cannot be differentiated where an average is taken. Here, however, the averages are for judgments concerning elements of the sentencing decision, for example, the scaling of seriousness for a case factor, where there is a particular aim of sentence in mind. This is a legitimate procedure that would provide interpretable estimates, providing the responses of the judges are not too disparate. If the responses were seriously disparate, then the source of the differences would have to be identified and resolved before the data could be used as a basis for detailed sentencing statistics.

Decomposed Scaling Procedures

Decomposed scaling represents an orientation to the analysis of decisions and is tied to a body of research known as multiattribute utility measurement (MAUM)—see, for example, Bunn, 1984; Edwards, 1977; Edwards & Newman, 1982; Fischer, 1976, 1977; Humphreys, 1977; Keeney, 1977; Keeney & Raiffa, 1976; Phillips, 1979; Stillwell, Barron, & Edwards, 1983. MAUM is both an approach to the study of how individuals make decisions as well as a set of techniques for analyzing and investigating decision making. Moreover, it is offered to decision makers to assist them in making assessments in the face of complexity—a decision is said to be complex where the objects of the assessment are characterized by a common set of conflicting attributes that require trade-offs. Determining a sentence so that it is proportional to the seriousness of the case is a complex decision. Here the judge must assess seriousness in terms of multiple case factors, where one factor may be both aggravating and extenuating relative to other factors in a case or to the same factors in other cases.

In using MAUM to understand how individuals make assessments, the researcher divides the decision task into its elements and then investigates the decision makers' intuitive assessments on these associated subtasks. MAUM identifies the constituent elements of these decisions, offers various models specifying possible ways in which the elements may be combined to form an overall assessment, and lays down the axiomatic basis of the models. To apply a model the researcher must investigate whether the individual's assessments are consistent with the model's underlying assumptions, or proceed on an article of faith that the assumptions are reasonable. However, even where an individual's assessments are consistent with the model's assumptions, it does not necessarily follow that an individual's overall intuitive assessments will be consistent with the assessments derived from the combination of the individual's responses to the subtasks.

How does MAUM characterize decision making and how does it apply in the present context? First, there is the decision. Here it is the assessment of the seriousness of offenses of burglary. (It should be noted that MAUM procedures cannot be applied directly to the study of sentencing, because determining an appropriate sentence for an element of a case is meaningless. Moreover, not all cases for which noncustodial sentences are imposed are equally serious.) Second, there are the criteria (offense attributes) on which the overall seriousness of the offense characteristics of a case is to be based. The offense characteristics identified in the archival burglary study were violence to the victims, organization, counts of burglary, and total value of the theft. Third, it is necessary to develop a seriousness scale for each attribute to show how seriousness varies with changes in the objective values (e.g., the number of counts) along each attribute. At this point an offense of burglary is represented by four assessments of seriousness—one for each attribute. Fourth, there is the determination of the relative importance (weight) of each of the attributes in the overall assessment. Finally, MAUM offers a number of formal models specifying how the single-attribute seriousness assessments may be combined, taking account of the weights, to provide an overall assessment of the seriousness of the offense characteristics of the case. It will be immediately obvious that MAUM's characterization of the structure of a decision is isomorphic with my legal model of the judicial determination of offense seriousness for a tariff sentence. Accordingly, it is appropriate to apply MAUM to the present problem.

In addition to offering an approach to the understanding of decision making, MAUM also provides a host of techniques for eliciting responses from the decision maker as a basis for developing the single-attribute seriousness scales and setting weights for these attributes. These techniques range from the complex and theoretically elegant indirect methods such as those of Keeney (1977) and Keeney and Raiffa (1976) to the simpler yet theoretically less sound direct methods of Edwards's Simple Multiattribute Rating Technique (SMART) (Edwards, 1977; Edwards & Newman, 1982; Stillwell et al., 1983). It is said that one may pay a high price for the theoretical soundness of the former, because they require complex preference and indifference judgments about hypothetical instances, and the consequence may be judgments of unacceptably low reliability and validity; where decision makers are not experienced in making the particular judgments or have not thought about the issues, they may fall back on unstable and artificial reference points and have little defense against biases associated with the elicitation techniques (Edwards, 1977). One must remember, however, that in this study the subjects (judges) are experienced in fixing quanta of sentence regarding the seriousness of cases.

In summary in the decomposed scaling procedures, the way that individuals make decisions is investigated by dividing a decision into its component parts and eliciting judgments in relation to the components. MAUM provides guidance on how the decision should be separated into its constituent elements and the judgments elicited.

There are two aspects to the understanding of decision making through MAUM. First, decision theory may be regarded as a model describing how people actually make particular assessments. The issue of validity here turns on whether an individual's overall assessments are consistent with the axioms and predicted judgments of a well-specified and internally consistent algebraic model that, on logical or psychological grounds, can be regarded as a plausible model of decision making. If this consistency is found, then a common view is that it is reasonable to assume that these judgments provide a valid indicator of the individual's real preferences. The underlying idea is that a valid scaling of preferences is possible only if a valid preference model has been specified (Fischer, 1977). This first aspect is decision theory as description. But decision theory may be applied with a prescriptive orientation. It may be applied to specify the evaluations people should make about complex phenomena according to their assessments of the (simpler) components of these phenomena so that their overall judgments are internally consistent (see Phillips, 1979). To apply decision analysis in the second sense, one must be able to specify the structure of the model on a priori grounds. Fortunately, this approach is possible here, because I have already developed such a model on the basis of legal analyses of appellate sentencing judgments—judgments laying down the correct curial approach to sentencing. This application of decision analysis would seem to be appropriate only where, as is the case here, the focus of the understanding is the thought processes judges attempt to follow as they apply sentencing policy, that is, thought processes free from the distortions that may arise from influences such as information overload and prejudice. This approach does nevertheless require the assumption that the decision makers' assessments on the subtasks validly indicate their true preferences.

These two aspects to the understanding of decision making through MAUM should not be seen as diametrically opposed. Rather, they represent differences in emphasis and orientation, not in kind. Nevertheless, the prescriptive orientation is an apparently more powerful and satisfactory application of decision analysis—its strength stemming from the a priori specification of a decision model. For this independent input would appear to free it from the circularity and potential logical inconsistency inherent in the (internal) validation procedure of a decision model in its descriptive role. Birnbaum (1982) has raised the problem of circularity; to determine whether a scale is valid, it is necessary to assume that the model is valid, but the validation of the underlying model requires the assumption of scale validity. The problem of circularity bears on the test of validity concerning whether an individual's overall assessments are consistent with the assumptions underlying the model. Then there is the problem of a potential logical inconsistency in the (external) validation strategy; this is concerned with assessing validity in terms of the relationship between an individual's overall assessments and the model's predictions. The raison d'être for decision analysis rests on two propositions. First, holistic assessments of complex (multiattribute) phenomena are not valid indicators of an individual's true preferences because information overload is responsible for errors of judgment. Second, the cognitive errors arising from overload can be averted by dividing a decision into its component parts and basing the overall assessment on an individual's assessments made in relation to these apparently simple (single-attribute) elements. To validate the use of a decomposition model, however, the researcher also must demonstrate that an individual's overall assessments are consistent with the model's predictions. Now, if the two are concordant, then one may conclude with some confidence that one has some understanding of that aspect of the individual's decision making and, consequently, in the future validly use decision analysis, without holistic judgments, in similar situations. The dilemma arises, of course, where the holistic and predicted assessments are disparate. Should one dismiss the validity of the criterion holistic judgments on the grounds of assumed cognitive error and hold to the model? Such a course would require an act of faith and provoke queries over the relevance of the validation study. However, if one were to dismiss the model on the basis of such results, then what is to be gained from decision analysis? (Pitz, Heerboth, & Sachs, 1980.) Decomposition procedures are employed to overcome possible cognitive errors induced by information overload not to predict them. Indeed, a high correlation between the decomposed and holistic assessments should perhaps lead one to question the validity of the decomposed strategy (Slovic et al., 1977; Stillwell et al., 1983). The problem raised here becomes increasingly significant as the number of attributes and, consequently, the complexity of the decision increases. A second problem here is that MAUM does not have an error theory. Accordingly, there is no standard against which a model can be rejected (Fischer, 1976; Fischhoff, 1983). Similar difficulties would arise where holistic judgments were used as a basis for comparing two decision models. Hence, the arrival at the earlier conclusion – it was fortunate that a prescriptive orientation could be adopted in this study.

Holistic Scaling Procedures

The fundamental feature of holistic scaling procedures, and one distinguishing them from decomposed scaling procedures, is that here the understanding of how individuals assess complex (multiattribute) phenomena is derived directly from their holistic assessments of these phenomena, rather than from assessments of the components (attributes) of the complex phenomena. In applying this approach to, say, the assessment of the seriousness of criminal cases, the decision maker would be required to assess seriousness for a set of cases that had been systematically varied in terms of characteristics germane to the evaluation of seriousness (number of counts, and so on). The output of the analysis may comprise subjective scale values (the scaling of seriousness for the objective values on each of the attributes) and a weight for each of the attributes. The scaling of these responses is made in terms of a model specifying the elements of the decision and how these elements are combined to form an overall evaluation. For this scaling procedure to be considered valid, however, it must be first demonstrated that the decision maker's holistic assessments are consistent with the axiomatic basis of the model. Again, there is a problem of circularity here (Brinbaum, 1982). The analysis therefore would seem to be on surer ground where the model's structure can be proposed on a priori grounds. Clearly, holistic scaling procedures are descriptively oriented, because the analysis is based on holistic judgments requiring simultaneous consideration of cross-currents of aggravating and extenuating factors as in real-life decisions. Nevertheless, the holistic approach offers information on a decision maker's use of scales and weights—the information sought in this study—and so it was considered here.

Two theoretically elegant holistic scaling procedures provide estimates of the decision maker's weights and subjective scale values: (1) conjoint analysis (see Green & Srinivasan, 1978, for a discussion of the application of conjoint analysis) and (2) Anderson's (1981) theory of functional measurement. These two approaches bear some conceptual and methodological similarities (e.g., see the exchange between Schönemann, Cafferty, & Rotton, 1973, and Anderson, 1973) and the preceding introductory comments are applicable to both. There are other holistic approaches, although they are not suitable for the present problem: the direct analysis of judgments by analysis of variance (Slovic, Fleissner, & Bauman, 1972) or the related technique of multiple regression (Hammond, Stewart, Brehmer, & Steinmann, 1975) do not provide subjective scale values, and the aggregation rule is based on the objective values (Slovic & Lichtenstein, 1971). Accordingly, these techniques do not lend themselves to the understanding of decision making in the context of the present study. With multiple regression one must distinguish between analyses based on real-life correlated data and those based on orthogonal fictitious data. Problems associated with the former were discussed in Chapter 2 in relation to Wilkins and his associates' (1978) development of descriptive guidelines, and the latter provides similar results to an analysis of variance (Phelps & Shanteau, 1978).

Relative Merits of the Decomposed and Holistic Scaling Procedures

Initially, this discussion turns to consider the advantages of decomposed scaling procedures. In the introduction to this series of studies concerning judicial input into the model of sentencing, the point was made that there is no explicit corporate judicial policy and there is perhaps lack of implicit agreement between judges, on many aspects of the sentencing decision. This leads to the first point. Clearly, the decomposed procedures lend themselves to the identification of these areas of indecision and inconsistency; moreover, they provide techniques that would assist decision makers in resolving these issues. Although holistic procedures are not bereft of value here, their potential contribution is not as great. If the holistic analyses were applied separately to individual decision makers, then the researcher would identify inconsistency, although not indecision, in the decision makers' assessments regarding particular elements. The source of any inconsistency would not be clear, however. Was it due to real differences in preferences, apparent differences that were an artifact of cognitive overload, or the absence of a considered view (indecision)? Finally, there are no procedures for developing policy and resolving differences between the decision makers.

A further point, made in the introduction to this stage of the project, related to the nature of the decision model being developed. What is required is a model of the sentencing policies and decision rules that judges attempt to follow as they determine sentence in accordance with sentencing policy, that is, a model of their thought processes free from the distortions that may be induced by information overload and prejudice. Clearly, this is a prescriptive problem and does not fit in with the descriptive orientation of the holistic approaches, where the analysis is of judgments made, as in real life, under cognitive complexity, a condition conducive to distortions in judgment caused by information overload. Rather, it is compatible with the prescriptive aspect of MAUM–what one should decide on an issue based on one's views regarding the elements of the decision so that one is coherent. This sentiment appears to tie in with Green and Srinivasan's (1978) conclusion that users of conjoint analysis generally have emphasized predictive validity and regarded explanation largely as a secondary objective.

These points in favor of the decomposed procedure relate to the reason for attempting to develop detailed sentencing statistics for the guidance of judges: to minimize sentencing disparity caused by (1) variation between judges in specific aspects of sentencing policy and (2) cognitive overload arising from the complexity of the factual basis of criminal cases. Clearly, the decomposed strategy addresses these very problems. The decision makers' policies are identified regarding the elements of the decision, and the judgments relevant to a decision are elicited in the absence of cognitive overload. Concerning this second point, however, it is important to stress that the holistic judgments required for this present task would be much simpler cognitively than sentencing judgments for actual cases. The present task is limited to offense characteristics of burglary and comprises cases varying on only four offense factors; whereas burglary cases determined in the courts comprise these four offense factors together with, on average, another nine offender factors, and the multifaceted factor of prior convictions (see Part Two, particularly Chapter 8).

Reviews of research on the effects of the number of dimensions on decision making have been made by Payne (1982), Slovic et al. (1977), and Slovic and Lichtenstein (1971). Examples of specific studies are Cook and Stewart (1975), Einhorn (1971), Olshavsky (1979), and Phelps and Shanteau (1978). Now, in addition to the inevitable doubts hanging over the internal validity of any study, the external validity of this research has been questioned (Einhorn & Hogarth, 1981; Levin, Louviere, Schepanski, & Norman, 1983; Slovic et al., 1977), and accordingly, the results of this research should be applied cautiously; the potential limitations arise from factors associated with subject and task characteristics. One cannot determine on the basis of this literature the degree of cognitive load above which decision making becomes suboptimal and characterized by noisy and otherwise poorly executed compensatory judgments or inappropriate noncompensatory strategies. All one can say is that probably few would disagree with the view that 13 plus factors (the minimum number of factors typically found in a case of burglary) clearly would exceed the cognitive limits of adults whereas 4 factors (the number of common factors describing an offense of burglary) generally would be regarded as within the range of human capability, although perhaps around the upper limit (see, e.g., Barron & Person, 1979; Fischer, 1977; Green & Srinivasan, 1978; Phelps & Shanteau, 1978). This capacity definitely should be within the limits of well-motivated professionals, such as the judges in this study, who realized that their responses might act as a basis for detailed sentencing statistics in the courts. Accordingly, then, on this score the holistic approach would seem valid for the analysis of the four offense factors of burglary; but it would not be appropriate for an analysis of mitigating case factors or criminal history.

There are three potential disadvantages of decomposed scaling procedures and attention has already been drawn to them. The first concerns the question of the reliability and validity of the decision makers' judgments made in relation to the constituent elements, especially where the subjects have not considered the issues or are not experienced in making the assessments in the particular form in which they are presented. Although this matter must remain somewhat problematic, one must remember that judges are experienced in these matters. In reaching decisions about sentence they speak freely about the seriousness of particular case factors and about the relative weights of various aspects of cases. Accordingly, judges would be expected to be cognitively comfortable with these tasks, and the underlying decision structure could not be reasonably described as artificial. Nevertheless, it behooves the researcher to ask the judges after they have completed the required judgments whether they experienced any difficulties in making these assessments, and if they responded affirmatively, how they thought this might have affected their judgments. Furthermore, indecisiveness exhibited by the decision makers in making their responses may provide powerful clues about possible problematic responses. Humphreys (1983) and Fischhoff, Slovic, and Lichtenstein (1980) have cast doubts on the usefulness of decomposed procedures where the decision makers do not have clear views on the issues, although these authors do not require the views to be consciously available to the subjects. The concern is that the elicitation process may shape the views of uncertain decision makers, induce noisy responses, and leave the decision makers at the mercy of perceptual biases. This position seems uncritically harsh, because these procedures facilitate the identification of uncertain areas and provide a means of resolving the matters at issue (Edwards, 1977; Keeney, 1977). Of course, this rebuttal is not intended to apply to other than professional decision makers who are responding in terms of a decision structure that has a prescriptive basis or has been otherwise independently validated. Regarding the validity of decomposed judgments, Slovic et al. (1977) have raised a potential advantage of the holistic approach. Individuals, especially experienced professionals, may be able to express holistic preferences more reliably and validly than they can make assessments relating to the component parts. This is a point of no minor importance here, because the decision makers in this study are judges experienced in the criminal jurisdiction. All one can say in defense is to reiterate an earlier point: judges in their deliberations and judgments refer not infrequently to the seriousness and appropriate weights of case factors in the course of determining sentences.

A second potential disadvantage of decomposed scaling procedures is that they should be validated against holistic judgments. This matter was canvassed at length earlier in this discussion. It is the conclusion that is important and bears restating: holistic validation is not necessary where decision analysis is used prescriptively in relation to a model that can be specified on a priori grounds. Such is the case here.

The final point is no more than an apparent disadvantage of the decomposed procedures. They cannot be used to study sentencing directly, because sentences are not imposed for parts of cases; and cases in which noncustodial sentences are imposed may nevertheless vary in seriousness. Accordingly, to proceed with the analysis it was necessary to introduce an intervening concept such as offense/case seriousness or offender culpability. Now, it will be recalled (see Chapters 1 and 4) that these concepts are central to the decision whether to impose a tariff or a rehabilitative sentence and, in the former circumstance, the quantum of sentence is made proportional to seriousness. Clearly, then, to understand the sentencing decision and to build a model faithful to the structure of judicial thought, the construct of seriousness (or some similar construct) must be used.

At this point no grounds have been offered for not incorporating both the decomposed and holistic approaches in the study so that the results could be compared. Concordant sets of scale and weight estimates could be taken to bolster one's confidence in the data. In addition disparate results could be used constructively. They would point to responses for which there should be some doubt whether they represented the decision makers' true preferences or were artifacts of the technique.

One objection to a holistic analysis is that the simultaneous consideration of multiple factors requiring compensatory judgments may exceed a person's cognitive capacity. This matter is not a significant problem here, however; it was argued earlier that a four-factor set would not be expected to exceed the capabilities of well-motivated judges. A second problem concerns the number of holistic judgments required of the subjects. It would be necessary to construct 64 cases for a fractional, four-factor four-level model, incorporating the main effects and two-way interactions. Again, such a large number of cases would not necessarily be an insurmountable problem for well-motivated subjects, although clearly it detracts from the technique's appeal where the subjects are busy professionals. The third problem is the damning one. It arises from the requirement of the analysis that the structure of the factor levels (the objective values on each of the factors) must be balanced across the factor set—the factors must be orthogonal. The likely undesirable effect of this is that some of the cases would comprise implausible combinations of factor levels, for example, a large number of counts, extensive organization but little or no money stolen in the burglaries. Where this occurred, one would expect the subjects, especially if they were professionals, to experience difficulty in assessing these particular cases. One effect of this might be reflected in the reliability and validity of their assessments for these cases. Another effect might be a general disillusionment with the task and a consequent lowering of the subjects' motivation. To check whether this would be a problem for the present study, the offense pattern of each of the 64 cases was examined. This revealed that just under 25% of the combinations would seem to be reasonably regarded as implausible. (Whether a particular combination is implausible is, to some extent, a subjective judgment and depends on the rigor of one's definition. The estimate therefore must be treated as approximate.) In my view, the percentage of implausible cases was too high for the holistic scaling procedure to be regarded as a viable means of estimating the decision makers' scale values and weights. Furthermore, the strategies proposed by Green and Srinivasan (1978) (see also, Barron & Person, 1979) for circumventing or minimizing the effects of this problem did not appear to be helpful here. Consequently, a holistic analysis was not pursued further.

Overview of the Analysis

This study, concerning judicial input into the model of sentencing for the scaling and weighting of offense factors in relation to seriousness and the relationship between seriousness and sentence for cases of burglary, comprised the following components. These matters are dealt with in detail subsequently in separate chapters.

Validity of the Technique of Fictitious Cases

In the exercises that were developed to elicit the judges' responses as input for the model of decision making, the judges were asked to make each decision as though it was part of a determination as to what is appropriate by way of sentence for an actual case being heard in court. This prompted a consideration of the external validity of their responses. To check this, a study was conducted in which the details of a number of cases already determined in the courts were presented to the judges and their task was to impose a sentence for each of these cases; these sentences then were compared with the actual sentences that had been imposed in the courts.

Multiattribute Utility Measurement Analysis

Standard MAUM procedures were used to ascertain how judges scale seriousness for the four offense factors of burglary and how they weight these factors.

Coherence and the Tariff

To be regarded as valid a judge's determination of the appropriate quantum of sentence for a particular combination of offense characteristics requires the assumption that this relationship is based in the mind of the judge on a reasonably stable, logical, and internally consistent set of rules and quantities that are applied reliably. This was tested for a set of fictitious cases by examining for each judge the relationships between (1) holistic assessments of overall offense seriousness, (2) calculated overall offense seriousness derived from the assessments of the scale values and weights for each of the component offense factors, and (3) quanta of sentence determined to be proportional to the seriousness of the offenses. (The distinction between the notion of coherence involving the relationship between seriousness assessed holistically and seriousness derived from decomposed judgments and Fischer's, 1977, use of convergent validity, referred to previously, is discussed in the chapter dealing with coherence—Chapter 16.)

The tasks designed to elicit information relating to these four matters were presented as four separate exercises to the one sample of County Court judges. Serious cases of burglary normally are heard in the County Court, and the archival study of sentencing in the higher courts was based on a sample of cases determined in that jurisdiction. The order of presentation of the exercises was (1) validity study of the technique of fictitious cases, determination of sentences for archival cases; (2) MAUM analysis, assessment of seriousness and weights for offense factors; (3) coherency study, holistic assessment of case seriousness for fictitious cases; and (4) coherency study, determination of the quanta of sentence for fictitious cases. The reason for leading with the fictitious-cases validity study was that in this exercise judges were required to determine sentences for cases taken directly from court records, and it was felt that this was the exercise with which the judges would feel most comfortable. The decision that the decomposed assessments of seriousness should precede the holistic judgments was made quite deliberately and in full recognition that this might induce in the judges an uncharacteristically sensitive analytic set toward the holistic judgments, especially because the offense factors were defined identically in these two exercises. This offered a favorable and yet valid test of the judges' ability to apply an internally consistent set of rules to the determination of offense seriousness. In addition there was the real possibility that the reverse order would have confounded the valid testing of this aspect of the coherence assumption. It was noted in the introduction to this stage of the analysis that the judges' scaling and weighting of offense factors might involve to some extent the development of sentencing policy, because they were required to provide detail on matters of sentencing policy as yet not stated explicitly and precisely and about which they might have given little conscious thought. If policy development did in fact occur in this way, then the ordering of the holistic judgments first would have lowered the validity of the test. Moreover, there is some empirical evidence for order effects in this type of task. Pitz, Heerboth, and Sachs (1980) found that subjects' decomposed judgments were less discriminating when they followed holistic assessments. Similar motivation underlay the decision that the holistic seriousness assessments should precede the fictitious sentencing exercise. If the sentencing exercise had been undertaken first, it might have confounded the testing of the assumption of coherency, because sentence necessitates judgments in addition to the assessment of seriousness.

13
The Validity of the Technique of Fictitious Cases

This chapter presents a discussion and empirical test of the validity of judges' responses to fictitious sentencing exercises as a basis for understanding how judges determine appropriate sentences for particular cases. Here, the terms *fictitious case* and *fictitious procedure or technique* are used interchangeably. The critical feature is that the judgment is not made as part of a determination as to what is appropriate by way of sentence for an actual case as it is being heard in court. The fictitious procedure sometimes is referred to as simulation in the literature.

In the subsequent chapters the analyses are concerned with ascertaining how judges scale and weight offense characteristics as part of their assessment of the seriousness of individual cases and the quanta of sentence deemed to be appropriate for various levels of case seriousness. As it has been already explained, the goal of the study is to develop a model of judicial decision making to which the archival data could be fitted to show the relationship between case fact and sentence as a basis for detailed sentencing statistics. To elicit this information, judges were required in a series of sentencing exercises to make assessments regarding the seriousness of elements of fictitious cases (e.g., weight the contribution of each constituent offense factor to the overall assessment of case seriousness), to assess holistically the seriousness of fictitious cases and to determine sentences for these cases. In this study the focus of these tasks is a multiattribute utility measurement analysis. The technique of fictitious cases, however, may be used also in conjoint analysis, functional measurement, and analysis of variance to study how judges determine sentence (or seriousness). In these approaches judges are required to determine sentences for cases (or to rate the seriousness of cases) comprising a set of case factors normally combined according to a full or fractional orthogonal factorial design. The alternative is an archival analysis of actual sentencing decisions using multiple regression.

Perhaps this is an appropriate point to pause and consider as a general issue the reasons why and circumstances under which an analysis of fictitious data might be preferred to one based on archival data. Clearly, the assessment of seriousness requires a fictitious procedure, because archival data do not include judges' assessments of the seriousness of cases or the elements of cases. Of course, this requirement does not apply to the analysis of sentencing data. Here, the researcher is able to choose between the archival and fictitious approaches.

In the analysis of sentencing data, the advantage of a fictitious procedure over an archival analysis is that it allows the researcher to exert a much greater degree of control over the definition and structure of the data (case factors) with the result that the internal validity of the analysis should be higher. More specifically, there are the following advantages (Blumstein et al., 1983a and Lovegrove, 1984b):

1. Cases can be formulated so that it is possible to examine experimentally the independent effects of individual case factors that in real life generally are correlated with other case factors.
2. It facilitates the detection of the curvilinear and configural use of information about cases.
3. This strategy overcomes the problem of measuring the effect of case factors on the dependent variable for cases in which there are multiple counts. Unless the offenses were split, one could not be sure to what extent a judge's sentence for the principal offense was influenced by his awareness that an offender's effective sentence had to cover multiple counts.
4. Case factor levels that are uncommon features of real-life cases and yet of material relevance to sentence can be incorporated in a sufficient number of fictitious cases so that their effects can be estimated reliably.
5. In principle, variables that should not be material to sentence cannot affect the determination of case factor weights in the analysis through their association with other factors. For, say, race to exert such an influence it would have to be written into the fictitious cases. Nevertheless, if judges believe, for example, that certain patterns of offending are more likely to be followed by particular types of offender and they allow this view to influence their assessment of cases in which the critical offender characteristics were omitted, then this potential advantage would be lost.

Another (already mentioned) feature of the fictitious procedure is that it allows the assessment of seriousness to be considered independently of the determination of sentence. This has the benefit of permitting the researcher to (1) study how judges differentiate cases at the lower levels of severity (levels associated with noncustodial sentences), (2) avoid confounding sentences fixed according to tariff principles with those in which the rehabilitation of the offender was the sentencer's main concern, and (3) investigate as a separate matter the relationship between the seriousness of the case and the quantum of sentence deemed to be appropriate.

The advantages of the fictitious procedure have been considered; this discussion now turns to the objections raised against its use. This issue has been addressed by many writers. A wide-ranging discussion can be found in Ebbesen and Konečni (1980) and Konečni and Ebbesen (1979, 1981, 1982), as well as in Blumstein et al. (1983a) and Levin et al. (1983). At issue here is the external validity of the results of this type of research. Six principal objections to the use of fictitious cases have appeared in the literature. (Of course, there are many simulation studies to which some of these points do not apply.)

1. No significant consequences (or different consequences) attend the assessments, and the prisoner is a "paper defendant" (Partridge & Eldridge, 1974). Under such conditions judges might give vent to personal biases in the absence of appellate review of sentence (e.g., a preference for harsher penalties) and curb other biases when under academic scrutiny (e.g., chivalrous sentencing of women), or other normally critical factors might not exercise their minds (e.g., considerations relating to mercy), or simply they might not pay due attention to the task.

2. Information describing the cases is presented more simply—fewer case factors, less redundancy, no conflicting evidence, more compact and readily comprehensible. In these circumstances the judges might give weight to factors that would otherwise be ignored because of information overload (Payne, 1982; Slovic et al., 1977; Slovic & Lichtenstein, 1971). There is another potential problem where information about common case characteristics is omitted. In such instances a judge might make inferences about these characteristics in the light of the given information.

3. Some of the cases comprise atypical characteristics or patterns of factors. Certain factorial combinations might be difficult to judge because they rarely occur in real life. Further, the decision-making strategy in other combinations might be affected by these atypical cells. Moreover, the use of atypical case factor levels together with the omission of both common and the more uncommon case factors might result in the significance of factors being overestimated because of their undue prominence. Finally, if the atypical cases appear to be unrealistic and comprise a significant proportion of the task, the judges might conclude that the task is irrelevant and as a consequence not apply themselves to it.

4. Decisions are made in the absence of potentially critical features of court procedures, such as (1) the pressures to decide cases fairly and yet as quickly as possible to minimize backlogs, (2) the presentation of information about cases by personal testimony, and (3) the complexity of many cases. These differences might affect the case factors that are taken into account and the weights given to them.

5. Response categories have no legal significance.

6. The subjects are not judicial officers and might exercise their judgment differently because of personality and intellectual differences, lack of experience with the task, and ignorance of sentencing law and policy.

According to Ebbesen and Konečni (1980) and Konečni and Ebbesen (1981, 1982) the validity of the fictitious technique is questionable if one accepts what they regard as the reasonable assumption that individuals' decision strategies are task and situation specific, because, they suggest, it follows that decision making would be expected to vary according to these differences between the real world and the laboratory. Konečni and Ebbesen therefore conclude that the appropriate data base for studies describing the process of sentencing is archival data incorporating transcripts of hearings and documents available to the judge.

The point of the following discussion is not to argue that Konečni and Ebbesen are wrong but to put the view that their approach may be interpreted in an unnecessarily narrow way unless it is firmly set in a broader context. Ready acceptance of their conclusion might restrict and stifle the application of psycholegal research for the understanding and consequent improvement in sentencing. The issue is the extent to which we can simulate the process of sentencing and yet offer valid information. In Konečni and Ebbesen's (1979) discussion of research methods, one finds a guiding principle: when one studies an intact, functioning social network, such as the criminal justice system, there are certain logical and practical criteria that lead one on a priori grounds to trust the conclusions reached by one method over those reached by another. The contentious issues surrounding simulation are examined in turn on this basis. Before moving on to this, it is necessary to consider the sort of information that is required from the analysis.

There are at least three different aspects to the understanding of judicial decision making. First, one may seek to understand how judges actually fix sentences as they hear and determine cases in court. Here, the decision processes they attempt to follow to determine appropriate sentences according to current sentencing law, policy, and practice may be distorted by information overload because of the complexity of cases, by pressures arising from the need to decide cases as quickly as possible to keep delays to a minimum, and by factors that may be legally immaterial and yet emotionally and personally compelling (e.g., sympathy for distressed relatives of the offender). Second, one may seek to understand the decision processes judges attempt to follow, that is, how judges would apply current sentencing policy if they were free from the influence of confounding factors such as information overload. It would seem intuitively clear that a model of ideal judicial decision making is the appropriate framework on which to fit data to show the relationship between case fact and sentence as a basis for detailed sentencing statistics. Finally, the attention of the researcher could be directed toward helping the judiciary to develop and reform sentencing policy—here, fictitious cases would be seen as a technique for assisting judges to decide afresh, perhaps in view of new considerations, the case factors that they should take account of, how seriousness should be related to these factors, how they should weight and combine this information, and the quanta of sentence appropriate to the various levels of case seriousness. These decisions would become the basis of what has been referred to earlier (Chapter 1) as numerical guidelines. These three faces of understanding judicial decision making range from a descriptive to a prescriptive orientation. For convenience they are labeled actual, ideal, and prescriptive judicial decision making. The present research comes within the scope of the latter two categories; although up to this point the study has addressed only the ideal orientation.

There can be no disputing that research following the first-mentioned orientation must rely on an archival data base, because one wants complete data, "warts and all." This is unfortunate because the statistical technique traditionally applied to such data is multiple regression; the use of the results of this type of analysis for the understanding of the nature and structure of judicial decision making is problematic. This point was made in Chapter 2 and need not be labored here. Nevertheless, under appropriate conditions responses to fictitious cases offer a valid basis for understanding what has been termed here ideal and prescriptive judicial decision making. To sustain this position, each of the previously mentioned points against simulation is reconsidered in turn in view of the notion of ideal and prescriptive decision making. (There is, of course, considerable overlap between some of these points.)

Inconsequential Decisions. Clearly, simulation is of suspect validity where it is used as a means of identifying what judges actually do. The validity, however, of exercises directed toward understanding ideal and prescriptive judicial decision making is a different matter. In these instances the consequences would be significant because the judges would be told that the results were to be used to develop a structure for representing detailed sentencing statistics or for setting numerical guidelines. Furthermore in relation to the prescriptive orientation, judges would be freer to exercise their personal discretion as they imposed sentence in the light of legislation, simply because their decisions would not be subject to appeal; accordingly, these data would be expected to be a more valid representation of judges' personal preferences.

Simplification of Case Details. Simplification takes the form of the concise and compact presentation of information. Clearly, such a data base would not be suitable for the development of a decision model representing courtroom sentencing practices. For the study of ideal and prescriptive decision making, however, distortions caused by information overload are not wanted. Accordingly, to the extent that fictitious cases minimize information overload, in this respect they hold a potential advantage. Of course, it is critical that all the major material legal factors are present, because factors might otherwise be inappropriately weighted, in part because inferences might be made about the nature of the missing information and also because the factors present might be given undue prominence. A related trap with simulations, which must be avoided, is the tendency of some researchers to classify information (to summarize it) rather than to present the material as case-specific factors, for example, describing a burglary as well planned, rather than listing the characteristics of the case bearing on organization and then leaving the judge to assess the degree of organization as part of the assessment of seriousness or sentence. Where this is practiced, the researcher is performing part of the judge's task and may be biasing the outcome. In developing the material for the sentencing exercises, the author tried to satisfy these two conditions; the cases were described in terms of a detailed and comprehensive set of factors, and the task of classifying the information was left to the judge.

Artificiality of the Task. Fictitious cases for which the descriptions comprise atypical case characteristics and/or omit both the common and the more uncommon case factors and, for this reason, appear to be unrealistic to the judges, present a validity problem for the three orientations to the study of judicial decision making. A related problem arises where the researcher has made no serious attempt to ensure as far as possible that the descriptions of the fictitious cases maintain the character of the descriptions in the official records. These problems were minimized in the sentencing exercises by basing the content of the fictitious material (i.e., the dimensions and their defining categories) on the real-life cases in the archival burglary study and having a researcher who was well-acquainted with the style of the official records write the fictitious cases in a similar vein. The fictitious cases did not, of course, cover the more uncommon case factors.

The occurrence of atypical combinations of case factors is more problematic. This potentially unavoidable problem arises from the requirement of some statistical analyses for systematic variations in the combination of case characteristics. This was not a significant problem in this MAUM analysis. In any case any air of unreality associated with some combinations was minimized through the judicious selection and description of behaviors satisfying the definitions of the case factor levels. Moreover, although some of the patterns of offending were uncommon combinations, factually improbable cases were not included in the exercises; and one must remember that not infrequently judges are amazed at the facts surrounding actual cases. Nevertheless, as a check, the researcher asked the judges whether they thought any of the case descriptions were unrealistic and implausible.

Procedural Infidelity. The absence of the essential features of a courtroom hearing would not appear to undermine in general the validity of the data as a basis for understanding ideal and prescriptive sentencing practices. One critical exception might be for information relating to an offender's rehabilitation prospects and based on impressions conveyed by witnesses in court. Nevertheless, for the reasons given previously, one might expect that the absence of procedural features that add complexity and immaterial information to the case might enhance the validity of the fictitious technique for these orientations. However, there is a positive point. It is that many judges appear to be comfortable with a practice analogous to the use of fictitious cases; both in Britain (Cross & Ashworth, 1981) and in Australia (Law Reform Commission—Australia, 1980) there is support for sentencing conferences as a means of providing information about the quantum of sentence, and yet the training material there comprises fictitious cases. The fictitious cases used in the sentencing exercises here therefore were modeled on cases that had been presented at judicial seminars in England. Moreover, judges use this approach in the courts. Surely, the use of the fictitious technique is analogous to procedures followed by the appellate courts? There, one of the judges' main sources of information about cases are the trial transcripts, and they determine and weight material factors largely on this basis. Similarly, law reports of cases determined by appellate courts rely on abridged versions of the facts of these cases.

The Dependent Measures Are Not Legally Significant. Unquestionably, no matter which orientation is guiding the analysis, the assessments of the cases must be in a form consistent with sentencing law and policy. This study required judgments of sentence and offense seriousness. Judges were asked to determine the sentences in accordance with current sentencing law. And a judge, in determining an appropriate sentence, must at least implicitly form a view about the seriousness of the offense characteristics of the case.

Nonjudicial Officers as Subjects. The decision making of judges cannot be assumed to be mimicked by subjects selected from the general population. Consequently, nonjudicial subjects are not suitable for studies of actual or ideal sentencing practices. Regarding the prescriptive orientation, there is another consideration; on the ground of judicial independence alone, there can be no doubt that the judiciary must determine sentencing policy. The results of the Law Reform Commission's (1980) survey show that Australian judges view their independence as sacrosanct and Ashworth (1983b) in his discussion of several proposals for reform in England drew attention to the sensitivity of judges to the issue of judicial independence. Nevertheless, when pretesting an empirical strategy to determine its adequacy, under certain circumstances it may be advisable to use barristers experienced in the criminal jurisdiction, because the cooperation of judges is hard won and, presumably, easily lost.

The preceding arguments defend the validity of the qualified use of simulation, according to the criteria advanced for understanding ideal and prescriptive aspects of the judicial approach to sentencing. These considerations cover matters raised in Anderson and Hayden's (1981) discussion of the three criteria for assessing the validity of a simulation: sociological, conceptual, and structural verisimilitude. They represent a more sophisticated view of simulation than that of Elwork et al. (1981), who state that the research methodology should be designed to eliminate artificiality as much as possible. Rather, this approach shows sensitivity to the warning of Elwork et al. (1981) and Monahan and Loftus (1982) that simulation is essential if we are to develop alternatives to existing procedures. Nevertheless, it is stricter than Houlden's (1981) view that verisimilitude is not critical when the purpose of the research is to test theory and propose interventions on the basis of the theory.

The Validity Study

The validity study investigated whether sentences determined by judges for cases presented in the form of a sentencing exercise are similar to the sentences determined for identical, real-life cases and heard as part of the normal business of the court. It affords an empirical test of the argument that the inconsequential nature of the decisions, simplification of case details (excluding the element relating to the presence of fewer factors), and procedural infidelity associated with the fictitious sentencing exercises in this study would not undermine the external validity of the results regarding the determination of sentence. It does not cover potential problems associated with the artificiality of the task or the judgments made on the dimensions of seriousness. Moreover, the empirical test is confined to the validity of fictitious cases as a technique for understanding actual decision making. Strictly, the argument that the fictitious cases technique provides a better basis than archival data for understanding ideal decision making is left open. Indeed, if the two types of decision making are substantially different, then sentences for actual cases would not be an appropriate criterion for this validity test, and clearly, differences between the sentences for the real-life cases and the same cases in their fictitious form would be expected. Of course, differences also would be expected because of an inevitable degree of intrajudge unreliability and interjudge differences in sentencing practice. The previous distinction therefore probably should be regarded as subtle. Nevertheless, unreliability would not be expected to contribute to substantial discrepancies in the general levels of sentence fixed under conditions of real life and simulation. The present empirical comparison of sentences for the real-life cases and the cases in their fictitious form therefore was regarded as an adequate test for the purposes of the present study. Indeed, it follows from the foregoing discussion that this measure is a conservative estimate of external validity. Accordingly, if the levels of sentence for the two sentencing conditions were found to be similar in this validity study and if the judges did not report discomfort over the artificiality of the fictitious cases or the means of assessing seriousness in the sentencing exercises, then one would be entitled to accept the responses to the fictitious cases in the sentencing exercises as a valid basis of understanding ideal and prescriptive sentencing.

The preceding considerations bear on the use of fictitious cases rather than archival data for developing a model of ideal and prescriptive judicial decision making in relation to the determination of sentence. Later in this book it is argued that there would be advantages to be gained from basing the detailed sentencing statistics on judges' sentences for fictitious cases rather than on sentences for actual cases determined in the courts, that is, sentences for fictitious cases (cf. actual cases) would be fitted to the model of judicial decision making to represent the relationship between case fact and sentence. This approach also would rest on the assumption that the sentences fixed by the judges for the fictitious cases would not have been substantially different if those judgments had been made for identical real-life cases determined as part of the normal business of the court. This use of fictitious cases is analogous to the ideal orientation and, accordingly, rests on the same assumptions.

Method

General

The previously described archival burglary study (see Part Two) provided an ideal basis for the present investigation. Actual cases were extracted from that original sample of 100 cases and were presented in fictitious form. The judges' task was to determine sentences for these cases. The degree of similarity between the two sets of sentences – the sentences imposed in the courts for these archival cases and the sentences imposed as part of the current exercise – was the measure of validity of the simulation.

The archival cases included in the sample for the validity study were heard in the County Court between June 1981 and November 1983. Since that time there have been legislative changes that might have influenced the judges' practices regarding the use and length of imprisonment. To avoid any potential problems arising from these changes in the interpretation of the results, judges were asked to determine sentences in accordance with sentencing law, policy, and practice as it was at the time of the original hearing of each of the cases.

There appear to have been only four potentially significant changes. First, the introduction of the pre-release program in 1984, under which prisoners serving sentences of at least 12 months could be released up to 12 months before the expiry of the minimum term but for a period not exceeding one third of their sentence and not less than 3 months; before the commencement of this validity study, the scope and impact of the program had been curtailed somewhat. The potential effect of this scheme is that some judges might impose longer sentences than they otherwise would have considered to allow for the effect of early release. Second, there are two new sentencing options (begun June 1986): the suspended and partly suspended sentence for prison sentences of 12 months or less, and the provision that for prison sentences of 3 months or less a community-based order also may be imposed. The potential effect of these provisions would be expected to be in the direction of the less frequent use of imprisonment and shorter periods of imprisonment for some of the less serious cases. Finally, there is now a legislative provision that imprisonment should be regarded as the sanction of last resort (begun June 1986). It is an open question whether this provision would result in the less frequent use and shorter terms of imprisonment, but one would be surprised if it did, especially in the higher courts. (See the *Corrections Act* 1986 and the *Penalties and Sentences Act* 1985 for these legislative changes.)

The effects of the introduction, however, of the pre-release program are so straightforward and the introduction of the latter three provisions so recent that the judges were expected to have little difficulty in determining sentences according to the sentencing provisions and practice in operation at the time of the hearings of the cases in the archival burglary study.

This validity study examined 36 cases from the archival study, and with adjusted case scores ranging from −8 to 31, these cases adequately covered this dimension (see Figure 11.1) from a level of seriousness just below the most serious case in the archival sample to a level well below that at which a custodial sentence was probable. For each case all the information that appeared to have been put before the court was included in the case description. This covered factors relating to the offense, prior record, and mitigation; it also included details of counts other than burglary. In the record of the plea, evidence called by counsel in support of an assertion was summarized briefly and its source identified. Information taken from the plea was confined to facts about the offender;

it did not include any pleading by counsel. Nevertheless, an attempt was made to capture the spirit and strength of the plea by using the defense counsel's own phrases, although the success of this attempt must be regarded as problematic. Because sentences were required for only the principal offender in each case, information of sole relevance to any other offender was excluded. Incidental material was not incorporated in the case summaries. Of course, it is possible that in some cases the court had additional material facts that were not in the file or mentioned in the plea, for example, that the offender had been remanded in custody. The information was presented with minimal redundancy, with little or no conflicting evidence, and was more compact than the real-life versions—the lengths of the descriptions of the fictitious versions of these cases ranged from one to four pages and were typically about one-and-a-half pages long, exclusive of the record of prior convictions—whereas for archival cases the file with the record of interview(s) and statement(s) of victim(s), together with accompanying documentation, is much more extensive and a plea lasting over 1 hour is not uncommon. The records of prior convictions were reproduced nearly verbatim. It is appropriate to mention at this point that in approximately two thirds of the cases the principal offender pleaded guilty. In this sort of offense there appears to be less information on record about the circumstances of the offense when there is a trial because the offender does not provide information about the modus operandi in the record of interview.

Procedure

The 36 cases together with the instructions were presented to the judges in a booklet with the cover title *Sentencing Research Exercise— Part 1.* The instructions were on the first page, followed by the descriptions of the cases. (A sample case is presented in Appendix 1.) One booklet was assigned to each judge unsystematically, and in each booklet the cases were presented in a different random order.

To select the judges for this study, I asked a senior judge of the County Court to identify about 10 judges who generally would be regarded as experienced in criminal work and who might be prepared to participate in a study examining the feasibility of providing judges with detailed sentencing statistics. (At this time just under 40 judges determined criminal matters in the County Court.) An invitation was extended to 11 judges to meet as a group with the author and a Justice of the Supreme Court of Victoria. At this meeting the author briefly outlined the nature of detailed sentencing statistics, the form that they might take, and how they could assist the sentencing judge. The point was made that to develop these statistics it was necessary to know which case factors are considered by judges to be material to sentence, how seriousness varies on each factor, and the weight attached to each factor in determining the quantum of sentence. The judges were told that their participation in this study would require a substantial commitment, because the study comprised four separate exercises. It was stressed to the judges that this was a feasibility study only and that should detailed sentencing statistics be introduced the information gathered from them as part of this study would not be incorporated in those statistics. Finally, the author explained that the Victorian Government's Sentencing Committee (of which the author and the previously mentioned Supreme Court judge and County Court judge were members) would draw on the results of this study to determine whether to recommend the introduction of detailed sentencing statistics into the courts.

Nine of the eleven judges agreed to participate in the study. (One judge was concerned about possible breaches of confidentiality, and the other judge felt that he did not have sufficient free time to give due attention to the task.) Clearly, this sample of judges was not representative of the County Court judges who determined criminal matters. This was not seen as a problem because the project was a feasibility study only. Rather, the bias was intentional and regarded as a strength; it was thought that this group would respond more consistently and would be more comfortable with the task. (The County Court judge who sought the cooperation of the other judges told them how they had been chosen.) A few weeks after the meeting, I arranged individual appointments. The booklets for the first exercise were handed to the judges personally at these subsequent meetings. Each judge was given an identification number and retained this number throughout the series of studies.

The following instructions were included at the beginning of each booklet. (The task also was explained informally to each judge by the author.)

This exercise is the first in the series concerned with understanding how judges determine what is appropriate by way of sentence. As you are aware, consideration is being given to providing the courts with more detailed sentencing statistics so that judges would have a clearer idea about the types and levels of sentence which are currently being imposed in the jurisdiction for cases comprising the various combinations of offense and offender characteristics. The data base for these statistics would be actual cases determined in the courts. However, in order to show the relationship between case characteristics and sentence, it is necessary to understand how judges construe information about cases to determine sentences. The information gathered in this series of studies will be analyzed for that purpose. Your responses will not become part of a sentencing statistics data base and will not be submitted as individual data to the Sentencing Committee.

The specific purpose of this first exercise is to investigate whether sentences imposed for cases presented in the form of a sentencing exercise differ from those which are imposed in court. In this booklet there are brief descriptions of 36 cases of burglary; the descriptions include facts relating to the offense(s), any prior convictions of the offender and relevant mitigating information about the offender. (The source of any evidence called by counsel in support of an assertion is indicated.) In some instances you will find that the case also includes counts other than burglary. Since a sentence is required for only one offender in each case, information of sole relevance to any other offender has been excluded. These case descriptions are summaries of actual cases which have been determined in the County Court.

You are asked to determine an appropriate sentence—a maximum and a minimum sentence—for each case. Exercise your discretion in accordance with sentencing law and sentencing policy (and practice) as it was to be found in relevant statutes and appellate judgments at the date of the plea: fix each sentence as though you were making the determination for an actual case being heard by you in your Court. You have been presented with a summary of all the information which was put before the Court and placed on record. Please write your sentence at the end of the outline of each case. Reasons are not required for your decision.

Please complete the cases in the order in which they appear in the booklet. Do not feel under any obligation to complete the task without a break. Finally, I should be grateful if you would refrain from discussing this exercise with your brother judges. They are fixing sentences for the same cases.

Before starting this exercise each judge was given the opportunity to ask questions about those aspects of the task that were unclear, and confusing matters were clarified. Furthermore, judges were given a copy of a document outlining the sentencing options and provisions in operation during the period in which these cases were determined in the courts. At the conclusion of the exercise, the judges were interviewed individually by me and asked whether they had experienced any difficulties in exercising their discretion in relation to the previous sentencing policy, and they were given the opportunity to express opinions that they might have formed about the exercise. The exercise was handed to the judges in February/March 1987 and typically was completed within a 2- to 3-month period.

Selection of the Cases

The sample comprised cases selected from the original archival burglary study. It was important that the sample in this analysis comprised only those cases for which tariff sentences were appropriate, and the quanta of sentence had been correctly fixed in proportion to the seriousness of the case. The researcher would, of course, face a problematic analysis if a substantial proportion of the sample consisted of cases for which the sentences generally would be regarded by judges as disparate— outside the normal range. Then, any discrepancies between the archival sentences and the sentences imposed by the judges for such cases in their fictitious form could not be confidently attributed to the distorting effects of the simulation but rather might reflect idiosyncratic approaches of the sentencing judges in the courts. In such circumstances the degree of correspondence between the two sets of sentences might well be an invalid measure of the verisimilitude of the fictitious technique (simulation). Accordingly, cases from the burglary sample were not included in this study where the sentence did not appear to be proportional to seriousness or where a custodial sentence was imposed but the case characteristics indicated that a rehabilitative sentence might have been appropriate. It does not follow that sentences for cases satisfying one of these criteria should be regarded as in error, because the sentence might have been based on material factors not incorporated in the guidelines. Rather, one should take the view that there is less doubt about the appropriateness of the sentences for the remaining cases. Of course, this approach rests on the assumption that these criteria can be measured.

Fortunately, the burglary study offered measures of seriousness and the appropriateness of a rehabilitative sentence. These were the only independent indicators available to the researcher, and the high degree of fit that had been found between sentence and seriousness in the burglary study (see Chapter 10) provided support for the view that the measure of seriousness had a substantial degree of validity. Accordingly, these measures were used here to increase the degree of precision of the analysis. To maximize the validity of these measures, cases characterized by significant offense or offender factors not included in the scoring system for the burglary study (see Chapters 6 and 8) also were excluded.

The three previously mentioned grounds on which cases were excluded from the archival burglary study for this analysis were operationalized by the following criteria (these categories are not mutually exclusive):

1. Cases with sentences that departed significantly from the line defining the proportionality between seriousness (defined by adjusted case score) and effective sentence (see Figure 11.1). This figure has been reproduced as Figure 13.1, but the figure includes the boundaries marking what was considered to be the normal range. These lines seemed to suggest themselves naturally and were widened gradually as the adjusted case score increased so that the normal range remained (roughly) proportionately constant.
2. Cases with sentences of youth training.
3. Cases for which a custodial sentence was imposed and yet the offender fell into one of the special categories – youth, first offense of dishonesty, substantial gap since last offense of dishonesty, exculpatory reason for the offense – and also was deemed to have favorable rehabilitation prospects (see Tables 10.2 and 10.3). Such offenders satisfy the criteria for an individualized measure. (Cases for which a noncustodial sentence was imposed were not excluded on this criterion, because there would have been an insufficient number of cases left across the lower part of the range of adjusted case score.)
4. Cases in which the majority of the offender's prior convictions could be explained by a reason that could have been coded −6 on the offender characteristic reason for the offense (see Table 8.1).
5. Cases in which the sentence for the unconnected offenses (including pending charges taken into account in the determination of sentence, and attempted burglaries) might have accounted for a substantial proportion of the effective sentence; this exclusion was applied to cases fulfilling one of the following criteria (see Table 10.11 and accompanying text):
   a. Three or more unconnected offenses;
   b. Total sentence for the unconnected offense(s) was greater than 12 months (exclusive of the effects of any concurrency orders with the burglary or burglaries);
   c. Any nonconcurrent component of the sentence(s) for the unconnected offense(s) increased the sentence by more than 6 months.
6. Cases in which the nonconcurrent component of the sentence(s) for the connected offense(s) increased the sentence by more than 6 months.

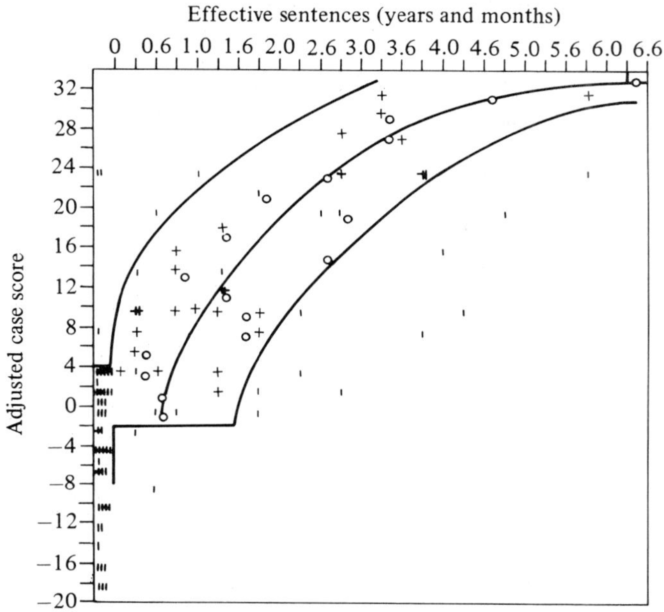

FIGURE 13.1. The proportionality between case seriousness and sentence and with lines marking the normal range of sentence. *Note.* The mean sentences for the various levels are indicated by the circles. The categories on effective sentences cover a range, with the upper limit of each category indicated. For example, the second category includes all custodial sentences up to and including a length of 3 months exactly. The categories on adjusted case scores cover a range, with the lower limit of each category indicated. For example, the top category includes case scores of 32 and 33. The crossed cases remained in the analysis for the validity study.

7. Cases in which the unconnected offense(s) captured the character of the offense; there was one such case—the offender broke into his brother's flat as a part of an escape from legal custody.
8. Cases with other significant material offense or offender factors that were not included in the scoring system for the archival burglary study or were odd variations of the factors in the model.

The numbers of cases with custodial and noncustodial sentences excluded on these grounds were 25 and 8, respectively. (Cases with both noncustodial sentences and adjusted case scores below −8 were not considered for inclusion in this analysis, because for the majority of these cases, the appropriateness of a noncustodial sentence appeared to be obvious.) Of the remaining cases with noncustodial sentences, 11 were excluded so that there was a manageable number of such cases; this was done unsystematically, except with the constraint that the cases should be well distributed across this part of the range of adjusted case score. As a consequence the final sample of cases comprised 24 custodial sentences and 12 noncustodial sentences (these are represented as the crossed cases in Figure 13.1).

Results

Sentencing Data

Before this analysis could proceed, it was necessary to determine the standard against which the judges' responses should be compared. There were three contenders. First, there were the actual sentences imposed by the sentencing judges in the court (actual sentence). A possible limitation of this criterion is that the sentencing judges' discretion may have miscarried in some of the cases, although the procedure for the selection of the cases was devised to minimize the chance of such cases being included in the analysis. Second, there is the sentence defined by the line marking the proportionality between case seriousness (adjusted case score) and the effective sentence (Figure 13.1) – proportional sentence. The problem with this criterion is that it does not allow for the possible effects on sentence of unusual material case factors, not to mention the effects of possible errors in the model, although the method of selecting cases for this study would have reduced the effects of these errors on the validity of this criterion. Finally, the standard may be taken as the mean of the actual and proportional sentences (criterion sentence). It may be that this index offers a reasonable compromise between the previous two measures. In any case the differences between the three indices would be expected to be minimal in view of the strategy for the selection of the cases.

The principal question addressed here is whether the levels of sentence determined for the cases presented in the form of a sentencing exercise were similar to the levels of sentence that had been fixed for the same cases during the normal business of the court. To answer this question the 36 cases were divided into four groups according to the criterion effective sentence. The first group comprised cases whose criterion effective sentence came within the range 2.9 to 5.4 years; for the second group the range was 1.1 to 1.8 years; the range of the third group was 0.3 to 0.9 years; the fourth group comprised all those cases, and only those cases, for which a noncustodial sentence had been imposed in the court by the sentencing judge. For the cases in the fourth group, the criterion effective sentence was 0 or 0.2 years (these latter cases had an adjusted case score within the range for which there was not a clear demarcation between noncustodial and custodial sentences; see Figure 11.1). Table 13.1 shows the mean effective sentence imposed in the sentencing exercise, for each judge and each level of sentence, compared with the mean criterion effective sentence and the mean actual court sentence.

As expected, there was a high degree of similarity between the mean criterion and mean actual court sentences for each of the four levels, and therefore it was concluded that at this level of analysis, the criterion sentence reasonably could be

TABLE 13.1. A comparison of the sentences in the validity study with the criterion sentence and actual court sentence for each judge and level of sentence: Effective sentence (years)

Level	No. of cases (n = 36)	Mean criterion sentence	Judges' mean sentences 1	2	3	4	5	6	7	8	9	Mean	Mean actual court sentence
1	7	3.7	3.3	3.6	3.9	5.1	2.0	1.7	3.3	3.2	3.9	3.3	3.8
2	9	1.4	1.4	1.5	1.4	1.8	0.6	1.0	2.0	0.8	1.3	1.3	1.4
3	8	0.7	0.7	0.9	0.9	0.6	0.3	0.1	1.2	0.1	0.9	0.6	0.7
4	12	0.1	0.3	1.2	0.8	0.8	0.1	0.3	0.9	0	0.9	0.6	0

regarded as a sound standard against which the judges' sentences from the exercise could be compared to assess the validity of the technique of fictitious cases. No account was taken of any concurrency order that the judge might have made in relation to any sentence an offender might have been serving at that time.

Concerning the matter under investigation, the first point to notice is that for the highest three levels of seriousness, the mean quanta of sentence for each of the nine judges are ordered according to the mean criterion sentence; moreover, within judges, the relative lengths of sentence across the levels generally are similar to the relative lengths of the mean criterion sentences. Clearly, these observations do not apply to the fourth level; the sentence lengths across the judges for this level are similar to those for the third level, even though the mean criterion sentences differ significantly between these two levels. An inspection of the raw data shows that for three of the cases in the fourth level, some of the judges imposed substantial terms of imprisonment, although there were no obvious differences between the characteristics of these cases and some of the other cases in this level for which only noncustodial or very short custodial sentences were imposed.

The means of the judges' sentences in the exercise are remarkably similar to the mean criterion sentences for the first three levels. And in each of these levels only two to three judges—and not always the same judges—differ significantly from the mean of the judges.

This analysis also was made on the data for the minimum sentences. Cases were placed in one of the four levels on the basis of their criterion effective sentence, so that each of the cases is considered in the same level in this analysis as it was for the analysis of effective sentences. The results are shown in Table 13.2, and it can be seen that the same trends are apparent for the minimum sentences as for the effective sentences. (To determine the proportional sentences and the criterion sentences for this analysis in relation to minimum terms, a graph showing the relationship between the adjusted case scores and minimum sentences was constructed, using the same format as in Figure 11.1.)

Finally, the relationship between the judges' mean effective sentence imposed in the validity study and the criterion effective sentence for each of the cases in the first three levels (n = 24) is shown in the graph in Figure 13.2.

TABLE 13.2. A comparison of the sentences in the validity study with the criterion sentence and actual court sentence for each judge and level of sentence: Minimum sentence (years)

Level	No. of cases (n = 36)	Mean criterion sentence	Judges' mean sentences 1	2	3	4	5	6	7	8	9	Mean	Mean actual court sentence
1	7	2.7	2.3	2.3	2.5	3.4	1.1	1.1	2.2	2.3	2.5	2.2	2.6
2	9	0.8	1.0	1.1	0.7	1.1	0.5	0.8	1.3	0.6	0.8	0.9	0.8
3	8	0.5	0.6	0.7	0.6	0.5	0.3	0.1	1.0	0.1	0.5	0.5	0.6
4	12	0.1	0.3	0.8	0.5	0.4	0.1	0.2	0.5	0	0.5	0.4	0

Clearly, a direct relationship exists between the judges' mean effective sentences and the criterion effective sentences for the 24 cases for which a custodial sentence was imposed at the actual court hearing, although there is some scatter. The product-moment correlation is 0.86. An equivalent analysis for the minimum sentence showed an almost identical relationship, except, of course, that the sentence lengths were proportionately shorter.

JUDGES' COMMENTS

Several judges made the point that in the fictitious versions vital information relating to the quality and extent of the plea was missing. For example, the weight given to the goal of rehabilitation may turn on the judge's assessment of a witness's honesty or of the strength of character, integrity, and competence of a person offering to assist in the rehabilitation of the offender. The effect of this factor is that judges would be more likely in some cases to impose a custodial sentence or a longer custodial sentence where their decision was based on the information in a sentencing exercise rather than the actual court appearance. In fact six of the judges had acted as the sentencer in a total of eight of the cases in the sample (one of these judges had presided in three of the cases), and some of these judges recognized the cases in which they had fixed the actual sentence. So the previous observation was based on personal experience and intuition. Nevertheless, several judges noted that the consideration of the offense characteristics is based largely on the written records of the depositions. Accordingly, it would appear that the problem associated with the quality and extent of information relates to the consideration of the offender characteristics as they are presented in the plea rather than to the consideration of the effects on sentence of the offense characteristics.

Several of the judges indicated that in some of the cases they would have liked more information to resolve an apparent contradiction in the evidence or to provide additional evidence material to sentence, for example, the sentences imposed on co-offenders and presentence reports about the offender. However, this was a significant problem for only one judge: he declined to fix a sentence in five of the cases (the cases were distributed across the levels of seriousness)

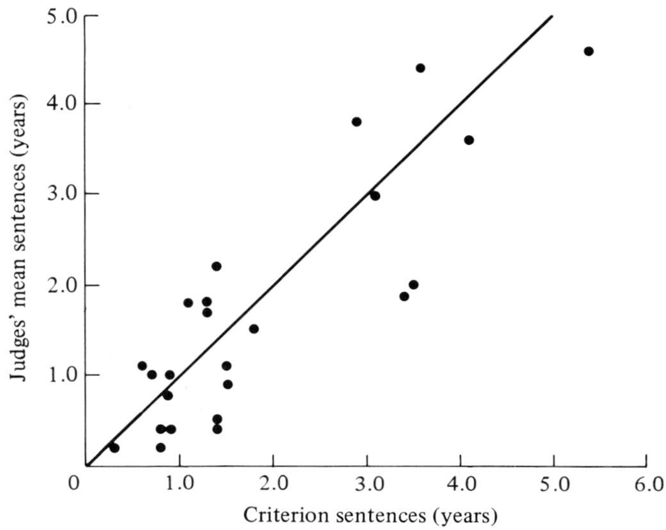

FIGURE 13.2. The relationship between the judges' mean sentences in the validity study and the criterion sentences for seriousness levels 1 to 3: Effective sentence.

because he felt that there was insufficient information to determine an appropriate sentence without a presentence report, and in these cases the sentencing judge had not called for a report.

None of the judges experienced any difficulties in exercising the sentencing discretion in relation to sentencing policy and practice as it was during the period in which the cases in this sample were determined in court. Indeed, there was a general view that sentencing practice had not obviously changed in regard to the use of imprisonment for the sort of case typically under consideration in the present study.

Discussion

In view of the similarity between the sentences imposed as part of the sentencing exercise and the sentences fixed in court for the same cases, together with the judges' comments about the exercise, it would appear reasonable to conclude that sentencing exercises are a valid means of understanding how judges determine the appropriate quantum of sentence, except in those cases in which the quality of the plea may be decisive. Most judges commented that the impact of a compelling plea is diminished and certain potentially mitigating information relating to the offender is lost when the material is presented in the form of a written summary. This may account for the finding that several of the cases for which a non-custodial sentence was imposed in court were dealt with harshly when presented in this exercise. Fortunately, this apparent limitation would not appear to be a problem in the present project, because the following sentencing exercises are concerned with the relationship between offense characteristics and quantum of custodial sentence.

There are four significant conditions that may underlie the validity of the present sentencing exercises and that should be borne in mind in any attempt to generalize the present results. First, it is likely that the judges would have been well motivated, because they were aware that the results might be the basis for innovations in sentencing practice. The judges participated in this study so that the Victorian Government's Sentencing Committee could assess the feasibility of providing the courts with detailed guidance for determining appropriate sentences. Second, the cases in their fictitious form were nevertheless very detailed; indeed, the cases contained virtually all the information that appeared to have been put before the sentencing judge. Therefore, in the subsequent sentencing exercises, the information about the offense and the offender were presented in a similar degree of detail. Third, the judges in the sample were experienced and, perhaps, less likely to be distracted by the form in which the information was presented. Finally, matters relating to the artificiality of the task were not addressed in this study, because the content and style of the fictitious cases were taken directly from actual cases.

The task of testing the validity of the technique of fictitious cases is deceptively simple. There are four principal problems. First, there is the problem of establishing a valid standard against which the responses to the sentencing exercises can be compared. The problem is, of course, that some of the sentences imposed in court may be in error or, at least, somewhat lenient or excessive. The criterion sentence and the method of selecting cases for this study were designed to reduce the significance of this potential problem. (Presumably it is obvious why separate standards could not be developed for each of the participating judges, and each judge given a set of cases in fictitious form, taken from cases he previously had sentenced in court; the reason is, of course, that judges appear to have an extraordinary capacity for memorizing details about cases long since past and they do not sentence particularly large numbers of cases.) The second problem relates to possible disparate sentencing by the judges participating in the exercise. This is a less significant problem when there is a sample, because it is possible to investigate whether a common standard is apparent. Indeed, an inspection of Tables 13.1 and 13.2 indicates that within each of the first three levels there seems to be a common standard, about which some of the other judges' sentences vary. The reassuring point is that this common standard and the criterion sentence are directly covariant across the levels; moreover, the several sentences that are apparently deviant within each level are, nevertheless, consistent across the levels for the particular judges who imposed them. The third problem is that not all the material information before the court is recorded; this would appear to be a particular problem in those cases for which the manner in which the plea material is presented and the nature of this evidence may be decisive. Finally, to interpret these data in support of the validity of the technique of fictitious cases, it must be assumed that the judges in this sample and the judges who fixed the sentences for the cases in the courts shared a common standard of sentence severity and that the judges in this exercise followed faithfully the instruction to "fix each sentence as though you were making the determination for an actual case being heard by you in your Court." For reasons related to these four points, the index of the validity of the technique of fictitious cases (the degree of correspondence between the sentences imposed in the exercise and the criterion sentence) would almost certainly underestimate the degree of external validity of a particular judge's responses in a sentencing exercise. Nevertheless, the results of this study of the validity of the technique of fictitious cases justify the use of the following sentencing exercises as a means of understanding how this sample of judges determines appropriate sentences in regard to the offense characteristics of cases.

14
Multiattribute Utility Measurement and the Model of Judicial Decision Making

The purpose of the MAUM analysis is to understand how judges construe the seriousness of offense characteristics of burglary as part of their determination of appropriate sentences for cases of burglary. Specifically, judicial input is sought on the scaling of seriousness in relation to the offense characteristics of burglary and the weighting of these case factors. This analysis comprises the following elements:

1. Identification and operational definition of the offense characteristics material to seriousness
2. Development of scales of relative seriousness for each offense factor
3. Determination of the relative importance of each offense factor in the assessment of seriousness
4. Calculation of the overall seriousness of the offense characteristics
5. Assessment of the sensitivity of the estimates of the weights for the offense factors

Identification and Operational Definition of the Offense Characteristics Material to Seriousness

For the reasons given earlier (Chapter 12), the offense criteria defining the seriousness of cases of burglary were not explored systematically with the judges at this stage in the development of the model of judicial decision making but were taken directly from the model. The four factors were violence to the victims, organization, counts of burglary, and total value of the theft, and each factor was defined by four categories (or levels). So that the results of these analyses could be related directly to the model, the judges' scaling of seriousness was based on descriptions taken directly from the objective case elements that were used to define these factors in the model (see Chapter 6). The following considerations governed the choice of the particular objective scale values (levels) selected for these assessments. First, the range of each of the factors should be closely tied to the distributions of actual cases on the corresponding offense factors in the (original) archival burglary study. The highest value on each factor was set around the value of the most extreme case on that factor; the lowest values were determined similarly. Accordingly, the levels marking the range of each factor could be properly described as maximum and minimum plausible values (Edwards, 1977). Second, for each factor the objective scale values (levels) for assessment should be at or about the values defining the categories in the corresponding offense factor in the model. Third, these levels should be well distributed across the range of each of the offense factors. Fourth, there should be a similar number of levels on each of the offense factors. One final point: for simplicity and experimental rigor, the type of premises always was a dwelling house. Of course, it could not be assumed that the judges' responses would be similar for other types of premises. With these general comments, each offense factor is considered in turn.

Violence to the Victims

The upper and lower levels for the factor of violence to the victims were defined by behavior that would fall at the upper extreme of the most serious category and the lower extreme of the least serious category, respectively, on this dimension in the model (see Table 6.1). Although the most serious category covered a physical assault on the victim, instances where the victim was terrorized (e.g., a knife held at the victim's throat), or required medical treatment for a physical injury as a result of a malicious and deliberate act or gross negligence by the offender, were excluded; in the (original) archival burglary study such rare instances (three) were considered qualitatively more serious and were coded as though there was a fifth category (see Chapter 10). The description chosen to mark the most serious level for scaling appeared to be at least as serious as any of the violent incidents coded as 4 in the burglary study. Six other levels were included for seriousness ratings on this factor. These were levels defined by behavior that appeared to mark the other upper and lower extremes of the four categories on this offense factor. As violence to the victims was described in the model, it covered both personal violence (confrontation) and property damage. To maintain control over the variation across this dimension, the degree of personal violence (confrontation) was varied, whereas the amount of property damage was kept constant at a minimal level. Of course, further development would require manipulation of this component of this factor as well. The eight behavioral descriptions marking the levels of seriousness—two for each category in the model—for the scaling of violence to the victims were composed by the author and are presented below in apparent order of ascending seriousness (Table 14.1). It was necessary to compose illustrative case events representing each of the levels because the definitions of the categories in the model were presented in the form of criteria.

These eight levels appeared to be related to the model's categories as defined in Table 6.1 and, accordingly, to mark different levels of seriousness, although clearly this was a subjective and somewhat imprecise exercise. It would not have

TABLE 14.1. Descriptions of the levels on violence to the victims for the scaling of seriousness

Level	Code[a]	Descriptions of levels[b]
1	1 (low)	No one was home during the burglary.
2	1 (high)	The burglar entered the home when the occupants were out. During the burglary he heard a car turn into the property, and he immediately left through the front door, running past the owner in the driveway.
3	2 (low)	The burglar entered the home when the occupants were out. During the burglary he heard a car turn into the property. He looked out from an upstairs window and saw a man entering the house. He continued to search the room but left by the window when he heard the owner come upstairs.
4	2 (high)	The burglar entered the home when the occupants were out. During the burglary he heard a car turn into the property. He looked out from an upstairs window and saw a man entering the house. He continued to search the room, even after the owner had come upstairs, until the owner entered the room. The owner ran toward him, whereupon he quickly climbed out of the window onto the roof of a ground-floor extension and made his escape.
5	3 (low)	The burglar entered the home when the occupants were out. During the burglary he heard a car turn into the property. He looked out from an upstairs window and saw a man entering the house. He continued to search the room, even after the owner came upstairs, until the owner entered the room, whereupon he went across to the window. The owner then ran across the room toward him. In response the burglar turned, waved his fist, and threatened to strike the owner. The owner withdrew, and the burglar immediately climbed out of the window onto the roof of a ground-floor extension and made his escape.
6	3 (high)	The burglar entered the home when the occupants were out. During the burglary he heard a car turn into the property. He looked out from an upstairs window and saw a man entering the house. He continued to search the room, even after the owner came upstairs, until the owner entered the room, whereupon the offender moved one pace toward him, waved his fist and threatened to strike him. The burglar then immediately ran across to the window and climbed out onto the roof of a ground-floor extension and made his escape.
7	4 (low)	The burglar entered the home when the occupants were out. During the burglary he heard a car turn into the property. He looked out from an upstairs window and saw a man entering the house. He continued to search the room, even after the owner came upstairs, until the owner entered the room, whereupon he went across to the window. The owner ran across the room toward him. In response the burglar picked up a table lamp with a metal base, threatened to strike him, and ordered him to stand with his hands behind his back. The burglar used the flex from the lamp to bind the owner's hands and feet. The burglar then immediately climbed out through the window onto the roof of a ground-floor extension and made his escape.

TABLE 14.1. *Continued.*

Level	Code[a]	Descriptions of levels[b]
8	4 (high)	The burglar entered the home when the occupants were out. During the burglary he heard a car turn into the property. He looked out from an upstairs window and saw a man entering the house. He continued to search the room, even after the owner came upstairs, until the owner entered the room, whereupon he picked up a table lamp with a metal base and ran at the owner, threatening to strike him and ordering him to stand with his hands behind his back. The burglar used the flex from the lamp to bind the owner's hands and feet. The burglar then immediately climbed out through the window onto the roof of a ground-floor extension and made his escape.

[a] This is the code that would fit this description, according to the model of judicial decision making (see Table 6.1).
[b] For all the levels, the only damage done was a broken lock on the rear door and minor disturbance to the contents, associated with the search.

been possible to have introduced more levels on the basis of these categories and have maintained confidence in the relative (rank) seriousness of the fictitious case events. One should not assume that an assessment of seriousness for a particular level as it was operationalized here would necessarily generalize to other possible behaviors marking that level.

Organization

In the archival burglary study the degree of organization was monotonically related to the number of components thought to be indicative of planning/organization/sophistication of approach (see Tables 6.2 and 6.3). Here, the lower and upper levels of this factor were set at one and eight components, respectively. One component was a necessary minimum since, for the holistic assessments in the (later) coherency study (see Chapter 16), some of the case combinations of these four offense factors involved multiple counts, and multiple counts is a component of organization. Indeed, the operationalization of organization in terms of the components therefore had to be slightly different for cases with single and multiple counts; cases with multiple counts comprised one less component of organization for an equivalent level of organization. (Actually, this distinction was not made in this MAUM analysis, because it would have required a different scale of organization in the weighting task when the comparison involved multiple counts and this would have been impracticable.) Even though the maximum number of elements of organization found in the (original) archival study to be associated with a burglary of a dwelling was six, eight was chosen, to some extent arbitrarily, as the maximum plausible upper limit. In this way each of the four categories on this factor in the model was represented by two levels of seriousness (one high, the other low); and the description of organization incorporating the eight components did not seem to be unrealistic or implausible.

Because the definitions of the components in the model were presented in the form of criteria, again the author had to compose illustrative case events

TABLE 14.2. Components comprising the levels on organization for the scaling of seriousness

Level[a]	Code[b]	Single count component	Multiple counts component
1	1	Jimmy	Multiple counts
2	1	Night	Jimmy
3	2	Fence	Night
4	2	Stole panel van	Fence
5	3	Preselected house	Stole panel van
6	3	Skeleton keys	Preselected house
7	4	Co-offender	Skeleton keys
8	4	Disconnected alarm	Co-offender

[a] The higher levels include the components comprising the lower levels.
[b] This is the code that would fit this description, according to the model of judicial decision making (Table 6.4).

representing these elements. Table 14.2 presents summary descriptions of the components used for the scaling of organization, for cases with single and multiple counts; detailed descriptions of these components are shown in Table 14.3. Where a component of organization was not part of an offense, it was considered desirable, for most of the elements, to indicate this clearly, and so in those instances reference was made in the fictitious descriptions to actions characteristic of their absence. The effect of this should have been to increase the precision of the description of the extent and nature of the organization. These descriptions are presented in brackets in Table 14.3.

Of course, the composition for each level of organization (Tables 14.2 and 14.3) was just one set of a potentially infinite variety of descriptions. Each com-

TABLE 14.3. Descriptions of the components of organization for the scaling of seriousness

Component	Description
Jimmy	The offender carried a jimmy to the burglary (the offender entered through an unlocked door or window)
Night	The offender committed the burglary at night (committed the burglary during the day)
Fence	The offender had a fence to whom he took the stolen goods immediately (the offender sold the goods in local pubs)
Stole panel van	The offender stole a panel van that was parked outside a house in a nearby suburb and then, after delivering the goods to the fence, abandoned it (the offender used his own panel van)
Preselected house	The offender, before committing the burglary, selected a prosperous area and selected suitable houses (e.g., ones offering camouflage) (the offender chose houses at random in a nearby suburb for convenience)
Skeleton keys	The offender carried a set of skeleton keys (no reference to this point)
Co-offender	The offender met a friend in a pub and asked him to help with a burglary for some easy money (i.e., two offenders) (the offender acted alone)
Disconnected alarm	The offender checked for and disconnected any alarm system (no reference to this point)

TABLE 14.4. Values for the levels on total value of the theft for the scaling of seriousness

Level	Value of theft ($)
1	100
2	2,000
3	5,000
4	15,000
5	30,000
6	50,000
7	70,000
8	90,000
9	105,000
10	115,000
11	120,000

ponent could be illustrated differently, and each level could comprise other combinations of components. One should not assume that an assessment of seriousness for a particular level as it was operationalized here would necessarily generalize to other possible descriptions of that level.

Total Value of the Theft

The upper and lower levels on this factor were set at $120,000 and $100, respectively. The figure of $120,000 was a little above the highest total value found in the (original) archival study (see Table 6.5) for a case of a theft from a dwelling. Now, although some burglaries are without profit, it was necessary to set the lowest level at a non-0 value, because for the holistic assessments in the coherency study, some of the case combinations of these four offense factors involved multiple counts, and it would have been unrealistic for such cases not to have had at least minimal material rewards; moreover, in any case of burglary there must be at least one count and minimal violence and organization. There were nine intermediate levels of seriousness whose values were set so that they fell on or near the criteria defining the four categories on this factor in the model and also were well distributed across the range (see Table 6.6). Table 14.4 shows the monetary values of the levels for the assessment of seriousness in relation to total value of the theft.

Counts of Burglary

The upper and lower levels on this factor were set at 37 counts and 1 count, respectively. The figure of 37 counts was a little above the highest number of counts for a case of theft from a dwelling in the (original) archival study, and there were cases involving one count (Table 6.7). There were eight intermediate levels of seriousness whose values were set so that they fell on or near the criteria defining the four categories on this factor in the model and also were well dis-

TABLE 14.5. Values for the levels on counts of burglary for the scaling of seriousness

Level	Number of counts
1	1
2	2
3	4
4	10
5	16
6	22
7	28
8	34
9	36
10	37

tributed across the range (see Table 6.8). Table 14.5 shows numbers of counts defining the levels for the assessment of seriousness in relation to counts of burglary.

General Matters

The nature of the first two scales, violence to the victims and organization, left the researcher with little freedom in determining how the levels for the scaling exercise should be distributed across the categories as they were defined in the model. It was not possible to differentiate more than two levels per category. For these two dimensions the levels were evenly distributed across seriousness, as it was defined in the model. Moreover, the levels, viewed independently of any particular construction of seriousness, would appear to be well distributed across these two dimensions, as they were defined in terms of objective case facts. However, for the case factors total value of the theft and counts of burglary, the nature of the distribution was left open. The levels could have been evenly distributed across seriousness, as it was defined in the model—two levels per category—or evenly distributed in terms of the objective case facts. An even distribution on one basis entailed an uneven distribution in relation to the other criterion. The second alternative was chosen. The levels of seriousness were distributed evenly in relation to the objective case factors of dollars and counts. Actually, they were symmetrically distributed about the midpoint of the objective scale. There were two reasons for this. The first alternative would have made the judges vulnerable to a rating bias. If the levels had been concentrated at the lower end of these two dimensions, then this might have conveyed to the judges an expectation that this is where the discriminations in seriousness should be made and might have influenced their assessments accordingly. Second, the levels for assessment still could be set at or about the values defining the categories on these two factors in the model.

It was considered desirable that the four case factors should be presented to each judge in a different random order. This was done with the constraint that organization was never presented first, because the operationalization of this dimension and the relevance of its individual elements to seriousness were thought at the time to be arguably problematic, at least to the extent that some judges might have been disorientated by it or perhaps become disenchanted with the exercise.

In setting maximum plausible values for the offense factors in the scaling exercise, regard was paid to the distributions on these factors of cases of burglary of a dwelling in the (original) archival study. It was thought that the archival study would provide more reliable estimates than those that would be obtained from the direct questioning of the judges. It must be remembered that individual judges do not sentence particularly large numbers of cases, and therefore their knowledge of how actual cases would lie on these offense dimensions, especially at the upper levels, might not be well founded. Clearly, though, the use of the archival study as a basis for these estimates was somewhat problematic, particularly for total value of the theft and counts of burglary, because the most extreme 5% to 10% of cases on these dimensions covered a wide range on the objective scales of dollars and counts, and the sample comprised only (approximately) 50 cases of burglary of a dwelling. Accordingly, as part of the scaling exercise, judges were asked whether they agreed that the values representing the upper levels on the offense factors reasonably could be regarded as maximum plausible values.

Development of Scales of Relative Seriousness in Relation to Each Offense Factor

This section of the study provided individual judges with the opportunity to explicitly express their value functions (in this case establish seriousness scales) for each of the four offense factors. These scaling judgments were made in terms of the levels identified in the analysis in the previous section. There, these levels were defined by objective offense characteristics for each of the offense factors.

The direct scaling methods advocated by Edwards in his SMART procedure (Edwards, 1977; Edwards & Newman, 1982; Stillwell et al., 1983) were applied here to the scaling of seriousness for each of the four offense factors. The instructions given to the judges on how to scale the objective scale values in relation to seriousness were consistent with interval scaling and were designed to encourage such a strategy. No attempt was made to assess the reliability of individual judge's ratings. It was thought that such a test would lack power because the judges would have been quite capable of remembering their answers within the period of time available for retesting and, moreover, a data base comprising the responses of a number of judges provided a measure of interjudge reliability. Of course, if this were low, it could be due to low intrajudge reliability or individual differences in the judges' value functions.

Edwards and Newman (1982) state that curvilinear value functions are unnecessary and that linear functions are adequate. Although they acknowledge that curvilinear relationships may provide more accurate representations of decision makers' true preferences, they argue that in most instances the more precise function would not change the overall evaluation and, if it did, the options would be so similar as to be interchangeable. In part, the validity of their argument depends on the degree of curvilinearity and the reliability of judges' assessments for the components of the decision. This is an empirical question. Of course, it would not be possible to determine which set of assessments was more valid. Even if one accepted holistic assessments in principle as a valid criterion of a decision maker's true preferences, whether the two sets of assessments were found to be differentially related to this criterion would depend on the reliability of the criterion judgments and the number of cases falling within that section of the distribution where the curvilinear and linear functions lay apart. In any case, if the judges' preferences are curvilinear and these functions were found to result in different (calculated) overall assessments, when allowance was made for inconsistencies in the value functions within and across the judges, then these judgments should stand. One would otherwise risk undermining the confidence of the decision makers in the technique and face a charge of adopting a scaling technique one did not believe in. This argument would appear to hold greater sway when the analysis is prescriptively based, because then the analysis is used to inform the decision makers about what overall evaluations they should make in view of their component judgments, and holistic judgments are not germane to the validity of the analysis. (Johnson & Mai, 1979, have warned that the correlation coefficient is an inappropriate measure of the degree of concordance between linear and curvilinear assessments, because it is insensitive to the expansion and contraction along a scale. Rather, Lyness and Cornelius's, 1982, measure of mean absolute deviations would seem to be a more appropriate measure, should casual inspection not suffice.)

Determination of the Relative Importance of Each Offense Factor in the Assessment of Seriousness

This section of the study provided individual judges with the opportunity to explicitly express how they weight each of the four offense factors (counts of burglary, organization, total value of the theft, and violence to the victims) in determining the overall seriousness of the offense characteristics of a burglary of a dwelling.

What is the significance of the weight of a factor? The meaning of weight is tied inextricably to the notions of importance and range. An offense factor is important to the extent that the assessment of seriousness in relation to that factor, independent of the range of the factor, determines the overall assessment of seriousness of the offense of which it is an element. Importance derives from the intrinsic nature of the factor. One may feel, for example, that physical injury is more serious than monetary loss. The more important a factor is in relation to the other factors, the greater is its relative influence on the decision. The range of a factor simply refers to the difference in seriousness between the minimum and maximum levels on the objective scale defining the factor. For example, a dimension of counts of burglary with maximum and minimum values of 100 counts and 1 count would cover a greater range than the same dimension with maximum and minimum values of 10 counts and 1 count; for a particular dimension, the greater the range of the dimension, the greater is its influence on the decision or contribution to the assessment.

Relative weight may vary across offense factors. Operationally, this means that the increase in perceived seriousness from the least serious (usually assigned a seriousness value of 0) to the most serious (usually assigned a seriousness value of 100) objective level of a factor may vary across the offense factors comprising offense seriousness. This occurs because the values of 0 and 100 may represent different degrees of seriousness across the factors, arising from differences in importance and range. As a consequence, the units of seriousness on different factors may not be equivalent. Weights can be quantified. When seriousness scale values on each of the component factors are multiplied by their appropriate relative factor weights, the units of seriousness on the various scales are made equivalent.

There are numerous direct and indirect methods for assessing weights (Anderson, 1982; Beach & Barnes, 1983; Cook & Stewart, 1975; Humphreys, 1977; Surber, 1985). The three most common direct methods appear to be the following:

1. Rating importance on a scale
2. Dividing 100 points between the component factors (Hoffman, 1960) in accordance with relative importance
3. Using the scaling technique of magnitude estimation (Edwards, 1977; Stillwell et al., 1983), in which the decision maker makes a ratio judgment to quantify the relative importance of one factor in terms of the modulus representing the arbitrary weight of a less important factor.

In my view the supposed simplicity of these methods is illusory, and the reason they can be described and applied so simply is that conceptual intricacies are handed over unstated and unraveled to the decision maker, who may neither be aware of them, nor understand them, nor be able nor willing to take account of them. It would appear that the concepts of range and importance are not always explained. Moreover, even where the role and interrelation of these two notions is explained, in my view these techniques do not facilitate the linking and consideration of range and importance in the decision maker's mind (Humphreys & McFadden, 1980; Wooler & Erlich, 1983). In any case the estimates of the ranges may vary across judges. Finally, unless the notion of range is introduced and explained, the decision maker may confound the effect of a factor on overall offense seriousness within a legal offense category (e.g., burglary) with the effect of that factor on the relative seriousness of two offenses (e.g., burglary and theft). By way of contrast, it would appear that Keeney and Raiffa's (1976) procedure for determining weights (scaling constants in their terms) in riskless decisions directs the decision maker's mind to the heart of the problem. Their approach therefore was followed here.

Extensive research deals with the appropriateness of unit weights. The research on this matter involves either predictions of outcomes for which there are external criteria or assessments made in the absence of a criterion measure (Dawes, 1979). In this literature there are both theoretical and empirical analyses of the conditions under which unit weights would be expected to be more appropriate than differential weights. Although many authors accept the utility and validity of unit weighting, it should be noted that whereas some authors appear to support it enthusiastically and conditional on only a few readily met requirements, others approve cautiously and with tight constraints (Camerer, 1981; Cattin, 1978; Dawes & Corrigan, 1974; Dorans & Drasgow, 1978; Keren & Newman, 1978; Parsons & Hulin, 1982; Wainer, 1976, 1978). Clearly, it is important to consider the relevance of these analyses in the light of the current problem.

The present project falls within the category of study in which there is no external criterion against which to compare the decision makers' judgments (in this case tariff sentences). Now, Einhorn and Hogarth (1975) conclude that in these circumstances only unit weights are appropriate. Although this argument may hold for a descriptive analysis, it does not apply to the prescriptive application of decomposed judgments, where one is concerned with the judgments individuals should make about complex phenomena in the light of their assessments of the components. Of course, in the absence of an external criterion, one may choose to model the decision makers' holistic assessments to derive their weights. Again, however, there is a problem here. Holistic assessments of seriousness are not appropriate as a source of the decision makers' weights or as a criterion for comparing differential- and unit-weighting schemes where the orientation is prescriptive, because the purpose of applying decision analysis is to improve on holistic judgments.

A critical difference between the thrust of this literature on weighting and the present problem is the goal of the analysis. Here the point of concern is decision—discriminating between cases in terms of seriousness—not prediction. Stillwell, Seaver, and Edwards (1981), Newman (1977), and Einhorn and McCoach (1977) have drawn attention to the significance of this distinction. In the present study the model is to be used to assess cases characterized by crosscurrents of aggravating and extenuating factors. Under such circumstances, the dimensions are negatively correlated and, accordingly, do not satisfy one of the requirements claimed to be necessary for the success of unit weights.

Moreover, one should not forget the judges' feelings in this matter. If in fact judges do believe that they weight factors differentially, then it would be foolish to proceed on the assumption that these perceived distinctions are not significant. Were one to pursue such a course in the absence of hard empirical evidence, then almost certainly it would be without the judges' cooperation (Newman, 1977).

It follows from this discussion that the research should test the validity of the differential- and unit-weighting schemes. And a sensitivity analysis is the appropriate means. If judges assess case factor weights differentially and if these weights were found to result in (calculated) overall assessments of seriousness different from those generated by equal weights, when allowance was made for inconsistencies in the assessed weights within and across judges, then the judgments of differential weight should stand.

One final point should be made regarding the assessment of weights. For the purposes of this study, it was not necessary to separate range and importance, because range was not determined arbitrarily and would be expected to show stability. The analysis therefore did not go down the track of Anderson and Norman (Anderson, 1982; Levin et al., 1983).

Calculation of the Overall Seriousness of the Offense Characteristics

To determine the overall seriousness of the offense characteristics of a burglary, the assessments of seriousness on each of the component offense factors must be aggregated, allowing for the factor weights. The foregoing sections dealt with the scaling of seriousness for the components and the assessing of relative factor weights. In this section the composition rule is the subject of attention. The question is: what form should the joint value function take to represent the judicial determination of offense seriousness accurately?

Two considerations are operative here. First, it will be remembered that this analysis has a prescriptive orientation. The focus is on the principles and rules that judges attempt to follow in applying sentencing policy—a model of their thought processes free from the distortions that may arise from influences such as information overload. The second is the principle of parsimony: the composition rule chosen should be the simplest one that is consistent with the prescriptions of sentencing policy for judicial decision making. Thomas (1979), on the basis of his analyses of the judgments of the English Court of Appeal (Criminal Division), has identified the line of reasoning that judges appear to attempt to follow to quantify offense seriousness on the basis of the facts of the offense (see Chapter 4). There it was concluded that judges arrive at a quantum judgment by adding (or subtracting), as it were, points for aggravating (or extenuating) circumstances surrounding the offense. Moreover, one may deduce implicitly that the determination of offense seriousness should be neither supra- nor subadditive. The overall assessment of seriousness, then, should not be greater or less than the sum of the components. Not greater because Thomas expressly provides for interaction only between certain combinations of mitigating factors, and not less because Thomas applies his totality principle, the import of which is that the quantum of sentence should increase at a rate less than in direct proportion to the seriousness of the case, only to the determination of sentence (cf. seriousness) for cases with multiple counts. In view of this discussion, the simplest veridical composition rule describing the judicial determination of the seriousness of an offense would be a weighted additive value function. This rule states that to determine the overall seriousness of an offense, one simply multiplies the single-attribute seriousness assessment on each offense factor by the appropriate factor weight and then sums these multiples; in this joint value function the relative weights add to unity. This aggregation rule is represented mathematically by the following equation:

$$V(O_j) = \sum_{i=1}^{n} w_i v_i\ (x_{ij}) \quad \text{and} \quad \sum_{i=1}^{n} w_i = 1$$

where

$V(O_j)$ is the seriousness of an offense (O_j)
$X_1 \ldots X_n$ are the n offense factors describing each offense (O_j)
x_i is a level on the objective scale of the ith offense factor
w_i is the weight of the ith offense factor
$v_i\ (x_{ij})$ is the seriousness on a 0 to 100 scale of the x_i of the jth offense.

The $v_i\ (x_{ij})$s are taken directly from each judge's seriousness scale for each offense factor. So, if a judge had rated 30 counts (x_{ij}) at 70 on the seriousness scale, then 70 would be the value of the $v_i\ (x_{ij})$ for a case (O_j) comprising 30 counts. The derivation of the w_is is a little more complex. Consider two factors, X_1 and X_2, where the weight of the first is greater, that is, $w_1 > w_2$. The determination of the relative weights is based on the assessed seriousness of level (x_1), such that the increase in seriousness between the highest and lowest levels on X_2 is equivalent to the difference in seriousness between this x_1 and the lowest level on X_1. Then,

$$w_2 = v_1 \frac{(x_1)}{100} w_1 \quad \text{and} \quad w_1 + w_2 = 1.$$

The weighted additive decomposition of a joint value function requires the assumption of mutual preferential independence of the set of attributes (case factors). For example, consider four attributes. One pair of attributes is preferentially independent of the others if the rate of trade-off between these two is independent of any fixed levels at which the other two attributes might be set. If the second pair also is preferentially independent of the first, then the two pairs satisfy the assumption of mutual preferential independence. This can be illustrated in the context of the present study. Assume that the assessed difference in seriousness between 1 and 20 counts (on counts of burglary) was judged to be equivalent to the difference in seriousness between \$100 and \$70,000 (on total value of the theft) when the levels on violence to the victims and organization were high, and the point of assessed equivalence (in this case, \$70,000) remained unchanged when the levels on violence to the victims and organization were lowered. This outcome is consistent with preferential independence. Now, if each pair of attributes is preferentially independent of its complement, then the assumption of mutual preferential independence is satisfied. (Actually, fewer tests are required to check the validity of this assumption; see Keeney & Raiffa, 1976.) Nevertheless, this assumption was not directly tested here because of the prescriptive orientation of the study; it is implicit in Thomas's model that the contribution of an offense factor to the overall seriousness of a particular offense is independent of the nature of that offense in terms of the other offense factors. Of course, this approach to the validity of the axiomatic basis of the decision model would not have been an option if the focus of concern had been a description of actual decision making (see Chapter 12).

It must be understood, however, that this approach to the independence assumption can be followed only when the set of offense factors are defined correctly and are interpreted appropriately by the judges. Each of these matters bears elaboration. First, it is possible that the technique used to elicit the judges' preferences might induce judgmental biases, in which case the judges' actual assessments would not be a veridical reflection of their true preferences. Second, the four offense factors, as defined in this study, might not be viewed by the judges as making independent contributions to the assessment of offense seriousness (i.e., the more detailed specification of Thomas's model through the operational definitions of the offense factors may be in error). Third, a judge might, when presented with a particular level on one offense characteristic, make inferences about the offense in terms of another offense characteristic; for example, a judge might assume that an offender who stole $120,000 in one count was well organized. Accordingly, in the weighting exercises it was necessary to investigate the effect of context on the assessments, that is, to check whether the trade-offs for the various combinations of offense factor pairs depended on the values of their complementary pairs. (This in effect tested preferential independence.)

To make these checks, each judge was asked to make a trade-off (find an equivalence point) between two particular factors by first considering them alone, then in the context of the complementary pair, each set at its least serious level and, finally, in view of variation in the levels of the complementary pair. This approach, in which the judges were in effect encouraged when making a trade-off to concentrate first and foremost on the actual two factors involved in the trade-off and as a consequence pay less attention to the complementary pair, was quite deliberate. It was considered that this was an adequate test of whether the trade-offs for the various pairs of offense factors were independent of the values of the complementary pairs. (In the holistic approach a judge in making a trade-off is forced to consider the seriousness of two cases; the seriousness of one of the factors in one of the cases is varied until equivalence is reached between the two cases. Of course, holistic assessments are necessary to test rigorously the assumption of preferential independence where the model purports to describe actual decision behavior.) Fortunately, this test was adequate; one of the reasons for adopting a decomposed orientation is to avoid judgmental errors induced by the cognitive overload associated with complex holistic judgments. In adopting this strategy in which the judges' focus of attention is on the two factors involved in the trade-off, one is conscious that judges are accustomed to making holistic case assessments and, accordingly, would be expected to be particularly alive to the potential import (cf. precise magnitude of effect) of the other offense factors for a particular trade-off. And so the test should not be insensitive to the possible role of the complementary factors and yet be less susceptible to the effects of cognitive overload.

This is the appropriate section to address an issue relating to the independence of two of the offense factors in this study. It should be noted that counts of burglary and total value of the theft are necessarily correlated; the total value of the money and merchandise stolen increases with the number of burglaries. This should be distinguished from an environmental correlation that is a consequence of a pattern of offending. For example, street muggings may be more likely than bank robberies to result in physical injuries to the victim because the victim is more likely to attempt to resist the attack, with a consequent (negative) correlation between violence to the victims and total value of the theft. In the former case a question arises whether the dimension of total value of the theft is a fair measure of the value of the theft because it could be construed as entailing double counting in the sense that an offender with multiple counts necessarily would obtain a higher score on total value of the theft. The matter of double counting does not arise, however, when the decision maker believes that the two offense factors should contribute independently to the overall seriousness of the offense. Indeed, it is assumed here that this position represents current sentencing policy. But perhaps an offense factor measuring the average value of the theft in each count would be fairer? The nature of the criteria defining offense seriousness was not explored systematically with the judges at this stage but, clearly, it is an area warranting further investigation. This again illustrates nicely how a quantitative approach fosters precision in the analysis of sentencing policy.

Assessment of the Sensitivity of the Estimates of the Offense Factor Weights

The purpose of a sensitivity analysis is to examine the effects of possible errors in the component judgments on the overall evaluation of the seriousness of the offense. Of concern is possible error in the judges' scaling of seriousness in relation to the objective offense factor scales and in their assessments of the relative weights of the offense factors. There are two potential sources of error. First, the judges may not have thought about some of the required assessments, at least not to an adequate level of precision, and the consequence of this might be instability in their judgments on these tasks. Second, the measurement techniques may induce biases, and these effects might be exacerbated to the extent that there was uncertainty over the assessments in the judges' minds. The strategy of a sensitivity analysis involves varying the assessed weights within the limits of possible measurement error and uncertainty and then observing the extent to which there are resultant changes in the measure of the composite assessment of offense seriousness. However, at this early stage in the development of the model of judicial decision making this was considered to be an inappropriately sophisticated analysis. Rather, it was considered sufficient to ask a more basic question, namely, whether the judges' assessed weights were significantly different from unit weights in terms of their effect on the calculated value of overall offense seriousness. This analysis was confined to the matter of weights, because it is clear from the literature that this is the contentious area in MAUM analysis. Moreover, the criterion was taken as the calculated value of overall offense seriousness, rather than the holistically assessed value, in view of the prescriptive orientation of the study.

The next problem in testing the sensitivity of the scaling concerned the selection of a sample of offenses that would act as a critical test. In a sensitivity analysis relating to the assessment of weight, the problem lies in the structure of the offenses; here *structure* refers to the way in which the offenses in the sample vary in relation to each other on the four constituent dimensions: counts of burglary, organization, violence to the victims, and total value of the theft. To test to what extent changes in weights would lead to changes in the overall assessments, the sample of offenses must provide a real decision problem. Technically, this means that there are no dominated options (offenses). An offense is dominated if there is another offense that is rated as more serious on at least one offense factor and is at least as serious on the other three offense factors. The work of Stillwell et al. (1981) suggests that the offense factors in such a set of offenses would be negatively correlated. The earlier discussion on weighting (preceding) referred to research showing that where the component dimensions are negatively correlated, equal and differential weights result in significantly different overall assessments. A proviso to this conclusion from the work of Stillwell et al. (1981) is that the negatively correlated factors must be differentially weighted.

Clearly, such a sample of offenses would make for a very conservative test and, relative to a representative sample of burglary offenses, would probably provide an overestimate of the significance of differential weighting, because in a representative sample there would be many dominated offense patterns. Nevertheless, it was decided to opt for the more stringent test on three grounds. First, for practical reasons the total number of offenses had to be relatively small, and it would have been impossible to represent adequately the patterns of offending among actual offenses. Second, because one of the main difficulties judges face in applying sentencing policy is thought to lie in their attempts at reconciling cross-currents of aggravating and extenuating circumstances, a sample of offenses satisfying this criterion seemed not inappropriate. Third, the present study is not a problem in prediction but rather an attempt at understanding and aiding decision making.

In establishing the offenses for this analysis, it was decided that there should be four levels on each of the four dimensions. Four levels provided a reasonable coverage of each dimension, facilitated comparisons with the model of judicial decision making, and yet did not require an unwieldy number of combinations for a sample of offenses covering the range of overall offense seriousness and

TABLE 14.6. Levels of seriousness on the four offense factors for the sensitivity analysis

Level	Factor			
	Violence to the victims[a]	Organization[b]	Total value of the theft	Counts of burglary
4	Tie-up victim—unprovoked	8	$120,000	37
3	Threaten victim—unprovoked	6	$50,000	16
2	Search premises until seen by victim	4	$15,000	4
1	Occupants not at home during burglary	1	$100	1

[a] See Table 14.1 for details.
[b] Number of elements; see Tables 14.2 and 14.3 for details.

TABLE 14.7. Structures of the offenses in samples A and B for the sensitivity analysis

Sample	Overall offense seriousness[a]	Offense factor			
		Counts	Organization	Violence	Value
A	14	4	4	3	3
	13	3	3	3	4
	12	3	1	4	4
	11	1	4	2	4
	10	1	4	4	1
B	9	4	1	2	2
	8	3	1	1	3
	7	1	1	1	4
	6	1	1	3	1
	5	1	2	1	1

Note. The patterns of offending are described in terms of the levels defined in Table 14.6.
[a] These figures assume the validity of the scoring system in the archival burglary study and so may only approximate overall offense seriousness as it was assessed by the various judges.

TABLE 14.8. Intercorrelations of the offense factors for the sensitivity analysis: Samples A and B

Sample	Organization	Value	Counts
A			
Violence	−.50	−.50	.13
Organization		−.47	−.34
Value			.37
B			
Violence	−.38	−.56	0
Organization		−.51	−.40
Value			.14

TABLE 14.9. Structures of the offenses in samples A′ and B′ for the sensitivity analysis

Sample	Overall offense seriousness[a]	Offense factor			
		Organization	Counts	Value	Violence
A′	14	4	3	4	3
	13	3	3	3	4
	12	3	1	4	4
	11	1	4	2	4
	10	1	4	4	1
B′	9	4	1	2	2
	8	3	1	1	3
	7	1	1	1	4
	6	1	1	3	1
	5	1	2	1	1

Note. The patterns of offending are described in terms of the levels defined in Table 14.6.
[a] These figures assume the validity of the scoring system in the archival burglary study and so may only approximate overall offense seriousness as it was assessed by the various judges.

providing some variation in the pattern of offending within each level of overall offense seriousness.

Table 14.6 presents descriptions of the objective scale values (levels) selected to represent each of the four offense factors. The descriptions for levels 2, 3, and 4 cover behaviors that appear to lie near the more serious boundaries of the equivalent categories in the model of judicial decision making and, for level 1, near the less serious boundaries (see Tables 6.1, 6.4, 6.6, and 6.8).

Ideally, weight sensitivity should be tested on a set of offenses covering the range of overall offense seriousness, since the significance of the effects of variation in the weights can be more readily appreciated in relation to the range of overall offense seriousness. This was not possible here, however. In a set of offenses spanning the range of seriousness, some of the patterns of offending that represent a high level of overall offense seriousness would have dominated patterns from the lower levels. Therefore, weight sensitivity was tested in two

TABLE 14.10. Intercorrelations of the offense factors for the sensitivity analysis: Samples A′ and B′

Sample	Organization	Value	Counts
A′			
Violence	.37	−.51	−.47
Organization		.46	−.61
Value			−.46
B′			
Violence	.14	−.56	−.51
Organization		0	−.40
Value			−.38

groups, each group comprising five undominated patterns of offending and together covering the range of overall offense seriousness; the selection of patterns was otherwise unsystematic. The columns were labeled so that none of the combinations of levels appeared to represent an implausible offense pattern. The structures of the offenses comprising these two groups are shown in Table 14.7; the structures are described in terms of the levels defined in Table 14.6. These structures cover all except the most and least extreme patterns of offending; only the most serious combination represented a level of seriousness that was not found in the (original) archival burglary study (see Tables 7.1 to 7.2). Table 14.8 presents the intercorrelations between these levels; most of these correlations are substantial and negative. Because the correlations are based on ranks they also would hold for the judges' assessments of the seriousness of these levels. This, of course, requires the very reasonable assumption that the judges' assessments of the seriousness of the levels are monotonically related to the levels' objective scale values.

Two additional samples, A′ and B′, were constructed and included in the test of weight sensitivity so that it was more rigorous; a finding of weight sensitivity or insensitivity in a sample of five offenses would indeed be tenuous. If the finding, however, were substantiated across four samples, two samples for each half of the dimension of seriousness, then one would have more confidence in the result. This additional pair of samples was created simply by interchanging the levels in the columns of counts and organization and also interchanging violence and value (see Table 14.7). Additionally, two of the levels had to be changed so that samples A and A′ did not share a common, the most serious, offense pattern. The structures of these two samples are presented in Table 14.9, and the resulting intercorrelations between the levels comprising the offense factors are shown in Table 14.10.

In comparing Table 14.8 and Table 14.10, it can be seen that within comparable samples (i.e., within A and A′ and within B and B′) at least one of the two intercorrelations for each pair of factors is substantial and negative.

15
Scaling of Seriousness and Assessment of Weights for Offense Factors of Burglary

MAUM Method

The instructions were presented to the judges in a booklet with the cover title *Sentencing Research Exercise—Part 2*. The first page gave a general introduction to the tasks followed on the next three pages by the instructions for the scaling of seriousness in terms of the offense factors and finally the instructions (two pages) for the weighting exercises. Associated materials for this task included sheets of paper on which the scaling problems were presented, graph paper with labeled axes for illustrating each judge's value (seriousness) functions and other sheets on which the weighting problems were presented.

The material for the scaling of each offense factor consisted of one A4 sheet per factor. The title of the offense factor was at the top of the page and under it the description of the factor in terms of the objectively defined levels for which seriousness ratings were required. The offense factor descriptions presented to the judges were the same as those shown in Tables 14.1 to 14.5, although the levels were labeled alphabetically, not numerically as in those tables. Moreover, for organization the description of each level incorporated all the components comprising that level in point form. The descriptions appeared in order from the least serious at the bottom of the page, with an identifying letter of the alphabet (A, B, C, etc.) to the left of the description of each level. In certain instances it was necessary to set the description of a factor in context to make the task less abstract (e.g., indicate the victim's means for total value of the theft); to ensure realism (e.g., limit a high level of violence to one offense in cases involving multiple counts); and to indicate precisely the nature of the levels of the factor (e.g., specify the time period for counts of burglary). The descriptions of the four factors each covered one A4 page. A rating scale was placed at the bottom of each description—a 100-mm line, horizontal and centered, with unlabeled marks at 10-mm intervals and the labels, *0*, and *100*, at the left and right ends, respectively, of the line. At the 0 point an A was written just above the line. Similarly, at the other end of the scale, the letter identifying the description of the most serious level on the factor was written above the 100. Accordingly, the two extreme levels on a factor defined the anchors for that factor. (See Tables 15.1 to 15.4.)

TABLE 15.1. The scale of total value of the theft: Scaling of seriousness

Scale label	Total value of the theft ($)
K	120,000
J	115,000
I	105,000
H	90,000
G	70,000
F	50,000
E	30,000
D	15,000
C	5,000
B	2,000
A	100

Note. Assume for all the levels that the victim was not poor; the property taken included cash and merchandise such as electrical goods.

The materials for the presentation of the weighting problems again simply consisted of sheets of paper with descriptions of the four offense factors—one A4 sheet per factor. They were set out in a similar fashion to the material for the scaling of seriousness, except that for organization and violence to the victims only summary descriptions were presented, and for counts of burglary and total value of the theft the intermediate levels were spaced in proportion to the objective scale values; also, the rating scales were omitted. The descriptions of each scale covered most of one page and were approximately the same length. (See Tables 15.5 to 15.8.)

The sample of judges participating in the first exercise was again used here. Each of the judges was interviewed by the author individually. Whereas in the previous exercise the judges were left to complete the task alone, in this exercise the author personally worked through the problems with the individual judges. The instructions were sent to each judge about 1 week before he undertook the exercise. This comprised the following material in quotation marks, but did not include the procedural asides or descriptions of the four offense factors. (One of the factors, counts of burglary, was included with the instructions to provide an example of the material.) The tasks also were explained informally to each judge at the beginning of the session. The text of the exercise booklet follows.

Text of Sentencing Research Exercise—Part 2

General Introduction

This exercise is the second in the series concerned with understanding how judges determine what is appropriate by way of sentence, and the information will be used to assist in developing a means of representing the relationship between case characteristics and sentence as a basis for detailed sentencing statistics. You are again reminded that your

TABLE 15.2. The scale of organization: Scaling of seriousness

Scale label	Organization
H	The offender carried a jimmy to the burglary. Committed the burglary at night. Had a fence to whom he took the stolen goods immediately. Stole a panel van that was parked outside a house in a nearby suburb and then, after delivering the goods to the fence, abandoned it. Before committing the burglary, selected a prosperous area and selected suitable houses (e.g., ones offering camouflage). Carried a set of skeleton keys. Met a friend in a pub and asked him to help with a burglary for some easy money (i.e., two offenders). Checked for and disconnected any alarm system.
G	The offender carried a jimmy to the burglary. Committed the burglary at night. Had a fence to whom he took the stolen goods immediately. Stole a panel van that was parked outside a house in a nearby suburb and then, after delivering the goods to the fence, abandoned it. Before committing the burglary, selected a prosperous area and selected suitable houses (e.g., ones offering camouflage). Carried a set of skeleton keys. Met a friend in a pub and asked him to help with a burglary for some easy money (i.e., two offenders).
F	The offender carried a jimmy to the burglary. Committed the burglary at night. Had a fence to whom he took the stolen goods immediately. Stole a panel van that was parked outside a house in a nearby suburb and then, after delivering the goods to the fence, abandoned it. Before committing the burglary, selected a prosperous area and selected suitable houses (e.g., ones offering camouflage). Carried a set of skeleton keys. Acted alone.
E	The offender carried a jimmy to the burglary. Committed the burglary at night. Had a fence to whom he took the stolen goods immediately. Stole a panel van that was parked outside a house in a nearby suburb and then, after delivering the goods to the fence, abandoned it. Before committing the burglary, selected a prosperous area and selected suitable houses (e.g., ones offering camouflage). Acted alone.
D	The offender carried a jimmy to the burglary. Committed the burglary at night. Had a fence to whom he took the stolen goods immediately. Stole a panel van that was parked outside a house in a nearby suburb and then, after delivering the goods to the fence, abandoned it. Chose houses at random in a nearby suburb for convenience. Acted alone.
C	The offender carried a jimmy to the burglary. Committed the burglary at night. Had a fence to whom he took the stolen goods immediately. Used his own panel van. Chose houses at random in a nearby suburb for convenience. Acted alone.
B	The offender carried a jimmy to the burglary. Committed the burglary at night. Sold the goods in local pubs. Used his own panel van. Chose houses at random in a nearby suburb for convenience. Acted alone.
A	The offender carried a jimmy to the burglary. Committed the burglary during the day. Sold the goods in local pubs. Used his own panel van. Chose houses at random in a nearby suburb for convenience. Acted alone.

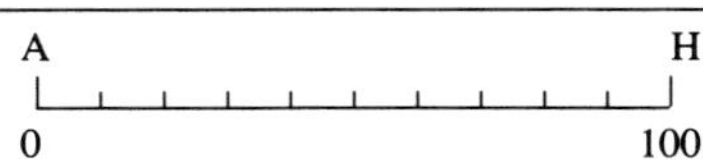

TABLE 15.3. The scale of counts of burglary: Scaling of seriousness

Scale label	Counts of burglary
J	37
I	36
H	34
G	28
F	22
E	16
D	10
C	4
B	2
A	1

Note. Assume that for each of the levels comprising multiple counts the offenses were committed over an extended period of time (several weeks to months), and this period was proportional to the number of counts.

responses will not become part of a sentencing statistics data base and will not be submitted as individual data to the Sentencing Committee.

This exercise comprises two stages. In the first stage your task is to develop four scales of seriousness, one for each of four offence factors of cases of burglary—*counts of burglary, organization, total value of the theft,* and *violence to the victims.* In the second you will be asked to consider how important each of these factors is in the determination of the overall seriousness of the offence characteristics of a case of burglary. In all instances you should assume that the factors relate to burglaries of private homes.

Assessment of Seriousness

Cases in which burglary is the principal count vary in a number of aspects, including the number of counts, extent of the organization, the total amount of money stolen, and the degree of violence, i.e., the objective scale values (number of counts, etc.) of each of these factors vary across cases of burglary. The objective scale values which an offence factor may assume are referred to as levels. For each offence factor you will be presented with a number of its potential constituent levels. Each level is described briefly and is identified by a letter of the alphabet (e.g., a series of numbers of counts for the offence factor *counts of burglary*). Your task is to assess, for each factor, the relative seriousness of its constituent levels by placing marks, together with the letter identifying the level, on the scale of seriousness at the bottom of the description of the factor. Each of the four factors is presented separately, and is to be considered in turn; you will be told the sequence in which the factors are to be assessed. One factor is shown on [a following] page . . . .

In determining what is appropriate by way of sentence a judge must, *inter alia*, form a view about the seriousness of the offence characteristics of the case. Clearly, a judge, in assessing the overall seriousness of the offence characteristics of a case, must at least implicitly form a view about the relative seriousness of the levels within each of the constituent offence characteristics—the number of counts, etc. These evaluations are the point of this task.

To assist you in making these assessments, you have been given rating scales; the most serious level on each factor has arbitrarily been assigned a seriousness rating of 100, and

TABLE 15.4. The scale of violence to the victims: Scaling of seriousness

Scale label	Violence to the victims
H	The burglar entered the home when the occupants were out. During the burglary he heard a car turn into the property. He looked out from an upstairs window and saw a man entering the house. He continued to search the room, even after the owner came upstairs, until the owner entered the room, whereupon he picked up a table lamp with a metal base and ran at the owner, threatening to strike him and ordering him to stand with his hands behind his back. The burglar used the flex from the lamp to bind the owner's hands and feet. The burglar then immediately climbed out through the window onto the roof of a ground-floor extension and made his escape.
G	The burglar entered the home when the occupants were out. During the burglary he heard a car turn into the property. He looked out from an upstairs window and saw a man entering the house. He continued to search the room, even after the owner came upstairs, until the owner entered the room, whereupon he went across to the window. The owner ran across the room towards him. In response the burglar picked up a table lamp with a metal base, threatened to strike him, and ordered him to stand with his hands behind his back. The burglar used the flex from the lamp to bind the owner's hands and feet. The burglar then immediately climbed out through the window onto the roof of a ground-floor extension and made his escape.
F	The burglar entered the home when the occupants were out. During the burglary he heard a car turn into the property. He looked out from an upstairs window and saw a man entering the house. He continued to search the room, even after the owner came upstairs, until the owner entered the room, whereupon the offender moved one pace toward him, waved his fist and threatened to strike him. The burglar then immediately ran across to the window and climbed out onto the roof of a ground-floor extension and made his escape.
E	The burglar entered the home when the occupants were out. During the burglary he heard a car turn into the property. He looked out from an upstairs window and saw a man entering the house. He continued to search the room, even after the owner came upstairs, until the owner entered the room, whereupon he went across to the window. The owner then ran across the room toward him. In response the burglar turned, waved his fist and threatened to strike the owner. The owner withdrew, and the burglar immediately climbed out of the window onto the roof of a ground-floor extension and made his escape.
D	The burglar entered the home when the occupants were out. During the burglary he heard a car turn into the property. He looked out from an upstairs window and saw a man entering the house. He continued to search the room, even after the owner had come upstairs, until the owner entered the room. The owner ran toward him, whereupon he quickly climbed out of the window onto the roof of a ground-floor extension and made his escape.
C	The burglar entered the home when the occupants were out. During the burglary he heard a car turn into the property. He looked out from an upstairs window and saw a man entering the house. He continued to search the room but left by the window when he heard the owner come upstairs.
B	The burglar entered the home when the occupants were out. During the burglary he heard a car turn into the property and he immediately left through the front door, running past the owner in the driveway.
A	No one was home during the burglary.

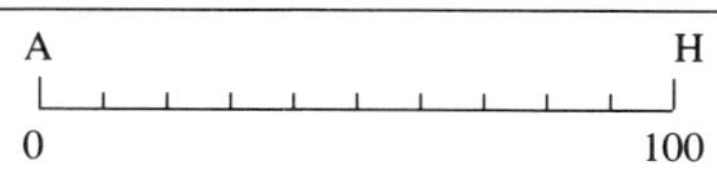

Note. For all the levels, the only damage done was a broken lock on the rear door and minor disturbance to the contents, associated with the search; and the owner was 45 years old.

TABLE 15.5. The scale of total value of the theft: Assessment of weight

Total value of the theft ($)
120,000
115,000
105,000
90,000
70,000
50,000
30,000
15,000
5,000
2,000
100

Note. Assume for all the levels that the victim was not poor; the property taken included cash and merchandise such as electrical goods.

TABLE 15.6. The scale of organization: Assessment of weight

Scale label	Organization
H	Jimmy carried, committed at night, goods taken immediately to fence, stolen van used, preselected houses offering some camouflage in prosperous area, skeleton keys carried, friend's help enlisted, checked for and disconnected alarm system
G	Jimmy carried, committed at night, goods taken immediately to fence, stolen van used, preselected houses offering some camouflage in prosperous area, skeleton keys carried, friend's help enlisted
F	Jimmy carried, committed at night, goods taken immediately to fence, stolen van used, preselected houses offering some camouflage in prosperous area, skeleton keys carried, acted alone
E	Jimmy carried, committed at night, goods taken immediately to fence, stolen van used, preselected houses offering some camouflage in prosperous area, acted alone
D	Jimmy carried, committed at night, goods taken immediately to fence, stolen van used, houses not preselected, acted alone
C	Jimmy carried, committed at night, goods taken immediately to fence, used own van, houses not preselected, acted alone
B	Jimmy carried, committed at night, sold the goods in local pubs, used own van, houses not preselected, acted alone
A	Jimmy carried, committed during the day, sold the goods in local pubs, used own van, houses not preselected, acted alone

the least serious level a rating of 0. Your rating of the seriousness of each level of a factor is to be made relative to these two anchors. Indicate your assessment of the degree of seriousness of each level by making a slash at the appropriate point on the rating scale and writing its identifying letter above the slash. (If you prefer, you may write the number quantifying your assessment of seriousness at the appropriate point on the scale, rather than making a slash.) For example, if you thought that the level before you (test level) was midway in seriousness between the two anchors you would make a slash at the mid-point of the rating scale. (The number quantifying your judgment in this instance would be 50.) This would mean that in your view the difference in seriousness between the test level and the least serious (anchor) level was equal to the difference in seriousness between the test level and the most serious (anchor) level. It is important to stress that this is not equivalent to the conclusion that the test level is thought to be half as serious as the most serious (anchor) level. The reason for this is that the least serious (anchor) level is not devoid of seriousness. Similarly, if you put a mark 25/100ths along the scale (or gave a rating of 25) it would mean that you thought that the increase in seriousness between the least serious (anchor) level and the test level was approximately 1/3rd of the increase in seriousness from the test level to the most serious (anchor) level; it would not follow that you thought that the test level was approximately 1/4 the seriousness of the most serious (anchor) level. It is crucial to keep in your mind that you are making interval not ratio judgments. An everyday example may help illustrate this distinction. Say that you were rating the heights of individuals on a 0-100 scale, and assume that the heights of these individuals fell within the range 5 ft to 7 ft. We could arbitrarily label a height of 5 ft as "0" and 7 ft as "100." Now, if you rated an individual's height as 50 on this scale, it would be concluded that you thought that the difference in height between this individual's height and the 5-ft

TABLE 15.7. The scale of counts of burglary: Assessment of weight

Counts of burglary
37
36
34
28
22
16
10
4
2
1

Note. Assume that for each of the levels comprising multiple counts the offenses were committed over an extended period of time (several weeks to months) and this period was proportional to the number of counts.

anchor was equivalent to the height difference between the individual's height and the 7-ft anchor; clearly, it would not follow that you thought the individual was one half of the height of the 7-ft anchor.

You should assess the seriousness of each level as you would assess seriousness if you were making this judgment as part of a determination as to what is appropriate by way of sentence for an actual case being heard by you in your court.

Before you start to make these ratings I should explain to you how the description of the most serious (anchor) level for each of the offence factors was determined. You may be aware that I have recently completed a study of cases of burglary determined in the County Court. As a part of that study I examined how those cases were distributed on these four offence factors. For *organization, total value of the theft,* and *counts of burglary* the description of the most extreme level on each factor has been set so that it is slightly more extreme than the events in the case that was found to be most extreme on that factor for actual burglaries of dwelling-houses. The same consideration applied to the setting of the upper level for *violence to the victims,* except that here it does not cover instances where the victim was injured physically or terrorized with a weapon.

In making your ratings of the seriousness of the various levels on a particular factor, you will be told the sequence in which the levels are to be assessed. You may change your

TABLE 15.8. The scale of violence to the victims: Assessment of weight

Scale label	Violence to the victims
H	Offender continued to search an upstairs room after the owner had returned home and come upstairs. When the owner entered the room, the offender picked up a metal-based lamp, ran at him, and threatened to strike him. The offender then tied the owner up with flex from the lamp, and left quickly by the window.
G	Offender continued to search an upstairs room after the owner had returned home and come upstairs. When the owner entered the room, the offender tried to get out through the window. The owner then ran toward him. In response, the offender picked up a metal-based lamp, and threatened to strike the owner. The offender then tied the owner up with flex from the lamp, and left immediately through the window.
F	Offender continued to search an upstairs room after the owner had returned home and come upstairs. When the owner entered the room, the offender moved one pace toward him, waved his fist, and threatened to strike him. The offender then left immediately through the window.
E	Offender continued to search an upstairs room after the owner had returned home and come upstairs. When the owner entered the room, the offender tried to get out through the window. The owner then ran toward him. In response the offender turned, waved his fist, and threatened to strike him. The owner withdrew, and the offender immediately left through the window.
D	Offender continued to search an upstairs room after the owner had returned home and come upstairs. The owner entered the room and, on seeing the offender, ran toward him. The offender left quickly through the window.
C	Offender continued to search an upstairs room after the owner had returned home. He left through the window when he heard the owner come upstairs.
B	Offender immediately left the house through the front door when he saw the owner enter the property. He ran past the owner in the driveway.
A	No one was at home during the burglary.

Note. For all the levels, there was only minor disturbance to contents and negligible damage. The owner was 45 years old.

assessments of already-rated levels in the light of your subsequent ratings. Indeed, you should first rate a level in relation to the anchors, and then in relation to the already-rated levels, as a check. For example, consider a level which you have just rated around (say) 50; you should then consider the difference in seriousness between this level and (say) a level already assigned a lower seriousness rating in relation to the difference in seriousness between this lower level and the least serious (anchor) level, and so on. Make any changes to your ratings until you feel they represent your true preferences and so there are no apparent internal inconsistencies.

Do not feel under any obligation to spread or to attempt to spread the levels evenly across the full range of seriousness on each case factor. Of course, if in order to reflect your true preferences you would have to spread these levels across the range, then do so. However, if you feel that most or the majority of levels are in your view more appropriately placed in either the lower half or upper half of the scale of seriousness for a factor (not necessarily evenly in each half) then make your ratings accordingly. Remember, each case factor is to be rated independently of the others so that the way in which you distribute your ratings may vary across the four case factors.

The descriptions of the four offense factors were presented to each judge in a different order, with the constraint that the dimension organization was never presented first. In contrast the levels on the factors were presented systematically. First, each judge was asked to rate one of the levels around the midpoint on the objective scale of a factor. Next followed a level that was midway between one anchor and this midlevel, and so on. For half the sample of judges, this second level was taken from above the midlevel and for the other half from below the midlevel. The judges completed each factor in turn and were not permitted to look back at their assessments on a factor after completing it.

When a judge rated the more serious levels on violence to the victims and organization, he was instructed to assume that for cases comprising multiple counts only one of the offenses was marked by a high level of violence but that most of the counts were characterized by a high level of organization.

Each judge was given the opportunity to have confusing points clarified at the beginning of the task or during the session. I supervised the checks on the internal consistency of the ratings on each factor to ensure that they were performed systematically. After a judge was satisfied with his ratings for a factor, I interpreted them for him in terms of the implied relationship between perceived seriousness and the objective levels. I drew a rough graph of the judge's value functions for counts of burglary and total value of the theft to facilitate the judge's understanding of the explanation. If a judge did not feel that these were an accurate picture of his true preferences, he was permitted to change his rating; he was asked to make such changes systematically in relation to the anchors and the other levels.

After a judge completed scaling seriousness for each of the four factors, he was asked several questions about the nature of the four offense factors and the assessment task. Specifically, the following matters were canvassed with each judge:

1. Did the judge feel that these four offense factors and, in the case of organization and violence to the victims, their components, were material to the determination of the seriousness of the offense characteristics of the burglary of private homes, whether other factors or components should be added, and whether the extreme levels were realistic upper limits (i.e., only rarely would there be a case that was more extreme on one of the factors)? If a judge was not satisfied with the content of these factors, he was asked to identify the difficulties and to explain how he thought these perceived difficulties might have affected his ratings.
2. Did the judge feel that before making these assessments he had already formed at least an implicit view on how these offense factors related to seriousness? If a judge did not feel he had formed such views, he was asked whether he had difficulties formulating such views and whether he thought his now expressed views would be stable.
3. Did the judge experience difficulties in assessing seriousness and using the scales as a means of expressing his preferences and, if so, what were the nature of those problems?

4. Did the judge experience other problems in completing these assessments? If so, he was asked to explain how he thought these perceived difficulties might have affected his ratings.

Weighting of the Offense Factors

The purpose of this second stage is to establish the relative weights of these four offence factors in your determination of the overall seriousness of the offence characteristics of a burglary of a private house, i.e., your view of the relative contributions of *counts of burglary, organization, violence to the victims* and *total value of the theft* to that assessment. Clearly, in order to determine what is appropriate by way of sentence a judge must form a view about the seriousness of the offence characteristics of the case. And consideration has just been given to how you assess relative seriousness for the objective scale values within each of the four offence factors. In assessing the overall seriousness of the offence characteristics of a case, a judge must also, at least implicitly, form a view about the relative importance of each of the constituent offence factors – the number of counts, etc. These evaluations are the point of this task. Again, you should weight the factors as you would if you were making the judgments as part of a determination as to what is appropriate by way of sentence for an actual case being heard by you in your court.

To assist you in making these assessments, I will ask you a series of questions with the help of these four sheets which carry the descriptions of the levels, ranked in order of seriousness from most to least down the page, of each of the four offence factors.

The four pages, 1 to 4, were placed before each judge in a different random order.

You are asked to consider the least serious and the most serious level on each of these factors. Assume that the four factors are all at their least serious levels. The issue is whether the increases in seriousness would be equal or different across these four factors if they were all changed to their most serious levels. To help you decide, I will present them in pairs for your consideration. Now turn to the first two – 1 and 2. (Assume, for the purposes of illustration, that these are *violence to the victims* and *total value of the theft*.)

The judge was first asked to consider these two factors alone and determine whether the increase in seriousness would be equal or different across these two factors if they were both changed to their most serious levels. After he had made this judgment, the assessment was made in more detail, as follows, to check his assessment in the context of a case. (It was made clear that these are alternative forms of the same question.)

Consider a case in which no-one was at home during the burglary (the least serious level of violence) with the other three factors also at their least serious levels and another case in which \$100 was the total value of the cash and merchandise stolen (the least serious level of the theft) with the other three factors also at their least serious levels. If in the first case the degree of violence was increased so that the offender tied up the victim and threatened to strike him (the most serious level of violence) and in the other case the value of the theft was changed to \$120,000 (the most serious level of theft), would the change in the degree of offence seriousness be greater for one of these two offence factors than the other or would the change be the same? (This is equivalent to asking whether one of the cases would be more serious.) If one difference is greater (or one case is more serious), identify the factor (or the case); this factor (or the factor in this case) is the more important factor. In making this assessment, remember that you should base your answer on the difference in seriousness between the most and least serious level of violence compared with the difference between the most and least serious level of theft, not the comparison between the most serious level of violence and the most serious level of theft. Also, you should say that there is a difference in the changes in seriousness (or that one case is more serious) even if the margin is small, as long as you are confident that in your view there is a difference. If you are not able to state confidently that there is a difference, then you should answer "same".

At this point, it was explained that the assessment relates to the effect of a factor on seriousness within an offense (burglary), not the effect of a factor on the relative seriousness between offenses (e.g., theft and burglary); so, for example, a judge could assign a trivial weight to violence here and yet hold that the component of violence is the main reason why, in general, burglary is viewed as more serious than theft.

Once you have completed the comparison for this pair, four of the other five factor combinations— 3/4, 1/4, 2/3, 1/3, 2/4—are to be assessed in a similar fashion.

In this procedure the judge was in effect encouraged to concentrate on the two factors being assessed in each comparison and as a consequence pay less attention to the two factors whose levels were fixed. Any inconsistencies in the assessments were identified and resolved.

The judges were not asked to compare counts of burglary and total value of the theft, because this would have involved improbable offense patterns. Also, when the counts of burglary dimension was compared with organization and violence to the victims, total value of the theft was not set at $100 (the value of the least serious level) but at $15,000.

This information on your rank-ordering of the importance of the four factors will be used now as a basis for quantifying their relative weights. First turn to the two which were given the highest two rankings. (Assume for the purposes of illustration that you assigned the highest ranking to *violence to the victims* and that *total value of the theft* was the next highest ranking.)

The judge was first asked to consider these two factors alone and determine an equivalence point. The assessment then continued, as follows. (It was made clear that these are alternative forms of the same question.)

Consider a case for which *total value of the theft* is at the most serious level and the levels on the other three factors are at their least serious, and contrast this with another case in which the levels on the four factors are at their least serious. Your task here is to move up through the levels on the dimension *violence to the victims* for this latter case until you feel the two cases are equally serious. In effect, this should be the level of violence for which the difference in seriousness between this level of violence and the least serious level of violence (no-one home during the burglary) is equal to the difference in seriousness between \$120,000 and \$100, when the other two factors are at their lowest levels. Before you on these eight sheets of paper are the descriptions of the two cases—four sheets (offence factors) per case, and you will notice that I have marked the critical levels that you must consider. You may find that this representation of the problem will help you conceptualize it; please mark the level on *violence to the victims* at which equivalence is reached. You may, of course, choose an equivalence value between two of the levels written on the sheet. Once you have assessed the first pair, four of the other five factor combinations— ⅓ (offence factors ranked first and third), ¼, ⅔, 2/4, ¾ —are to be compared similarly.

Again, in this procedure the judge was in effect encouraged to concentrate on the two factors assessed in each comparison and as a consequence pay less attention to the two factors whose levels were fixed. Any inconsistencies in these judgments were identified and resolved.

To investigate for the possible effects of context on these judgments, each judge made the assessments for the five factor combinations under two conditions. In the first condition the two factors not under consideration were set at their least serious levels (except, as indicated above, when counts of burglary was being assessed); the factor being varied was set at its least serious level, and each judge was asked to move up through the levels until equivalence was reached. (This condition is illustrated in the preceding description of the procedure.) In the second condition the factor being varied was again set at its least serious level, however the two factors not under consideration were set at higher levels of seriousness. The complementary factors could be set at their most serious levels for only three of the five possible combinations, because assessments involving comparisons with total value of the theft would have required improbable offense patterns. In both conditions each judge was told to assume, where cases involved multiple counts in a comparison, that the counts were characterized by a common degree of organization but only one of the counts was marked by a high degree of violence. Moreover, when establishing an equivalence point in each condition, each judge was encouraged to consider levels above his tentative equivalence point and to move down through the levels until equivalence was reached. Each judge completed all the assessments for one factor combination before moving on to the next combination. The order in which the two conditions were presented was the same for all the judges and was in the same sequence as described here.

After these assessments had been made, the relative weight of a particular factor for a judge could be determined simply through reference to the judge's value functions. By way of illustration, assume that a judge felt that 30 counts was equivalent to a (total) theft of \$120,000, and the judge had rated 30 counts at 70 on the seriousness scale for this factor, then for this judge the factor of total value of the theft would be 0.7 times the weight of counts of burglary.

Each judge was given the opportunity to have confusing points clarified at the beginning of the task or during the session. I supervised the checks of the internal consistency of the weight assessments across factors to ensure that they were performed systematically. After a judge was satisfied with his weight assessments, I interpreted them for him. If a judge did not feel that these were an accurate picture of his true preferences, he was permitted to change his assessments; in such instances he was shown the implications of these changes for his trade-off assessments and asked to consider his revised judgments in this light. This final assessment of relative factor weights was included because it permitted a check on the assessments of the relative offense factor weights in intuitive terms with its concomitant advantage that the assessments were free from the difficult equivalence and difference judgments and yet constrained by an implicit range for each factor.

After a judge had completed weighting the four factors, he was asked several questions about the assessment procedures. Specifically, the following matters were canvassed with each judge:

1. Did the judge feel that before making these assessments he had already formed at least an implicit view on the relative weights of these four factors? If a judge did not feel that he had formed such views, he was asked whether he had difficulties formulating such views and whether he thought his now expressed views would be stable.
2. Did the judge experience difficulties in assessing weight and using trade-offs as a means of expressing his preferences and, if so, what were the nature of these problems?
3. Did the judge experience other problems in completing these assessments? If so, he was asked to explain how he thought these perceived difficulties might have affected his determination of the relative weights.

On completion of this exercise each judge was asked to refrain from discussing it with the other judges. Each judge was asked to make an appointment to undertake this exercise after he had finished the first task. It was always completed in a single sitting of approximately 2 hours.

Results and Discussion

These analyses are based on the responses of seven of the nine judges who completed the first exercise. One of the two other judges went on extended leave just after he had finished the first exercise. The second of these two judges began this second exercise but felt that he required more time to think through the matters raised in the exercise than was possible in a single session. He intimated that he preferred to work through the exercise in his own time; he sought further detailed instructions on the procedure, and promised to complete the exercise as soon as possible. However, this judge had not completed the exercise at the time this report was written.

For five of the seven judges, it had been possible to analyze their responses to the first exercise before the second session; each of these judges was shown the results of the analysis of his responses at the beginning of the second session.

Identification and Operational Definition of the Offense Characteristics Relevant to Seriousness

In general the judges believed that the four offense factors (total value of the theft, counts of burglary, organization, and violence to the victims) and their components, as described in the exercise, were material to the determination of the seriousness of the offense characteristics of burglaries of private homes, that the descriptions covered the more common variations in this sort of burglary, and that the extreme offense factor levels on each of the scales represented realistic upper and lower levels of seriousness. There was only one significant departure from this view. For one judge the factor of counts of burglary was not material to seriousness as an independent factor; rather, his position was that the number of counts contributes indirectly to offense seriousness, in that he regarded cases with multiple counts as better organized, and of course, the total amount stolen in a particular case increases with additional offenses. This particular judge (no. 3) therefore was unable to scale or weight counts of burglary in relation to seriousness. This judge, however, said that the number of counts did affect the way he constructed concurrency orders in cases comprising multiple counts. He agreed that, in general, cases with multiple counts would attract higher quanta of sentence, but insisted that such considerations were unrelated to the seriousness of the offense.

Although six of the judges accepted the relevance and definitions of the four factors, and the seventh judge accepted this for three of the four factors, several modifications were suggested by some of the judges. The most commonly proposed change related to the factor of organization. Five judges commented that the range could have been somewhat greater; although they all agreed that the limits, as described in the study, were not unrealistic, cases departing from them, however, were not so uncommon as to not be within the experience of many judges. For some of these judges the elements in this scale did not capture those aspects of an operation that normally would lead to the description *professional*, nor did the elements cover a carefully planned burglary of a specially selected victim; and several of these judges perceived that at the lower end of the scale there was insufficient provision for differentiating the burglary committed by an offender on the spur of the moment and without regard to the modus operandi.

Three of these judges also proposed one or more additional factors as being material to seriousness under certain circumstances, although these suggestions carried no implication that these additions should be regarded as common factors. They included the offender significantly underestimated the value of the stolen merchandise; breach of the victim's trust by the offender; the effect of the theft on the victim; a gap in the pattern of offending in cases comprising multiple counts; the offender intended to steal far more than was actually taken; and the burglary committed at night as a component of violence.

TABLE 15.9. Judges' seriousness scales for total value of the theft

	Level: Objective scale value[a]								
Judge[b]	B	C	D	E	F	G	H	I	J
1	14	20	40	57	66	76	90	96	99
2	10	25	40	50	70	80	95	99	100
3	15	30	50	64	78	87	94	98	99
4[c]									
5	10	20	40	60	70	80	88	93	98
6	10	30	50	80	85	89	93	97	99
7	10	20	35	48	62	73	85	92	97
8	20	30	40	53	66	74	84	93	98
9[d]									
Mean	13	25	42	59	71	80	90	95	99
SD	4	5	5	10	7	6	4	3	1

Note. Where a judge's seriousness rating for a particular level differed from the curve of apparent best fit by more than 3, the real value was taken as the mean of these two figures. This occurred very rarely.

Several of the judges did not differentiate some of the levels. In these instances the real values were taken from the curve of apparent best fit.

[a] For the definitions of these levels in case-specific terms, see Table 14.4.
[b] These identifying numbers correspond to the numbers in Table 13.1.
[c] This judge completed the first exercise only.
[d] This judge has yet to complete this exercise.

TABLE 15.10. Judges' seriousness scales for counts of burglary

	Level: Objective scale value[a]							
Judge[b]	B	C	D	E	F	G	H	I
1	5	14	40	54	82	86	90	95
2	10	20	40	50	63	80	98	99
3	—	—	—	—	—	—	—	—
4[c]								
5	20	40	80	85	90	94	97	99
6	10	20	40	60	73	87	98	99
7	10	23	46	63	74	84	94	98
8	20	30	60	70	80	90	98	99
9[d]								
Mean	13	25	51	64	77	87	96	98
SD	6	8	15	11	8	4	3	1

Note. Where a judge's seriousness rating for a particular level differed from the curve of apparent best fit by more than 3, the real value was taken as the mean of these two figures. This occurred very rarely.

Several of the judges did not differentiate some of the levels. In these instances the real values were taken from the curve of apparent best fit.

[a] For the definitions of these levels in case-specific terms, see Table 14.5.
[b] These identifying numbers correspond to the numbers in Table 13.1.
[c] This judge completed the first exercise only.
[d] This judge has yet to complete this exercise.

TABLE 15.11. Judges' seriousness scales for organization

Judge[b]	Level: Objective scale value[a]					
	B	C	D	E	F	G
1	10	20	50	65	73	80
2	0	30	40	50	50	80
3	10	30	35	70	70	95
4[c]						
5	20	50	60	70	80	90
6	20	40	60	80	90	90
7	40	50	60	70	80	90
8	30	40	50	70	80	80
9[d]						
Mean	19	37	51	68	75	86
SD	12	10	9	8	12	6

[a] For definitions of these levels in case-specific terms, see Tables 14.2 and 14.3.
[b] These identifying numbers correspond to the numbers in Table 13.1.
[c] This judge completed the first exercise only.
[d] This judge has yet to complete this exercise.

Scales of Relative Seriousness in Relation to Each Offense Factor

Tables 15.9 to 15.12 show for each of the judges the scaling of the constituent levels of total value of the theft, counts of burglary, organization, and violence to the victims regarding seriousness. The relation between the mean seriousness scale values across the seven judges and the constituent levels of the first two factors are shown in Figures 15.1 and 15.2. In general there is a fairly high degree of uniformity across judges in their assessments of the relative seriousness of the constituent levels on each of the four offense factors: the agreement is particularly high across all judges on total value of the theft, and there is perhaps only one disparate judge for several of the levels on counts of burglary (judge no. 5).

For total value of the theft seriousness increases sharply up to about $30,000 and from that point appears to increase steadily at a fairly uniform rate; there is no obvious sign that $120,000 is an upper limit, in the sense that further increases in the value of the theft would not significantly increase the seriousness of the offense (see Figure 15.1).

The pattern of the relationship between the number of counts and seriousness would appear to be similar. The turning point on counts of burglary is around 10 counts (see Figure 15.2).

For organization, when the effect on seriousness of each additional element of organization is considered across the seven judges, the increase appears to be relatively uniform. A more detailed inspection of the data, however, shows that whereas this holds in general at the level of the individual judge, for most of the judges one level – and not the same level – had a much greater impact on seriousness than the others taken individually. Among the elements in the more serious half of the scale (levels E to H), only one element for only one judge shows this

TABLE 15.12. Judges' seriousness scales for violence to the victims

	Level: Objective scale value[a]					
Judge[b]	B	C	D	E	F	G
1	30	20	40	60	65	95
2	10	10	30	60	60	80
3	0	20	25	50	50	80
4[c]						
5	10	14	20	70	75	93
6	0	20	40	70	70	90
7	10	20	30	50	60	90
8	0	30	50	70	80	90
9[d]						
Mean	9	19	34	61	66	88
SD	10	6	10	8	9	6

[a] For the definitions of these levels in case-specific terms, see Table 14.1.
[b] These identifying numbers correspond to the numbers in Table 13.1.
[c] This judge completed the first exercise only.
[d] This judge has yet to complete this exercise.

differential effect on seriousness; it is not clear to what extent this might be related to a possible tendency for increases in levels on a factor to have less impact with successive increases in seriousness.

For violence to the victims a fairly minor assault on the victim (levels G/H) was sharply distinguished from a threat of an assault (levels E/F), and this, in turn, was regarded as far more serious than the next (lower) level of seriousness in which the offender ran off when seen by the victim (level D). Up to this last-mentioned level, the effect of each additional level of seriousness is fairly uniform. This pattern is similar for most of the judges, although there is some variation across judges in the actual ratings of the perceived seriousness of each of the levels.

Because the level of uniformity is so high across the judges, there could be little argument over the use of averages for representing each of these elements of sentencing policy.

Figures 15.1 and 15.2 and Tables 15.11 and 15.12 are the numerical representations of the judges' sentencing policy concerning that element of policy covering the relationship between objective offense factor levels and seriousness for each of the material factors.

In the individual interviews on the completion of this exercise, each of the judges agreed that, in determining appropriate sentences, a judge must form a view about the seriousness of the case in regard to each of the material offense factors. They all reported that they had, before undertaking this exercise, a qualitative impression in their own minds how seriousness varied with changes in the levels across each of the offense factors. Finally, none of the judges appeared to have any obvious problems in using the scales to express his prefer-

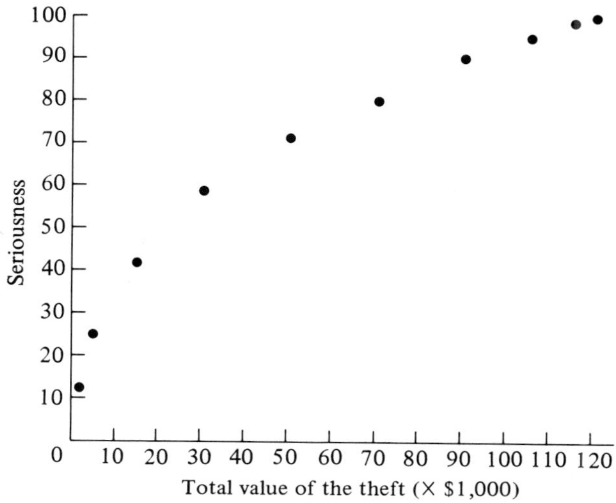

FIGURE 15.1. Judges' mean seriousness scale values for total value of the theft.

ences. From the casual asides made by the judges in the course of making the assessments, my impression was that at least some of the judges did not distinguish between seriousness and quantum of sentence or at least considered the differential effects of the various levels of a factor on sentence to make the assessment in relation to seriousness.

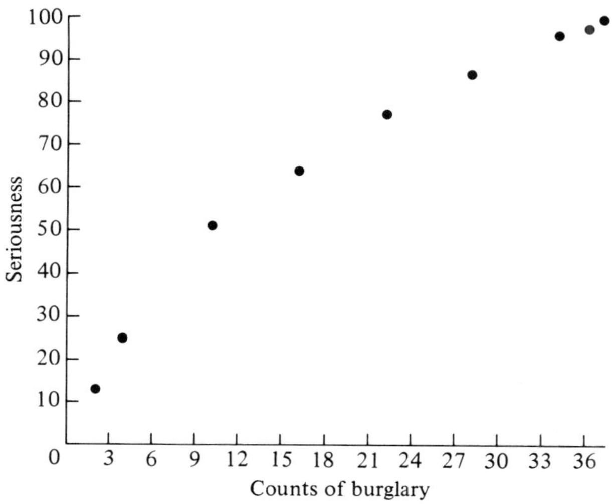

FIGURE 15.2. Judges' mean seriousness scale values for counts of burglary.

TABLE 15.13. Judges' weights for the relative importance of the four offense factors

	Judge[a]										
Offense factor	1	2	3	4[b]	5	6	7	8	9[c]	Mean	SD
Total value of the theft	22	30	37		18	10	16	14		21	9
Counts of burglary	31	11	0		8	20	32	14		17	11
Organization	22	22	35		34	20	20	24		25	6
Violence to the victims	25	37	28		40	50	32	48		37	9

[a] These identifying numbers correspond to the numbers in Table 13.1.
[b] This judge completed the first exercise only.
[c] This judge has yet to complete this exercise.

The value functions of the judges, both individually and taken as a group, clearly are curvilinear rather than linear for the total value of the theft and counts of burglary. The question must be raised whether a linear function would distort these two seriousness scales significantly. The answer is clearly in the affirmative. Consider imaginary lines representing linear functions in Figures 15.1 and 15.2. First, seriousness gauged on the basis of these lines would be significantly underestimated for cases comprising thefts under $30,000 and cases with fewer than 10 counts; the vast majority of cases involving burglaries of dwelling houses fell within this range—83% for total value of the theft (see Table 6.5) and 87% for counts of burglary (see Table 6.7) in the (original) archival study. Second, there is a potential problem at the other end of the two scales. Consider those rare instances where a case would not come within the range of one of these scales; in such instances a judge would have to extrapolate from the graph to estimate how the higher levels of such extreme cases should relate to seriousness. Clearly, the use of a linear relationship would lead the judge to overestimate the effects of large amounts of money stolen or numbers of counts on seriousness.

Relative Importance of Each Offense Factor in the Assessment of Seriousness

Table 15.13 shows for each of the judges the perceived relative weights of the four offense factors (total value of the theft, counts of burglary, organization, and violence to the victims) in the assessment of the overall seriousness of a case involving residential burglary; in Table 15.14 there are rank data for the same relationship. For the judges as a group, violence to the victims was considered to make the greatest contribution to the assessment of the overall seriousness of the offense, organization was seen as important, but significantly less so than the former factor, whereas counts of burglary and total value of the theft were regarded similarly and as somewhat less important than the second offense factor. Nevertheless, a detailed analysis by judge revealed marked individual differences among the judges. Clearly, averages could not

TABLE 15.14. Judges' rankings of the importance of the four offense factors

	Judge[a]									
Offense factor	1	2	3	4[b]	5	6	7	8	9[c]	Mean
Total value of the theft	3.5 (2.5)	2 (2)	1 (1)		3 (3)	4 (3)	4 (3)	3.5 (3)		3.0
Counts of burglary	1	4	4		4	2.5	1.5	3.5		2.9
Organization	3.5 (2.5)	3 (3)	2 (2)		2 (2)	2.5 (2)	3 (2)	2 (2)		2.6
Violence to the victims	2 (1)	1 (1)	3 (3)		1 (1)	1 (1)	1.5 (1)	1 (1)		1.5

Note. The figures in parentheses are the judges' rankings of the relative importance of total value of the theft, organization, and violence to the victims, when counts of burglary is excluded.
[a] These identifying numbers correspond to the numbers in Table 13.1.
[b] This judge completed the first exercise only.
[c] This judge has yet to complete this exercise.

be used to represent this aspect of sentencing policy. The most significant disparity occurred for the offense factor of counts of burglary; for this factor four of the seven judges perceived it to be the least or equal least important factor, whereas two judges regarded it as the most or equal most important factor. When the rankings for counts of burglary are put to one side, disparity is evident for two of the other three factors but does not split the sample so clearly. Indeed, respecting both total value of the theft and violence to the victims, only one judge's (the same judge) rankings of relative importance are substantially at variance with the general trend.

Table 15.13 is the numerical representation of the judges' sentencing policy in respect of that element of policy covering the relative weights of the material offense factors.

All the judges gave considerable thought to each of the assessments; this is evidenced by the length of time taken to administer this exercise—typically 2 hours. In the individual interviews at the completion of the task, the judges reported that, in determining appropriate sentences for particular cases, they do differentiate offense factors in terms of their potential contribution to the overall seriousness of an offense and that the use of trade-offs was a legitimate way of tapping their views on this aspect of policy. It appeared that all of the judges had previously formed a view about the relative weights of the four factors, although not in such formal and precise terms. None of the judges experienced difficulties in ranking the relative contributions of the four factors; and although almost all of the judges showed evidence of inconsistencies when quantifying, pair by pair, the relative contribution of each of the factors, these were only minor, and none of the judges had difficulty in resolving the differences. Only one of the judges (no. 5) experienced problems with the exercise; this was revealed by serious inconsistencies in his assessments of the relative contributions of the factors, assessed pair by pair, and his inability to resolve these readily. (He had comfortably ranked the factors in order of importance.) To help the judge to complete

TABLE 15.15. Differences in calculated offense seriousness based on unit and judges' assessed weights for the four samples in the sensitivity analysis: Rank correlations

Sample[b]	Judge[a] 1	2	3	4[c]	5	6	7	8	9[d]
A	1.0	0.9			0.7	0.9	1.0	0.8	
B	1.0	0.9			−0.1	0.5	0.9	0.7	
A′	0.9	0.9			1.0	0.9	0.8	1.0	
B′	1.0	0.9			0.9	0.7	1.0	0.9	

[a] These identifying numbers correspond to the numbers in Table 13.1.
[b] The structures of the offenses in these samples are shown in Tables 14.7 and 14.9.
[c] This judge completed the first exercise only.
[d] This judge has yet to complete this exercise.

this aspect of the exercise, I told him to consider the four factors together (rather than proceeding pair by pair) and to assess their relative weights intuitively. After the judge had done this, I showed him the results of these assessments in relation to the levels at which equivalence had implicitly been reached. Finally, he was given the opportunity to revise his assessments in view of this information. This judge thought that his difficulties arose because the model of the determination of sentence underlying the task was at variance with his own approach. In fixing a quantum of sentence for a case in which there were multiple counts, he said that he tended to determine a sentence for each offense and then, in view of the individual sentences, set a sentence for the case. Nevertheless, he proceeded with the exercise because he agreed that multiple counts constitute an aggravating factor; he also felt that perhaps he preconsciously considered the seriousness of the case as a whole in determining an effective sentence covering multiple counts. Again, one could not help but feel that at least some of the judges had the notion of sentence in the forefront of their minds when making the assessments in this exercise.

Finally, a comment should be made on the checks that were made to investigate whether the trade-offs for the various combinations of offense-factor pairs depended on the values of their complementary pairs. First, it must be remembered that the effect of context was not tested comprehensively, because some of the assessments would have required improbable offense patterns. This might have been problematic if the purpose of these additional assessments had been to test the assumption of mutual preferential independence. There can be no issue, however, where the potential effect of context on the trade-offs is the point of the assessments, because improbable offense patterns would not occur in the context of an actual case. Second, some of the judges, when given the opportunity of comparing the relative importance of the pair of offense factors under consideration in the context of two cases or in view of changes in the levels of the other two (complementary) offense factors, indicated that it would make no difference to their assessments of the relative importance of the two factors, and for this reason did not proceed to make the related assessments. Of the judges for whom the effect of context was tested, only one showed evidence of preferential depen-

TABLE 15.16. Differences in calculated offense seriousness based on unit and judges' assessed weights for the offenses (n = 20) in the sensitivity analysis: Frequencies

Magnitude of difference	Judge[a]								
	1	2	3	4[b]	5	6	7	8	9[c]
0–5	19	11			8	8	11	8	
6–10	1	7			4	3	7	4	
11–15		2			3	5	2	3	
16–20					3	3		2	
21–25					2	1		3	

[a] These identifying numbers correspond to the numbers in Table 13.1.
[b] This judge completed the first exercise only.
[c] This judge has yet to complete this exercise.

dence in relation to context. This occurred in one assessment where total value of the theft, as a complementary factor, was changed from its lowest to highest level. However, questioning revealed that the judge changed his assessment of the relative contribution of the two factors under consideration in view of this change because he had assumed that the large amount of money stolen indicated greater organization. When told that he must assume that the degree of organization was constant, he then concluded that the relative contribution of the two factors would remain unchanged, despite the change in the complementary factor (total value of the theft).

Sensitivity of the Estimates of the Offense Factor Weights

The purpose of this sensitivity analysis is to compare the calculated values of overall offense seriousness based on unit weights with those based on the judges' assessed weights. In these calculations the seriousness of the constituent levels was taken from the judges' assessments. (Judge no. 3 could not be included in this analysis, because he did not scale counts of burglary.) Table 15.15 shows the Spearman rank-order correlations for each of the judges and for the four samples in the sensitivity analysis (see Tables 14.7 and 14.9). Clearly, for two or three of the six judges—judges nos. 5 and 6 and, perhaps, 8—is there evidence that the assessed weights result in a significantly different rank order of offenses regarding overall seriousness. The limitation of rank correlations, however, is that no account is taken of the magnitude of the differences on the scale of offense seriousness. The problem is that in a set of offenses ranked similarly, there nevertheless could be marked discrepancies in relative offense seriousness. This difference is of particular significance when the analysis is not being used to make a choice at the top end of a scale but rather to determine relative seriousness across a range. Table 15.16 therefore was constructed to show the magnitude of the differences in the calculated values of overall offense seriousness between the two weighting schemes—unit and assessed weights—for each of the six judges and across the 20 offense patterns in the sensitivity analysis.

Clearly, Table 15.16 shows that for five of the six judges there are dramatic differences in the calculated values of overall offense seriousness for a substantial number offense patterns. The adjective *dramatic* is used here advisedly; from an inspection of Figure 16.1, which shows the relationship between offense seriousness and sentence for one judge, it can be seen that relatively small differences in offense seriousness translate into not insignificant differences in the associated length of the effective sentence for an offense attracting a substantial prison term. (The data in Figure 16.1 were collected in the coherency study, Chapter 16.) The reason for the lack of concordance between the two sets of data – offense seriousness scores and ranks – is that in the present context ranks provided a very crude test; to construct samples consisting solely of undominated options and, accordingly, ensure weight sensitivity, the analysis was based on samples of no more than five offense patterns. Now, since the five offense patterns in each of the samples covered a range of approximately 40 on an offense seriousness scale with an effective range of 10 to 90, in many instances the offense seriousness scores of any two offense patterns could change greatly with little or no concomitant change in their rank order.

16
Coherence and the Tariff

The analysis to this point has dealt with the scaling of offense seriousness. As a consequence of this work there is now a model of judicial sentencing behavior that specifies how judges scale the relationship between seriousness and the objective levels of each offense factor, the relative weight of each factor, and the rule for aggregating the decisions on each of these components. Now it is possible to determine the relative overall offense seriousness of various patterns of offending. Clearly, this construction of seriousness is of minimal practical assistance to judges in their task of sentencing unless it is related to the quantum of sentence. The task of this chapter is to prepare the way for that final step. At the outset, however, the scope of the chapter should be delimited. Of concern here is the tariff sentence—a sentence in which the quantum of sentence is made proportional to the seriousness of the offense and in regard to an offender's plea in mitigation and prior convictions. The notion of proportionality implies monotonicity—mutual increase (or decrease) in values on both dimensions—but not necessarily a direct relationship. Indeed, the totality principle (Thomas, 1979) provides that after a certain level of seriousness is reached, the rate of increase in the quantum of sentence should decrease with further increases in case seriousness.

The aggregation rule makes it possible to show the relationship between any combination of offense characteristics (pattern of offending) and relative overall offense seriousness. (It is reasonable to assume that seriousness is quantified as a score on an interval scale.) Here, the purpose of the analysis is to extend this to show the relationship between any pattern of offending and the appropriate tariff sentence. To develop detailed sentencing statistics, the offense characteristics of cases of burglary determined in the courts are construed according to the model and thereby each case placed at the appropriate point along the dimension of offense seriousness; the sentences fixed in the courts for these cases then are related to this scale of seriousness. This relationship may be shown readily in graphical or tabular form by plotting for every case the actual sentence in relation to the score quantifying offense seriousness. This was in fact done earlier, in the first draft of the detailed sentencing statistics, where my model of judicial decision making was used as a basis for the statistics (see Figure 11.1); the nature of the representation envisaged here is identical, the only difference being that the model would be modified in view of the input from the judiciary and is limited to offense characteristics.

This simple representation of the relationship between offense seriousness and sentence rests on an important assumption, an assumption that should be tested. The second task of this chapter, then, is to explain the nature of this assumption and then to test its validity. The assumption is that the judges have a coherent understanding of the tariff for burglary; that is, they explicitly know how the offense factors are scaled, weighted, and aggregated in the determination of case seriousness, how seriousness is related to quantum of sentence, and finally, they apply these rules with a high degree of reliability. If this assumption is true, then it may be concluded that the tariff is coherent, that is, the relation between the quanta of sentence and the various combinations of offense factors is based in the mind of each judge on a reasonably stable, logical, and internally consistent set of rules and quantities that are applied reliably. The validity of this assumption would be particularly open to doubt if judicial input in regard to the scaling and weighting of the offense factors to some extent involved in effect the development of sentencing policy. This was a real possibility here because the judges were required to provide detail on matters of sentencing policy that are not stated explicitly and precisely and about which they might have given little conscious thought.

It should be understood that the problem addressed here is not one of the external validity of the fictitious procedure. It may be that the necessary characteristics of this procedure (inconsequential decisions, simplification of case details, artificiality of the task and procedural infidelity) ensure that the responses made under these conditions differ from real-life assessments of seriousness. This potential problem was the point of Chapter 13; associated matters were examined there, together with an empirical examination of the assumption that the fictitious procedure is externally valid. The assumption under test in this chapter should also be distinguished from the considerations relating to the validity of the MAUM procedures. In Chapter 12 I canvassed the possibility that the judges' assessments in terms of the scaling and weighting of the offense factors may be unreliable and invalid because the judges were forced to make assessments to which they might have given little conscious thought and to express these judgments through means foreign to them. Nevertheless, although this issue is not the point of this chapter, the data would fail to support the assumption of judicial coherency in tariff sentencing if these procedures induced unreliable and invalid responses. Similarly, this present study requires the assumption that the weighted additive value function is a faithful representation of the way the judges aggregate their assessments regarding each of the elements of the offense.

How, then, was this assumption tested? The model of judicial decision making was used to formulate systematically a series of burglary cases whose combinations of offense characteristics, according to the model, placed them across the range of the dimension of overall case seriousness. (My model of judicial decision making from the archival burglary study was used to place the cases on this range because this study was planned before the judges had completed the scaling and weighting exercises. Of course, the structure and content of the offense characteristics of these burglary cases were based on the offense factors and offense factor levels used in the MAUM analysis.) Judges were asked individually to assess intuitively the overall seriousness of each of the cases and to determine an appropriate sentence. Several cases were used to represent each level of seriousness (determined according to the archival model) so that the assessments of overall case seriousness and judgments of what was an appropriate sentence could not be considered to be an artifact of any one set of combinations of offense characteristics. The coherency hypothesis was tested for the determination of case seriousness as well as sentence, even though the latter concept was the focus of concern. There were two reasons for this. First, it was possible that the quanta of sentence imposed by the judges for these cases might not have provided an adequate measure for a rigorous test of this hypothesis. The discrimination between the cases in terms of the quanta of sentence might not have been sufficiently fine. Moreover, a significant number of the sentences might have been noncustodial and, accordingly, not offered any differentiation on the dimension of seriousness. (The cases in this exercise were formulated so that on the basis of the model and the relationship established between case seriousness and sentence in the archival study [see Figure 11.1] it would be predicted that only custodial sentences would be appropriate, but of course, this assumed the validity of the archival analysis.) There was a second reason for measuring seriousness. The seriousness of a case is an important intervening construct in the determination of sentence. Clearly, the quantitative analysis would not have been complete if this link had not been explored.

So that the judges could determine a sentence for each of the cases, it was necessary to incorporate offender characteristics (prior convictions and mitigation) with the offense characteristics. Three considerations governed the construction of the offender characteristics. First, the focus of the study was tariff sentencing. Second, how judges scale case seriousness in relation to offender characteristics was not of interest here. Third, the sentences should all be custodial and cover the range of this type of sentence. Accordingly, the offender characteristics had to be related to the offense characteristics so that judges would attempt to make the sentence proportional to the seriousness of the case (rather than impose a sentence for which the main or substantial aim was rehabilitation) and would not be able to allow for mitigation. From the earlier discussion on the legal basis of the model of sentencing (see Chapter 4), it follows that these conditions would be satisfied where the cases were characterized by an extensive record of prior convictions and there was very little credit available by way of the plea in mitigation. The three sentencing principles of import here are: (1) As an offender's past record increases in seriousness there is a corresponding decrease in the allowance for the effect of any mitigating offender characteristics until a point is reached where mitigating characteristics can have no effect on the determination of case seriousness. (2) Prior convictions do not aggravate case seriousness beyond the level set by the overall seriousness of the offense characteristics. (3) A tariff sentence is imposed when an individual's rehabilitation prospects do not appear favorable. (Where there is little available to an offender by way of mitigation in the characteristics of a case then the offender's rehabilitation prospects would not appear favorable; see Chapter 4.) Because the point of interest here was the judges' determining of sentence in relation to offense seriousness, the offender characteristics, including criminal history, were held constant across cases.

This analysis provides a test of the assumption that the judges have a coherent understanding of the determination of the tariff. The validity of the assumption would be upheld if there was a substantial degree of correspondence between overall case seriousness calculated on the basis of each judge's assessments of scale value and weight in the MAUM analysis and case seriousness assessed holistically, and if similar sentences were set for cases falling within the same level of case seriousness, again calculated from the MAUM data, and more (or less) severe sentences for the higher (or lower) levels of case seriousness. Of course, a negative result could be attributed to distortions in the judges' assessments induced by the MAUM procedures or the invalidity of the model rather than to an incoherent tariff. One should not seek more than a reasonable degree of correspondence, because allowance must be made for the possible distorting effects of cognitive overload on the holistic judgments. It should be noted parenthetically that this was not expected to be a significant problem in this instance, because four factors should be within the cognitive limits of well-motivated professionals (see Chapter 12).

This analysis places a somewhat different emphasis on the notion of the convergent validity of the decision-making model from that found in the similar analyses of Fischer (1977) and Stillwell et al. (1983), in which assessments of seriousness based on decomposed and holistic judgments were intercorrelated. This position follows logically from the orientation of this project, which is not concerned with how judges actually determine sentence but rather is focused on how judges should make decisions in accordance with current sentencing policy. Consequently, the degree of coherence cannot be measured by the numerical value of the correlation between the decomposed and holistic assessments, because the holistic assessment is not an appropriate criterion. Rather, in the context of this present project, offense seriousness calculated on the basis of the decomposed assessments is regarded as the criterion of the judges' true preferences. This view is more akin to Humphreys and McFadden's (1980) view of the relationship between coherence and convergence. On a related matter, the case against the use of correlation for testing the appropriateness of a cognitive (algebraic) model has been well-argued (Anderson & Shanteau, 1977; Birnbaum, 1973). It is perhaps unnecessary to make the point that the present use of the notion of correlation—correspondence—is not considered inappropriate in view of their arguments, because the prescriptive orientation does not require the empirical validation of the underlying model.

Of course, if the "coherent tariff" hypothesis is not supported, then the source of the problem would have to be identified and resolved before the model could be used as the basis of detailed sentencing statistics.

Method

Formulation of Cases: Offense Factors

Two sets of offense patterns were formulated. The first comprised the four groups (samples A, B, A', B'), which were used in the sensitivity analysis; the previously advanced reasons underlying the choice of those patterns of offending apply here also (see Tables 14.7 and 14.9, together with the accompanying text). This set comprised offense patterns characterized by cross-currents of aggravating and extenuating offense factor levels.

The second set consisted of two samples and was formulated on different grounds, although the four levels comprising each of the four dimensions again were defined similarly (see Table 14.6). In setting up the patterns of offending for each level of overall offense seriousness and labeling the columns, four conditions were satisfied. First, the offense factor levels comprising each pattern covered the smallest range (e.g., 4333 was preferred to 4441). Second, an attempt was made to ensure that the frequencies of each of the four levels within each offense factor were similar across (but not within) the four dimensions. Third, none of the combinations of levels represented an implausible offense pattern. Fourth, there were no identical offense patterns within and between the two sets. The selection of the patterns was otherwise unsystematic. Following these criteria, the resulting sample (C) of offenses comprised the patterns of offending shown in Table 16.1. An inspection of Table 16.1 shows that most of the offense patterns do not pose real decision problems because they are dominated. Not surprisingly, the rank-order correlations among these levels are high (see Table 16.2). Accordingly, this sample of offenses would not be expected to be weight sensitive.

The value of this sample of offense patterns is that it offers a weaker and less demanding test of coherence because the offenses do not involve cross-currents of aggravating and extenuating factors. Accordingly, a finding of incoherence among the judges for this sample of offenses could not be attributed to inconsistency in their attempts at reconciling cross-currents of offense factor levels.

According to the scoring system in the archival burglary study, the scores quantifying the offense seriousness of these patterns of offending range from 3 (5 for the cases in Exercise 3, presented later in this chapter) to 33+ (see Table 10.1); the lower limit of the range for the samples in the sensitivity analysis was 5 and the upper limit again 33.

So that there were two similarly constructed patterns of offending per level of overall offense seriousness in the second set, an additional sample (D) of offenses

TABLE 16.1. Structures of the offenses in sample C for the coherency analysis

Overall offense seriousness [a]	Offense factor			
	Violence	Organization	Value	Counts
14	3	3	4	4
13	3	4	3	3
12	3	3	3	3
11	2	3	3	3
10	3	3	2	2
9	3	2	2	2
8	2	2	2	2
7	2	1	2	2
6	1	2	2	1
5	2	1	1	1
4[b]	1	1	1	1

Note. The patterns of offending are described in terms of the levels defined in Table 14.6.
[a] These figures assume the validity of the scoring system in the archival burglary study and so may only approximate overall offense seriousness as it was assessed by the various judges.
[b] This pattern could not be used for the seriousness ratings in Exercise 3 because it acted there as an anchor case.

was formulated. This additional sample was created simply by changing the offense factors assigned to particular columns; value, counts, violence, and organization were substituted for violence, organization, value, and counts, respectively. Also, four of the levels had to be changed to satisfy the just previously mentioned third and fourth criteria. The resulting offense structures are shown in Table 16.3, and the factor intercorrelations are shown in Table 16.4.

The coherency analysis now comprised 41 cases—samples A, B, A′, B′, C, and D.

History of Prior Convictions

In the earlier discussion, it was made clear that the cases had to be characterized by an extensive record of prior convictions, especially in relation to convictions for offenses of dishonesty. Since an offender's record comprises not only offenses but also sentences imposed judicially, the safest means of ensuring realism for an extensive record is for the criminal history to be based substantially on an actual

TABLE 16.2. Intercorrelations of the offense factors for the coherency analysis: Sample C

	Organization	Value	Counts
Violence	.65	.59	.71
Organization		.79	.75
Value			.95

Note. These rank correlations require the assumption that the judges' assessments of the seriousness of the levels are monotonically related to the levels' objective scale values.

TABLE 16.3. Structures of the offenses in sample D for the coherency analysis

Overall offense seriousness[a]	Offense factor			
	Value	Counts	Violence	Organization
14	3	3	4	4
13	3	4	3	3
12	4	3	3	2
11	2	3	3	3
10	3	3	2	2
9	3	2	2	2
8	2	2	1	3
7	2	1	2	2
6	1	2	2	1
5	2	1	1	1

Note. The patterns of offending are described in terms of the levels defined in Table 14.6.
[a] These figures assume the validity of the scoring system in the archival burglary study and so may only approximate overall offense seriousness as it was assessed by the various judges.

case. And so it was here. A record was selected and slightly adapted from one of the archival cases on the basis of the definitions and scoring system developed for prior convictions in that burglary study. The criminal history developed for this present study is shown in Table 16.5, and Table 16.6 presents the analysis of this history in relation to the components and scoring of prior convictions in the archival study (see Tables 8.3, 8.12, and 8.13).

According to the scoring system for aggregating the effects of the components of prior convictions and for setting the relative weight of prior convictions in relation to the mitigating effects of the other offender characteristics, the score quantifying the aggravation associated with prior convictions in this criminal record is 15 (see the section dealing with the coding and scoring of a case in Chapter 11 and see Table 9.1). Only 18% of the principal offenders in the (original) archival burglary study had a more extensive criminal history (see Table 9.1).

Mitigating Offender Characteristics

In the earlier discussion, it was concluded that for the cases in the present study the characteristics of the offender should offer no more than minimal credit by

TABLE 16.4. Intercorrelations of the offense factors for the coherency analysis: Sample D

	Organization	Value	Counts
Violence	.63	.48	.70
Organization		.34	.58
Value			.54

Note. These rank correlations require the assumption that the judges' assessments of the seriousness of the levels are monotonically related to the levels' objective scale values.

TABLE 16.5. The criminal history used in the coherency analysis

Court	Charges	Sentence
1. Children's Court 12/17/69	Illegal use of a motor car Armed with an offensive weapon Unlicensed driver	7 days Youth Training Center (YTC) 7 days YTC Fine $14 in default 7 days Total: YTC 14 days
2. Children's Court 1/24/70	Unlawful assault Indecent language	Fine $20 in default 10 days Fine $20 in default 5 days
3. Children's Court 2/7/70	Illegal use of a motor car (2 charges) Larceny (2 charges) Schoolhouse breaking and stealing (2 charges)	YTC 12 months on all charges
4. Magistrates' Court 4/7/71	Shopbreaking and stealing Schoolbreaking and stealing Illegal use of a motor car (3 charges) Larceny (5 charges) Dangerous driving Unlicensed driver	YTC 3 months on each of charges 1–5 Convicted without penalty on charges 6–10 and 12 YTC 1 month on 11th charge Total: YTC 16 months
5. Magistrates' Court 6/15/71	Illegal use of a motor car Escaping from legal custody	2 months 1 month (concurrent) Total: 2 months
6. Magistrates' Court 1/20/73	Assault by kicking	1 month
7. County Court 5/28/74	Burglary (3 counts) Theft (2 counts)	Probation: 2 years
8. County Court 5/18/78	Burglary (3 counts)	10 months on each count (counts 2 and 3 concurrent with each other) Total: 20 months
9. Magistrates' Court 5/11/80	Assault with a weapon Assaulting a member of the police force in the lawful execution of his duty Being drunk and disorderly	7 days on each of charges 1 and 2 (concurrent) Convicted without penalty on charge 3
10. County Court 8/27/83	Burglary (3 counts)	2 years 6 months on count 1 and 12 months on each of counts 2 and 3 (concurrent with each other and with count 1) Total: 2 years 6 months Minimum 18 months

TABLE 16.6. Analysis of the criminal history used in the coherency analysis

Prior convictions category	Case characteristic	Code
Counts, dishonesty	29 counts	4
Appearances, dishonesty	7 appearances	4
Time since last count, dishonesty	30 months	2
Average time between appearances, dishonesty	27 months	2
Sum of custodial sentences, dishonesty	81 months	4
Appearances, nondishonesty	3 appearances	3
Counts, nondishonesty	7 counts	3
Sum of custodial sentences, nondishonesty	1 month	1

Note. For the definitions of the categories and the coding system, see Tables 8.3 and 8.12.

way of mitigation. Again, the construction of case seriousness in the archival burglary study was used to develop and represent an appropriate plea in mitigation. Table 16.7 presents the mitigation associated with the cases in terms of the categories of the offender characteristics as they were defined in the archival burglary study (see Table 8.1).

According to the scoring system in the archival burglary study, the score quantifying the degree of exculpation associated with these offender characteristics (excluding consideration of the criminal history) is 10. Only 13% of principal offenders in the (original) archival burglary study had a score indicating less mitigation (see Table 9.2).

Adjusted Case Score

According to the scoring system in the archival burglary study, the scores quantifying the overall seriousness of the cases in the coherency study range from 3 (5 for the cases in Exercise 3) to 33+. This is the same as the range for offense seriousness, because the total mitigation is effectively zero. The exculpation arising from the mitigating offender factors actually is outweighted by the aggravating effects of the offender's criminal history, but the offense sets the ceiling on case seriousness.

The sentencing statistics for the (original) archival burglary study (see Figure 11.1 and accompanying text) show that the least serious case in the coherency study is at a level of seriousness for which custodial and noncustodial sentences were imposed. This level of case seriousness is around the upper limit for the imposition of a noncustodial sentence. And the notional effective (maximum) tariff sentence for cases at this level of seriousness is approximately 9 months.

Procedure for the Holistic Assessment of Case Seriousness

Four practice cases and 40 test cases, together with the instructions and two anchor cases, were presented to the judges in a booklet with the cover title

TABLE 16.7. Analysis of the plea in mitigation used in the coherency analysis

Factor	Category description	Code
Age	32 years (born: 7/15/53).	0
Previous good character	Left school at 16 years of age, had a series of jobs as a laborer, longest continuous period of employment was 12 months. Periods during which he was out of work were caused by no available employment. Not employed for 1 month at the time of the offense.	2
Reason for the offense	On unemployment benefits at the time of the offense and felt financially insecure.	0
Remorse–confession	Plea of guilt at the preliminary hearing and admitted the charges to the police during the interview.	2
Remorse–reconciliation	Sold the stolen merchandise; he is not in possession of any of the goods and has spent the proceeds.	0
Remorse–current character	Since the current offense(s) the offender has not committed any offenses, and there are no matters outstanding.	3
Remorse–rehabilitation prospects	Offender was looking for work at the time he was arrested but had been unsuccessful.	0
	He has a girlfriend who is employed as a shop assistant. They have been living together for 18 months.	1
	He does not have any association with known criminals.	1
	There is no obvious medical or psychological condition motivating his criminal behavior.	1
Deprived family background	Lived at home until 16 years of age when his mother died. He then drifted, staying with various friends and acquaintances. His father disappeared when he was about 12 months old. He married at 22 but has been separated about 5 years (he is now divorced). His wife has remarried and has taken responsibility for the care of their two children, girls aged 8 and 10.	0

Note. For the definitions of the categories and the coding system, see Table 8.1. The plea was dated April 1987.

Sentencing Research Exercise–Part 3. The instructions were on the first three pages, followed by the descriptions of the two anchors, then the descriptions of the practice cases and, finally, the test cases. The descriptions of the offense characteristics for the two anchor cases also were included in the booklet on loose sheets for ready reference during the rating task. The description of each case began on a new page, and a rating scale was placed at the end of each case–a 100-mm line, horizontal and centered, with unlabeled marks at 10-mm intervals and the labels, *0* and *100* at the left and right ends, respectively, of the line. These arbitrary ratings of 0 and 100 were defined by two anchors comprising the least and the most serious combinations of levels of offense seriousness–1,1,1,1 (L) and 4,4,4,4 (M), respectively–on the four dimensions (total value of the theft, counts of burglary, violence to the victims, and organization; see Table 14.6 for a description of these levels). The letters *L* and *M* were written over the *0* and *100* labels, respectively, on the scale to represent the location of the two anchors.

TABLE 16.8. Structures of the practice offenses for the holistic scaling of seriousness

Overall offense seriousness[a]	Offense factor			
	Violence	Organization	Value	Counts
7	2	1	3	1
9	3	3	2	1
11	2	2	4	3
13	4	4	3	2

Note. The patterns of offending are described in terms of the levels defined in Table 14.6.
[a] These figures assume the validity of the scoring system in the archival burglary study and so may only approximate overall offense seriousness as it was assessed by the various judges.

The description of each case was set out in five sections: (1) the number of counts, with a list of the value of the money and goods stolen in each count, a description of the nature of the property stolen, and the period of offending; (2) information from the statement(s) of the victim(s); (3) information from the interview with the offender; (4) record of the offender's prior convictions; and (5) the plea in mitigation. (The history of prior convictions and plea in mitigation were common to all cases.) The lengths of the descriptions of the cases ranged from approximately three A4 pages for the cases with the least serious combination of levels—three 1s and one 2—to approximately four pages for the cases with the most serious combination—two 4s and two 3s. The structures of the offense characteristics of the practice cases are set out in Table 16.8; these cover the dimension of offense seriousness and do not describe any implausible patterns of offending. One booklet was assigned to each judge unsystematically, and in each booklet the test cases were presented in a different random order. (A sample fictitious case is presented in Appendix 2.)

In certain instances it was necessary in this exercise, as it had been in the previous exercise, to set the description of a factor in context to make the task less abstract, to ensure realism, and to indicate precisely the nature of the level of the factor (e.g., limit a high level of violence to one offense in cases with multiple counts). Of course, this additional detail was kept constant, or a constant proportion, across cases. Moreover, these considerations had to be borne in mind when combining the various sets of the component levels to form cases. For example, for cases with multiple counts and the theft of a motor vehicle as part of the organization, it did not appear realistic to record the offender as having been charged with a connected offense for every count. Where there were 37, 16, or 4 counts of burglary, the number of connected counts was set at 6, 3, and 2, respectively.

The sample of judges used here was the same as in the previous exercise. Each of the judges was seen individually by me, and the booklets were handed to the judges personally. The judges were left to work through the cases in their own time.

The following instructions were set out at the beginning of each booklet. (The task also was explained informally to each judge.)

This exercise is the third in the series concerned with understanding how judges determine what is appropriate by way of sentence, and the information will be used to assist in developing a means of representing the relationship between case characteristics and sentence as a basis for detailed sentencing statistics. You are again reminded that your responses will not become part of a sentencing statistics data base and will not be submitted as individual data to the Sentencing Committee.

The point of this exercise is to study how you as a judge assess the overall seriousness of cases of burglary. You are being presented with a series of brief descriptions of cases; each case comprises details about the offense(s) and personal information about the principal offender. You are asked to rate the seriousness of each of these cases on a scale. Now, a judge in determining what is appropriate by way of sentence must, *inter alia*, form a view about the overall seriousness of the characteristics of the case. Nevertheless, it is recognized that the relationship between seriousness and sentence is complex. One, in order to give effect to the aim of rehabilitation, a judge may decide not to attempt to make the sentence proportional to the seriousness of the offense or the case. Two, seriousness and sentence are different attributes and, consequently, even where a judge attempts to make one proportional to the other, the scales on which these two attributes are quantified may increase at different rates; for example, a case which on the scale of seriousness is midway between the most serious case of burglary and the seriousness of a case of burglary which just requires imprisonment may not be deemed to require a sentence which is half the length of the sentence for the most serious case – the appropriate sentence may be greater or less. Remember, you are being asked to assess seriousness not sentence (or relative sentence) and it is recognized that had you been asked to determine the latter then your relative numerical assessments of the cases may have been different.

The booklet contains 40 case descriptions of burglaries of private homes, which have been varied systemically on the following four offense factors: total amount of money stolen in the burglaries; number of counts of burglary; the amount of violence inflicted on the victim(s) (violence is interpreted broadly, and ranges from simple entry to a home in the absence of the occupant(s) to an assault upon an occupant), and degree of organization. (The descriptions also include a common history of prior convictions and plea in mitigation.) Each case is described separately, and your task is to indicate the seriousness of each particular case of burglary by placing a mark on the scale at the end of the description of the case. It is inevitable that there will be a lot of repetition among the elements of the case descriptions, although in each case the combination of the case factors is unique. Remember, in making your ratings, treat each case as independent of the others and assume that each of the cases relates to a different offender. To assist you in making each assessment, you have been given a rating scale; the most serious case has arbitrarily been assigned a seriousness rating of 100, and the least serious case a rating of 0. These two cases – the scale's anchors – are described on the pages following these instructions. Once you have finished reading these instructions you should read and re-read the two anchor cases carefully so that these reference points are fixed clearly in your mind.

Your rating of the seriousness of each test case is to be made relative to these two anchor cases. (These seriousness ratings are to be made on the same basis as in the previous exercise.) For example, if you thought that the test case before you was midway in seriousness between the two anchors you would make a slash at the mid-point of the rating scale. (If you prefer, you may write the number quantifying your judgment at the appropriate point on the scale – in this instance it would be 50.) This would mean that in your view the difference in seriousness between the test case and the least serious (anchor) case was equal to the difference in seriousness between the test case and the most serious (anchor) case. It is important to stress that this is not equivalent to the conclusion that the test case is thought to be half as serious as the most serious (anchor) case. The reason for this is that the least serious (anchor) case is not devoid of seriousness. Similarly, if you put a mark 25/100ths along the scale (or gave a rating of 25) it would mean that you thought that the increase in seriousness between the least serious (anchor) case and the test case was approximately 1/3rd of the increase in seriousness from the test case to the most serious (anchor) case; it would not follow that you thought that the test case was approximately 1/4 the seriousness of the most serious (anchor) case. It is crucial to keep in your mind that you are making interval not ratio judgments. An everyday example may help illustrate this distinction. Say that you were rating the heights of individuals on a 0–100 scale, and assume that the heights of these individuals fell within the range 5 ft to 7 ft. We could arbitrarily label a height of 5 ft as "0" and 7 ft as "100". Now, if you rated an individual's height as 50 on this scale, it would be concluded that you thought that the difference in height between this individual's height and the 5-ft anchor was equivalent to the height difference between the individual's height and the 7-ft anchor; clearly, it would not follow that you thought the individual was one half of the height of the 7-ft anchor.

You are asked to assess the seriousness of each test case as you would assess seriousness if you were making this judgment as part of a determination as to what is appropriate by way of sentence for an actual case being heard by you in your Court– i.e., seriousness should be determined according to case factors considered material and appropriately weighted in the light of current sentencing policy and practice. You may assume that you have been presented with all the information which is required to fix a just sentence: no material case information has been omitted.

There are four practice cases for helping you to get a feel for the task. These are set out in this booklet, following the descriptions of the two anchor cases. You are asked to read and re-read the anchor cases and then complete the practice cases. Once you have completed these, re-read the anchor cases and then proceed to the test cases. Please complete the cases in the order in which they appear in the booklet, and do not look back at the cases you have rated or the assessments you have made. You should feel free to re-read the anchor cases at any time. Do not rate too many cases without a break–consider say ten as a maximum; nevertheless, it is advisable not to spread the whole task over too long a period. Whenever you have a substantial break, please re-read the anchor cases before proceeding with the rating task. Finally, I should be grateful if you would refrain from discussing this exercise with your brother judges. They are rating the same cases.

Before starting the exercise each judge was given the opportunity to have confusing points clarified.

The judges were handed this exercise at the end of the session for the second exercise and generally completed this task within a 2- to 3-month period. After the assessments were made, each judge was interviewed by me and asked whether he found any of the case descriptions unrealistic and implausible, and whether he had difficulty or was uncomfortable in assessing seriousness and using the scales as a means of expressing his preferences. If the judge replied in the affirmative, he was asked to explain the nature of these problems and how he thought this might have affected his assessments. Also, each judge was reminded of the relative weights he had assigned to each of the four offense factors in the MAUM analysis and asked whether he thought that these assessments represented the relative importance that he had attached to each of these factors in his determination of the overall seriousness of the cases in this exercise.

Procedure for Determining the Quanta of Sentence

The 41 cases together with the instructions were presented to the judges in a booklet with the cover title *Sentencing Research Exercise—Part 4.* The instructions were on the first page, followed by the descriptions of the fictitious cases. The descriptions of the cases were identical with the cases used in the third sentencing exercise. The (least serious) anchor case was included in this exercise as a test case. There were no practice cases.

One booklet was assigned to each judge unsystematically, and in each booklet the fictitious cases were presented in a different random order. The sample of judges used here was the same as in the previous two exercises. Each of the judges was seen by the author individually, and the booklets were handed to the judges personally. The judges were left to work through the cases in their own time.

The following instructions were set out at the beginning of each booklet. (The task was also explained informally to each judge.)

This exercise is the fourth in the series concerned with understanding how judges determine what is appropriate by way of sentence, and the information will be used to assist in developing a means of representing the relationship between case characteristics and sentence as a basis for detailed sentencing statistics. You are again reminded that your responses will not become part of a sentencing statistics data base and will not be submitted as individual data to the Sentencing Committee.

The booklet contains 41 case descriptions of burglaries of private houses, which have been varied systematically on the following four offense factors: total amount of money stolen in the burglaries; number of counts of burglary; the amount of violence inflicted on the victim(s) (violence is interpreted broadly, and ranges from simple entry to a home in the absence of the occupant(s) to an assault upon an occupant), and degree of organization. (The descriptions also include a common history of prior convictions and plea in mitigation.) Each case is described separately, and your task is to determine a sentence for the (principal) offender in each case. It is inevitable that there will be a lot of repetition among the elements of the case descriptions, although for each case the combination of the case factors is unique. Remember, treat each case as independent of the others and assume that each of the cases relates to a different offender.

You are asked to determine an appropriate sentence—a maximum and a minimum sentence—for each case. Exercise your discretion in accordance with sentencing law and sentencing policy (and practice) as it is currently to be found in the relevant statutes and appellate judgments: fix each sentence as though you were making the determination for an actual case being heard by you in your Court. You may assume that you have been presented with all the information which is required to fix a just sentence: no material case information has been omitted. Please write your sentence at the end of the description of each case. You are not required to give reasons for your decisions.

Please complete the cases in the order in which they appear in the booklet. When determining a sentence for a particular case, do not refer to any of the cases for which you have already fixed sentences. Do not feel under any obligation to complete the task without a

TABLE 16.9. Relationship between the judges' decomposed and holistic assessments of case seriousness: Product-moment correlations

	Judge[a]								
Sample	1	2	3	4[b]	5	6	7	8	9[c]
Sensitivity	.92	.80	.88		.62	.91	.87	.70	
Coherency (including sensitivity)	.93	.85	.91		.72	.88	.89	.78	

[a] These identifying numbers correspond to the numbers in Table 13.1.
[b] This judge completed the first exercise only.
[c] This judge has yet to complete this exercise.

break, although it is advisable not to spread the whole task over too long a period. Finally, I should be grateful if you would refrain from discussing this exercise with your brother judges. They are fixing sentences for the same cases.

Before starting this exercise each judge was given the opportunity to have confusing points clarified.

The judges began this task after they had completed the third exercise and typically completed it within a 2- to 3-month period. On returning the booklet, each judge was interviewed by me and asked whether he found any of the case descriptions unrealistic and implausible. If the judge replied in the affirmative, he was asked how he thought this might have affected his determination of sentence. The judges were asked whether in any of the cases there was any mitigation associated with the offender's plea, after allowing for the criminal record, for which credit was given; whether a more severe sentence would have been imposed in any of the cases if the offender's history of prior convictions, especially for dishonesty, had been more extensive and serious; and whether the sentences had been discounted for the plea of guilty. Finally, each judge was asked again to comment on the appropriateness of his factor weights from the MAUM analysis in regard to the determination of sentence for the cases in this exercise.

Results and Discussion

Relationship Between Decomposed and Holistic Assessments of Case Seriousness

Table 16.9 shows product-moment correlations between overall case seriousness calculated on the basis of the assessments of scale value and weight in the MAUM analysis (see Chapter 15) and the holistic assessments of case seriousness elicited in Exercise 3, for each of the judges. Data are presented for the 40 cases comprising the coherency analysis and separately for the 20 cases from the sensitivity analysis (see Tables 14.7, 14.9, 16.1, and 16.3). (This latter sample forms part of the sample of cases in this coherency study.)

The correlations for the 40 cases in the coherency sample reveal substantial to very high correlations for five of the seven judges (nos. 1, 2, 3, 6, and 7), and moderate correlations for the other two judges. A more rigorous test of the coherency hypothesis is provided by the data from the 20 cases in the sensitivity analysis, because this set of cases is weight sensitive. For this sample four of these five judges (nos. 1, 3, 6, and 7) again exhibited substantial to very high correlations. It is reasonable to conclude on the basis of these data that four of the judges demonstrated a coherent understanding of their holistic assessments of case seriousness (i.e., they are aware of the way the material offense factors are scaled, weighted, and aggregated in the determination of offense seriousness and are able to make and apply these judgments reliably). And for these four judges, the magnitudes of their correlations are similar for both the weight-sensitive sample (the 20 cases from the sensitivity analysis) and weight-insensitive sample (the 20 extra cases formulated for this coherency study). (The approximate size of the correlations for the set of weight-insensitive cases can be deduced from the data in Table 16.9, because the sensitivity sample forms part of the coherency sample.) In contrast, the discrepancies between the correlations for the weight-sensitive and weight-insensitive samples would be substantial for the three judges who did not demonstrate coherency as assessed by the weight-sensitive sample. Indeed, the correlations for two of these three judges would be substantial to very high for the weight-insensitive sample. It is not possible to identify directly the reason for this discrepancy. Perhaps these judges lacked insight into the relative weights of the factors underlying their holistic assessments of case seriousness. Another reason may lie in the nature of the cases comprising the weight-sensitive sample. Unlike the cases in the weight-insensitive sample, these cases involved cross-currents of aggravating and extenuating factors, clearly a more complex cognitive task. Now, perhaps, this additional complexity induced unreliability into the holistic assessments of these judges. And there are other possible explanations.

Of course, one of the limitations of the correlation coefficient is that it is influenced unduly by extreme pairs of high and low values and is influenced more by the rank order of pairs than their relative numerical values. This is a real limitation in the context of the present study, because judges would be expected to have little difficulty in identifying the more serious and less serious cases.

To investigate whether these correlations were hiding incoherency in the midrange of seriousness and were, accordingly, an artifact of extreme values, Table 16.10 was constructed to examine the relationship between seriousness calculated on the basis of the decomposed judgments and the holistic assessments of case seriousness, across the range of case seriousness, for each of the judges.

In Table 16.10 coherency would be marked by three characteristics: sequential increases in assessed seriousness as calculated case seriousness increases; relatively small standard deviations; and correspondence between the magnitudes of assessed and calculated case seriousness. On these grounds it may be concluded that two of the judges (nos. 1 and 3) exhibit a high degree of coherency and for another three judges (nos. 2, 6, and 7) there is evidence of substantial coherency. These are the same five judges who were identified as coherent in the

TABLE 16.10. Relationship between the judges' decomposed and holistic assessments of seriousness across the range of case seriousness for the coherency sample: Means and standard deviations

Calculated case seriousness	Judge[a] 1	2	3	4[b]	5	6	7	8	9[c]
0–9	20–0	23–3	18–8		8–2	19–7	23–3	29–8	
10–19	29–6	22–9	22–9		29–10	25–4	33–11	31–15	
20–29	40–13	50–15	40–6		43–33	37–12	31–7	36–20	
30–39	46–10	52–13	48–6		21–7	60–8	47–14	28–3	
40–49	58–8	65–5	52–10		34–16	56–18	56–11	40–14	
50–59	67–14	60–10	53–2		55–26	66–7	58–12	38–2	
60–69	68–4	76–3	62–9		48–24	75–5	75–5	54–19	
70–79	85–4	80–7	66–4		67–10	79–10	83–4	70–14	
80–100	88–3	85–0	80–7		75–11	80–9	83–5	78–8	

Note. Cases were assigned to the levels on the basis of the calculated case seriousness scores of each of the judges. Accordingly, the means and standard deviations within a level are not necessarily for the same cases.
[a] These identifying numbers correspond to the numbers in Table 13.1.
[b] This judge completed the first exercise only.
[c] This judge has yet to complete this exercise.

correlational analysis. Clearly, the correlational analysis in providing a global measure leads one to form an unrealistic impression of the degree of coherence. As intended, this accompanying detailed analysis acts to correct such an impression. However, the concomitant danger is that the detailed data in Table 16.10 may create a false impression of the level of incoherence; in interpreting these data it must be remembered that the divisions across the range of calculated case seriousness are relatively narrow and in each of the cells there is an average of only four and one-half cases.

Relationship Between Holistic Assessments of Case Seriousness and Effective Sentence

Chapter 15 dealt with judicial input into the three elements of sentencing policy, namely, the identification of material case factors, and the scaling and weighting of these factors. This section is concerned with the fourth element of sentencing policy for which judicial input was required—the quanta of sentence considered appropriate for various levels of case seriousness for burglaries of private homes. The relevant data are presented in Table 16.11, and are based on the 41 cases in the coherency study.

In interpreting Table 16.11 it must be again remembered that the divisions across the range of case seriousness are relatively narrow, and in each of the cells there is an average of only four and one-half cases. The import of this caveat is that for each of the judges the mean sentences in the intermediate levels cannot be considered in isolation but must be viewed in the context of the judge's sentences for the other levels. Moreover, the mean sentences in the highest and

TABLE 16.11. Relationship between the judges' holistic assessments of case seriousness and effective sentence (months) for the coherency sample: Means and standard deviations

Case seriousness (holistic assessment)	Judge[a]								
	1	2	3	4[b]	5	6	7	8	9[c]
0–9	12–0	0–0	14–2		34–10	0–0	9–0	6–0	
10–19	–[d]	0–0	27–9		30–5	6–0	24–0	9–0	
20–29	24–8	0–0	15–0		43–7	8–3	30–7	13–4	
30–39	34–8	18–12	26–11		50–6	14–9	34–9	18–2	
40–49	45–9	33–3	41–24		60–0	–[d]	36–10	22–4	
50–59	48–0	38–5	45–19		93–15	10–4	45–11	30–4	
60–69	58–11	44–9	68–23		65–11	27–10	36–0	40–6	
70–79	61–10	60–9	76–23		81–20	26–13	55–4	38–6	
80–100	77–6	73–6	81–2		83–17	32–14	72–9	50–4	

Note. Cases were assigned to the levels on the basis of case seriousness as it was assessed holistically by each of the judges. Accordingly, the means and standard deviations within a level are not necessarily for the same cases.

Because the ranges of sentence vary across judges, the standard deviations are not directly comparable as measures of dispersion.

[a] These identifying numbers correspond to the numbers in Table 13.1.
[b] This judge completed the first exercise only.
[c] This judge has yet to complete this exercise.
[d] There were no cases in this cell.

lowest levels can be regarded as no more than a rough guide to a particular judge's range of sentence. Notwithstanding these limitations associated with the interpretation of these data, one is led to the tentative conclusion that there is a marked variation across judges in the range of sentence considered appropriate for the more serious cases of residential burglary. Although there is no methodological consideration that would prevent one from averaging the sentences across judges as the index of this element of sentencing policy, it is suggested that the disparities are so substantial that they could not be properly resolved arithmetically. Indeed, these differences across the judges in what are considered appropriate sentences for the upper and lower extremes of case seriousness for this sample of cases appear to reflect what is commonly considered harsh and lenient sentencing. Now, this is a matter of sentencing policy and should be resolved in jurisprudential terms by an appellate court, sentencing council, or the legislature.

There is another reason why the mean sentences in the upper and lower levels of seriousness in Table 16.11 may provide a misleading impression about each judge's range of sentence. Such a conclusion would require the assumption that seriousness and sentence are interchangeable concepts in the sense that the assessments on both dimensions are governed by a similar consideration of the same factors. The substantial concordance between case seriousness assessed holistically and effective sentence as it is shown by the data in Table 16.11 suggests that this appears to be a sound assumption for all but judge no. 3 and perhaps judges nos. 5 and 6. It will be recalled that judge no. 3 said that the number of counts was not material to the assessment of seriousness but that it did bear upon the determination of sentence (see Chapter 15).

TABLE 16.12. Judges' highest and lowest effective sentences for the cases in the coherency analysis

Effective sentence (months)	Judge[a]								
	1	2	3	4[b]	5	6	7	8	9[c]
Highest	84(48)	84(60)	108(96)		108(42)	45(36)	90(60)	54(54)	
Lowest	12	0	12		24	0	9	6	

Note. The figures in parentheses are the highest effective sentences imposed by the judges in the 36 cases in the study examining the validity of the fictitious cases technique (see Chapter 13).
The sentences within a level are not necessarily for the same cases.
[a] These identifying numbers correspond to the numbers in Table 13.1.
[b] This judge completed the first exercise only.
[c] This judge has yet to complete this exercise.

Table 16.12 shows the highest and lowest effective sentences imposed by each of the judges for the 41 cases in the coherency analysis.

The data in Table 16.12 are consistent with the data in Table 16.11 and confirm the conclusion that judges differ in terms of what they regard as an appropriate upper limit on the quantum of sentence for the more serious cases of residential burglary. Moreover, these individual differences across judges regarding the highest effective sentence imposed in this coherency study largely are consistent with the rank severity of the judges' sentences for the cases taken from court records in the validity study of the technique of fictitious cases (see Chapter 13). With the exception of judges nos. 1 and 5, the judges who imposed the harshest sentences there also imposed the most severe sentences in this coherency study.

Relationship Between Decomposed Assessments of Case Seriousness and Effective Sentence

By way of introduction, the point should be made that it is possible to examine directly the notion of coherency in terms of the relationship between case seriousness calculated on the basis of the assessments of scale value and weight in the MAUM analysis (see Chapter 15) and the effective sentences imposed in this exercise because the data satisfied two conditions. First, the vast majority of the sentences imposed were custodial sentences. Accordingly, the effective sentence could be used as a basis for differentiating cases in terms of their seriousness across the range of seriousness covered by the cases. Second, for each of the judges the sentences for the 41 cases in the coherency study were well distributed across a substantial range, and this permitted fine discriminations. It should also be noted that the preceding analysis (see Table 16.11) showed that for six of the seven judges there was moderate to high concordance between the holistic assessments of case seriousness and the quanta of sentence. Accordingly, sentence could be directly related to case seriousness calculated on the basis of the decomposed assessments and in this way used as an index of seriousness.

TABLE 16.13. Relationship between the judges' calculated case seriousness scores (decomposed assessments) and effective sentence: Product-moment correlations

	Judge[a]								
Sample	1	2	3	4[b]	5	6	7	8	9[c]
Sensitivity	.94	.82	.49		.42	.73	.82	.68	
Coherency (additional cases)	.98	.92	.91		.84	.91	.88	.94	
Coherency (including sensitivity)	.96	.87	.67		.62	.81	.82	.77	

[a] These identifying numbers correspond to the numbers in Table 13.1.
[b] This judge completed the first exercise only.
[c] This judge has yet to complete this exercise.

Table 16.13 shows for each of the judges product-moment correlations between case seriousness calculated on the basis of the assessments of scale value and weight in the MAUM analysis (see Chapter 15) and the effective sentences fixed for the 40 cases (20 weight-sensitive cases from the sensitivity analysis and the additional 20 weight-insensitive cases) in Exercise 4.

The correlations between calculated case seriousness and effective sentence for the 40 cases in the coherency sample reveal that for only one judge (no. 1) the correlation can reasonably be described as very high. The significance of this result is confirmed by the data for the weight-sensitive sample. (It is worth noting here that for this judge the discrepancy between the magnitudes of the correlations for the weight-sensitive and weight-insensitive samples is small.) Clearly, only one of the judges demonstrated a coherent understanding and application of his tariff-sentencing principles. In contrast the correlations for the six other judges are only moderate to substantial for the cases in the coherency sample. The striking feature, however, for four of these judges (nos. 3, 5, 6, and 8) is the substantial difference between the magnitudes of the correlations for the weight-sensitive and weight-insensitive sets of cases, and the high correlations for this latter sample of cases. Notwithstanding the limitations of the correlation coefficient, these data lead one to suppose that these four judges may have provided a set of very reliable sentences but not have made valid representations in the MAUM analysis of their understanding of the basis of tariff sentencing. Indeed, so great was the discrepancy between the correlations for the weight-sensitive and weight-insensitive samples that it seemed worthwhile to make a detailed analysis of these four judges' responses for the purpose of attempting to identify the error in their representation of the relative factor weights. Clearly, a casual inspection of the data could not be expected to detect other than a major mis-weighting of a single factor for any one judge. The picture for the other two judges (nos. 2 and 7) is less clear. For these judges the correlations between their calculated assessments of case seriousness and effective sentences for the sensitivity sample, although substantial, are insufficiently high for one to conclude that these judges' understanding of the tariff has been adequately captured by the MAUM analysis, and yet the discrepancies between the correlations for the weight-sensitive and weight-insensitive samples are not sufficiently great to offer

TABLE 16.14. Relationship between the judges' calculated case seriousness scores (decomposed assessments) and effective sentence (months) across the range of case seriousness for the coherency sample: Means and standard deviations

Calculated case seriousness	Judge[a] 1	2	3	4[b]	5	6	7	8	9[c]
0–9	14–1	0	20–10		32–10	5–3	21–11	12–5	
10–19	28–3	2–3	16–1		47–8	8–3	34–11	17–9	
20–29	40–5	34–17	44–27		63–32	12–7	32–6	21–13	
30–39	47–3	39–11	33–15		41–12	13–12	38–10	18–0	
40–49	50–5	50–11	55–22		57–14	17–8	49–8	26–12	
50–59	64–9	45–3	59–14		56–19	17–9	50–8	22–1	
60–69	68–7	63–7	60–19		54–10	26–11	67–13	34–12	
70–79	77–5	70–8	80–26		73–18	35–9	71–9	38–9	
80–100	84–0	81–3	74–12		89–17	40–4	68–6	48–6	

Note. Cases were assigned to the levels on the basis of the calculated case seriousness scores of each of the judges. Accordingly, the means and standard deviations within a level are not necessarily for the same cases.

Because the ranges of sentence vary across judges, the standard deviations are not directly comparable as measures of dispersion.

[a] These identifying numbers correspond to the numbers in Table 13.1.

[b] This judge completed the first exercise only.

[c] This judge has yet to complete this exercise.

one much hope of detecting a possible misweighting of an offense factor. (The discussion returns to the detailed analysis of the four judges' responses shortly.)

To examine the correspondence between calculated case seriousness and effective sentence across the range of case seriousness for each of the judges, Table 16.14 was constructed. It is based on the 41 cases in the coherency sample. The data in Table 16.14 confirm the very high degree of correspondence between the calculated values of case seriousness based on the MAUM analysis and effective sentence for judge no. 1 and the substantial discrepancies between these two indices for the other six judges, especially judges nos. 3, 5, 6, and 8.

Figure 16.1 presents the relationship between calculated case seriousness and effective sentence for judge no. 1, together with the line of apparent best fit. This line marks this judge's view of the proportionality between case seriousness and quantum of sentence. The line appears to show a slight curve; as case seriousness increases there is a corresponding decrement in the additional quantum of sentence. Figure 16.1 is the numerical representation of this judge's sentencing policy respecting that element of policy covering the relationship between the seriousness of a case and what is considered an appropriate sentence.

Figure 16.1 shows that for judge no. 1 there are at least two cases for which there might be considered to be a substantial discrepancy between calculated case seriousness and sentence. This raises the question whether this reflects unreliability in the judge's assessments or perhaps is a sign that the weighted additive model is an oversimplification of the rules followed by this judge in aggregating his assessments for each of the component offense factors to determine the overall seriousness of a case. To decide between these alternative explanations, the judge should be asked to consider whether he preferred the sentences he imposed

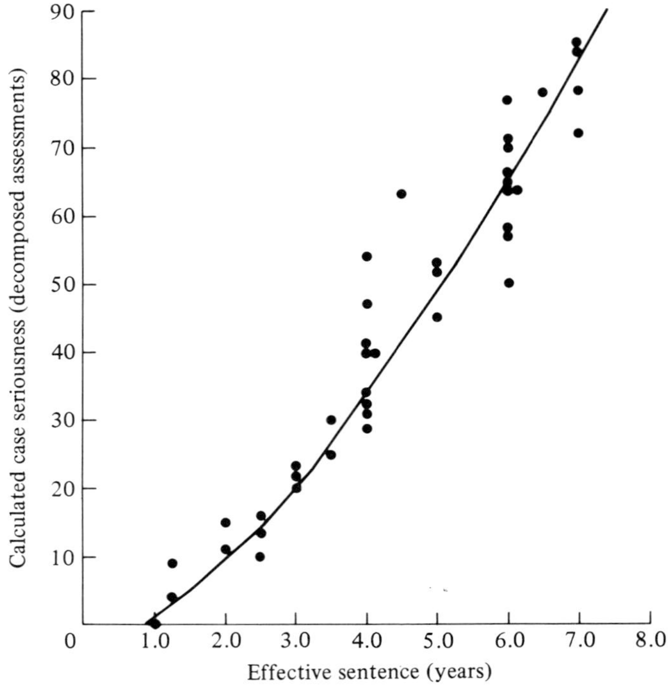

FIGURE 16.1. Relationship between calculated case seriousness and effective sentence: judge no. 1.

or the quanta of sentence consistent with calculated case seriousness. If he preferred or, at least, felt that the latter sentence was not inappropriate, then it would seem reasonable to conclude that the weighted additive model is an acceptable representation of his aggregation rule. Again, the prescriptive orientation of this study places this argument on surer ground. If, however, the effect was traced to the judge's preference for an interaction between offense factors, then it could be treated as a unique factor for which allowance could be made in relation to the effect of the common factors.

This discussion now turns to a detailed consideration of the responses of the four judges (nos. 3, 5, 6, and 8) for whom the correlations between calculated case seriousness and effective sentence were much lower for the weight-sensitive sample than for the weight-insensitive sample (see Table 16.13). To determine whether a particular factor has been misweighted by a judge, it is necessary, first, to identify those cases in the sensitivity analysis for which there was a substantial discrepancy between the judge's calculated value of case seriousness and the corresponding quantum of sentence and, then, to examine the nature of the relationship between the patterns of the levels on the four offense factors comprising these cases and the corresponding discrepancies. If the quanta of sentence tend

TABLE 16.15. Judges' weights for the relative importance of three of the four offense factors: Weights as a proportion of the most important factor

	Judge[a]							
Offense factor	1	2	3	4	5	6	7	8
Total value of the theft	.88	.81	1		.45	.20	.50	.29
Organization	.88	.59	.95		.85	.40	.63	.50
Violence to the victims	1	1	.76		1	1	1	1

[a]These identifying numbers correspond to the numbers in Table 13.1.

to be excessive in relation to the calculated values of case seriousness when one of the factors is set at its highest level (4) and inadequate when the same factor is set at its lowest level (1) then it is likely that the judge has underestimated the relative importance of that factor. This systematic inspection of the data indicated that these four judges had seriously underestimated the relative importance of the factor of counts of burglary, and that rather than its being a relatively unimportant factor in their decision it was in fact exerting a very substantial effect on the assessment of what was considered appropriate by way of sentence.

Accordingly, it was decided to recalculate the case seriousness scores of each of the judges on the basis that counts of burglary was an important factor. Of necessity, this analysis was "rough-and-ready," because the values of the substituted weights for counts of burglary could be based on no more than a "guesstimate."

Consider the judges' assessments of the relative importance of total value of the theft, organization, and violence to the victims when counts of burglary is excluded. These were recalculated on the basis of the data in Table 15.13 and are shown in Table 16.15 in terms of importance as a proportion of the most important factor.

Clearly, Table 16.15 shows that judges nos. 5, 6, 7, and 8 assess the relative importance of the total value of the theft, organization, and violence to the victims in a somewhat similar manner. Now, judge no. 7 ranked counts of burglary as equally as important as violence to the victims. Accordingly, the calculated values of case seriousness based on this judge's decomposed assessments in the MAUM analysis were compared with the effective sentences imposed by each of the judges nos. 5, 6, and 8 for the 40 cases (20 weight-sensitive cases from the sensitivity analysis and the additional weight-insensitive cases) in this coherency study. The results (product-moment correlations) are shown in Table 16.16 and are directly comparable with the data in Table 16.13.

Now, judge no. 7's MAUM assessments could not be used for judge no. 3, because their rankings of the relative importance of the other three offense factors differ. An inspection of the discrepancies between the calculated values of case seriousness and effective sentence seemed to indicate that this judge was in effect giving a very high relative weight to counts of burglary. Accordingly, for judge no. 3 this factor was reweighted so that its new weight was substantially higher than the weight for the factor (total value of the theft) that judge no. 3 con-

TABLE 16.16. Product-moment correlations between the judges' calculated case seriousness scores (decomposed assessments) and effective sentence: Reweighting of counts of burglary

	Judge[a]			
Sample	3[b]	5[c]	6[c]	8[c]
Sensitivity	.89	.74	.89	.87
Coherency (additional cases)	.98	.91	.93	.97
Coherency (including sensitivity)	.93	.82	.91	.90

[a] These identifying numbers correspond to the numbers in Table 13.1.
[b] Case seriousness calculated on the basis of a substantial weight for counts of burglary and lesser weights for the other three factors in accordance with this judge's weights.
[c] Case seriousness calculated on the basis of judge no. 7's decomposed assessments.

sidered the most important factor in the MAUM analysis; the relative weights for this judge of the other three factors were left unchanged. Clearly, the actual value of the new relative weight assigned to counts of burglary is somewhat arbitrary. There are many values that would satisfy the condition that the weight for counts of burglary be substantially higher than for total value of the theft. In this reanalysis of the relationship between calculated case seriousness score and effective sentence, the relative weights of counts of burglary, total value of the theft, organization, and violence to the victims for judge no. 3 were set at 37, 23, 22, and 18, respectively. Since judge no. 3 did not scale the levels on counts of burglary in relation to seriousness, these values were taken as the average values for these levels across the seven judges (see Table 15.10). The result of this reweighting of counts of burglary on the relationship between calculated case seriousness and effective sentence for judge no. 3 also is shown in Table 16.16.

The correlations showing the relationship between calculated case seriousness and effective sentence are substantial to very high (see Table 16.16). They are based on the 40 cases in the coherency sample. When these data are compared with the results in Table 16.13 for these particular judges, it is clear that the reweighting of counts of burglary has led to a dramatic increase in the correlations for the sensitivity sample and to a small increase in the already high correlations for the 20 weight-insensitive cases in the coherency sample. It follows that the previously low correlations for these judges did not signify unreliability in their sentencing of the cases in the sensitivity sample but rather that the assessments they made in the MAUM analysis misrepresented their true preferences in regard to the relative importance of counts of burglary as a determinant of sentence. Moreover, the correlations between calculated case seriousness and effective sentence are sufficiently high for the cases in the sensitivity sample that it seems reasonable to conclude that three of these four judges (nos. 3, 6, and 8) also may be considered to have demonstrated that they do apply the tariff coherently. In drawing this conclusion it must be borne in mind that the values of the substituted weights for counts of burglary were almost certainly suboptimal. For judge no. 5 the correlation between these assessments of case seriousness (reweighted) and effective sentence for the sensitivity sample is insufficiently

TABLE 16.17. Relationship between the judges' calculated case seriousness scores (decomposed assessments) and effective sentence (months) across the range of case seriousness for the coherency sample: Means and standard deviations for the reweighting of counts of burglary

Calculated case seriousness	Judge[a]			
	3[b]	5[c]	6[c]	8[c]
0–9	18–9	34–10	4–3	10–4
10–19	21–3	34–8	6–3	15–7
20–29	28–6	46–8	10–3	17–1
30–39	36–5	48–10	13–6	22–2
40–49	40–5	66–24	22–7	34–11
50–59	62–22	62–15	21–9	30–5
60–69	73–10	77–15	37–1	40–8
70–79	78–2	86–14	40–5	49–2
80–100	99–11	94–11	38–3	54–0

Note. Cases were assigned to the levels on the basis of the calculated case seriousness scores of two of the judges (nos. 3 and 7). Accordingly, the means and standard deviations within a level are not necessarily for the same cases.
Because the ranges of sentence vary across judges, the standard deviations are not directly comparable as measures of dispersion.

[a] These identifying numbers correspond to the numbers in Table 13.1.

[b] Case seriousness calculated on the basis of a substantial weight for counts of burglary and lesser weights for the other three factors in accordance with this judge's weights.

[c] Case seriousness calculated on the basis of judge no. 7's decomposed assessments.

high for one to conclude that his understanding of the tariff has been adequately captured by the MAUM analysis.

Table 16.17, which shows for the 41 cases in the coherency sample the correspondence between calculated case seriousness and effective sentence across the range of case seriousness for each of these four judges, confirms the conclusions drawn on the basis of the correlations in Table 16.16. Compare the data in Table 16.17 with the data for these judges in the corresponding table (Table 16.14) in which the weights are based on each judge's own assessments in the MAUM analysis; it can be clearly seen that as a result of the reweighting of counts of burglary the mean values of their effective sentences increase more uniformly with increases in the calculated value of case seriousness and the standard deviations are substantially smaller.

There are several important consequences of this finding to which attention should be drawn. First, it is necessary to revise the conclusion, based on the judges' assessments in the MAUM analysis, that there is significant disparity among judges regarding the relative importance of counts of burglary in determining the appropriate quantum of sentence (see Table 15.14 and the associated discussion); the secondary analysis showed that counts of burglary is one of the most important offense factors for six of the seven judges in the sample. Nevertheless, one judge's weighting of counts of burglary clearly was different, and of course there may be some disparity among the other six judges on this point. The analysis of the reweighting was too crude to make firm conclusions, and in any case, the technique is an inappropriate means to identify a judge's underlying decision strategy from holistic assessments. Moreover, when the importance of counts of burglary is excluded, it would appear that significant disparity still remains among the judges regarding the relative importance of the other three factors (see Tables 15.13, 15.14, and 16.15). Again, the nature of the analysis does not permit one to take this conclusion further. Of course, it must be borne in mind that a considerable number of the County Court judges who were not included in this sample would be regarded widely as experienced in the criminal jurisdiction. This sample may not have captured the diversity of their views regarding the relative importance of these four factors in determining sentence. Clearly, at this point in time, judicial sentencing policy on this matter could not be represented numerically as the average importance of the factors taken across the judges. Not until there was agreement across judges, or at least those judges whose views were being taken as a basis for policy, over the rank order of the importance of the offense factors could one contemplate using the average as a means of representing this aspect of sentencing policy.

Second, to ascertain the appropriate weight of the factor of counts of burglary in relation to the other three offense factors, it would be necessary to repeat the MAUM analysis for the judges for whom there were significant discrepancies between the calculated value of case seriousness and sentence. Before this step, it might be helpful to point out to each judge these discrepancies and to draw his attention to the effect the number of counts had on his determination of sentence so that he could determine with greater insight which of the two sentences—the imposed sentence or the quantum of sentence consistent with calculated case seriousness—he considered more appropriate, for each of the patterns of offending. Indeed, in view of the prescriptive orientation of this study, it would be necessary for the judges to make this comparison and to reconcile the differences so that there was no longer any incoherence in their understanding of the tariff.

Third, the substantial discrepancies between calculated case seriousness and sentence for four of the judges (nos. 3, 5, 6, and 8) lead one to doubt the validity of the MAUM procedures as a means of tapping (in this instance) a judge's true preferences relating to offense factor weights in the determination of sentence. It will be recalled that a judge's preferences regarding the relative weights were assessed in the MAUM analysis (see Chapter 14) by first having the judges assess pairs of factors and then check this assessment in the context of a case. It may be that this later test is not a powerful check on the judgments of relative weight. This conclusion can be treated as no more than speculative, because some of the judges did not check their assessments in the context of a case or did so in a cursory fashion.

Judges' Comments

In responding to these two exercises, none of the judges reported difficulties attributable to unrealistic case descriptions. For two of the judges (nos. 3 and 5), however, the concept of seriousness was regarded as problematic in those cases comprising multiple counts (this point is elaborated on later). Notwithstanding the preceding point, all of the judges appeared comfortable in assessing case seriousness by means of the scales.

Only one judge (no. 8) felt, in view of his experience in assessing overall case seriousness and fixing sentences for the cases in these two exercises, that his MAUM assessments of the relative weights of the four offense factors might not have accurately reflected his decision making. In the MAUM exercise this judge assessed counts of burglary as the least important factor, but on reflection he thought that it was probably second in importance only to violence to the victims. In fact the secondary analysis indicated that counts of burglary made an important contribution in this judge's determination of sentence.

Four of the judges (nos. 1, 6, 7, and 8) felt that the sentences they had imposed could reasonably be regarded as "ceiling" sentences for each of the 41 combinations of case facts; three of these judges said that their sentences included a small discount for the guilty plea, whereas one of the judges (no. 6) had given a substantial (25%) reduction in the quantum of sentence for this factor. Nevertheless, two of these judges identified factors that if present would cause them to modify the ceiling sentences. For example, one judge said that if the offender's guilty plea had involved his admitting to a large number of counts that would not otherwise have come to the attention of the police, then this would have justified a substantial discount, or that if the current offense(s) had been committed in the early stage of the offender's parole then one would have had to consider a longer term of imprisonment. All of these four judges held that the plea contained little by way of mitigation and that the criminal history was near the upper limit of seriousness.

The sentences of the other three judges (nos. 2, 3, and 5) could not be regarded as setting a ceiling for each of the offense patterns. Although they too agreed that the offender's plea was of little consequence, these three judges stated that they would have been prepared to impose substantially more severe sentences if the offender's record of prior convictions had been more serious and that this consideration would have been particularly significant for the more serious cases among those presented to them in the exercise.

17
Toward Deliberative Sentencing and Numerical Guidelines

This chapter first considers the implications for the development of detailed sentencing statistics of the results of the judges' assessments relating to the model of judicial decision making. Then a proposal is made to use fictitious cases as a basis for statistics describing current sentencing policy and practice and as a means to develop and reform sentencing policy. Finally, an overview is presented of the course this study has taken in its attempt to open the judges' exercise of the sentencing discretion to further quantification.

The analyses in the archival burglary study (see Part Two) were based on a model of judicial decision making developed by the writer. To construct this model showing the relationship between the characteristics of the offense and the offender and the overall seriousness of the case, I intuited what definitions, weights, and aggregation rules judges apply to these case factors as they determine the sentence for a case. This area of sentencing policy is the preserve of the judiciary and, accordingly, a MAUM analysis was adopted to provide judicial input on these matters as they relate to offense characteristics of burglary (see Chapters 14 and 15). An earlier study provided no evidence for doubting that the judges' responses to cases presented in fictitious form were a valid indication of the way they assessed the seriousness of offense characteristics in relation to quantum of custodial sentence (see Chapter 13). A subsequent study demonstrated that the judges' assessments of seriousness and sentence were coherent and of a high quality (see Chapter 16). This series of exercises sets the scene for the final step in the development of detailed sentencing statistics showing the relationship between various combinations of the characteristics of cases and the actual sentences imposed for those cases in the courts. That is, the seriousness of the 100 cases in the archival burglary study would be reassessed in terms of the now-modified model of judicial decision making and the statistics would show the relationship between these assessments of seriousness and the corresponding sentences imposed in the courts.

For several reasons this final step cannot be taken as part of the present study. First, the model was modified in regard to offense characteristics only; factors associated with prior convictions and the plea in mitigation have yet to be scaled by the judges. This limitation for this present analysis lies in the fact that these latter factors exert a substantial weight in determining an appropriate sentence for a case of burglary and, accordingly, a reanalysis of the archival data relating to the model modified only in terms of the offense factors would be pointless. One need no more than recall the poor relationship between offense (cf. case) seriousness and sentence in the (original) archival study to appreciate this point (see Table 7.1). Second, doubt remains over the values of the relative offense factor weights that would provide the most accurate representation of the judges' average sentencing policy. In part the resolution of this matter would require discussion among the judges and a detailed consideration of the reasons underlying their various assessments. Third, of course, there is the problem of the extent to which the present sample of judges represents the population of sentencing judges. Fourth, the objective case facts used to operationalize the levels on violence to the victims and organization are but specific instances of a wide variety of offense characteristics that would satisfy the levels on these two offense factors. It is unclear whether the observed relationship between assessed seriousness and the objective scale values (levels) for each of these factors would vary significantly if other behaviors were used to illustrate the constituent levels. Finally, the judges' assessments did not cover commercial premises or variations in that element of violence to the victims relating to property damage.

The discussion concludes on what must be regarded as a problematic element in this analysis: the role of the factor of counts of burglary in the determination of overall case seriousness as well as the appropriate effective sentence for a particular case. There was a hint of disparity in the review of authority on this matter (see Chapter 4). The judgment of the Victorian Court of Criminal Appeal in *Tutchell* (1979) stated clearly that in determining the effective sentence for a case comprising multiple counts, a judge should take a global view of the seriousness of the characteristics of the offense. In this approach the factor of counts of burglary is properly considered as one of the four offense factors in the determination of offense seriousness and sentence. Five of the seven judges said that this was their approach. Nevertheless, one of these five judges thought that this global strategy in sentencing is not easy to follow for those case in which one of the counts is much more serious than the other counts. This particular position seems to fit the circumstances covered in Thomas's (1979) statement on the application of the totality principle. Nevertheless, this judge took the view that this circumstance did not apply to the cases in the third and fourth exercises, because it could be reasonably assumed that the offender had a propensity to resort to this highest level of violence in all of the counts, but that this propensity could not have been assumed if the highest level on violence to the victims had been more extreme. One judge believed that the factor of counts of burglary is important but cannot be treated similarly to the other three factors. This judge believed that the proper course is to impose an appropriate sentence for each count and then determine orders of concurrency and partial concurrency so that the effective sentence is not crushing. Then there was another judge who clearly favored this latter view but thought that the overall seriousness of the case may unconsciously influence his determination of the effective sentence. Not only was there apparent disparity among authorities and the judges in the sample on this matter, but also the coherency analysis revealed that four of the seven judges were not aware of the role played by counts of burglary in their determination of a tariff sentence. Related to the role of counts of burglary is the question whether the effect of the value of the property taken in a series of burglaries is more properly considered as the average across the counts or as the total of all of the counts. The issue is that use of the total amount may be considered to overweight the combined effects of the number of counts and the value of the theft.

Fictitious Cases as a Basis for the Description of Current Sentencing Policy: Detailed Sentencing Statistics

The primary purpose of the four exercises undertaken by the judges was to provide judicial input into the model of decision making relating to the circumstances of the offense and quantum of sentence and, in this way, refine the model in terms of the definition of the material offense factors, and the scaling and weighting of those factors. To develop the detailed sentencing statistics, the relative seriousness of actual cases heard in the courts would be determined in terms of this model and the statistics would show the relationship between these assessments of seriousness and the corresponding sentences imposed in the courts. In this approach the elements of policy concerned with the definition, scaling, and weighting of the case factors would be taken from a sentencing exercise (a MAUM analysis), and that element of policy covering the appropriate quanta of sentence for the various levels of case seriousness would be based on actual sentencing decisions imposed in the courts. In this context the point of the fourth exercise, in which judges imposed sentences for fictitious cases, was to test whether the judges' policies regarding the elements of the sentencing decision (definitions of factors, etc.) were coherently related to the final decision, namely, the appropriate quantum of sentence for a case. Nevertheless, one cannot help but consider whether that element of sentencing policy covering the quantum of sentence might not be taken from a sentencing exercise, as it would be done for the other elements of sentencing policy. Clearly, it is feasible. The judges did not report any difficulties in imposing sentences for the fictitious cases. Moreover, the limited evidence available supports the external validity of their responses. First, the nature of the fourth exercise was similar to the first exercise. In the first, judges fixed sentences for cases taken from court records and the results showed that across a range of seriousness the levels of sentence fixed in the exercise corresponded to the levels of the actual sentences for those cases for which the court had imposed a custodial sentence (see Chapter 12). Second, the notional sentence for the least serious of the fictitious cases (see Table 16.1), as it was calculated on the basis of the detailed sentencing statistics developed in this project (see Figure 11.1 and accompanying text), was approximately 9 months. (Even if a straight line had been fitted to the data in Figure 11.1, the notional sentence at this level of seriousness would not have been significantly different.) And an inspection of the sentences imposed in the fourth exercise showed that all but one of the judges imposed an effective sentence within the range of 0 to 12 months for the least serious fictitious case (see Table 16.12). (An attempt to determine on the basis of the archival study notional sentences for all of the fictitious cases and in this way examine further the external validity of the sentences imposed in the fictitious cases would be problematic because the notional sentences are not based on differential weighting and the appropriateness of the curvilinear relationship is open to question. Both these differences would significantly limit the validity of comparisons at the higher levels of case seriousness.) Finally, the judges, with two exceptions, who imposed the harshest sentences for the cases taken from the court records (the first exercise) also imposed the most severe sentences in the coherency study (see Table 16.12 and the associated discussion).

In the assessment of the present approach to the development of detailed sentencing statistics based on archival data, it was concluded that this approach has advantages over some of the earlier attempts but, nevertheless, shares several common problems (see Chapter 11). The following analysis argues that if sentences imposed for fictitious cases were used as a basis for detailed statistics describing current sentencing policy and practice, rather than actual sentences imposed in the courts, then the remaining problems associated with the present approach would be overcome. Each matter is considered in turn.

First, when an appellate court enunciated a new policy, its effect on the determination of sentence could be readily incorporated in the statistics. Where the change related to the general level of sentences, the change could be recorded by the stroke of a pen. In those instances involving significant changes to the weighting of case factors for a particular legal category of offense, for example, the weight assigned to violence, the judges would simply be required to make a series of judgments, similar to the ones described in the MAUM exercise, and to set sentences for a series of cases to test the coherency of the new policy.

Second, sentencing statistics could be developed for those legal offense categories for which offenders come before the courts relatively infrequently.

Third, because the fictitious cases comprise only material case factors, the guidance provided by sentences determined for fictitious cases would not be open to distortions arising from the surreptitious influence of material or immaterial case factors (e.g., race). Of course, it is important that the descriptions of the fictitious cases should be comprehensive and detailed because the judges might otherwise make inferences about the missing information, based on typical patterns of offense and offender characteristics, and in this way immaterial case factors could unintentionally be incorporated in the guidelines.

Fourth, because policy concerning appropriate quanta of sentence for the various levels of seriousness—the relationship between case seriousness and sentence—is based on changes in only a small number of factors (four for offense), distortions in the judgments arising from the limitations of human information processing would be expected to be substantially less significant than the errors in the determination of archival sentences where the cases vary across a large number of offense and mitigating offender factors as well as factors covering prior criminal history.

Finally, fictitious cases provide a means of identifying individual differences in judges' sentencing policies. The technique also provides a means of reconciling these differences coherently, because it would be possible to detect whether a changed judicial attitude toward an element of policy (e.g., the weighting of a case factor) was associated logically with what would be necessary changes in the assessments of the relative seriousness of various cases.

There would be expected to be an added bonus in having judges participate in the process by which their current sentencing policies were identified for the purpose of developing sentencing statistics. The judges would be expected to have a clearer understanding of how the case factors were related to sentence in the guidelines, a process that would be facilitated where the only variation in the case factors was for those factors incorporated in the detailed sentencing statistics. If judges acquired a greater understanding of the basis of the statistics, they would be better placed to consider accurately the effects on sentence of the unique factors in relation to the common factors and, accordingly, use the guidance more effectively as an aid in the exercise of the sentencing discretion.

It is therefore important that the form of the presentation of the detailed sentencing statistics should be designed to facilitate the judges' understanding of the relationship between the sentence and the definition, scaling, weighting, and combination of the factors. A possible format is described following. The scaling of the offense factors of violence to the victims and total value of the theft in relation to seriousness are illustrated in Figure 17.1. The summary definitions are based on the archival burglary study, and the scale values are the average (mean) values taken from the judges' assessments in the MAUM analysis (see Tables 14.1 and 15.12 for violence to the victims and Tables 14.4 and 15.9 for total value of the theft). For violence to the victims, the guideline also would include detailed definitions of the various levels of seriousness (see Table 6.1) together with illustrative examples in concrete, case-specific terms, and for total value of the theft there also would be a graph showing the relationship between seriousness and amount of money (see Figure 15.1).

Figure 17.2 illustrates the relative contributions of violence to the victims and total value of the theft to overall offense seriousness. The value is based on the mean relative contribution across the judges (see Table 15.13). It also shows the relative impact on offense seriousness across the two factors of changes in seriousness in relation to the levels assessed by the judges. It would not directly assist a judge in exercising a deliberative judgment and probably does little more than add detail to the following figure, Figure 17.3. Moreover, it carries the danger that judges might perhaps erroneously equate the seriousness of adjacent levels across the two scales.

The purpose of Figure 17.3 is to demonstrate how the individual assessments of seriousness on the four offense factors combine in determining overall offense seriousness, with particular reference to violence to the victims and total value

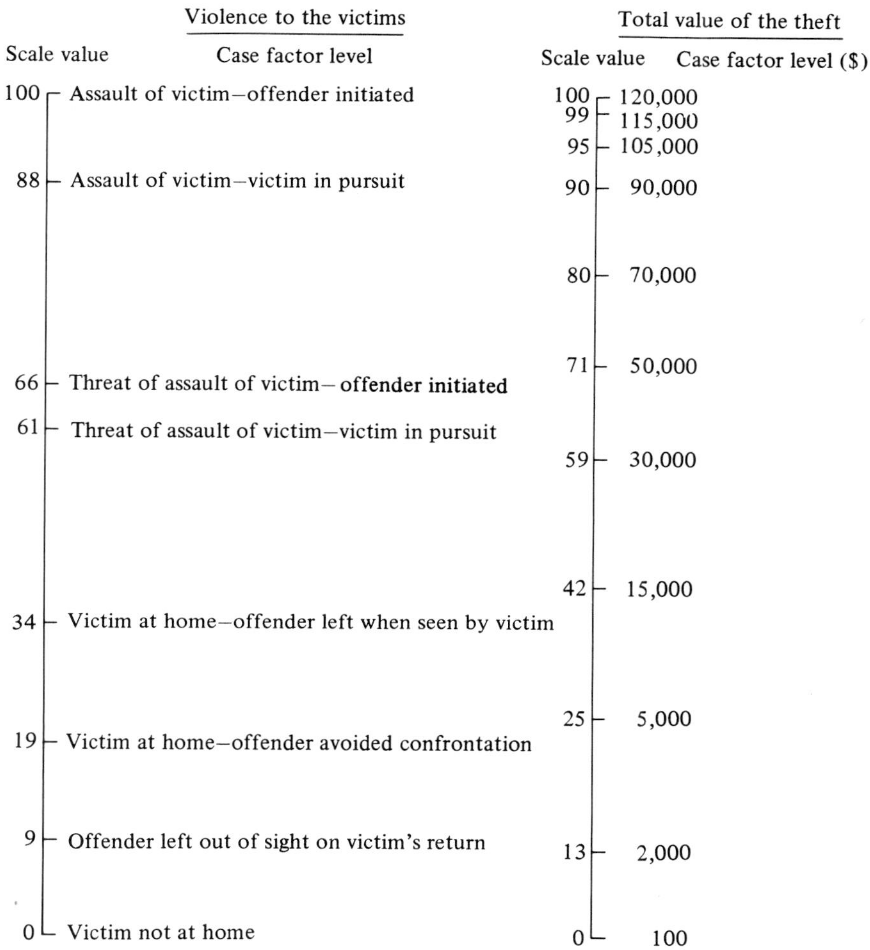

FIGURE 17.1. Illustrative scaling of violence to the victims and total value of the theft in relation to seriousness for residential burglaries.

of the theft—for these two factors the scale values of the offense factor levels assessed by the judges are shown. The mean values of the relative contributions of the factors are taken from Table 15.13. This figure, in association with the detailed definitions of the factors and the chart showing how seriousness varies across the offense factor levels for each of the factors (Figure 17.1) should assist a judge in allowing for the effects of offense factors or offense factor levels not included in the guidance in relation to those elements in the system. Figures 17.1 and 17.3 should be of particular value to a judge in considering the effects on sentence of more serious offense factor levels; together they show how seriousness increases over levels on a particular factor and also the relative contribution

FIGURE 17.2. Illustrative weighting of the relative contributions of violence to the victims and total value of the theft to offense seriousness for residential burglaries.

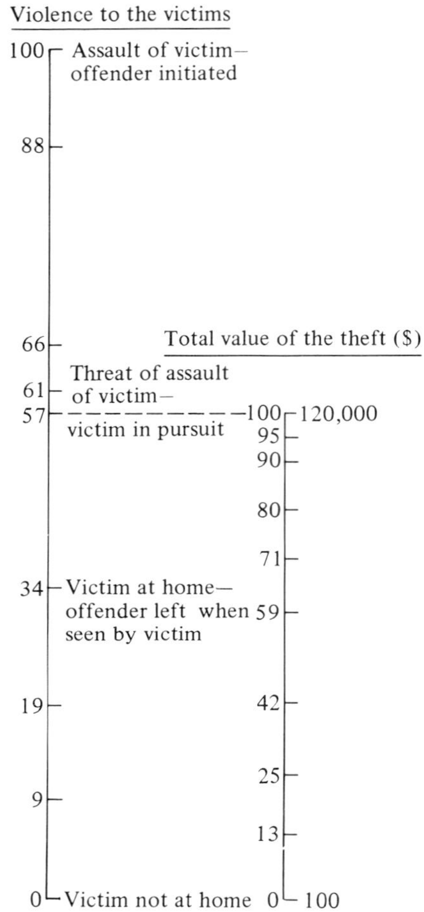

of that factor to overall seriousness. This feature of the guidance might be critical. Hood (1972) in his study of magistrates formed the view that disparities in the sentencing of unusual cases might arise out of too great a reliance on systems for achieving uniformity in run-of-the-mill cases.

The final element in the guidance would be a graph showing the relationship between overall offense seriousness and sentence. (A graph representing this element of sentencing policy for one of the judges in the sample is shown in Figure 16.1.) Of course, the aggregation of the individual assessments of seriousness in the determination of the appropriate quantum of sentence for a case would be done by computer.

The detailed sentencing statistics at this stage of development would show the upper limit, or ceiling, of the quantum of sentence for any combination of levels for the offense factors incorporated in the guidelines. To determine the appropriate quantum of sentence, a judge then would be required to determine whether,

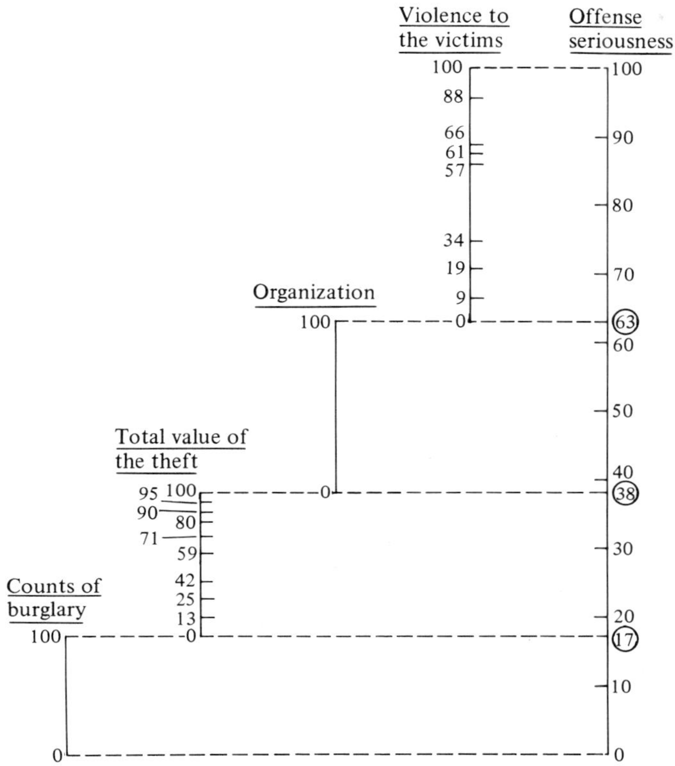

FIGURE 17.3. Illustrative combination of the four offense factors in relation to offense seriousness for residential burglaries with particular reference to violence to the victims and total value of the theft.

in view of the offender's criminal history, allowance could be made for any mitigating considerations, and the judge's task would be to exercise discretion to determine how much the ceiling sentence should be reduced in accordance with the offender's claims to mitigation. And, of course, the judge also would be required to allow for the effects on sentence of any material case factors outside of the guidelines.

To provide guidance on the effects of offender characteristics, the judges would be required to undertake another series of sentencing exercises. My personal view is that in developing the statistics, prior criminal history should be incorporated in the guidance before the system was made operational. Sentencing exercises could be readily formulated to provide for assessments of seriousness relating to criminal history and such a system would provide extensive guidance to a sentencing judge. In the early stages of the implementation of a system of numerical guidance, it might be unwise to attempt to incorporate mitigating offender characteristics in the system, or at least more than a few of the major and more objective ones; sentencing judges might doubt the amenability of these apparently qualitative factors to quantification, and a system incorporating them might seem overwhelmingly complex. It would appear preferable in the first instance to allow judges to become accustomed to a system comprising mainly offense characteristics and criminal history; the proposed approach would so increase the precision in the determination of sentence that to the legal mind it might appear as a revolutionary change, rather than what it would be, an evolutionary development in sentencing. Nevertheless, it might be advisable in the early stages to develop the indicators for determining whether the sentence should emphasize the seriousness of the offense (tariff sentence) or whether the rehabilitation prospects of the offender should be the salient consideration (individualized measure).

Fictitious Cases as a Basis for the Development and Reform of Sentencing Policy: Numerical Guidelines

The analysis to this point has been concerned with describing current sentencing policy and practice, that is, developing detailed sentencing statistics showing the relationship between patterns of offending and sentence. Here the discussion turns to the development and reform of sentencing policy. In developing sentencing policy the focus mainly is on filling in gaps in policy; for example, explicitly specifying case factor weights. So that the model of judicial decision making could be used as a basis for describing current sentencing practice, it would be necessary to develop sentencing policy to this limited extent. Reform, however, involves more; it involves changes in sentencing policy, for example, the reweighting of offense factors or disallowing consideration of certain case factors such as, perhaps, employment status. The guideline judgments of the Lord Chief Justice of England and the Minnesota Sentencing Guidelines Commission's guidelines involve both the development and reform of sentencing policy, although the emphasis in England is on development and in Minnesota the changes are more appropriately characterized as reform.

Development and reform may relate to the determination of material case factors, the operational definition (including description and scaling) of these factors, their weights, the rules for aggregating these elements, and the quanta of sentence deemed appropriate for the various combinations of case characteristics. The earlier empirical work demonstrated the value of the model as a basis for developing a description of current sentencing policy in respect of these five elements. It would require but a small step to use the model as a basis for a systematic examination of current policy with a view to reform. The model would be, as it were, a first quantitative draft of current sentencing policy and in this way offer a basis for moving toward uniformity of approach by providing a framework for directing attention to critical questions about sentencing policy and representing the answers with precision. Changes could be contemplated to the existing model (e.g., case factors could be redefined and reweighted), and perhaps new types and quanta of sentence could be approved for various combinations of offense and offender characteristics. Moreover, the methods adopted in the development of the model of judicial decision making provide a strategy for eliciting answers to the questions raised by the model and also offer a means of testing the coherence of these judgments in regard to the five interconnected elements of sentencing policy. Of course, in the process of both development and reform, individual judges would differ initially in their assessments relating to the various elements of policy. The advantage of the model is that differences in determining appropriate sentences could be traced back to their source in the sentencing judgment. Clearly, if the MAUM analysis were to be used in the development of sentencing policy then it would require the participating judges to provide and discuss the reasons for their assessments. Recently, Pease examined several of the guideline judgments of the Court of Appeal (Criminal Division) in England with a view to plotting the Court's formulation of the relationship between certain case characteristics and sentence for several offenses. He concluded that if such guidance were scaled in this way it would serve to facilitate discussion of these judgments and add precision to the formulation of them (Harvey & Pease, 1987; Pease, 1987).

The concepts and techniques considered in the present project offer a structure and procedure for the development and representation of guideline judgments by an appellate court (see Ashworth, 1984) or sentencing guidelines by a sentencing commission or council (see Ashworth, 1983b; Canadian Sentencing Commission, 1987; Law Reform Commission–Australia, 1980). This sort of guidance has a prescriptive orientation; to distinguish these guidelines from detailed sentencing statistics, which involve the description of current sentencing policy and practice, they may be referred to as numerical guidelines.

Overview and Conclusion

The purpose of this project has been to explore how and to what extent the exercise of the sentencing discretion might be amenable to further quantification. In this quest two specific goals gave direction to the analysis: (1) the provision of detailed sentencing statistics for use in the courts to show for specific legal offense categories the relationship between various combinations of offense and offender characteristics and the type and quantum of sentence and (2) the introduction of empirical techniques to facilitate the development and reform of sentencing policy. Significant numbers of judges, academic lawyers and criminologists, and members of law reform bodies have drawn attention to the significant value of these two tasks. The description and development of current sentencing policy is seen as important because in the absence of a detailed and comprehensive policy, individual sentencing judges are forced to formulate and apply policy as they determine particular cases, and inevitably some of their views will be divergent. Moreover, there are commentators and practitioners who are dissatisfied with what appear to be some of the policies applied in the courts. In the absence of a precise description of current policy, however, it is impossible to identify the gaps and idiosyncratic views or to discuss satisfactorily the policies and applications of those policies that the community believes would lead to the just treatment of its criminals. The need for greater guidance, indeed assistance, for the judge in sentencing is also predicated on the grounds that to apply sentencing policy the judge must consider and integrate a large number of factors, and the complexity of the required decision making exceeds the putative limits of human information processing, with error being the inevitable consequence.

In this project the decisions whether or not to imprison and, for those cases in which prison is considered appropriate, the length of the term, were the focus of attention. An analysis of sentencing judgments showed that these decisions are characterized by a high degree of imprecision, apparently because the underlying assessments are unnecessarily subjective and qualitative. In particular, this imprecision is manifest in the selection, classification, and aggregation of information relating to the scaling of case seriousness and the indicators of an offender's rehabilitation prospects. A move toward greater quantification is compatible and consistent with the intrinsic nature of the sentencing judgment as it is now understood. The final decision is quantitative (the amount of the fine, years of imprisonment, etc.), and in many instances the quantum of sentence is tied to a judgment about the seriousness of the case; moreover, the courts constantly refer to the weighting of matters in the course of determining sentence.

The major problem inherent in other approaches to the development of detailed sentencing statistics (Doob, 1986; Doob & Park, 1987; Hogarth, 1986a, 1986b; Wilkins et al., 1978) and numerical guidelines (Court of Appeal—Criminal Division in England—see Ashworth, 1984; Minnesota Sentencing Guidelines Commission, 1984; United States Sentencing Commission, 1987) is that the problem of how to represent quantitatively the aggregation of the various elements in the sentencing decision is ignored (Court of Appeal—Criminal Division in England; Hogarth; Doob; Minnesota Sentencing Guidelines Commission) or it is dealt with inappropriately (Wilkins; United States Sentencing Commission). In the present study the attempt to solve this problem involved developing a legal model of the way judges should determine an appropriate sentence in view of the facts of a case; it is a model of ideal decision making relating to current policy, because it takes no account of the limitations of human information processing.

To use the model as a basis for determining the appropriate sentence for a particular case according to current sentencing policy, the case would be construed in terms of the model (i.e., the case factors would be selected, scaled, weighted, and aggregated as prescribed in the model) to determine the relative seriousness of that particular combination of case factors and then reference made to a table showing the sentence or the range of the sentences imposed previously in the courts (or considered appropriate by an appellate court or sentencing council) for cases falling at that level of seriousness. This sentence or range of sentences would provide the standard against which the judge could exercise the sentencing discretion to allow for the effect of factors or particular combinations of factors that were not incorporated in the guidelines, perhaps not even covered in current policy, and yet were considered by the judge as material to sentence in the particular case.

The development and application in this way of a model of judicial decision making faithful to the structure of judicial thought has the potential to provide the most accurate and comprehensive representation of the tariff. Moreover, where the guidance was to act as a standard against which judges would further exercise their discretion, it would be difficult for them to allow properly for the unique case factors in relation to the common case factors if they did not understand how the standard was derived. Finally, a model of ideal judicial decision making is essential when the description of sentencing policy is to act as a basis for policy development and subsequent numerical guidelines.

If the proposals and strategies formulated in this project were implemented, to what extent would the twin goals of the control of disparity and the development of policy in sentencing be achieved? One would show great naivety as well as an ignorance of the literature in concluding confidently that the introduction of detailed sentencing statistics and numerical guidelines would result in a reduction in sentencing disparity. In the context of the present study it would depend on the extent to which disparity arises from the judges' ignorance of sentencing policy, the limitations of human information processing, the absence of a detailed and comprehensive policy, and the degree to which the factors incorporated in the guidelines cover the variations occurring in the nature of offending and the circumstances of offenders within a particular legal offense category, as well as the significance for sentence of those factors not included in the system of guidance. The scope and effect of these matters are largely unknown. All one can conclude is that the present proposals offer a means of plugging several notorious gaps. Furthermore, in providing greater structure to the exercise of the sentencing discretion, the model might facilitate the identification of other sources of disparity. Then, of course, there are potential sources of disparity outside of the bounds of the present study, such as possible adaptive responses by other participants within the criminal justice system.

Nevertheless, one can be more positive and confident about the contribution of the present analysis to the goal of the description of current sentencing policy and the development of a detailed and comprehensive policy. This study sought to identify and introduce concepts that would facilitate the representation of policy and permit judicial input into the development of policy. The empirical work showed that the empirical techniques adopted made it possible to elicit from judges a coherent set of judgments covering the classification and aggregation of case facts in the course of determining the quantum of sentence. Moreover, it was possible to represent these descriptions of sentencing policy in a way that would facilitate discussion about the appropriateness of the assessments relating to each component of sentencing policy.

It is appropriate now to consider possible criticisms of such a move toward introducing further quantification and a higher degree of precision into the sentencing judgment—criticisms that almost certainly would find fertile ground in many legal minds. A common view is that this sort of approach entails a mechanical, rather than, presumably, a human approach to the administration of justice. Which perceived characteristics of the mathematical and behavioral science underpinnings of the proposed approach might lead to this pejorative use of "mechanical" or, alternatively, what are the peculiarly human capabilities that so reassure us about the ability of the wise judge to dispense justice fairly? Perhaps it is the belief that with increasing precision through quantification there is a necessary reduction in the capacity of the system of guidance to provide for individualized punishment. Surely, in such a system the number of case variables that could be incorporated in the decision would be severely limited? Surely, it would not be possible to allow for apparently qualitative variables like the degree of organization? And would not the system be refractory to gradual and continual changes in sentencing policy, in that a sentencing judge would find it difficult to allow for the effects of a particular combination of factors not yet covered by the guidance and in that it would not be possible to incorporate readily and coherently in the guidance changes to sentencing policy as they were enunciated by the appellate court? Nothing could be further from the truth. Nothing could represent a greater misunderstanding of the approach developed in this present study. Let it be clear, what is in contention here is not that a system that failed to meet these requirements would be unacceptable. Indeed, the Wilkins et al. (1978) approach to the development of detailed sentencing statistics was criticized and rejected on these very grounds. What is in contention here is that these undesirable features are necessary characteristics of a system of guidance providing structure and precision in the sentencing judgment through quantification.

It is presumably necessary at this point to no more than remind readers of some of the aspects of the present strategy designed to minimize or obviate these (and other) everpresent hazards threatening the successful development of numerical guidance. To ensure that the guidance was not based on an impoverished set of case factors, the criterion for the inclusion of a case factor was that an analysis of appellate and first-instance judgments revealed it was material to sentence; this contrasts with the traditional approach of selecting variables from a correlational analysis of archival data. This alternative approach was made possible because I concomitantly developed a model of the structure of the sentencing decision, including an aggregation rule, and so it was then possible to interrelate a large number of case factors in the decision. Moreover, the empirical analysis demonstrated that qualitative case factors like organization can be operationalized validly in terms of concrete, case-specific characteristics. Of course, it was not practicable to incorporate in the analysis the less common manifestations of the common case factors, and it was impossible to anticipate all case factors or combinations of case factors that might at some time in the future arise and be deemed by a sentencing judge or an appellate court to be material to sentence. Accordingly, it is essential that the guideline sentences should act as no more than a standard against which the sentencing judge could exercise a further discretion. The standard therefore was based on a model faithful to the structure of judicial thought, and this would be expected to assist the judge in allowing coherently for the unique elements in relation to the common case factors. Finally, the technique of fictitious cases provided a method for the description and development of sentencing policy that would facilitate the ready and coherent incorporation of changes to current sentencing policy as they were enunciated by an appellate court.

A second matter of possible concern to lawyers is that any attempt to implement such a system of guidance would become unwieldy and for that reason be impracticable. The reason underlying this view is valid. The potential number of matters of relevance to any one sentencing decision are manifold. This is moderated by the fact that, as Thomas (1979) put it, "Innovation in crime . . . is relatively rare" (p. 29) and, one may add, it is possible to refer to types of offenders. Nevertheless, there is innovation in crime, and offenders are found in different circumstances, and this is why a system of guidance should be designed to facilitate the exercise of discretion by the sentencing judge. Indeed, because the sentencing decision is so complex and because there are limits to human information processing, it is desirable to reduce the load on judges as much as possible without oversimplifying or otherwise modifying the determination of sentence.

A third consideration perhaps underlying the lack of enthusiasm of some for a quantitative approach is that the sentencing process appears to be largely based on the application of rules and, accordingly, any worthwhile system for structuring the sentencing discretion would be rule based rather than quantitative. Although it is true that sentencing is rule based, many of the rules relate to quantification, because in tariff sentencing the judge's task is to make the quantum of sentence proportional to the seriousness of the case. Nevertheless, there are many aspects of the sentencing decision where the rules do not deal with quantity. More importantly, there are matters which, if considered solely in numerical terms, would be oversimplified. An apposite example here is the consideration of an offender's prior criminal history in regard to the decision whether to impose a period of imprisonment. In principle, an offender could accrue a high score on the scale measuring this case factor, and yet in the mind of the sentencing judge, the offender may not have had the benefit of an appropriate noncustodial option. Clearly, the sentencing judgment cannot be reduced to a mathematical equation.

Some may say that even though this system of guidance might alleviate many of the problems associated with the current level of imprecision in the sentencing judgment, it is possible that the greater precision would give rise to new difficulties. Because the effect of a judge's decision in regard to each element of the sentencing judgment would be clear, counsel may conclude that much is to be gained from contesting every matter, with the inevitable result being drawn-out sentencing hearings. This, it must be admitted, is a real danger, and presents a problem that must be addressed. To prevent this unintended consequence, the guidance should comprise only those case factors that have a substantial objective component and can be described in concrete, case-specific terms, and moreover, each dimension should be defined in terms of a substantial number of subdivisions or categories. Under these circumstances it would be difficult to more than quibble, and little would be gained (or lost) if the offender were given the benefit of the doubt, and accordingly, a case were described in terms of a lower rather than a higher category or division on a particular scale, because the factor still would have a similar impact on seriousness and, accordingly, on sentence (see, e.g., Figures 16.1, 17.1, and 17.3). Perhaps this point would become clearer if it was illustrated in terms of an inappropriately defined dimension. Consider a dimension designed to assess violence and defined in terms of only two categories, one labeled *violence* and the other labeled *no violence*. Little imagination is needed to realize that under such circumstances counsel would have much scope for contesting an unfavorable application of the category of violence, because it is undefined, and would have much to gain from a successful bid. A dimension defined in this way should be contrasted with the way the dimensions were defined in the multiattribute utility analysis (see, e.g., Tables 6.1 and 14.1) to appreciate why this problem would not be expected to be significant in the proposed system. (A second problem associated with such vague definitions of case factors is that considerable room is left for subjectivity and, consequently, disparity, in applying the guidance in particular cases.)

Finally, some may argue that the development of this system of guidance would be too demanding of judicial time and too slow to be practicable. In considering this point of view, the following matters should be borne in mind. At the outset it is important to appreciate that to provide a set of sentences acting as a ceiling for various combinations of offense characteristics for a particular legal offense category, it would not be necessary for judges to undertake all of the exercises in the present series of feasibility studies. Indeed, in the light of the understanding gained from these studies of the nature of judicial decision making in relation to sentencing, judges would be required to complete a MAUM analysis (Exercise 2)—Chapter 15—and determine sentences for selected cases as in the coherency analysis (Exercise 4)—Chapter16. The MAUM analysis would provide information on the scaling and weighting of the material offense factors, and the latter exercise would set quanta of sentence across the range of offense seriousness. It would be unnecessary for judges to set sentences for more than several cases at each of the highest, lowest, and intermediate levels of seriousness—perhaps two to three cases at each of these three levels. This, of course, requires the assumption that the judges have a coherent understanding of the tariff.

Now, it would take some years to provide tariffs covering offense and selected offender characteristics for the full range of legal offense categories. Nevertheless, the process of development would proceed more quickly than in the traditional curial approach to the provision of guidance to sentencers, and additionally, the product would be expected to be more satisfactory. Moreover, this process should of itself be profitable; it would encourage the judiciary to engage in a hard examination of the basis and application of the tariff.

There are, of course, wider criminological considerations relating to possible unintended consequences of guidelines in general and numerical guidance in particular. As intimated in the introduction to this study, however, these are outside the scope of the present project, which is confined to an analysis of the conceptual and methodological problems associated with the introduction of precision into the sentencing judgment in the course of developing detailed sentencing statistics and numerical guidelines.

The system developed in this study for classifying cases and then determining appropriate sentences may seem quite complex. Indeed, it is complex in the sense that it incorporates a large number of decisions and elements of information. The complexity is not intrinsic to the system but rather arises from what has been a serious attempt to represent the complexity of the sentencing process. The decisions and information specified in this system merely cover many of the decisions and much of the information that judges must now consider intuitively every time they determine sentence. One advantage of this system is that it would be expected to make the task of determining sentence easier because it specifies the decisions that must be made and offers guidance on the way that the information normally should be classified and combined. A second advantage is that it spells out these rules and defines the case characteristics with a reasonable degree of precision and thereby would facilitate analyses of the jurisprudence of sentencing.

It is suggested that the critical question is whether the model is sufficiently complex to account for judicial thought processes adequately and yet its representation of the relationship between case fact and sentence simple enough to be practicable for use in the courts. In developing any model of behavior there is necessarily a balance to be struck between accuracy and simplicity. One should guard against rejecting detailed sentencing statistics and numerical guidelines on the ground that the underlying model oversimplifies judicial thought processes before first considering whether sentences determined on the basis of these statistics might be more reliable and valid than those determined intuitively. In relation to this point, the exercises concerned with judicial input into the model of sentencing demonstrated that it is possible to describe comprehensively in a small set of factors the common variation in the offense of burglary, obtain judges' assessments for the scaling and weighting of these offense factors, and finally, account for the judges' sentences for a sample of these offenses in terms of their assessments for the constituent offense characteristics.

The purpose of this research project has been to explore the amenability of the sentencing judgment to further quantification and, in doing this, introduce concepts and methods that would facilitate this development. It set out to offer no more than a numerical aid to the common law approach. The results of the empirical analyses demonstrated that the sentencing process could be more finely honed or, at least, made less blunt, and profitably so. In this way the exercise of the sentencing discretion would become more objective and quantitative and, accordingly, less intuitive and more deliberative.

Appendix 1
A Sample Case in Exercise 1

New Case

Date of Plea: 6/2/81

Presentment

One count receiving; three counts burglary.

Plea

Guilty.

First Count

Receiving, 6/22/78. This involved a T.V. valued at $560, which was recovered.

Second Count

Burglary, 10/29/80.

Victim's Statement. He left his flat locked at 11:00 a.m. When he returned at 1:10 p.m. it was still locked but the color T.V. was gone. Value, $400.

Record of Interview. The accused could not recall with whom he had broken in. He had sold the T.V.

Third Count

Burglary, 11/6/80.

Victim's Statement. He had gone to work at 7:00 a.m. When he returned at 4:40 p.m., the front door was unlocked. His wife had gone out at midday. Missing property: books, vacuum cleaner, kettle, and ornaments. Value, $350.

Record of Interview. The accused broke in with another offender but did not recall how they had entered.

Fourth Count

Burglary, 11/17/80.

Victim's Statement. He left for work at 8:30 a.m. and left the flat locked. When he returned at 6:00 p.m., he discovered the premises had been entered. Missing property: T.V., radio/cassette recorder, bag, two cassettes, $20, pillowcase. Value, $437.

Record of Interview. The accused stated that he had broken in with another offender. They went in his girlfriend's car and had used "plastic to slip the lock open." He sold the property in the hotel.

Priors

1. Magistrates' Court 7/26/76	Burglary	Probation 2 yrs
	Being an unlicensed driver	Fine $150 in default 5 days, disqualified from obtaining a license for 6 months
2. Magistrates' Court 12/5/78	Stealing	Fine $75 in default 21 days
3. Magistrates' Court 5/3/79	Attempt to steal	Fine $50 in default 14 days
4. Magistrates' Court 8/3/79	Illegal use of a motor vehicle (3 charges)	3 months on charges 1 and 2
	Unlicensed driver	Probation 3 years on charge 3 Fine $60 in default 21 days, disqualified from obtaining a license for 6 months on charge 4
	In possession of property suspected of being unlawfully obtained	Fine $50 in default 21 days
	Using obscene language	Fine $50 in default 21 days
	Resisting a member of the police force in the lawful execution of his duty	Fine $75 in default 28 days
5. Magistrates' Court 1/17/80	Willfully destroying property	Fine $50 with $98 restitution in default imprisonment 1 month

Plea

The accused was born on 4/28/59. He has now been in custody 162 days. The accused finished Form 5 at technical school and had regular employment for quite some time. He was unemployed and went to Queensland and had some employment there. He was charged with handling stolen goods and absconded. Earlier this year he was fined in Victoria for a breach. He and his de facto wife were expecting a child. He was unemployed at the time of these offenses and was behind in the rent. The male persons sharing his flat at that time suggested that he come with them and share in the proceeds and that would get him out of trouble. The co-offender was dealt with for three burglaries and several other offenses and received 9 months at an Attendance Center. The co-offender is about 21 now and did not have many priors.

He intends to marry his de facto, and their child is now 8 months old. They are living with his mother. He intends to return to his mother when he is released. His mother was annoyed that he did not realize he could go to her for help. He now realizes that he can go to his family.

He has been offered immediate employment for at least 1 year building swimming pools.

A Salvation Army witness saw him at least eight times while he was in custody, has noted his willingness to co-operate, and feels he has good rehabilitation prospects.

A considerable number of items were recovered, and $700 cash was found in the flat and is in the possession of the police.

Appendix 2
A Sample Fictitious Case in Exercise 3 and Exercise 4

New Case

Date of Plea: April 1987

Presentment

Sixteen counts burglary; three counts theft of motor vehicle with intent.

Plea

Guilty.

Dates of Offenses

February 12 to March 28, 1986

Statements of Victims. The 16 victims provided evidence of the break ins of their homes. In all cases the victims were absent from their properties for part of the night and, on returning late at night, entered the front door to find that the contents were slightly disturbed. Entry apparently was through the back or side door, which in most cases showed signs of having been forced open by breaking the lock.

In one case the owner, aged 45, had then gone upstairs to continue his check and had entered one of the upstairs rooms. The offender was in the room and, on seeing the owner, had moved one pace toward him, and waved his fist at the owner, threatening to strike him. The offender then ran immediately to the window, climbed out, and escaped.

Missing Property. Cash, \$750; jewelry, \$7,500; silverware, \$3,000; electrical equipment, \$3,000; cameras, \$750. Counts 1–16:

\$ 937	\$ 280	\$ 190	\$1,020
\$2,055	\$1,210	\$2,400	\$ 90
\$ 350	\$ 60	\$1,540	\$1,040
\$ 940	\$ 350	\$1,600	\$ 938

Total value, \$15,000.

Record of Interview (Signed). The offender stated that before committing any of the burglaries he had chosen a prosperous area and had selected a number of houses that looked "suitable," e.g., that offered some camouflage. He had acted alone and said that all the burglaries were carried out at night. The offender took a jimmy with him and would steal a panel van from a hotel parking lot or from outside a house in a nearby suburb and drive to the house he had selected. He entered by forcing the back or side door. After the burglary the offender took the goods straight to a fence he knew and then abandoned the vehicle in a nearby suburb.

During one burglary the offender heard a car turn into the drive while he was upstairs searching. He looked out of the window and saw a man about to enter by the front door. The offender continued his search even after the man came upstairs. The man entered the room he was in, and the offender admitted that he had taken one step toward the man and had waved his fist and had threatened to hit him. He had then run immediately to the window and climbed out onto the roof below and escaped.

Priors

1. Children's Court	12/17/69	Illegal use of a motor car	7 days Youth Training Center (YTC)
		Armed with an offensive weapon	7 days YTC
		Unlicensed driver	Fine $14 in default 7 days Total: YTC 14 days
2. Children's Court	1/24/70	Unlawful assault	Fine $20 in default 10 days
		Indecent language	Fine $20 in default 5 days
3. Children's Court	2/7/70	Illegal use of a motor car (2 charges) Larceny (2 charges) Schoolhouse breaking and stealing (2 charges)	YTC 12 months on all charges
4. Magistrates' Court	4/7/71	Shopbreaking and stealing Schoolbreaking and stealing Illegal use of a motor car (3 charges)	YTC 3 months on each of charges 1–5
		Larceny (5 charges) Dangerous driving Unlicensed driver	Convicted without penalty on charges 6–10 and 12 YTC 1 month on 11th charge Total: YTC 16 months
5. Magistrates' Court	6/15/71	Illegal use of a motor car	2 months
		Escaping from legal custody	1 month (concurrent) Total: 2 months
6. Magistrates' Court	1/20/73	Assault by kicking	1 month
7. County Court	5/28/74	Burglary (3 counts) Theft (2 counts)	Probation: 2 years
8. County Court	5/18/78	Burglary (3 counts)	10 months on each count (2 and 3 concurrent with each other) Total: 20 months

Priors cont.

9. Magistrates' Court	5/11/80	Assault with a weapon Assaulting a member of the police force in the lawful execution of his duty Being drunk and disorderly	7 days on each of charges 1 and 2 (concurrent) Convicted without penalty on charge 3
10. County Court	8/27/83	Burglary (3 counts)	2 years 6 months on count 1 and 12 months on each of counts 2 and 3 (concurrent with each other and with count 1) Total: 2 years 6 months Minimum 18 months

Plea

The accused was born on 7/15/53 and was 32 years old at the time of these offenses.

His father disappeared from the family home when the accused was 12 months old. The accused lived at home with his mother until he was 16, when his mother died, after which he moved from place to place staying with various friends and acquaintances. He left school at this age and had a series of laboring jobs with the longest continuous period of employment being 12 months. There were periods when he was out of work because no work was available.

When he was 22 years of age the accused married, and there are two children of this marriage, two girls aged 10 and 8. He has been separated from his wife for 5 years, and they are now divorced. His wife has remarried and has taken responsibility for the care of the two children.

At the time of the first offense, the accused had been out of work for 1 month and felt financially insecure. He was looking for work when he was arrested but had been unsuccessful. The accused admitted the charges to the police during the interview and pleaded guilty at the preliminary hearing. He is not in possession of the goods and says that he sold all the stolen property and has spent the proceeds.

Since the current offenses the accused has not committed any offenses and there are no matters outstanding.

The accused receives unemployment benefits and has been living with his girlfriend for the past 18 months. She has regular employment as a shop assistant. He has no associations with known criminals.

References

Adams and others. (1972, October). New South Wales Court of Criminal Appeal, unreported.

Advisory Council on the Penal System. (1978). *Sentences of imprisonment: A review of maximum penalties.* London: Her Majesty's Stationery Office.

American Law Institute. (1962). *Model penal code – Proposed official draft.* Philadelphia: A.L.I.

Anderson, J.K., and Hayden, R.M. (1981). Questions of validity and drawing conclusions from simulation studies in procedural justice: A comment. *Law and Society Review, 15,* 293–303.

Anderson, N.H. (1973). Comments on the article of Hodges and of Schönemann, Cafferty and Rotton. *Psychological Review, 80,* 88–92.

Anderson, N.H. (1981). *Foundations of information integration theory.* New York: Academic Press.

Anderson, N.H. (1982). *Methods of information integration theory.* New York: Academic Press.

Anderson, N.H., and Shanteau, J. (1977). Weak inference with linear models. *Psychological Bulletin, 84,* 1155–1170.

Aramah. (1982). *Criminal Appeal Reports (Sentencing), 4,* 407–410.

Aschenbrenner, K.M. (1977). Influence of attribute formulation on the evaluation of apartments by multi-attribute utility procedures. In H. Jungermann and G. de Zeeuw (Eds.), *Decision making and change in human affairs* (pp. 81–97). Dordrecht: Reidel.

Ashworth, A. (1983a). Reducing the prison population in the 1980s: The need for sentencing reform. In A.M.G. Christopher (Chm.), *A prison system for the 80s and beyond* (pp. 1–20). London: National Association for the Care and Resettlement of Offenders.

Ashworth, A. (1983b). *Sentencing and penal policy.* London: Weidenfeld and Nicolson.

Ashworth, A. (1984). Techniques of guidance on sentencing. *Criminal Law Review,* 519–530.

Ashworth, A. (1987). Devising sentencing guidance for England. In M. Wasik and K. Pease (Eds.), *Sentencing reform: Guidance or guidelines?* (pp. 81–104). Manchester, England: Manchester University Press.

Ashworth, A., Genders, E., Mansfield, G., Peay, J., and Player, E. (1984). *Sentencing in the Crown Court: Report of an exploratory study.* Oxford, England: Centre for Criminological Research.

Baldwin, R., and Hawkins, K. (1984). Discretionary justice: Davis reconsidered. *Public Law,* 570–599.

Barber, R. (1974). Judge and jury attitudes to rape. *Australian and New Zealand Journal of Criminology, 7,* 157–172.

Barron, F.H., and Person, H.B. (1979). Assessment of multiplicative utility functions via holistic judgments. *Organizational Behavior and Human Performance, 24,* 147–166.

Bateman. (1977, June). Victorian Court of Criminal Appeal, unreported.

Beach, L.R., and Barnes, V. (1983). Approximate measurement in a multiattribute utility context. *Organizational Behavior and Human Performance, 32,* 417–424.

Beach, L.R., Townes, B.D., Campbell, F.L., and Keating, G.W. (1976). Developing and testing a decision aid for birth planning decisions. *Organizational Behavior and Human Performance, 15,* 99–116.

Bibi. (1980). *Criminal Appeal Reports (Sentencing), 2,* 117–180.

Birnbaum, M.H. (1973). The devil rides again: Correlation as an index of fit. *Psychological Bulletin, 79,* 239–242.

Birnbaum, M.H. (1982). Controversies in psychological measurement. In B. Wegener (Ed.), *Social attitudes and psychophysical measurement* (pp. 401–485). Hillsdale, NJ: Erlbaum.

Blumstein, A., Cohen, J., Martin, S.E., and Tonry, M.H. (Eds.). (1983). *Research on sentencing: The search for reform* (Vols. 1 and 2). Washington, DC: National Academy Press.

Bottoms, A.E., and Preston, R.H. (Eds.). (1980). *The coming penal crisis: A criminological and theological exploration.* Edinburgh: Scottish Academic Press.

Bray, R.M., and Kerr, N.L. (1979). Use of the simulation method in the study of jury behavior: Some methodological considerations. *Law and Human Behavior, 3,* 107–119.

Brewster. (1980). *Criminal Appeal Reports (Sentencing), 2,* 191–192.

Bunn, D.W. (1984). *Applied decision analysis.* New York: McGraw-Hill.

Camerer, C. (1981). General conditions for the success of bootstrapping models. *Organizational Behavior and Human Performance, 27,* 411–422.

Canadian Sentencing Commission. (1987). *Sentencing reform: A Canadian approach.* Ottawa: Canadian Government Publishing Centre.

Cattin, P. (1978). A predictive-validity-based procedure for choosing between regression and equal weights. *Organizational Behavior and Human Performance, 22,* 93–102.

Champagne, A., and Nagel, S. (1982). The psychology of judging. In N.L. Kerr and R.M. Bray (Eds.), *The psychology of the courtroom* (pp. 257–283). New York: Academic Press.

Chan, J. (1987). The limits of sentencing reform. In I. Potas (Ed.), *Sentencing in Australia: Issues, policy and reform* (pp. 445–483). Canberra: Australian Institute of Criminology.

Clarke, R.V.G. (Ed.). (1978). *Tackling vandalism.* London: Her Majesty's Stationery Office.

Cook, B.B. (1973). Sentencing behavior of federal judges: Draft cases – 1972. *University of Cincinnati Law Review, 42,* 597–633.

Cook, R.L., and Stewart, T.R. (1975). A comparison of seven methods for obtaining subjective descriptions of judgmental policy. *Organizational Behavior and Human Performance, 13,* 31–45.

Criminal Statistics: England and Wales 1985. (1986). London: Her Majesty's Stationery Office, 1986.

Cross, R., and Ashworth, A. (1981). *The English sentencing system* (3rd ed.). London: Butterworths.

Daunton-Fear, M.W. (1977). *Sentencing in Western Australia.* St. Lucia, Australia: University of Queensland Press.

Daunton-Fear, M. (1980). *Sentencing in South Australia*. Sydney: Law Book Co.

Davis, K.C. (1969). *Discretionary justice: A preliminary inquiry.* Baton Rouge: Louisiana State University Press.

Dawes, R.M. (1979). The robust beauty of improper linear models in decision making. *American Psychologist, 34,* 571–582.

Dawes, R.M., and Corrigan, B. (1974). Linear models in decision making. *Psychological Bulletin, 81,* 95–106.

de Havilland. (1983). *Criminal Appeal Reports (Sentencing), 5,* 109–118.

Diamond, S.S. (1981). Exploring sources of sentence disparity. In B.D. Sales (Ed.), *The trial process* (pp. 387–411). New York: Plenum Press.

Diamond, S.S. (1982). Growth and maturation in psychology and law. *Law and Society Review, 17,* 11–20.

Diamond, S.S. (1983). Order in the court: Consistency in criminal-court decisions. In C.J. Scheirer and B.L. Hammonds (Eds.), *Psychology and the law* (pp. 119–146). Washington, DC: American Psychological Association.

Doob, A.N. (1986). *Sentencing aids: An information system.* Unpublished manuscript, Centre of Criminology, University of Toronto.

Doob, A.N., and Park, N.W. (1987). Computerized sentencing information for judges: An aid to the sentencing process. *Criminal Law Quarterly, 30,* 54–72.

Dorans, N., and Drasgow, F. (1978). Alternative weighting schemes for linear prediction. *Organizational Behavior and Human Performance, 21,* 316–345.

Ebbesen, E.B., and Konečni, V.J. (1980). On the external validity of decision-making research: What do we know about decisions in the real world? In T.S. Wallsten (Ed.), *Cognitive processes in choice and decision behavior* (pp. 21–45). Hillsdale, NJ: Erlbaum.

Ebbesen, E.B., and Konečni, V.J. (1981). The process of sentencing adult felons. In B.D. Sales (Ed.), *The trial process* (pp. 413–458). New York: Plenum Press.

Edwards, W. (1977). How to use multiattribute utility measurement for social decision making. *IEEE Transactions on Systems, Man, and Cybernetics, SMC-7,* 326–340.

Edwards, W., and Newman, J.R. (1982). *Multiattribute evaluation*. Beverly Hills: Sage, 1982.

Einhorn, H.J. (1971). Use of nonlinear, noncompensatory models as a function of task and amount of information. *Organizational Behavior and Human Performance, 6,* 1–27.

Einhorn, H.J., and Hogarth, R.M. (1975). Unit weighting schemes for decision making. *Organizational Behavior and Human Performance, 13,* 171–192.

Einhorn, H.J., and Hogarth, R.M. (1981). Behavioral decision theory: Processes of judgment and choice. *Annual Review of Psychology, 32,* 53–88.

Einhorn, H.J., Kleinmuntz, D.N., and Kleinmuntz, B. (1979). Linear regression *and* process-tracing models of judgment. *Psychological Review, 86,* 465–485.

Einhorn, H.J., and McCoach, W. (1977). A simple multiattribute utility procedure for evaluation. *Behavioral Science, 22,* 270–282.

Elwork, A., Sales, B.D., and Suggs, D. (1981). The trial: A research review. In B.D. Sales (Ed.), *The trial process* (pp. 1–68). New York: Plenum Press.

Farrington, D.P., and Hawkins, K. (1979). Psychological research on behaviour in legal contexts. In D.P. Farrington, K. Hawkins, and S.M. Lloyd-Bostock (Eds.), *Psychology, law and legal processes* (pp. 3–34). London: Macmillan.

Fischer, G.W. (1976). Multidimensional utility models for risky and riskless choice. *Organizational Behavior and Human Performance, 17,* 127–146.

Fischer, G.W. (1977). Convergent validation of decomposed multi-attribute utility assessment procedures for risky and riskless decisions. *Organizational Behavior and Human Performance, 18,* 295–315.

Fischhoff, B. (1983). Decision analysis: Clinical art or clinical science? In L. Sjöberg, T. Tyszka, and J.A. Wise (Eds.), *Human decision making* (pp. 68–94). Bodafors: Doxa.

Fischhoff, B., Slovic, P., and Lichtenstein, S. (1980). Knowing what you want: Measuring labile values. In T.S. Wallsten (Eds.), *Cognitive processes in choice and decision behavior* (pp. 117–141). Hillsdale, NJ: Erlbaum.

Fisher, F.M., and Kadane, J.B. (1983). Empirically based sentencing guidelines and ethical considerations. In A. Blumstein, J. Cohen, S.E. Martin, and M.H. Tonry (Eds.), *Research on sentencing: The search for reform* (Vol. 2, pp. 184–193). Washington, DC: National Academy Press.

Fitzmaurice, C., and Pease, K. (1982). On measuring distaste in years. In J. Gunn and D.P. Farrington (Eds.), *Abnormal offenders, delinquency and the criminal justice system* (pp. 91–110). Chichester, England: Wiley.

Fitzmaurice, C., and Pease, K. (1986). *The psychology of judicial sentencing.* Manchester, England: Manchester University Press.

Forst, M.L. (Ed.). (1982). *Sentencing reform: Experiments in reducing disparity.* Beverly Hills: Sage.

Fox, R.G. (1983). *Victorian criminal procedure* (4th ed.). Clayton, Australia: Monash Law Book Co-operative.

Fox, R.G., and Freiberg, A. (1985). *Sentencing: State and federal law in Victoria.* Melbourne, Australia: Oxford University Press.

Fox, R.G., and O'Brien, B.M. (1975). Fact-finding for sentencers. *Melbourne University Law Review, 10,* 163–206.

Frankel, M.E. (1973). *Criminal sentences: Law without order.* New York: Hill & Wang.

Freiberg, A., and Fox, R. (1986). Sentencing structures and sanction hierarchies. *Criminal Law Journal, 10,* 216–235.

Fuller, L.L. (1966). An afterword: Science and the judicial process. *Harvard Law Review, 79,* 1604–1628.

Galegher, J., and Carroll, J.S. (1983). Voluntary sentencing guidelines: Prescription for justice or patent medicine? *Law and Human Behavior, 7,* 361–400.

Galligan, D.J. (1981). Guidelines and just deserts: A critique of recent trends in sentencing reform. *Criminal Law Review,* 297–311.

Gardiner, P.C., and Edwards, W. (1975). Public values: Multiattribute-utility measurement for social decision making. In M.F. Kaplan and S. Schwartz (Eds.), *Human judgment and decision processes* (pp. 1–37). New York: Academic Press.

Gibson, J.L. (1980). Environmental constraints on the behavior of judges: A representational model of judicial decision making. *Law and Society Review, 14,* 343–370.

Gottfredson, D.M., Wilkins, L.T., and Hoffman, P.B. (1978). *Guidelines for parole and sentencing.* Lexington, MA: Heath.

Gottfredson, M.R., and Gottfredson, D.M. (1980). *Decision making in criminal justice: Toward the rational exercise of discretion.* Cambridge, MA: Ballinger.

Gould and others. (1983). *Criminal Appeal Reports (Sentencing), 5,* 72–75.

Green, P.E., and Srinivasan, V. (1978). Conjoint analysis in consumer research: Issues and outlook. *Journal of Consumer Research, 5,* 103–123.

Grossman, J.B. (1966). Social backgrounds and judicial decision-making. *Harvard Law Review, 79,* 1551–1564.

Grossman, J.B. (1967). Social backgrounds and judicial decisions: Notes for a theory. *Journal of Politics, 29,* 334–351.

Hammond, K.R., Stewart, T.R., Brehmer, B., and Steinmann, D.O. (1975). Social judgment theory. In M.F. Kaplan and S. Schwartz (Eds.), *Human judgment and decision processes* (pp. 271–312). New York: Academic Press.

Hampel, G. (1978). Plea making: Concepts, preparation and presentation of pleas. *Law Institute Journal, 52,* 99–107.

Haney, C. (1980). Psychology and legal change: On the limits of a factual jurisprudence. *Law and Human Behavior, 4,* 147–199.

Harvey, L., and Pease, K. (1987). Guideline judgments and proportionality in sentencing. *Criminal Law Review,* 96–104.

Hewitt, J.D., and Little, B. (1981). Examining the research underlying the sentencing guidelines concept in Denver, Colorado: A partial replication of a reform effort. *Journal of Criminal Justice, 9,* 51–62.

Hoffman, P.J. (1960). The paramorphic representation of clinical judgment. *Psychological Bulletin, 57,* 116–131.

Hogarth, J. (1971). *Sentencing as a human process.* Toronto: University of Toronto Press.

Hogarth, J. (1986a, March). *Computers as an aid to sentencing.* Paper presented at the conference on the role of courts in society. Jerusalem, Israel.

Hogarth, J. (1986b). Sentencing data base study: Demonstration package. Unpublished manuscript, Law Courts, Vancouver, BC.

Hogarth, R.M. (1980). *Judgement and choice: The psychology of decision.* Chichester, England: Wiley.

Hood, R. (1972). *Sentencing the motoring offender: A study of magistrates' views and practices.* London: Heinemann.

Hood, R., and Sparks, R. (1970). *Key issues in criminology.* London: World University Library.

Houlden, P. (1981). A philosophy of science perspective on the validity of research conclusions: Response to Anderson and Hayden. *Law and Society Review, 15,* 305–316.

Humphreys, P. (1977). Application of multi-attribute utility theory. In H. Jungermann and G. de Zeeuw (Eds.), *Decision making and change in human affairs* (pp. 165–207). Dordrecht: Reidel.

Humphreys, P. (1983). Decision aids: Aiding decisions. In L. Sjöberg, T. Tyszka, and J.A. Wise (Eds.), *Human decision making* (pp. 14–44). Bodafors: Doxa.

Humphreys, P., and McFadden, W. (1980). Experiences with MAUD: Aiding decision structuring versus bootstrapping the decision maker. *Acta Psychologica, 45,* 51–69.

Johnson, L.C., and Mai, N. (1979). Decomposition techniques: Linear vs nonlinear models. *Organizational behavior and human performance, 24,* 60–66.

Johnson, S. (1980). Misuses of applied social research. In M.J. Saks and C.H. Baron (Eds.), *The use/nonuse/misuse of applied social research in the courts* (pp. 39–41). Cambridge, MA: Abt.

Kalven, H., Jr. (1968). The quest for the middle range: Empirical inquiry and legal policy. In G.C. Hazard, Jr. (Ed.), *Law in a changing America* (pp. 56–74). Englewood Cliffs, NJ: Prentice-Hall.

Kapardis, A. (1985). *Sentencing by English magistrates as a human process.* Nicosia: Asselia.

Keeney, R.L. (1977). The art of assessing multiattribute utility functions. *Organizational Behavior and Human Performance, 19,* 267–310.

Keeney, R.L., and Raiffa, H. (1976). *Decisions with multiple objectives: Preferences and value tradeoffs.* New York: Wiley.

Keren, G., and Newman, J.R. (1978). Additional considerations with regard to multiple regression and equal weighting. *Organizational Behavior and Human Performance, 22,* 143–164.

Konečni, V.J., and Ebbesen, E.B. (1979). External validity of research in legal psychology. *Law and Human Behavior, 3,* 39–70.

Konečni, V.J., and Ebbesen, E.B. (1981). A critique of theory and method in social-psychological approaches to legal issues. In B.D. Sales (Ed.), *The trial process* (pp. 481–498). New York: Plenum Press.

Konečni, V.J., and Ebbesen, E.B. (Eds.). (1982). *The criminal justice system: A social-psychological analysis.* San Francisco: Freeman.

Kress, J.M. (1980). *Prescription for justice: The theory and practice of sentencing guidelines.* Cambridge, MA: Ballinger.

Law Department–Victoria, Management Information Section. (1983). *Sentencing statistics, higher criminal courts, Victoria 1982.* Melbourne, Australia: Law Department.

Law Department–Victoria, Management Information Section. (1984). *Sentencing statistics, higher criminal courts, Victoria 1983.* Melbourne, Australia: Law Department.

Law Department–Victoria, Management Information Section. (1985). *Sentencing statistics, higher criminal courts, Victoria 1984.* Melbourne, Australia: Law Department.

Law Department–Victoria, Research Section. (1982). *Sentencing statistics, higher criminal courts, Victoria 1981.* Melbourne, Australia: Law Department.

Law Reform Commission–Australia. (1980). *Sentencing of federal offenders.* Canberra: Australian Government Publishing Service.

Lawrence, J., and Homel, R. (1987). Sentencing in magistrates' courts: The magistrate as a professional decision-maker. In I. Potas (Ed.), *Sentencing in Australia: Issues, policy and reform* (pp. 150–189). Canberra: Australian Institute of Criminology.

Lawrence, J.A. (1984). Magisterial decision-making: Cognitive perspectives and processes used in courtroom information processing. In D.J. Müller, D.E. Blackman, and A.J. Chapman (Eds.), *Psychology and law: Topics from an international conference* (pp. 319–331). Chichester, England: Wiley.

Lemon, N. (1974). Training, personality and attitude as determinants of magistrates' sentencing. *British Journal of Criminology, 14,* 34–48.

Levin, I.P., Louviere, J.J., Schepanski, A.A., and Norman, K.L. (1983). External validity tests of laboratory studies of information integration. *Organizational Behavior and Human Performance, 31,* 173–193.

Lloyd-Bostock, S.M. (1981a). Introduction: Does psychology have a practical contribution to make to law? In S.M. Lloyd-Bostock (Ed.), *Psychology in legal contexts: Applications and limitations* (pp. xi–xix). London: Macmillan.

Lloyd-Bostock, S.M. (1981b). Psychology and the law: A critical review of research and practice. *British Journal of Law and Society, 8,* 1–28.

Lovegrove, A. (1983, October). *Towards detailed sentencing statistics: A feasibility study for offence characteristics of armed robbery.* Report to the Victoria Law Foundation. Unpublished manuscript.

Lovegrove, A. (1984a). An empirical study of sentencing disparity among judges in an Australian criminal court. *International Review of Applied Psychology, 33,* 161–176.

Lovegrove, S.A. (1984b). Structuring judicial sentencing discretion. In D.J. Müller, D.E. Blackman, and A.J. Chapman (Eds.), *Psychology and law: Topics from an international conference* (pp. 301–317). Chichester, England: Wiley.

Lovegrove, A. (1986). Judges, sentencing, and experimental psychology. *Journal of Community Psychology, 14,* 253–266.

Lovegrove, A. (1987). An evaluation of judicial models for sentencing guidelines. In D.C. Pennington and S. Lloyd-Bostock (Eds.), *The psychology of sentencing: Approaches to consistency and disparity* (pp. 133–142). Oxford, England: Centre for Socio-Legal Studies.

Lyness, K.S., and Cornelius, E.T., III. (1982). A comparison of holistic and decomposed judgment strategies in a performance rating simulation. *Organizational Behavior and Human Performance, 29,* 21–38.

Mackay, A.L. (1977). *The harvest of a quiet eye: A selection of scientific quotations.* London: Institute of Physics.

Maguire, M. (1982). *Burglary in a dwelling: The offence, the offender and the victim.* London: Heinemann.

McCarthy, J., Jr. (1978). *Report of the sentencing guidelines project to the administrative director of courts.* Unpublished manuscript, Administrative Office of the Courts, New Jersey.

McCormack and others. (1981). *Victorian Reports,* 104–112.

McKenna, B. (1969). The judge and the common man. *Modern Law Review, 32,* 601–614.

McKnight, C. (1981). Subjectivity in sentencing. *Law and Human Behavior, 5,* 141–147.

Meehl, P.E. (1971). Law and the fireside inductions: Some reflections of a clinical psychologist. *Journal of Social Issues, 27(4),* 65–100.

Minnesota Sentencing Guidelines Commission. (1984). *The impact of the Minnesota sentencing guidelines: Three year evaluation.* St. Paul, MN: M.S.G.C.

Mischel, W. (1968). *Personality and assessment.* New York: Wiley.

Monahan, J., and Loftus, E.F. (1982). The psychology of law. *Annual Review of Psychology, 33,* 441–475.

Morris, N. (1979). The sentencing disease: The judge's changing role in the criminal justice process. *Judges Journal, 18,* 8–13 and 50.

Mungham, G., and Thomas, P.A. (1981). Studying lawyers: Aspects of the theory, method and politics of social research. *British Journal of Law and Society, 8,* 79–96.

Nagel, S.S. (1962). Judicial backgrounds and criminal cases. *Journal of Criminal Law, Criminology and Police Science, 53,* 333–339.

Nagel, S.S., and Neef, M.G. (1979). *Decision theory and the legal process.* Lexington, MA: Heath.

National Institute of Law Enforcement and Criminal Justice. (1978). *Multijurisdictional sentencing guidelines program test design.* Washington, DC: United States Department of Justice.

Newman, J.R. (1977). Differential weighting in multiattribute utility measurement: When it should not and when it does make a difference. *Organizational Behavior and Human Performance, 20,* 312–325.

Newton, J.E. (1979). *Cases and materials on sentencing in Queensland.* Canberra: Australian Institute of Criminology.

Nicholson, C.G.B. (1981). *The law and practice of sentencing in Scotland.* Edinburgh: W. Green.

Nicholson, C.G.B. (1985). *The law and practice of sentencing in Scotland. First supplement.* Edinburgh: W. Green.

Nisbett, R.E., and Wilson, T. DeC. (1977). Telling more than we can know: Verbal reports on mental processes. *Psychological Review, 84,* 231–259.

Olshavsky, R.W. (1979). Task complexity and contingent processing in decision making: A replication and extension. *Organizational Behavior and Human Performance, 24,* 300–316.

Palys, T.S., and Divorski, S. (1984). Judicial decision-making: An examination of sentencing disparity among Canadian provincial court judges. In D.J. Müller, D.E. Blackman, and A.J. Chapman (Eds.), *Psychology and law: Topics from an international conference* (pp. 333–344). Chichester, England: Wiley.

Parsons, C.K., and Hulin, C.L. (1982). Differentially weighting linear models in organizational research: A cross-validation comparison of four methods. *Organizational Behavior and Human Performance, 30,* 289–311.

Partridge, A., and Eldridge, W.B. (1974). *The second circuit sentencing study: A report to the judges of the second circuit.* Washington, DC: Federal Judicial Center.

Payne, J.W. (1982). Contingent decision behavior. *Psychological Bulletin, 92,* 382–402.

Payne, J.W., Braunstein, M.L., and Carroll, J.S. (1978). Exploring predecisional behavior: An alternative approach to decision research. *Organizational Behavior and Human Performance, 22,* 17–44.

Pease, K. (1987). Psychology and sentencing. In D.C. Pennington and S. Lloyd-Bostock (Eds.), *The psychology of sentencing: Approaches to consistency and disparity* (pp. 36–45). Oxford, England: Centre for Socio-Legal Studies.

Phelps, R.H., and Shanteau, J. (1978). Livestock judges: How much information can an expert use? *Organizational Behavior and Human Performance, 21,* 209–219.

Phillips, L.D. (1979). *Introduction to decision analysis.* London: London School of Economics and Political Science.

Pitz, G.F., Heerboth, J., and Sachs, N.J. (1980). Assessing the utility of multiattribute utility assessments. *Organizational Behavior and Human Performance, 26,* 65–80.

Pitz, G.F., and Sachs, N.J. (1984). Judgment and decision: Theory and application. *Annual Review of Psychology, 35,* 139–163.

Pitz, G.F., Sachs, N.J., and Heerboth, J. (1980). Procedures for eliciting choices in the analysis of individual decisions. *Organizational Behavior and Human Performance, 26,* 396–408.

Radzinowicz, Sir Leon, and Hood, R. (1981). The American volte-face in sentencing thought and practice. In C.F.H. Tapper (Ed.), *Crime, proof and punishment: Essays in memory of Sir Rupert Cross* (pp. 127–143). London: Butterworths.

Rich, W.D., Sutton, L.P., Clear, T.R., and Saks, M.J. (1982). Sentencing by mathematics. *State Court Journal, 6(3),* 33–41.

Rinaldi, F. (1979). Whitelaw. *Criminal Law Journal, 3,* 119–120.

Rinaldi, F. (1980). Kellow and Townsend. *Criminal Law Journal, 4,* 55–56.

Robinson, P.H. (1987). Dissent from the United States Sentencing Commission's proposed guidelines. *Journal of Criminal Law and Criminology, 77,* 1112–1125.

Ruby, C.C. (1980). *Sentencing* (2nd ed.). Toronto: Butterworths.

Ruby, C.C. (1986). Range of sentence. *Criminal Law Quarterly, 28,* 447–453.

Saks, M.J. (1982). Innovation and change in the courtroom. In N.L. Kerr and R.M. Bray (Eds.), *The psychology of the courtroom* (pp. 325–352). New York: Academic Press.

Saks, M.J., and Hastie, R. (1978). *Social psychology in court.* New York: Van Nostrand Reinhold.

Saks, M.J., and Kidd, R.F. (1980). Human information processing and adjudication: Trial by heuristics. *Law and Society Review, 15,* 123–160.

Sawyer. (1985). *Criminal Law Review,* 332–333.

Scarr, H.A. (1973). *Patterns of burglary* (2nd ed.). Washington, DC: United States Department of Justice.

Schönemann, P.H., Cafferty, T., and Rotton, J. (1973). A note on additive functional measurement. *Psychological Review, 80,* 85–87.

Shapland, J. (1981). *Between conviction and sentence: The process of mitigation.* London: Routledge & Kegan Paul.

Shapland, J. (1987). Who controls sentencing? Influences on the sentencer. In D.C. Pennington and S. Lloyd-Bostock (Eds.), *The psychology of sentencing: Approaches to sistency and disparity* (pp. 77–87). Oxford, England: Centre for Socio-Legal Studies.

Skinner, Sir Harry. (1984). Roehampton report. *Bulletin of the Judicial Studies Board*, No. 1, 10–13.

Slovic, P., Fischhoff, B., and Lichtenstein, S.(1977). Behavioral decision theory. *Annual Review of Psychology, 28,* 1–39.

Slovic, P., Fleissner, D., and Bauman, W.C. (1972). Analyzing the use of information in investment decision making: A methodological proposal. *Journal of Business, 45,* 283–301.

Slovic, P., and Lichtenstein, S. (1971). Comparison of Bayesian and regression approaches to the study of information processing in judgment. *Organizational Behavior and Human Performance, 6,* 649–744.

Smith, E.R., and Miller, F.D. (1978). Limits on perception of cognitive processes: A reply to Nisbett and Wilson. *Psychological Review, 85,* 355–362.

Smith and Woollard. (1978). *Criminal Appeal Reports, 67,* 211–213.

Sparks, R.F. (1983). The construction of sentencing guidelines: A methodological critique. In A. Blumstein, J. Cohen, S.E. Martin and M.H. Tonry (Eds.), *Research on sentencing: The search for reform* (Vol. 2, pp. 194–264). Washington DC: National Academy Press.

Stevens, S.S. (1975). *Psychophysics: Introduction to its perceptual, neural and social prospects.* New York: Wiley.

Stillwell, W.G., Barron, F.H., and Edwards, W. (1983). Evaluating credit applications: A validation of multiattribute utility weight elicitation techniques. *Organizational Behavior and Human Performance, 32,* 87–108.

Stillwell, W.G., Seaver, D.A., and Edwards, W. (1981). A comparison of weight approximation techniques in multiattribute utility decision making. *Organizational Behavior and Human Performance, 28,* 62–77.

Surber, C.F. (1985). Measuring the importance of information in judgment: Individual differences in weighting ability and effort. *Organizational Behavior and Human Decision Processes, 35,* 156–178.

Sutton, L.P. (1978). *Variations in federal criminal sentences: A statistical assessment at the national level.* New York: Criminal Justice Research Center.

Tanke, E.D., and Tanke, T.J. (1979). Getting off a slippery slope: Social science in the judicial process. *American Psychologist, 34,* 1130–1138.

Tapp, J.L. (1976). Psychology and the law: An overview. *Annual Review of Psychology, 27,* 359–404.

Taylor and O'Meally. (1958). *Victorian Reports*, 285–300.

Thomas, D.A. (1963). Sentencing—The case for reasoned decisions. *Criminal Law Review,* 243–253.

Thomas, D.A. (1977). Equity in sentencing. Sixth Annual Pinkerton Lecture. School of Criminal Justice, University of Albany

Thomas, D.A. (1979). *Principles of sentencing: The sentencing policy of the Court of Appeal Criminal Division* (2nd ed.). London: Heinemann.

Thomas, D. (1982). *Current sentencing practice.* London: Sweet and Maxwell.

Thomas, D. (1983). Sentencing discretion and appellate review. In J. Shapland (Ed.), *Decision making in the legal system* (pp. 61–71). Leicester, England: British Psychological Society.

Thomas, D. (1985). Sawyer. *Criminal Law Review,* 332–334.

Thomas, D.A. (1987). Sentencing: Some current questions. In D.C. Pennington and S. Lloyd-Bostock (Eds.), *The psychology of sentencing: Approaches to consistency and disparity* (pp. 13–23). Oxford, England: Centre for Socio-Legal Studies.

Tonry, M.H. (1982). More sentencing reform in America. *Criminal Law Review,* 157–167.

Tonry, M.H., and Morris, N. (1978). Sentencing reform in America. In P.R. Glazebrook (Ed.), *Reshaping the criminal law* (pp. 434–448). London: Stevens.

Tonry, M., and Zimring, F.E. (Eds.). (1983). *Reform and punishment: Essays on criminal sentencing.* Chicago: University of Chicago Press.

Tutchell. (1979). *Victorian Reports*, 248–258.

Twentieth Century Fund Task Force on Criminal Sentencing. (1976). *Fair and certain punishment.* New York: McGraw-Hill.

United States Sentencing Commission. (1987). *Sentencing guidelines and policy statements.* Washington, DC: U.S.S.C.

Vining, A.R., and Dean, C. (1980). Towards sentencing uniformity: Integrating the normative and the empirical orientation. In B.A. Grosman (Ed.), *New directions in sentencing* (pp. 117–154). Toronto: Butterworth.

von Hirsch, A. (1976). *Doing justice: The choice of punishments.* New York: Hill & Wang.

von Hirsch, A. (1981). Desert and previous convictions in sentencing. *Minnesota Law Review, 65,* 591–634.

von Hirsch, A. (1985). *Past or future crimes: Deservedness and dangerousness in the sentencing of criminals.* New Brunswick, NJ: Rutgers University Press.

von Hirsch, A. (1987). Guidance by numbers or words? Numerical versus narrative guidelines for sentencing. In M. Wasik and K. Pease (Eds.), *Sentencing reform: Guidance or guidelines?* (pp. 46–69). Manchester, England: Manchester University Press.

von Hirsch, A., Knapp, K.A., and Tonry, M. (1987). *The sentencing commission and its guidelines.* Boston: Northeastern University Press.

Wainer, H. (1976). Estimating coefficients in linear models: It don't make no never-mind. *Psychological Bulletin, 83,* 213–217.

Wainer, H. (1978). On the sensitivity of regression and regressors. *Psychological Bulletin, 85,* 267–273.

Walker, N. (1985). *Sentencing: Theory, law and practice.* London: Butterworth.

Wasik, M. (1987). Guidance, guidelines and criminal record. In M. Wasik and K. Pease (Eds.), *Sentencing reform: Guidance or guidelines?* (pp. 105–125). Manchester, England: Manchester University Press.

Wilkins, L.T. (1980). Sentencing guidelines to reduce disparity? *Criminal Law Review,* 201–214.

Wilkins, L.T., Kress, J.M., Gottfredson, D.M., Calpin, J.C., and Gelman, A.M. (1978). *Sentencing guidelines: Structuring judicial discretion.* Washington, DC: United States Department of Justice.

Williscroft and others. (1975). *Victorian Reports,* 292–304.

Wooler, S., and Erlich, A. (1983). Interdependence between problem structuring and attribute weighting in transitional decision problems. In P. Humphreys, O. Svenson, and A. Vari (Eds.), *Analysing and aiding decision processes* (pp. 321–334). Amsterdam: North-Holland.

Young, Sir John McI. (1979). Sentencing reference: Survey of judges and magistrates. *Justinian*, August, 8.

Yuill and Besson. (1975, June). Victorian Court of Criminal Appeal, unreported.

Zalman, M. (1978). The rise and fall of the indeterminate sentence. *Wayne Law Review, 24,* 857–937.

Zouras. (1984, July). Victorian Court of Criminal Appeal, unreported.

Author Index

Subject Index